LAW IN THE CITY

LAW IN THE CITY

Proceedings of the Seventeenth British Legal
History Conference, London, 2005

ANDREW LEWIS, PAUL BRAND
& PAUL MITCHELL

EDITORS

FOUR COURTS PRESS

Typeset in 10.5pt on 12.5pt EhrhardtMt by
Carrigboy Typesetting Services for
FOUR COURTS PRESS LTD
7 Malpas Street, Dublin 8, Ireland
e-mail: info@four-courts-press.ie
and in North America for
FOUR COURTS PRESS
c/o ISBS, 920 N.E. 58th Avenue, Suite 300, Portland, OR 97213.

© the several authors and the publishers 2007

A catalogue record for this title is available
from the British Library.

ISBN 978–1–84682–038–0

All rights reserved.
Without limiting the rights under copyright
reserved alone, no part of this publication may be
reproduced, stored in or introduced into a retrieval system,
or transmitted, in any form or by any means (electronic, mechanical,
photocopying, recording or otherwise), without the prior
written permission of both the copyright owner and
publisher of this book.

Printed in England by MPG Books, Bodmin, Cornwall.

Contents

LIST OF CONTRIBUTORS	vii
THE BRITISH LEGAL HISTORY CONFERENCE	ix
PREFACE	xi

The City and the common law: the contribution of London to modern English law
  Penny Tucker — 1

Glanvill Continued: a reassessment
  Sarah Tullis — 15

Consanguinity and the common law: 'idle ingenuities' in *Bracton*?
  Samantha Worby — 24

The making of English thirteenth-century legislation: some new evidence
  Paul Brand — 42

Thirteenth-century legislation on mortmain alienations in Flanders and its influence upon France and England
  Dirk Heirbaut — 54

Feodo de Compedibus Vocato le Sewet: the medieval prison 'oeconomy'
  Jonathan Rose — 72

The trust beneficiary's interest before *R. v. Holland* (1648)
  N.G. Jones — 95

Localism *v.* centralism: tensions in the administration of tax in nineteenth-century England and America
  Chantal Stebbings — 119

The will theory of contract in the nineteenth century: its influence and its limitations
  Warren Swain — 163

The 'creation' of the default judgment in nineteenth-century
English procedural reforms
   Carla Crifò   181

Poor law in the city: a comparative analysis of the successful
legal resistance to the implementation of the Poor Law Amendment
Act 1834 in the cities of Chester and Liverpool
   Lorie Charlesworth   206

The lord chancellor, the poets and the courtesan: public
morality and copyright law in the early nineteenth century
   Isabella Alexander   230

Legal education in England and the German historical
school of law in the nineteenth century
   Marcel Senn   249

Law and India at King's College London
   Paul Mitchell   262

Dragging the law into disrepute
   Ruth Paley   283

What *were* the principles of nineteenth-century contract law?
   Stephen Waddams   305

Urban commons: from customary use to community right
on Scotland's bleaching greens
   Andrea Loux Jarman   319

Contributors

ISABELLA ALEXANDER is the Beachcroft LLP fellow in law and director of studies in law at Robinson College, Cambridge.

PAUL BRAND is senior research fellow and academic secretary at All Souls College, Oxford. Amongst his publications are three volumes of *The Earliest English Law Reports* for the Selden Society.

ANDREA LOUX JARMAN (née Loux) is a senior lecturer in law at the University of Westminster.

LORIE CHARLESWORTH is senior lecturer at the Law School, Liverpool John Moores University, UK. She is editor in chief of the *Liverpool Law Review* and on the editorial board of *Crimes and Misdemeanors: deviance and the law in historical perspective.*

CARLA CRIFÒ is a lecturer in law at the University of Leicester.

DIRK HEIRBAUT is a professor at Ghent University and publishes in the fields of medieval customary law in Flanders and nineteenth-century Belgian private law.

N.G. (NEIL) JONES is a fellow of Magdalene College, Cambridge, and editor of the *Journal of Legal History*.

ANDREW LEWIS is professor of comparative legal history at University College London.

PAUL MITCHELL is a reader in law at King's College London. He is the author of *The Making of the Modern Law of Defamation* (2005) and an editor of *Chitty on Contracts.*

RUTH PALEY works at the History of Parliament.

JONATHAN ROSE is professor of law and Willard H. Pedrick distinguished research scholar at Arizona State University College of Law. He is currently working on the operation of the justice system in fifteenth-century England.

MARCEL SENN is professor of legal history and philosophy of law and the vice-dean of the faculty of law at the University of Zürich. He is the president of the Swiss Association for Philosophy and Social Philosophy of Law.

CHANTAL STEBBINGS is professor of law and legal history at the University of Exeter.

WARREN SWAIN is lecturer in law at the University of Durham.

PENNY TUCKER is a freelance researcher whose primary interest is in the place of law in local government, particularly the administration of the law in medieval London. Her book on medieval London's administration of the law will be published by Cambridge University Press.

SARAH TULLIS is a doctoral student at St Hugh's College, Oxford, where she is in the process of completing a thesis on Glanvill.

STEPHEN WADDAMS is Goodman/Schipper professor of law and university professor, University of Toronto.

SAMANTHA WORBY was one of the first graduates in law and history from University College London after which she completed her PhD there on Consanguinity.

The British Legal History Conference

The first British Legal History Conference was held in 1972 in Aberystwyth on the initiative of Professor Dafydd Jenkins. Since then there have been meetings at London/Cambridge (1974 and 1975), Edinburgh (1977), Birmingham (1979), Bristol (1981), Norwich (1983), Canterbury (1985), Cardiff (1987), Glasgow (1989), Oxford (1991), Exeter (1993), Durham (1995), Cambridge (1997), Edinburgh (1999), Aberystwyth (2001) and Dublin (2003). The Conference has become established as a leading forum for the discussion of all aspects of the history of law in Britain, and indeed further afield.

Proceedings of the Conference have been published as follows:

Legal History Studies 1972, ed. D. Jenkins (University of Wales Press, Cardiff, 1975).

Legal Records and the Historian, ed. J.H. Baker (Royal Historical Society, London, 1978).

Law-making and Law-makers in British History, ed. A. Harding (Royal Historical Society, London, 1980).

Law, Litigants and the Legal Profession, ed. E.W. Ives and A.H. Manchester (Royal Historical Society, London, 1983).

Law and Social Change in British History, ed. J.A. Guy and H.G. Beale (Royal Historical Society, London, 1984).

Customs, Courts and Counsel, ed. A. Kiralfy, M. Slatter and R. Virgoe, in *Journal of Legal History*, 5 (1984), and as a separate volume (Frank Cass, London, 1985).

The Political Context of Law, ed. Richard Eales and David Sullivan (The Hambledon Press, London, 1987).

Legal Record and Historical Reality, ed. Thomas G. Watkin (The Hambledon Press, London and Ronceverte, West Virginia, 1989).

Legal History in the Making, ed. W.M. Gordon and T.D. Fergus (The Hambledon Press, London and Rio Grande, Ohio, 1991).

The Life of the Law, ed. Peter Birks (The Hambledon Press, London and Rio Grande, Ohio, 1993).

Law Reporting in Britain, ed. Chantal Stebbings (The Hambledon Press, London and Rio Grande, Ohio, 1995).

Community and Courts in Britain, 1150–1900, ed. Christopher W. Brooks and Michael Lobban (The Hambledon Press, London and Rio Grande, Ohio, 1997).

Learning the Law: Teaching and the Transmission of English Law, 1150–1900, ed. Jonathan A. Bush and Alain Wijffels (The Hambledon Press, London and Rio Grande, Ohio, 1999).

The Dearest Birthright of the People of England: The Jury in the History of the Common Law, ed. John W. Cairns and Grant McLeod (Hart Publishing, Oxford and Portland, Oregon, 2002).

Legal Cultures, Legal Doctrine, ed. Richard W. Ireland, in *Cambrian Law Review*, 33 (2002).

Adventures of the Law: Proceedings of the 16th British Legal History Conference, Dublin 2003, ed. Paul Brand, Kevin Costello and W.N. Osborough (Four Courts Press, Dublin, 2005).

Law in the City: Proceedings of the 17th British Legal History Conference, ed. Andrew Lewis, Paul Brand and Paul Mitchell (Four Court Press, Dublin, 2007).

Preface

The Seventeenth British Legal History Conference was held in London at University College London 4–7 July 2005. For those who were present on the final morning of the Conference, the whole event will have been coloured by memories of the explosions on public transport in the near vicinity. Owing to the efficiency and good humour of the police operating in conditions of great stress, we were able to conclude our business with minimal disruption and we are grateful for the opportunity to play a small part in maintaining normal conditions of work in a time of emergency.

The conference theme was Law in the City which was typically understood in an extended sense. Visits were made to two important sites in the City of Westminster: Westminster Hall in the Houses of Parliament, home of the common law courts into the modern period; and the library of Westminster Abbey. For facilitating these visits the conference organizers are grateful to Lord Rodger of Earlsferry and Dr Tony Trowles respectively. The conference dinner was held in the splendid surroundings of the Hall of Bart's Hospital on Wednesday 6 July. On Tuesday 5 July sessions of the conference were held at the London base of Notre Dame University in Suffolk Street through the kindness of Professor Geoffrey Bennett and the good offices of the late Professor Martin Dockray of City University to whom the organizers would wish to pay especial tribute for his support and encouragement.

The organizers would wish to thank Lisa Penfold, UCL Laws, not only for her unfailing efficiency which relieved them of a good deal of the burden of detailed arrangements but also for her good will and enthusiasm which infected the whole atmosphere of the conference and contributed to its success.

Together with the editors of this volume a significant contribution to the organization of the conference was made by Professor Michael Lobban of Queen Mary, University of London.

ANDREW LEWIS

The City and the common law: the contribution of London to modern English law

PENNY TUCKER

THE CONTRIBUTION OF ENGLISH local custom to the national common law is not a popular subject among legal historians. It is not that it has been entirely unacknowledged: anyone who has read the works of Professors Plucknett, Kiralfy, Milsom or Baker will have encountered the suggestion that a number of legal remedies adopted by the national common-law courts at Westminster could well have been modelled on ones already available in the local courts, especially in London.[1] But if there was perhaps occasional borrowing from London custom by the national common law, that is hardly evidence of a significant contribution.[2]

So, if the contribution of local custom to the English common law as a whole has not been entirely overlooked, it has certainly not been rated highly. It is argued here that it has in fact been greatly underrated: that local custom – in particular, the custom of the city of London – had a critical influence on the development of the common law in the two centuries after 1350; and that there was a point in time, between about 1450 and about 1550, when the rival attractions of other courts – in particular, the courts of the city of London – helped to bring the two oldest and most important central common-law courts, King's Bench and the Common Pleas, close to moribundity, if not extinction.

There are several reasons why the influence of local custom on the common law has been underrated. The first is that custom generally is regarded by common lawyers as inferior to common law (by which they mean, above all, the common law as approved by and applied in the central

---

[1] T.F.T. Plucknett, *Legislation of Edward I*, pp 89–90, A. Kiralfy, 'Custom in mediaeval English law', *Journal of Legal History [JHL]*, 19 (1988), 26–49, especially 28, 34–6, S.F.C. Milsom, *Historical foundations of the common law* (2nd edn, London, 1981), pp 329–32, 343, J.H. Baker, *The Oxford history of the laws of England: vi, 1483–1558* (Oxford, 2003), pp 15, 283.

[2] R.C. Palmer, *English law in the age of the Black Death, 1348–81* (Chapel Hill & London, 1993), pp 186–90, 253–4, 275–8, especially fn. 38, but see also p. 190, for the suggestion of London influence on the central courts' treatment of 'horse doctor' liability.

Court of Common Pleas), and its practitioners as inferior to common lawyers. Its differences, as soon as a national law worthy of the name started to emerge, increasingly came to 'be seen [by common lawyers] at best as exceptional and at worst as exceptionable'.[3] The habit of contrasting the national common law, which Serjeant Fletewode described in the late sixteenth century as the 'full and perfect Conclusions of reason', with local customs, which were 'such things as through much often and long usage, through simplicity or ignorance, gain an entry and become hardened & then defended as firme & stable Lawes', is probably as old as the English legal profession.[4] How could common lawyers, reasonable men that they were and are, possibly allow their law to be influenced to any great extent by local custom, that 'slovenly' assortment of principles and practices followed by generations of ignorant butchers, bakers and candlestick-makers?[5]

There are two further reasons why the contribution of London's custom in particular has been underrated. One is that the courts of the capital tend to be regarded as being open only to a limited class of persons: simply put, to townspeople and merchants.[6] On the contrary, its Court of Husting, though it probably never entertained more than 150 cases a year even at its peak in the 1310s,[7] was open to almost anyone who owned or occupied property in London,[8] including those who held or lived in the private city jurisdictions, the sokes.[9] By the 1270s London also had a separate Sheriffs' Court, each of the two sheriffs holding one 'side' of the Court; and, by the 1300s at the latest, each sheriff also held sessions of his Court for Foreigns,

---

3   J.H. Baker, *An introduction to English legal history* (4th edn., Oxford, 2002), p. 14; see also T. Littleton, *Tenures*, ed. E. Wambaugh (Washington, 1903), Book II, ch. 11, s. 212; N. Doe, *Fundamental authority in late medieval English law* (Cambridge, 1990), pp 78–83.

4   London Guildhall Library, MS 9384, 'Observations on statutes & customes ...', fos. 1–9v, especially fo. 2.

5   It was Henry Brougham who in 1830 described borough Courts of Requests, presided over as they were by 'tradesmen who know nothing of the law', as providing 'slovenly justice': C. Hanly, 'The decline of civil jury trial in nineteenth-century England', *JHL*, 26 (2005), 253–78. For similar attitudes among MPs and common lawyers in the 17th-century, see C.W. Brooks, *Pettyfoggers and vipers of the Commonwealth: the 'lower branch' of the legal profession in early modern England* (Cambridge, 1986), pp 99–100.

6   F. Pollock, F.W. Maitland, *The history of the English law before the time of Edward I*, 2 vols (2nd edn., Cambridge, 1923), ii, 643–4; Baker, *An introduction to English legal history*, p. 7.

7   For estimates of the numbers of cases brought in the city's courts in the Middle Ages, see P. Tucker, 'Relationships between London's courts and the Westminster courts in the reign of Edward IV' in D.E.S. Dunn (ed.), *Courts, counties and the capital in the later Middle Ages* (Stroud, 1996), pp 117–37, especially 119–22.

8   See, e.g., Corporation of London Record Office [CLRO], Husting Roll of Common Pleas [HR CP] 27/5, CLRO Husting Roll of Pleas of Land [HR PL] 24/13 (cases in which the dowager countess of Cornwall and the earl of Hereford were litigants).

9   CLRO, HR CP3, m. 3, HR CP12, m. 3v (*Smith v. Prior of Holy Trinity* and *Le Tannere v. Master of St Bartholomew's West Smithfield*).

that is, parties who were not city residents (later, city freemen). Anyone whose cause of action lay in the city – the bargain had been struck, the goods were to be delivered, the debt was due to be repaid there – could sue or be sued on one side or another of the Sheriffs' Court.[10] And even these limitations did not apply, if the parties were merchants or the debt was 'de mercandisa' (an exemption which applied to other English cities and towns which were 'markets').[11] Given the dominance of the medieval capital city as a national and regional market, entrepot and financial centre, its Sheriffs' Court was in practice open to almost anyone who wanted to use it;[12] and even in the early fourteenth century it was probably entertaining several thousand civil pleas a year. By the mid fifteenth century, its workload could well have increased substantially (see below, for post-1350 developments in borough courts generally); and the city's main governmental and administrative court, the Mayor's Court, was also entertaining a modest number of personal pleas, perhaps around 400 a year, brought by anyone whose case fell within the city's jurisdiction, including the king.[13] Finally, in the early sixteenth century the city established its Court of Requests, a small claims tribunal in which jury trial was not available.[14] This was also open to anyone with a suitable case. Its early records, whatever they were (and it is likely that they were very brief and/or extremely informal in character)[15] have not survived, and there seems to be no way of knowing how many cases it heard. As it was initially ordered to sit on two days a week[16] and its procedures were (very) summary, however, it was certainly capable of handling many hundreds of cases a year, and the demand could well have been that high.[17]

10 H.T. Riley (ed.), *Munimenta Gildhallae Londoniensis: Liber Albus, Liber Custumarum, et Liber Horn*, 4 vols (London, 1859–62), i, 215–16, *Journals of the House of Lords*, 98 (London, 1866), pp 504, 505, ibid., 99 (London, 1868), pp 239–95 (*City of London v. Cox*). It was evidently not sufficient to ground an action in the city that a disputed bond, made and recording an agreement arising elsewhere, had been acknowledged before witnesses in the capital; had the acknowledgement itself been recorded in the Mayor's Court, however, that court might well have had jurisdiction: A.H. Thomas (ed.), *Calendar of early Mayor's Court rolls, 1298–1307* (Cambridge, 1924), pp 69–70 (*Weylond v. Mouncy*).
11 Ibid., 69 (*Weylond v. Mouncy*); Hampshire Record Office, Winchester City Court Rolls, W/D1/4, mm. 16v, 14 [sic] (*Thame v. Brydeport*).
12 For non-freemen suing or being sued in the Sheriffs' Court, see, e.g. CLRO, Sheriffs' Court Roll (1320), m. 7v (Henry Cook of Westminster), or, at the other end of the social scale, P.E. Jones (ed.), *Calendar of plea and memoranda rolls [CalPMR], 1458–1482* (Cambridge, 1961), pp 234 (the earl of Essex).
13 E.g., CLRO, Mayor's Court File of Original Bills MC1/3A, items 1, 14, 33, 61; ibid., item 15.
14 CLRO, MS Repertory 10, fo. 137.
15 See below, pp 5–6.
16 CLRO, MS Letterbook N, fo. 71.
17 In the late 1450s, around 100 of the civil cases brought in the Mayor's Court each year are likely to have involved claims for under £2 (based on the first 100 cases recorded in CLRO, Mayor's Court File of Original Bills, MC1/3A). In 1320, perhaps 500 of the civil cases

The other major reason why the extent of the influence of London custom on English national law has been underestimated is that London's custom tends to be regarded as being applicable to a limited type of case: simply put, to commercial cases, dealt with according to a mix of local custom and merchant law. On the contrary, the Husting, by 1300, dealt mainly with disputes over rights in and arising out of real property brought by writ.[18] By the same date the Sheriffs' Court handled a wide range of personal pleas brought informally, by oral [com]plaint and bill.[19] The Husting cases were heard according to a mix of common law and city custom.[20] This was also normally true of the Sheriffs' Court (increasingly so, from the later fourteenth century onwards) and of the formal side of the Mayor's Court. In addition, however, the latter court was from the outset receiving a sprinkling of petitions.[21] Out of this, from the 1360s onwards, it developed a jurisdiction in conscience, or 'equity', with disputes which could not be determined according to common law and city custom being heard and adjudged in separate, closed sessions in the Inner Chamber, a room used for meetings of the city's Court of Aldermen, its principal governing body.[22] In the late fourteenth century, it also took over from the Sheriffs' Court cases determined according to merchant law, which were similarly heard in the Inner Chamber.[23] By the time the city's Court of Requests was established, the Husting was largely moribund and the Sheriffs' Court was probably beginning to become more professionalized, formal, and perhaps also therefore slow and expensive, than it had once been.[24] The Mayor's Court, however, retained its summary character into the nineteenth century on both

    brought in the Sheriffs' Court that year involved claims for under £2 (based on all cases in CLRO, Sheriffs' Court Roll (1320); values are however often not given in this roll and the calculation assumes that the proportion of low-value claims in both courts was similar at the two periods, which is far from certain).

18 With only the very rare and anomalous exception, the latest personal pleas to be brought in the Husting are from the early 1300s; and, apart from actions known as pleas of naam (equivalent to replevin), which were almost always brought informally, by the same period even the few personal pleas seem usually to have been brought by writ (see, e.g. CLRO, HR CP28, m. 12v, HR CP29, m. 15, HR CP30, m. 3).

19 Although debt and trespass predominated, detinue, covenant, account, deceit and even the occasional plea *de re addirata* are to be found; and these categories covered a wider range of disputes than was then the case in the central common-law courts: CLRO, Sheriffs' Court Roll (1320), especially m. 12.

20 Riley, *Munimenta Gildhallae*, i, 186, 291.

21 See Thomas, *CalEMCR*, 196, for a session held in 1305 'concerning plaints and petitions'.

22 CLRO, Mayor's Court Files of Original Bills, MC1/1, items 19, 32, 24, 17, 18, 122.

23 CLRO, MS Liber Dunthorne, fo. 68, A.H. Thomas (ed.), *CalPMR 1381–1412* (Cambridge, 1932), pp 251–3.

24 [W.] Bohun, *Privilegia Londini: or the laws, customs, and priviledges of the city of London* ... (London, 1702), p. 192.

its formal, common-law side and on its informal, 'equity' side, as did the Court of Requests.²⁵

The belief that London's courts were severely limited as to persons and types of cases that came within their jurisdiction helps to account for any assumption that the influence of its custom, likewise, can only have been limited. It is not possible to do justice to the contrary argument as a whole here: in particular, to discuss the extent to which the remedies available in London, and the legal principles which underlay them, may have influenced those offered not only in other borough courts but also in the central courts.²⁶ What can be said, however, is that, although most of the London remedies which have previously been identified as models for common-law ones were indeed of a commercial nature, this is by no means true of all the possible exemplars. At least, 'commercial' seems an odd description of cases brought against surgeons alleging negligent treatment, against householders whose carelessness meant that their fires got out of control and damaged their neighbours' property, or even people who offered to keep other people's possessions safe and failed to do so.²⁷ Such cases are to be found in London's courts in the early fourteenth century, and might well have provided exemplars which helped to shape similar actions when they appeared in the central courts later in the century.

Instead, this paper will focus on two less obvious questions, which have to do with a trend in the common law of the later Middle Ages towards what might indeed, if a little unkindly, be called 'slovenly' justice. The first question to be discussed is the extent to which, as the medieval economy developed, the informal ways of London's courts may have prompted more relaxed practices in the central courts in relation to the conduct of and record-keeping in civil cases. The second is the possibility that London's example may have had an effect on the development of the legal profession in the late medieval and early-modern period, helping middle-ranking lawyers to carve out a substantial niche for themselves as advocates even in the central common-law courts. This, too, could be viewed as leading to more slovenly justice, assuming that the serjeants of the day regarded the less experienced pleader much as modern barristers tend to regard the solicitor-advocate.

Briefly, developments in the capital were as follows: As writ-initiated actions went out of fashion over the course of the fourteenth century, oral plaint and, increasingly, written bills became the main means of bringing a

---

25 Bohun, *Privilegia Londini*, pp 190, 399–404, W. Brandon, 'Observations on county courts and local municipal courts as courts for the recovery of small debts' (London, 1868) (copy available at the CLRO), pp 12–20.
26 These issues are discussed in detail in P. Tucker, *Law courts and lawyers in the city of London, 1300–1550* (Cambridge, 2007).
27 CLRO, Sheriffs' Court Roll (1320), m. 17v; Thomas, *CalEMCR*, p. 139; A.H. Thomas (ed.), *CalPMR 1323–64* (Cambridge, 1926), pp 220–1, CLRO, HR CP36, m. 18.

case.[28] The rise of the bill was accompanied by a fall in standards of record-keeping. The practice of keeping a formal court roll may have been abandoned in the Sheriffs' Court and Mayor's Court as early as the 1360s. The roll was probably replaced in part by a 'book of causes', perhaps giving very brief details of the case and process on it under session headings, as was the case in the Husting after 1448, and in part by files of bills and associated materials, which could be used if necessary to compile a formal record of a case.[29] Bills were simply filed on leather thongs, with process being scribbled in the margins.[30] At some stage before the 1450s, a record of the parties' pleadings began to be filed separately, probably being brought together with the bills only on determination.[31] These pleadings may well have been produced by, or were based on notes submitted by, the parties or their attorneys, since in 1345 the city responded to complaints about the inaccuracy of records of pleadings in the Husting by ordering attorneys to supply the court clerks with their own notes.[32] What appear to be examples of written pleadings survive in the Mayor's Court files of the later fourteenth century.[33] It was no doubt the growing number and variety of such 'papers', as they were known, which led to the establishment of a third clerkship in the sheriffs' offices in or by 1393, a clerk whose duty was specifically to keep the papers.[34]

There were several reasons why the clerks in the Mayor's and the Sheriffs' Courts could afford to abandon any attempt to keep a separate record of their own, at least wherever the parties were legally represented. One is that the records, including the original bill and the pleadings, could be freely amended until the case went to jury, law or judgment.[35] The other is that the clerks could normally rely on attorneys working in the city courts to keep an honest record because, for almost all of the fourteenth century, it is likely that

---

[28] Writs are only rarely mentioned in Sheriffs' Court cases brought on error even before 1350: CLRO, HR CP40, m. 23 (1315, writ of account), HR CP49, m. 16 (writ *ex gravi querela*, 1324–5); *CalEMCR*, pp 69, 99, 132–3, 140–1; *CalPMR 1323–64*, p. 213 (1344). Thereafter, they all but disappear from the record. The last reference (involving a writ of *justicies*) is from 1385: *CalPMR 1381–1412*, p. 93.

[29] CLRO, MS Sheriffs' Register of Writs, fo. 26; CLRO, Mayor's Court File of Original Bills, MC1/1 (this file contains, not only the bills themselves, but also notes of summons, attachments, receipts, attorney appointments, and jury and wardmote inquest verdicts).

[30] E.g. (among many other instances), CLRO, Mayor's Court File of Original Bills, MC1/1, item 4, which is annotated at the top and down the left-hand side.

[31] CLRO, Mayor's Court File of Original Bills, MC1/3A, items 16, 192, which refer to 'X pleading as on the file'.

[32] CLRO, MS Letterbook F, fo. 105, Riley, *Munimenta Gildhallae*, i, 473.

[33] CLRO, Mayor's Court File of Original Bills, MC1/1, items 133, 134, and 135.

[34] CLRO, MS Letterbook H, fo. 86.

[35] R.R. Sharpe (ed.), *Calendar of letter-books [CalLB] preserved among the archives of the corporation of the city of London at the Guildhall: letter-book H* (London, 1907), p. 374, *Munimenta Gildhallae*, i, 218.

they were usually city officials or officials' servants. Of around one hundred attorneys who appeared in the city's courts between 1300 and 1399 (excluding the few who only did so in joint appointments, since they were normally 'foreign' attorneys), twenty-six definitely held city offices, and another eleven undertook duties, such as acting as summoners and pledges to prosecute, which seem to have been discharged by city officials or their underlings. Given that junior clerks were among those who were most likely to act as attorneys later on, when more information about lower-status officers becomes available, and that this was probably also the case in the fourteenth century, even a quarter represents a considerable proportion.

Clerks continued to monopolize work as attorneys in the Mayor's Court into the early modern period;[36] and, since Mayor's Court clerk-attorneys also monopolized what little work there was in the Husting at that date, this was true of that Court as well. In the Sheriffs' Court after 1393, however, men had to be formally admitted as city, or, as they were usually known, common, attorneys.[37] Sheriffs' clerks were forbidden thereafter to act as attorneys or counsel, and, by and large, they did not. In 1518, the city also established offices known as common pleaderships.[38] This decision probably merely formalized an arrangement which existed by the 1450s, when it appears that attorneys who were senior enough to be selected to read at their inn of court for the first time were regarded as being qualified to act as advocates. Thomas Bryan, who was retained to act in several cases heard at Guildhall from 1448 onwards, was described and paid as an attorney until January 1450, but thereafter received the higher 'advocate's' rate of pay; he seems to have read for the first time in the autumn of 1450.[39] The early sixteenth-century common pleaders had reached a similar stage of their legal education.[40]

There are several other aspects of the conduct and practice of the city courts which merit notice. One is that they continued until 1550 at least to be presided over by lay magistrates: the mayor, sheriffs and, in practice if not initially in theory, the aldermen in the Husting; the mayor and a quorum of aldermen in the Mayor's Court, and a quorum of aldermen and commoners in the Court of Requests; and a single sheriff on each side of the Sheriffs' Court. Only in the Husting, where the recorder sat at the mayor's right hand,

---

36 E.g., apart from two men (Thomas Segrym and Giles Nase) appointed jointly together with a Mayor's Court clerk, all the attorney appointments noted in a file of bills of the 1440s and 1450s were of clerks: CLRO, Mayor's Court File of Original Bills, MC1/3, the exception being item 242.
37 CLRO, MS Letterbook H, fo. 286, printed in Riley, *Munimenta Gildhallae*, i, 519.
38 CLRO, MS Repertory 3, fo. 207.
39 Guildhall Library, Churchwardens' Accounts, St Peter's, West Cheap, 1435–1601, fos. 222v, 223; S.E. Thorne, J.H. Baker (eds), *Readings and moots at the inns of court in the fifteenth century*, Selden Society, 2 vols, 71, 105 (1954, 1989), i, p. xxxii.
40 Baker, *Introduction to English legal history*, p. 161.

can we be certain that men whom contemporaries probably regarded as professional lawyers, at least after 1400, formed part of the bench when the court was in full rather than administrative session. (Administrative sessions dealt with matters like the granting of bail and the valuation of arrested goods.) Another is the willingness of the bench in the Mayor's and Sheriffs' Courts to examine witnesses under oath and unsworn, in open court and in private rooms, and to put specific questions to them on the parties' behalf, although there was no system of formal, written interrogatories.[41] Also of note is that, although the two courts proceeded according to common law and custom, the jury was no more an 'essential part' of their procedure in civil cases than were wager of law, the peremptory oath or proof by witnesses.[42] Finally, from the middle of the fourteenth century onwards, proceedings in the Sheriffs' Court were almost certainly being conducted in English.[43]

Much of this appears to anticipate developments in the central courts and elsewhere, if only just. Parliamentary legislation ordering that English be employed for pleadings in the central and seignorial courts, enacted in 1362, post-dated the London ordinance by a mere six years.[44] The petition which sought to prevent records clerks in the central courts and assizes from acting as counsel and attorneys was submitted to Parliament at almost exactly the same time as London passed the ordinance forbidding these activities to Sheriffs' Court clerks.[45]

Although the 1393 parliamentary petition was unsuccessful, and for many years, indeed, several centuries afterwards, central court clerks continued to act as attorneys,[46] that may not have been true of the 1362 statute of pleading. If Sir John Fortescue is to be trusted, in the first half of the fifteenth century French was only used for the formal declaration, or count, upon the writ, for technical legal terms, and for reporting cases for the benefit of law students.[47] Here as elsewhere, conflicts between Fortescue's account and other evidence can perhaps be resolved by assuming that he was describing the practice of King's Bench when he presided over it, in the 1440s and 1450s, and that this differed from the practice of the Common Pleas. So it

---

41 E.g., CLRO, MS Journal 4, fos. 123–4, MS Journal 7, fos. 114v, 125v, 130, 124v.
42 *Pace* M. Blatcher, *Court of King's Bench, 1450–1550: a study in self-help* (London, 1978), p. 14. About 28% of fully contested Sheriffs' Court cases in 1320, and about half of such cases in the Mayor's Court in the 1450s, went to a jury, trespass being, unsurprisingly, the type of action most likely to be determined in this way.
43 R.R. Sharpe (ed.), *CalLBG* (London, 1905), p. 73; CLRO, HR CP146, mm. 3–3v.
44 *Statutes of the realm: I: 20 Henry III–50 Edward III (1236–1376/7)* (1810), pp 375–6.
45 *Rotuli parliamentorum; ut et petitiones et placitata in parliamento*, 6 volumes (Record Commission, 1783), iii, 306B.
46 M. Hastings, *The Court of Common Pleas* (Ithaca, NY, 1947), p. 111, Baker, *Legal profession and the common law*, p. 82, Baker, *Oxford history of the laws of England*, vi, 336–7, 25–6, Brooks, *Pettyfoggers and vipers*, p. 143.
47 S.B. Chrimes (ed.), *Sir John Fortescue: De laudibus legum Anglie* (Cambridge, 1949), p. 115.

could be that the statute enjoyed more success than has sometimes been assumed.[48] It may even be that the presence of former London undersheriffs like Fortescue on the bench of King's Bench from the 1440s onwards encouraged the use of English in that court.[49] As for the men who worked as advocates in the central courts, by 1500 common lawyers of similar status to Thomas Bryan fifty years earlier were beginning to colonize the Courts of King's Bench, Chancery and Requests, replacing the clerks of the latter two courts as counsel.[50] London's formal recognition in 1518 of the pleader as a man who was, or was about to become, a bencher at his Inn of Court also pre-dated formal recognition of these middle-ranking lawyers in the central courts. It was not until nearly thirty years later, in 1547, that it was decreed that only utter barristers of at least eight years' standing would be granted audience there.[51]

In the absence of adequate evidence for the early development of written pleadings, even in London, it is not possible to assert that a habit of employing them spread from the capital to Westminster.[52] In London, however, this habit seems to have been a by-product of the lax recording practices encouraged by procedure by bill, perhaps particularly in personal pleas, where the need to retain records for years was less than in real actions. It is possible that the early expansion and development of bill procedure in King's Bench in the fifteenth century was accompanied by certain other practices associated with procedure by bill,[53] including the use of written pleadings, and that all these developments owed something to the presence on the bench of a succession of former London undersheriffs between the 1440s and 1480s, and to the close links at the time between that court and the London sheriffs' offices (the London sheriffs being also sheriffs of Middlesex, and undersheriffs of Middlesex being, for much of the fifteenth century, King's Bench clerks).[54] If so, that might help to explain why King's

---

48 See W.M. Ormrod, 'The use of English: language, law, and political culture in fourteenth-century England', *Speculum*, 77 (2003), 750–84, especially 772–4, *pace* F.W. Maitland (ed.), *Year books of 1 & 2 Edward II, (1307–1308 & 1308–1309)*, Selden Society, 17 (1903), p. xxxiv, J. Vising, *Anglo-Norman language and literature* (London, 1923), p. 23.

49 Three successive chief justices between 1442 and 1481 were former city undersheriffs (John Fortescue, John Markham and Thomas Billyng); and until 1469 they normally had another former city law officer as one of their two junior colleagues: J.C. Sainty, *Officers of the Exchequer*, List & Index Society Special Series, 18 (1983), pp 8–9.

50 See below, p. 10 and fn. 59. In addition, Robert Pynkney appears to have begun to work as a pleader in Chancery on resigning as a London common attorney in 1500: TNA (PRO), Early Chancery Proceedings, C1/88, item 90; CLRO, MS Repertory 1, fo. 71.

51 Baker, *Introduction to English legal history*, pp 161–3 and fn. 27.

52 In the city they seem to have remained primarily aides-memoire for the clerks, at least until 1550. For the much more sophisticated use made of them by the central courts in the sixteenth century, see Baker, *Oxford history of the laws of England*, vi, 338–9.

53 S. Jenks, 'Bills of custody in the reign of Henry VI', *JHL*, 23 (2002), 197–222.

54 Blatcher, *Court of King's Bench*, pp 42–3.

Bench had acquired a clerk of the papers by 1533 at the latest, whereas the Common Pleas had not.[55]

But all this highlights a counter-argument. Even if every hypothesis just advanced has some truth in it, might it not simply be that London provided a base from which middle-ranking common lawyers could draw financial and moral support as they began to carve a distinct place for themselves within the Westminster courts and wider profession? There was, for instance, something of a Gray's Inn mafia which dominated the city's law offices (the recordership, the common serjeanty and the undershrievalties) in the middle decades of the fifteenth century. At least sixteen, perhaps twenty-one, of the twenty-eight appointments made between 1420 and 1470 were of members of that inn.[56] That this figure is swollen by the number of appointments (up to twelve) which went to Gray's Inn men who had previously held another city law office serves merely to confirm the strength of their grip on this part of London's administration.[57] And as soon as common lawyers began to appear as legal representatives in the conciliar courts, in the years around 1500, men who held city law offices, pleaderships and attorneyships were to be found among them: Robert Southwell, Robert Sheffelde and Henry White, serving common serjeant, recorder and undersheriff respectively, appeared as counsel in the central Court of Requests in 1502, 1505 and 1529, for example.[58] It may be that these men themselves saw their city offices merely as useful steppingstones to careers at Westminster. This is far from certain, however. The more junior of them in fact appeared in the Court of Requests before they obtained office in the city as pleaders or attorneys, and some remained in those offices for quite long periods.[59] It seems more likely that they viewed opportunities within the city of London much as they viewed opportunities in King's Bench and the conciliar courts, as acceptable ends in themselves.

Even if that is not so, it does not follow that they remained unaffected by their experience of the way in which the law was administered in London.

---

55 Baker, *Introduction to English legal history*, p. 82, Baker, *Oxford history of the laws of England*, vi, 337.
56 The eight law officers who cannot be associated, even tentatively, with a particular inn of court are excluded.
57 The law officers in question being Alexander Anne and Thomas Billyng (who both held all three offices), and Thomas Ursewyk, Guy Fairfax and Thomas Rigby (who each held two).
58 L.M. Hill (ed.), *The ancient state authoritie and proceedings of the Court of Requests by sir Julius Caesar* (London, 1975), pp 64, 78, 122.
59 Of the men who appeared in the central Court of Requests as an attorney, Roger Cholmondley (common pleader, 1518–?26, recorder, 1535–45) appeared in 1516, William Heydon (Mayor's Court clerk-attorney, 1521–9, if the identification is correct) in 1502 and 1504, and John Hichcoke (common attorney, 1534–?45) in 1529 (the fact that he appeared together with Undersheriff White, however, suggests that he was already working in the

This was particularly likely to be the case in the fifteenth century, when differences between the practice and personnel of the city and Westminster courts were greater than they would be a hundred years later. Much that was characteristic of and different about the city's courts and custom had been established before 1400, at a time when even the recordership was only rarely held by men who are known to have practised in the central courts;[60] and almost all of it survived the professionalization of the fifteenth century. Unlike several of their successors (men like Serjeant Fletewode, a former recorder, whose loyalties clearly lay with his profession rather than his sometime employer), the city law officers who went on to higher things in the national common-law courts during the fifteenth century could usually be relied upon to show a 'good & lovyng mynde' towards the city and its courts and customs.[61] There is nothing inherently contradictory about acknowledging, on the one hand, that the undersheriffs who advised and conducted London's Sheriffs' Court during the fifteenth century may well have contributed to the process by which the court became more strictly a court of common law and city custom; and, on the other hand, that those who went on to preside over King's Bench may also have contributed to the process by which the court developed its own custom in ways that their colleagues in Common Pleas regarded as contrary to the custom of that court, if not clearly contrary to the common law.[62]

It is of course true that it is impossible to demonstrate conclusively that the city of London influenced the national common law and legal profession in the ways just outlined, just as it is impossible to prove that its remedies provided models for those adopted by the central common-law courts from the later fourteenth century onwards. That the boroughs were invited to present their grievances to the 1362 parliament which passed the statute of pleading, as well as some other legislation likely to have been of interest to them,[63] is no evidence that it was London's governors, or others impressed by London's example, who urged the adoption of English as the language of pleading in the central and seignorial courts.[64] Likewise, we cannot show any direct link between the 1393 parliamentary petition and the 1393 London

---

city as White's underclerk or 'servant'): Hill, *The ancient state ... of the Court of Requests*, pp 91, 68, 74, 122.
60 Of the recorders who served before 1400, only two, Geoffrey de Hertpole (who served briefly in 1320) and Hugh de Sadelynstanes (1359–61), were certainly professional lawyers; conversely, Sadelynstanes' predecessor, Roger de Depham (1338–59), had previously served as a sheriff's clerk and as the city's common or town clerk.
61 CLRO, MS Repertory 9, fo. 186v.
62 Blatcher, *Court of King's Bench*, pp 140–1, 148, 143–4, 146.
63 *CalLBG*, p. 145 (the legislation itself, including the statute of pleading, is also recorded in Letterbook G, fos. cv–cvi).
64 Ormrod, 'The use of English', 752.

ordinance prohibiting certain court clerks from acting as counsel and attorneys. But if it is accepted, on a balance of probabilities, that we have some causal links here and not just coexisting events, then, with all due respect to Professor Maitland, borough custom (or the custom of London, at least) was indeed suffered to do harm to the national common law,[65] in the sense that it had a significant impact upon it.

Arguably, the developments in remedies and procedures which occurred from the later fourteenth onwards were beneficial, indeed, vital to the continued existence of the two main national common-law courts in the longer term.[66] But it is certainly also arguable that the short-term effects of other developments in English law during the fifteenth and early sixteenth century threatened to render these two courts as semi-moribund by the middle of the sixteenth century as the London Court of Husting then was.[67] Between 1450 and 1490, the number of civil pleas they entertained seems to have halved from perhaps 8–9,000 a year, thereafter continuing, if erratically, downwards to a nadir of under 2,000 a year in the mid 1520s.[68] This cannot simply have been the effect of a growth in the activity-levels of the equitable side of Chancery and of the other conciliar courts.[69] Even in combination and at a relatively late stage in the decline of the Westminster common-law courts (up to 1520), the volume of business in the conciliar courts was comparatively modest. Chancery, the busiest of them, was probably receiving no more than 900 petitions a year in the later fifteenth and early sixteenth centuries.[70] Even under Wolsey in the 1510s and '20s, the Star Chamber is said to have dealt with a modest 120 civil pleas or so a year on average.[71] Borough courts, too, saw a sharp increase in their activity-levels in the hundred years after 1350,[72] and some of them were still handling substantial quantities of civil pleas in the later fifteenth and early sixteenth centuries.[73]

---

65 Pollock, Maitland, *The history of the English law*, i, 644.
66 Blatcher, *Court of King's Bench*, pp 24–6.
67 Ibid., pp 32–3.
68 Brooks, *Pettyfoggers and vipers*, pp 86–7, and Blatcher, *Court of King's Bench*, p. 21.
69 For the debate over this question, see, e.g., E.W. Ives, *The common lawyers of pre-reformation England: Thomas Kebell, a case study* (Cambridge, 1983), pp 190–210.
70 P. Tucker, 'The early history of the Court of Chancery: a comparative study', *EHR*, 115 (2000), 791–811, especially 799, 793.
71 Blatcher, *Court of King's Bench*, p. 28.
72 E.g., civil pleas in Winchester's City Court rose from some 265 cases a year in 1375/6 to around 450 (based on 313 cases in the main court and 125 in the piepowder court rolls for 1425/6 and 1424/5 respectively) in the mid-1420s: HRO, Winchester City Court Rolls, W/D1/21, /37, 56 & Winchester Piepowder Court Rolls, W/D2/1. A similar pattern, though with differences in the timing of the peak period, is to be found in Colchester, where totals more than doubled between 1372/3 and 1398/9: R.H. Britnell, 'Colchester courts and court records, 1310–1525', *Essex Archaeology and History*, 17 (1984), 133–40, especially 134.
73 Even the court of a modest town like Sandwich was probably handling over 100 civil pleas

The City and the common law

Even in the 1470s, when the city of York was in decline, its Sheriffs' Court was entertaining 8–900 civil pleas a year, numbers similar to or greater than the number of petitions then being received by Chancery.[74] Given that London's commercial dominance increased between 1350 and 1550 and its population was perhaps ten times York's in the 1470s, its Sheriffs' Court alone may well have dealing with many more civil pleas in the later fifteenth century than the conciliar courts then did. Indeed, although the London Sheriffs' Court itself suffered a sharp drop in business in about 1550,[75] a quarter-century earlier it might conceivably have been handling more business than all the central courts, common-law and conciliar, combined.

The origins of this late-medieval boom probably lies partly in the commercialization of the economy after 1350[76] and partly (perhaps in consequence) in the greater accessibility and effectiveness of borough courts. By the fifteenth century, the courts of the leading provincial cities and towns were as open to foreigns as London's courts had long been. In Winchester, this change occurred in the late fourteenth century.[77] It seems to have been facilitated by quietly abandoning the earlier restriction that only foreigns who were merchants could sue one another in the borough's courts[78] and permitting anyone whose cause of action arose in the borough to do so.[79] At some stage, certainly by the early fifteenth century, it evidently became possible to exploit the national reach of the central courts in order to track down and arrest defendants and force them to appear in a local court,[80] thus eliminating one of the drawbacks of these courts.

a year in 1473, judging by the number of entries in its court roll for July of that year: East Kent Archives, Sandwich Court Roll. Winchester's city court was still handling at least 224 cases then (the roll is damaged, and insufficient records survive to show what happened in the piepowder court), although it too had suffered a severe decline by 1549: HRO, Winchester City Court Rolls, W/D1/63, /80.

74 Based on P.M. Stell (ed. and trans.), *Sheriffs' Court books of the city of York for the fifteenth century* (York City Archives, 2000), pp 114–264.
75 CLRO, MS Journal 12/2, fos. 262v–3.
76 Britnell, 'Colchester courts', 134.
77 E.g. Hampshire Record Office [HRO], Winchester City Court Rolls, W1/D1/21 (1375/6), m. 14, *Red* ['merchant' added] *v. Capoun butcher* ['merchant' added] and *Coupere of Eastgate v. Slek of Eastmone*.
78 Lawsuits involving, and, by the fifteenth century, between, foreigns became increasingly numerous in borough courts from the late fourteenth century onwards. In Nottingham, 'foreign pleas' came to dominate the court's workload: W.H. Stevenson, *Records of the borough of Nottingham, vol. 2: 1399–1485* (Nottingham, 1883), p. xi. In Colchester, the Court of Pleas was known from 1410 on as the *Curia Forinsec*: Britnell, 'Colchester courts', p. 136.
79 T. Foulds, J. Hughes, M. Jones, 'Nottingham borough court rolls: the reign of Henry VI (1422–57)', *Transactions of the Thoroton Society of Nottinghamshire*, 97 (1993), 74–87, especially 75; Britnell, 'Colchester courts', 133; W.A. Champion, 'Litigation in the boroughs: the Shrewsbury *Curia Parva*, 1580–1730', *JLH*, 15 (1994), 201–22, especially 203.
80 HRO, Winchester City Court Recorda, W1/D1/112, m. 41 [*recte*, 42], *Alfold v. Pulter*

So it was not (or not just) Chancery and the other conciliar courts which turned King's Bench and the Common Pleas, if only briefly, into 'two inconsiderable courts in a complex of courts',[81] but the availability of accessible, cheap, speedy justice – summary justice – in a variety of other courts. It was not civil lawyers who circumvented, undermined and eventually destroyed the serjeants at law, but the activities of their fellow common lawyers,[82] men of middling professional status who built up their positions and influence while, and quite possibly by, working in the other courts. It was not the civil law (or equity) which was the main influence that helped to transform the national common law, but the example of another part of the common law itself, local custom. And insofar as the surviving records allow one to tell, it was the custom of London and its courts, and the attitudes and actions of some of the common lawyers who worked in the city in the fifteenth and the early sixteenth centuries, which were the most influential of all.

(arrest achieved as a result of a subsequently-abandoned action in the Common Pleas, c.1410); CLRO, MS Journal 8, fo. 81 (costs awarded to plaintiff by the London Mayor's Court, incurred in that court and also in King's Bench, Common Pleas and Chancery, during a successful attempt to force an elusive defendant to answer there, 1474).

81 Blatcher, *Court of King's Bench*, p. 31.
82 Baker, *Introduction to English legal history*, pp 158–9. For what may be a reflection of contemporary serjeants' disapproval of the 'disloyalty' of the more junior common lawyers who worked in and supported the activities of Chancery and the other conciliar courts in the early sixteenth century, see J.A. Guy, *Christopher St German on Chancery and statute*, Selden Society Supplementary Series, 6 (London, 1985), p. 104. Although the dominance of former city undersheriffs in King's Bench between the 1440s and 1480s is particularly striking, the influence on developments in the conciliar courts of men like Edmund Dudley and Thomas More (undersheriffs of London, 1496–1502 and 1510–18 respectively) ought not to be overlooked.

Glanvill Continued: a reassessment

SARAH TULLIS

THE TEXT THAT WE CALL *Glanvill* is the late twelfth-century legal treatise generally accepted as the first textbook of the common law.[1] It was almost certainly not written by chief justiciar Rannulf de Glanvill(e), whose name it has borne since at least the fourteenth century.[2] The popularity of the treatise is attested by its survival in forty-one known manuscripts, which occur in a variety of forms and belong to various dates. This paper will focus more specifically on two of the best known of these manuscripts. H.G. Richardson drew attention to British Library, MSS Additional 25005 and Harley 323 (designated *C* and *H* respectively) in a well-known article in the *Law Quarterly Review* in 1938.[3] He considered these two volumes to constitute a distinct 'version' of the treatise and to represent a significant attempt at expanding and modernizing *Glanvill* for a mid-thirteenth-century audience, to catch up with the rapidly developing common law. He christened his so-called 'version' of the treatise *Glanville Continued*, based largely on the material with which the treatise is bound up in these two volumes. I shall start by giving a summary of Richardson's arguments about *Glanvill Continued* and then go on to discuss some of the problems with his thesis.

Richardson believed that the two manuscripts of his 'version' both dated from the reign of Edward I, but that they were later copies of a once more extensive earlier collection made in around 1240. He described *H* (Harley 323) as the more accurate but unfinished text, and *C* (Additional 25005) as being neater and fuller than *H*, but particularly error-ridden. He showed the

---

[1] The best and most recent edition of the treatise is *Tractatus de Legibus et Consuetudinibus Regni Anglie qui Glanvilla Vocatur*, ed. and trans. G.D.G. Hall (Oxford, 1965).

[2] The immediate parallel here is with the *De Legibus et Consuetudinibus Angliae*, the traditional attribution of at least the majority of which to Henry of Bracton now seems unlikely (*Henrici de Bracton. De Legibus et Consuetudinibus Angliae*, ed. G.E. Woodbine, revised and trans. S.E. Thorne, 4 vols (Cambridge, MA, 1968–77). A disproportionate amount of *Glanvill* scholarship has been devoted to trying to find an author to fit the treatise. See, for example, R.V. Turner, 'Who was the author of Glanvill? Reflections on the education of Henry II's common lawyers', in *Judges, administrators and the common law in Angevin England* (London, 1994), pp 71–101. However, the text generally reads to me as if it had been written by someone altogether humbler than has traditionally been suggested

[3] H.G. Richardson, 'Glanville Continued', *Law Quarterly Review*, 54 (1938), 381–99.

comparable sections of both manuscripts to begin with a *beta* version of *Glanvill*, the more functional and slightly later of the treatise's manuscript traditions, which is sub-divided for ease of reference into books and chapters. Richardson noticed that both manuscripts then continued with the same miscellaneous collection of twenty-one statutes, writs and ordinances of Henry III. He listed this collection, ranging from the 1225 Magna Carta and Charter of the Forest to the 1236 Provisions of Merton and showed that all but seven of its items could be precisely dated to between April 1233 and January 1236. This collection contains a variety of general writs and ordinances as well as several concerning the changing fortunes of three connected parties: Richard Siward, the Basset family and the disgraced justiciar Hubert de Burgh, all implicated in rebellion against Henry III, but subsequently pardoned.[4] Several writs in this section also deal with a 'Robert of London', upon whose identity – if he existed as more than just a scribal fiction – contemporary chancery rolls do not throw any more light. Richardson described the better manuscript (*H*) as breaking off after this collection, but the more careless *C* as continuing with a contemporary register of writs and a version of the short treatise *Judicium Essoniorum*, which – following Woodbine's incorrect dating of the *Judicium's* composition – he wrongly deemed to have been a later addition to the volume.[5]

The essence of Richardson's view of the significance of these manuscripts is twofold. First, he believed that the collection of statutes, ordinances and writs which follows the treatise in both manuscripts should be viewed as a deliberate continuation of the treatise, and that it comprised material specifically chosen to fit with and expand *Glanvill* and bring it up to date.[6] Second, he believed that the nature of this 'continuation' section proved that the collection as a whole was put together by a chancery clerk. He believed that this section evidenced the clerk's efforts in the mid 1230s at collecting a variety of precedents and memorabilia, largely avoiding conventional charters or writs *de cursu* that he might find in existing chancery formularies. Rather, Richardson argued, the clerk set out to collect 'the kind of thing that

---

4 For background, see D. Crouch, 'Siward, Sir Richard (d. 1248)', *Oxford dictionary of national biography*, 50 (Oxford, 2004), pp 814–15; or F.M. Powicke, *King Henry III and the Lord Edward* (Oxford, 1950), especially pp 129 and 140–1.

5 Woodbine erroneously dated the composition of the short treatise to 1267–75 (*Four thirteenth century law tracts*, ed. G.E. Woodbine (New Haven, 1910), pp 116–42). However, Brand has shown the treatise in fact to have been written in c.1218/9–30, meaning that it no longer needs to be explained away as a late inclusion in MS *C*: P. Brand, '"Nothing which is new or unique?" A reappraisal of "Judicium Essoniorum"', in P. Birks (ed.), *The life of the law*, Proceedings of the 10th British Legal History Conference, Oxford 1991 (London, 1993), pp 1–7.

6 For Richardson's discussion of this section, and his attribution of it to the chancery, see in particular 'Glanville continued', 388–92.

would strike an intelligent man as useful, curious or important'.[7] Richardson stressed the very miscellaneous and unusual nature of some of these items to assert that they must have been copied in the chancery. He cited in particular one of the section's ordinances of four articles concerning relations between Christians and Jews, and providing for the expulsion of those Jews who were not serviceable to the king.[8] He deemed that, because the ordinance does not survive anywhere else, but appears authentic, it must have come from within the chancery. Although primarily basing his chancery ascription on this miscellaneous section of statutes, writs and ordinances, Richardson argued that the register which follows this section in the better manuscript (*C*) further substantiated the collection's putative chancery origin. He based this on the register's expanded discussion of the writ of peace and the grand assize, that is, the writ directed to a feudal or county court to stop proceedings in an action for the recovery of a proprietary right and to compel trial by grand assize jury rather than battle (examples of which may be seen at *Glanvill*, book II, chapters 8 and 9). Basing his judgement largely on the fact that *C*'s register adds to the information in *Glanvill* itself on this writ and the procedure of obtaining it – from the chancery – Richardson believed that: 'the register which was added as a supplement to Glanville was originally compiled in the chancery of Henry III, for the guidance of chancery clerks, and that it gave them something that Glanville did not give'.[9]

To emphasize the significance of his collection, Richardson drew explicit parallels between *Glanvill Continued* and the more famous attempt at updating and actually revising the text of the treatise, discussed and described by Maitland as 'Glanvill Revised'.[10] Indeed, following what we now know to be Maitland's mis-dating of *Glanvill Revised* to *c*.1265, Richardson believed his collection to be of particular significance as the earlier of the two notable 'attempt[s] at modernizing Glanville'.[11]

In summary, if Richardson's 'strong presumption' that the collection originated in the chancery was correct, this would indeed make this collection interesting: only one other *Glanvill* manuscript has any suggested 'official' connection and that a notably unsubstantiated one.[12] If he was right that his

---

7 Ibid., 391.
8 Ibid., 392–4, and printed in full on 393.
9 Ibid., 388.
10 F.W. Maitland, 'Glanvill Revised' in *The collected papers of Frederic William Maitland*, ed. H.A.L. Fisher, vol. 2 (Cambridge, 1911), pp 266–89. This version of the treatise exists in Cambridge University Library, MS Mm.1.27 and Gonville and Caius College, Cambridge, MS 205/111. In fact, however, Hall showed that Maitland's suggested dating of *Glanvill Revised* to the mid 1260s, based on only one of its two manuscripts, to have been about thirty years too late: *Glanvill*, pp 195–8.
11 'Glanville continued', 381.
12 Balliol College, Oxford, MS 350 includes a transcript of that part of the Exchequer

collection did indeed represent a specific attempt at continuing and modernizing the treatise which would sit alongside *Glanvill Revised*, *Glanvill Continued* would indeed be significant in the broader context of *Glanvill* scholarship and could be used to throw light at once on the treatise and its transmission and development over time, the changing common law that it embodied and the relationship between the two. In other words, it would provide a neat view in microcosm of the crossover between the theory and practice of the developing common law.

Richardson's thesis has been generally accepted. It received a short, but ringing, endorsement by Powicke, who deemed our hypothetical chancery clerk to have been indeed 'a man with an historical mind'.[13] Although Derek Hall, the text's last editor, made rather less of *Glanvill Continued* than might have been expected, he too followed Richardson's assessment.[14] Despite, or perhaps because of, this general acceptance, there has been almost no critical work on *Glanvill Continued* since Richardson.

However, I will argue that Richardson's thesis now warrants reconsideration on several levels. There are reasons for doubting some of his factual description of these manuscripts. More importantly, his characterization of their significance as a modernized version of *Glanvill* that originated in the chancery of Henry III is at best questionable.

Richardson seems to have made some factual errors in the dating and description of the contents of these two manuscripts. He dated both manuscripts of *Glanvill Continued* to the reign of Edward I.[15] Derek Hall, following him, dated both manuscripts – more specifically – to around 1300.[16] In fact, however, whilst this dating may be accepted at least for the earlier parts of the composite MS *H*, *C*, the fuller of the two volumes, is considerably earlier and may instead be dated to the mid thirteenth century.[17] In other

---

Domesday relating to Herefordshire (fos. 1r–42r), which almost certainly originated in the royal scriptorium, and which dates from c.1160–70: V.H. Galbraith and J. Tait (eds), *Herefordshire Domesday, circa 1160–1170: reproduced by collotype from facsimile photographs of Balliol College manuscript 350* (Pipe Roll Society, 63: London, 1950). The Herefordshire Domesday is immediately followed in the volume by an early *alpha* text of *Glanvill* (fos. 43r–72r), pricked in a manner consistent with the previous section, but in a different, and slightly later hand of around 1200. It is possible that this section, too, was produced in the Exchequer.

13 Powicke, *King Henry III and the Lord Edward*, p. 770.
14 *Glanvill*, pp lvii–iii.
15 'Glanville Continued', 381.
16 *Glanvill*, p. lviii.
17 This dating is largely based on internal evidence. The hand responsible for *C* is clearly considerably earlier than those responsible for *H*. Similarly the register in *H* (fos. 69r–88r), although in a different hand to that manuscript's *Glanvill*, is later in date than that in *C* (fos. 67v–73v). E. De Haas and G.D.G. Hall (eds.), *Early registers of writs*, Selden Society vol. 87 (London, 1970) date the register in *C* to earlier than 1236 and that in *H* to before

words, C may be the original manuscript of this collection and not, as Richardson was forced to argue, a later copy. Richardson's argument that there must once have been substantially more of the manuscript, and in particular more of the miscellaneous collection of statutes, writs and ordinances of which he made so much, is based more on H, in which many sections including its *Glanvill* are either unfinished or incomplete. However, with the apparently complete C as the earlier, possibly original, manuscript of the collection, there is no evidence for anything being missing.

Moreover, Richardson also made some surprising omissions in his description of the contents of these two volumes. He failed, for example, to note the contents of the earliest folios of C, which precede *Glanvill* and, as with the rest of the volume, are written in the same hand as the treatise.[18] He also failed to mention specifically that MS H only opens mid-way through the treatise and that its second section – of statutes, writs and ordinances – is not as full as that in C, breaking off unfinished before the Provisions of Merton. Although these are small variants, and sections of the two manuscripts are undoubtedly very similar, it may be argued that Richardson over-simplified his description of the contents of both volumes in order to enhance their similarities.

Second, Richardson's firm ascription of *Glanvill Continued* to the chancery warrants reappraisal. As has been noted, the evidence for this attribution essentially comes down to the nature of the miscellaneous collection of statutes, writs and ordinances which comes after the treatise in both manuscripts, and to the register which follows them in C. Richardson argued that the unusual and lesser-known nature of the miscellaneous section following the treatise supports its supposed chancery origins. In fact, however, this argument is entirely based on conjecture. The unusual nature of many of these items is not particularly surprising in a period where there was still no general enrolment of legislation. It is therefore not a compelling argument that they could only have been collected in the chancery. Indeed, if this was the case and they were put together by a chancery clerk with broad access to draft material and presumably wide professional interests, why does the collection only represent such a short chronological period? This seems particularly surprising if – as has been suggested – Richardson may not have

---

1275 (at p. xxiii). In other words, the register in C predates the 1236 Statute of Merton, whilst that in H must have been written after it.

18 These folios include an outline summary schema of *Glanvill* which has not been found in any other manuscript of the treatise; a short section in French on distinctions of lettering and numbering; a French copy of the *Expositio Vocabulorum*; a Norman ducal genealogy down to the succession of John; a discussion of the longitude and latitude of England, also giving the country's size, its main roads, its counties, bishoprics and some of its laws and the Assize of Bread.

been correct in his view that the original collection was once much fuller that what now survives.

Indeed, it might be argued that this section's pronounced local flavour – something not commented upon by Richardson – might rather imply private compilation. All of the items in this section which are not either statutes, general ordinances or the four writs relating to Richard Siward and others may be connected with Lincolnshire. Writs concerning Boston Fair would seem to have held more interest to a local man of business whose interests included law and legal administration than to a chancery clerk. The same is true of a copy of a general summons of the Lincolnshire eyre of September 1234. The otherwise unidentifiable 'Robert of London' who features in a number of the items in this section, is described as having held land in Wainfleet, Lincolnshire, in which county he acted as coroner, and is distrained in another of the items in the section to appear as a witness at the next Lincolnshire county court.[19] It is conceivable that Robert might have fitted the bill as the Lincolnshire-based man of business who would have been a more plausible original compiler than our anonymous chancery clerk.[20]

Richardson also based his chancery ascription on the early register of writs which follows the section of statutes, writs and ordinances in *C* only. Although he was correct to notice the extended description of the writ of peace and the grand assize in this register, this is not unique. Indeed, there are at least two other registers of a similar date which contain virtually identical discussion at this point. These are the second of the two registers in Corpus Christi College, Cambridge MS 297 (fos. 115v–23r) and the register in British Library, MS Additional 8167 (fos. 107r–13r). More importantly, although the register does contain, albeit not uniquely, extended explanatory notes on the writ of peace, a writ – like many others – obtainable from the chancery, there is no compelling reason as to why this should have been produced by and for chancery clerks, as Richardson suggested. The added detail in the register in *C* on the process of the demandant obtaining the writ – over and above its briefer description in *Glanvill* itself – would have been at least as useful to a litigant or his advisor as to a chancery clerk, and arguably perhaps even more so. The register nowhere reads as if it were

---

19 The undated writ addressed to the sheriff of Lincolnshire on f. 66r orders the election of a new coroner in place of Robert. He is distrained to appear in court together with three other knights, 'William, Thomas and Gilbert' in a writ on f. 65v.

20 It is just possible that Robert might even have himself been implicated in rebellion or perceived rebellion against the king in the 1230s, which would explain his interest in the cases of Siward et al. This suggestion might be supported by the evidence of one of the writs in question which grants the customs and services at Wainfleet, earlier given by Robert 'as ransom', to Hawise (de Quincy), sister and coheir of Ranulf, last earl of Chester and Lincoln (osp. 1232). The reference to 'ransom' sounds sufficiently implausible that it might just be true.

specifically written for those in the chancery as opposed to outsiders dealing with it. Moreover, there is nothing else in the manuscript's register which particularly seems to reflect the sort of routine day–to–day activities of the chancery which one might expect if this were a collection, as Richardson suggested, specifically designed for chancery clerks.

Thus, it seems that even if a chancery clerk were responsible – and there is no specific or compelling evidence that he was – he must have undertaken the collection in a private capacity and unofficially. A simpler argument, and one for which there is at least as much evidence, is that the collection was compiled by a private individual with Lincolnshire connections, just possibly 'Robert of London'.

Finally, the third major area in which issue may be taken with Richardson's argument is his emphasis on *Glanvill Continued*'s status as a 'version' of the treatise. Nowhere in his article does he talk specifically about the text of the treatise itself as it appears in these two manuscripts. Extensive comparison of the two has shown widespread textual similarities to the extent that the later *H* must have been copied from another manuscript very like, but probably not actually, *C*. There are some points of intrinsic interest in these texts which make them noteworthy amongst other known *Glanvill* manuscripts. However, there are no substantial or legally significant textual variants in the treatise as it survives in these manuscripts, and certainly no serious engagement with, or modernization of, the text itself. It therefore seems dubious to characterize the manuscripts on this basis as containing a particular, identifiable, version of the treatise.

If, on the other hand, Richardson's assessment of the collection's 'version' status was made purely on the basis of the material with which the treatise is bound up in these manuscripts then this, too, is decidedly shaky. First, there is no particular connection between the treatise and the other material, in particular the miscellaneous section which follows it. There are no internal cross–references between them. The second section and the register of writs in *C* undoubtedly add to the information contained in the treatise. But if this automatically provided grounds for seeing the remainder of the collection as a deliberate continuation of the treatise, and in this respect a 'version' of it, then the majority of the other 39 manuscripts of the treatise in which *Glanvill* is bound up with a wide variety of material, most of which might be seen to add substantively to the information in the treatise, might similarly be described as *Glanvill Continueds*.[21]

21 The treatise is generally bound up with other material, often including a mixture of Anglo–Saxon laws and law codes, twelfth-century statutes and other legal literature and miscellaneous other material, usually although not exclusively of a legal nature. MS *H*, although clearly composite and possibly only bound together at a relatively late date, is highly unusual for the coexistence of the treatise together with canonical material, including letters and dicta relating to the Roman curia (ff. 1r–12v) a heavily glossed later

Not only did Richardson make some small errors and surprising omissions in his description of these two manuscripts, but his attribution of them to the chancery, and his claims for them of a status as a *bona fide* modernized version of the treatise are, at best, much shakier than has traditionally been thought. The collection in these manuscripts is unusual, particularly for its inclusion of some of the lesser enactments of Henry III. If anything, however, as it has been argued, the collection's unusual status derives from its very miscellaneous and local nature, rather than for any official connection. If there are reasons for doubting Richardson's attribution of the collection to a chancery clerk, it may be suggested instead that it was produced by a private individual associated with Lincolnshire, whose interests included law and legal administration. If the thesis of private compilation is accepted, this makes the collection significant not for its suggested official status, but as a notably early example of a private statute collection, a genre which only became common from the 1280s. There was no ready access to written legal enactments before the coming to prominence of the Statute Roll in the course of the fourteenth century, and there are very few other early private statute collections until the 1280s and '90s.[22]

How then should these two manuscripts be seen in the context of other *Glanvill* texts? We may reluctantly have to abandon their putative 'official' connection and their exalted status as a legitimate 'version' of the treatise. The manuscripts should not be seen, as they traditionally have been, alongside other recognized attempts at making the text of the treatise more serviceable over time. Richardson's own comparison with *Glanvill Revised* ironically only brings this into clearer focus. *Glanvill Revised* stands very much as the exception to prove the rule that there was very little genuine attempt in the thirteenth century and beyond to engage with, and modernize, the treatise for a later audience. Furthermore, it is worth noting here that even *Glanvill Revised* seems to have been abandoned unfinished in failure. Richardson was wrong to predicate the treatise's continuing usefulness over time on its being kept 'reasonably up to date' – this is simply not borne out

---

fragment of the *Constitutionum Clementinarum* (ff. 13r–22v), part of book II of the Decretals of Gregory IX (fos. 23r–38v), Innocent III's 'Tractatus de miseria humane condicionis' (fos. 89r–100v) and Bernard of Pavia's *Breviarum Extravagantium* (fos. 101r–187v).

22 P. Brand, 'English thirteenth century legislation', in ...*colendo iustitiam et iura condendo... Federico II. Legislatore del Regno di Sicilia nell'Europa del Duecento*, ed. A. Romano (Rome, 1997), pp 325–44, and particularly 342–3. For a study of statute books after the 1280s, see D.C. Skemer, 'Reading the law: statute books and the private transmission of legal knowledge in late medieval England', in J.A. Bush and A. Wijffels (eds), *Learning the law: teaching and the transmission of law in England, 1150–1900: Proceedings of the 13th British Legal History Conference, Cambridge 1997* (London, 1999), pp 113–31 and for a general overview, see H.G. Richardson and G.O. Sayles, 'The early statutes', *Law Quarterly Review*, 50 (1934), 201–23 and 540–71.

by the evidence.[23] This in turn has implications for our view of the function of the treatise over time. However, just because there was no serious attempt to bring the text of the treatise in these two manuscripts up to date does not mean that they were not designed to be, or that they did not function as, useful legal texts in the mid to late thirteenth century. If anything, these manuscripts, in particular the earlier *C*, are notable for the manifest and extended – probably private – use of the treatise that they evidence. If we may no longer call them '*Glanvill Continued*', they at least represent the continuing use of *Glanvill*.

---

23 'Glanville Continued', 381.

Consanguinity and the common law: 'idle ingenuities' in *Bracton*?

SAMANTHA WORBY

MAITLAND'S OPINION OF THE canon law rules on marriage (particularly about the extremes of the kinship rules, ranging from consanguinity and affinity to the impediment of public honesty and spiritual kinship) was not high. He said: 'Behind these intricate rules there is no deep policy, there is no strong religious feeling; they are the idle ingenuities of men who are amusing themselves by inventing a game of skill which is to be played with neatly drawn tables of affinity and doggerel hexameters.'[1]

These technical and academic kinship rules, particularly about the canon law of consanguinity, are usually found in purely canon law manuscripts, but also occur in common law manuscripts of the late thirteenth and early fourteenth centuries. In fact, about ten percent of the surviving manuscripts of *De Legibus et Consuetudinibus Angliæ* (which I will continue to call *Bracton* because the name is a convenient shorthand) contain canon law kinship treatises and trees.[2] These appear to have been copied or chosen by common lawyers, or by men with some association with the common law. Although information about the ownership and genesis of these late thirteenth- and early fourteenth-century *Bracton* manuscripts is scarce, the amount and

---

1 Frederick Pollock and Frederic William Maitland, *The history of English law before the time of Edward I*, 2nd edn, with a new introduction and select bibliography by S.F.C. Milsom, 2 vols (Cambridge, 1968), ii, 389.
2 About fifty *Bracton* manuscripts survive. These are listed by Woodbine in Bracton, *De legibus et consuetudinibus Angliæ*, ed. by G.E. Woodbine and translated (with revisions and notes) by Samuel E. Thorne, 4 vols (Cambridge, MA & London, 1968–77), i, 5–20 [henceforth *Bracton*]; and in J.H. Baker, *A catalogue of English legal manuscripts in Cambridge University Library; with codicological descriptions of the early manuscripts by J.S. Ringrose* (Woodbridge, 1996), p. 68. Five contain canon law treatises or trees: BL MS Additional 41258, fos. 37r–38v; BL MS Harley 653, fos. 40v–43r; Oxford Bodleian Library MS Rawlinson C 160, fos. 36r–38r; Cambridge University Library MS Dd.vii.6, Part III, fos. 66r–68v; and Worcester Cathedral Library MS F 87, fos. 28v–29r [Oxford Bodleian Library will be abbreviated to OB; Cambridge University Library to CUL]. On the authorship and process by which the text we call *Bracton* was written see: *Bracton* iii, pp xiii–lii per Samuel Thorne. This dating is now generally accepted: Paul Brand, 'The age of Bracton', in John Hudson (ed.), *The history of English law: centenary essays on 'Pollock and Maitland'* (Oxford, 1996), pp 65–89 at 66–73.

manner of the textual variation in the general run of *Bracton* manuscripts suggests that they were copied by men who understood the common law. More particularly, two of the manuscripts with canon law consanguinity treatises alongside *Bracton* are associated with men knowledgeable about the common law: Worcester Cathedral Library MS F 87 was used by a lawyer in Hereford and Worcester before 1400 and Cambridge University Library MS Dd.vii.6 was glossed by John de Longeville, an MP for Northamptonshire who died c.1324 (however, this manuscript may have been designed but not copied by him).[3] One of the manuscripts containing an (adapted) *arbor consanguinitatis* can also be connected to a common lawyer: Cambridge University Library MS Dd.vii.14 contains a common law adaptation of the arbor consanguinitatis that shows the arms of Walter de Langton (d.1321) who was bishop of Coventry and Litchfield, and treasurer of Edward I and Edward II; perhaps it belonged to a lawyer in his employ.[4] This manuscript has been connected with John de Solers, a tax collector for Hereford and Gloucestershire in 1313, and 1319 and a lawyer for the abbey of Winchcombe, though he too may only be an early owner.[5]

Five different treatises about canon law kinship occur in *Bracton* manuscripts. Some are merely copied: the canonist Johannes de Deo's *Arbor versificata* occurs in BL MS Harley 653, fos. 41v–43r; an anonymous treatise, beginning *Sciendum est*, occurs in BL MS Additional 41258, fos. 38rv incomplete at the end, and in OB MS Rawlinson C 160, fos. 36r–38r incomplete at the beginning; *Ad arborem*, a treatise on canon law kinship, apparently by the theologian and later archbishop of Canterbury Robert Kilwardby, occurs in CUL MS Dd.vii.6, Part III, fos. 66r–68v.[6] Some treatises were adapted, and these are discussed in more detail below. Four *Bracton* manuscripts include trees of consanguinity or affinity (though common lawyers were less interested in affinity – kinship through sex or marriage – than consanguinity – blood kinship).[7] Figure 1 is an example of a

---

3 R.M. Thomson, *A descriptive catalogue of the medieval manuscripts in Worcester Cathedral Library with a contribution on the bindings by Michael Gullick* (Worcester, 2001), p. 56. On CUL MS Dd.vii.6 see J.H. Baker, *Catalogue*, p. 68, cf. Dorothea Oschinsky, *Walter of Henley and other treatises on estate management and accounting* (Oxford, 1971), p. 24.

4 J.H. Baker, *Catalogue*, p. 83.

5 Dorothea Oschinsky, *Walter of Henley*, pp 25–6; Paul Brand (ed.), *The earliest English law reports: Volume I, Common Bench reports to 1284; Volume II, Common Bench reports 1285–1289 and undated reports 1279–1289*, Selden Society vols 111–12 (London, 1996), i, pp xxxii–xxxiii [henceforth *EELR*].

6 It is identified as his in R.A.B. Mynors, *Catalogue of the manuscripts of Balliol College Oxford* (Oxford, 1963), p. 4.

7 BL MS Additional 41258, fo. 37rv contains an out-of-date seven-degree *arbor consanguinitatis* and *arbor affinitatis*, and the four-degree *arbor consanguinitatis*, on which Figure 1 is based; BL MS Harley 653, fo.42r contains a ten-degree half *arbor consanguinitatis* drawn by an annotator; OB MS Rawlinson C 160, fo.37v contains the frame for a four-degree *arbor*

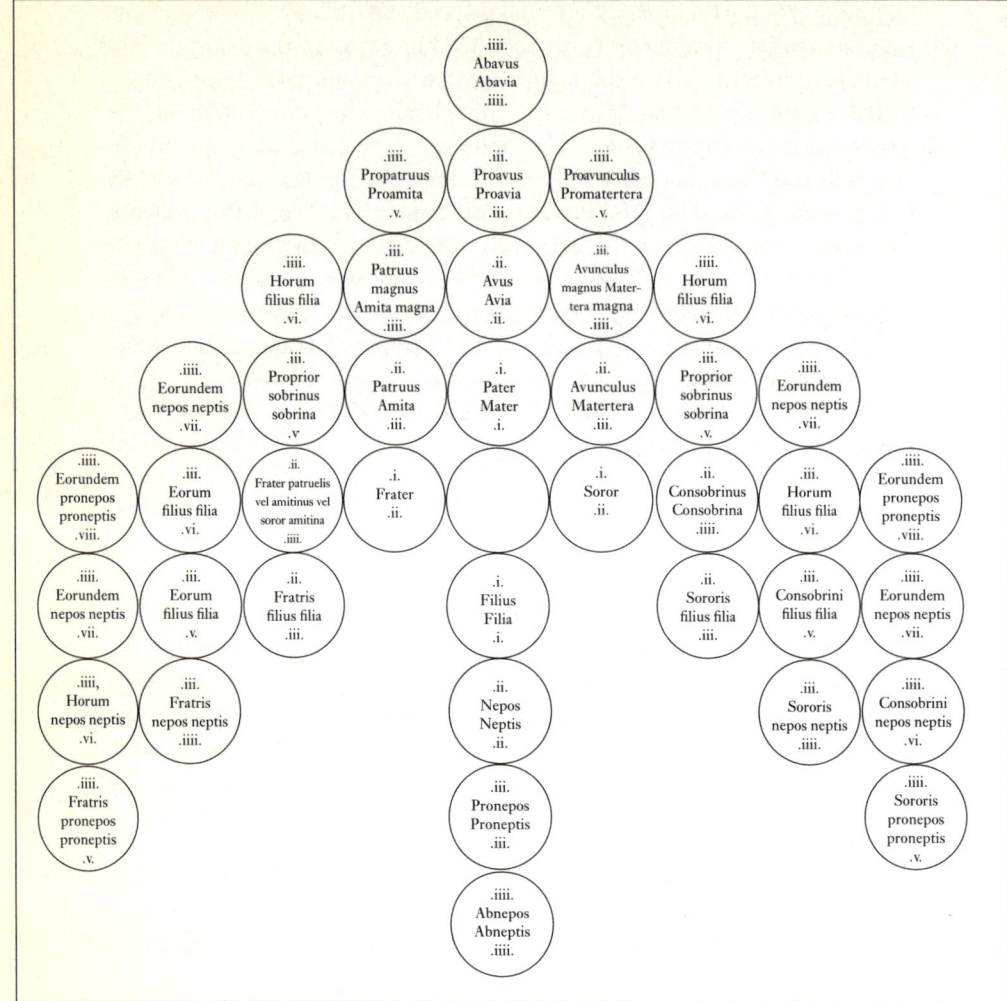

Figure 1: A four-degree canon law style *arbor consanguinitatis*, based on one copied into a *Bracton* manuscript: BL MS Additional 41258, fo. 37v.

typical four-degree canon law *arbor consanguinitatis* copied from a *Bracton* manuscript.[8] Other trees were adapted by common lawyers; and various copied and adapted trees occur in manuscripts of *Britton* (an Anglo French adaptation and abbreviation of Bracton from the 1290s).[9] Figure 2 is an

affinitatis and seems likely to once have contained an *arbor consanguinitatis*, though the folio is now removed; and CUL MS Dd.vii.14, fo.410r contains an adapted Bractonian *arbor consanguinitatis* but no treatise.
8 Copied from BL MS Additional 41258, fo.37v.
9 F. M. Nichols (ed.), *Britton: the French text carefully revised with an English translation,*

example. It comes from beside *Britton*'s section on the actions of cosinage, aiel and besaiel.[10] It is clearly based on the canon law model, but adapted and shortened, with the degrees and empty central cell removed. It has become a guide to common law actions – to aiel (by which a claim could be asserted to the possession of land held by a grandparent at the time of their death), besaiel (for land held by a great-grandparent) and cosinage (for land held by cousins or collateral kinsmen). In the canon law context Maitland thought the material in these treatises and trees was an example of 'exuberant learning'; canon law kinship was logic 'misapplied', it could segue into 'idle ingenuities'.[11] Hence the question implied in my title, were the canon law treatises and trees in common law manuscripts 'idle ingenuities' for the common lawyers who copied them (or had them copied)?

The very existence of this discussion implies that the answer is no, they were not idle ingenuities. This paper will go on to explain what aspects of the scholarship of canon law kinship common lawyers were interested in; to explain why it was there; to suggest possible uses for this material and to examine a few instances where canon law kinship ideas seem to have had practical impact on cases at common law.

THE TREATISES AND ADAPTATIONS

The canon law trees and treatises that occur in common law manuscripts belong to a genre of introductory texts, probably linked to canon law education at the universities, but also probably useful and interesting for a wider range of non-experts. Many kinship monographs were written in the thirteenth century after the changes to the church's marriage law introduced by the Fourth Lateran Council in 1215 and the contents of these treatises are very similar. Most such treatises occur in manuscripts of the *Decretum* or *Decretals* of Gregory IX, the great teaching texts for medieval canon law; and

---

introduction and notes, 2 vols (Oxford, 1865) [henceforth *Britton*]. There are several genres of trees in *Britton* manuscripts. Adapted *arbores consanguinitatis* occur in: CUL MS Dd.vii.6, Part III, fo.47v; OB MS Bodley 562, fo.98r; OB MS Rawlinson C 898, fo.154v; BL MS Harley 3644, fo.164r; and BL MS Harley 493A, fo.11r (this manuscript contains extracts from *Britton*). BL MS Harley 3644, fo.164r can be seen in Paul Brand, 'Family and inheritance, women and children', in Chris Given-Wilson (ed.), *An illustrated history of late medieval England* (Manchester & New York, 1996), pp 58–81 at p. 76. Cosinage trees or schemata occur in: OB MS Rawlinson C 898, fo.126r; BL MS Harley 3644, fo.132v; OB MS Bodley 562, fo.78r; BL MS Egerton 1842, fos. 257r, 317rv; CUL MS Dd.vii.6, Part III, fo.37r; BL MS Lansdowne 652, fo.71v; BL MS Lansdowne 1176, fo.101r; and BL MS Lansdowne 574, fo.118v. The most popular trees are mort d'ancestor figures. Examples are CUL MS Dd.vii.6, Part III, fo.30v and OB MS Rawlinson C 898, fo.106v.

10 Copied from BL MS Harley 3644, fo.132v.
11 Pollock and Maitland, *History of English law*, ii, 386, 389.

their contents seem to accord well with Helmholz's account of canon law teaching based on the statutes of Oxford university.[12] They are relatively short and simple texts. They teach the technical basics of canon law kinship, and so they teach the reader how quantify the distance of relationships by counting in degrees. The canon law degrees are in the tree in figure 1; they are the numbers at the top of each cell; the numbers at the bottom are civil law degrees. Briefly, for canon law degrees, you take the two people whose distance of relationship you are trying to measure and count the number of degrees from each of them to the common ancestor. If they are equally distant from the common ancestor then that is the number of degrees that separate them for the purpose of calculating whether they are too closely related to marry; if one is more distant from the common ancestor than the other, then the number of degrees of the more remote person is the number of degrees that separate them. The person you count from is *ego*, represented by the empty central cell in figure 1, also called the *truncus or protheus* in medieval canon law scholarship. The treatises also give instructions on how to draw trees like figure 1. They define certain concepts important to canon law kinship; so consanguinity is 'a bond of people descending from the same *stipes*, joined by propagation through the flesh'.[13] They include a few interesting points and commonplaces, but they only teach the bare minimum about canon law marriage rules: they explain that kinsmen related by four degrees cannot marry (that is anyone within four generations related by a common great-great-grandfather). They give no detail about the operation of these rules in practice or in canon law courts. The treatises are more about structures and background than practical marriage law.

Two works on canon law kinship were adapted and occur together in two surviving *Bracton* manuscripts copied in the early fourteenth century.[14] One, *Quibus modis*, named here from the opening words of the rubric from BL MS Harley 653, fos. 40v, is an adaptation of a minor canon law kinship treatise, the *Summa Magistri Iohannis Ispanii Super Arborem de Consanguinitate*.[15] The other, *Triplex est* (again, named here for the opening words) is an adaptation of the section *De cognatione carnali* from the canonist Raymón de Penyafort's

---

12 R.H. Helmholz, *The Oxford history of the laws of England: volume 1: The canon law and ecclesiastical jurisdiction from 597 to the 1640s* (Oxford, 2004), pp 189–90.
13 'Est enim consanguinitas vinculum personarum ab eodem stipite descendentium carnali compagine [*alternatively:* propagatione] contractum' BL MS Harley 653, fo.41r, with the alternative reading from St Raymundus de Peniafort, *Summa de poenitentia et matrimonio* [A facsimile of the Rome edition of 1603] (Farnborough, 1967), p. 533.
14 In BL MS Harley 653, fos 40v–41v and Worcester Cathedral Library MS F 87, fos 28v–29r.
15 The full version of the monograph has been edited: Isaias da Rosa Pereira, 'Lectura Arborum Consanguinitatis et Affinitatis Magistri Ioannis Egitaniensis', *Studia Gratiana* 14, Collectanea Stephan Kuttner 4 (1967), pp 155–82 at pp 165–82.

(1180/85–1275) *Summa de matrimonio* of c.1235.[16] Material from *Bracton*, a reference to a figure that will make 'how the degrees of kinship are computed and the number of degrees that separates one from another in the line of descent or ascent, [...] appear more clearly to the eye', is included at the end of the pair of adapted treatises; thus, it appears that they were originally adapted (and probably later copied) by common lawyers, specifically for this context in *Bracton* manuscripts.[17] In fact, due to the number of mistakes and misreadings in the texts of the treatises and the lack, in both manuscripts, of the promised figure, it seems that neither of the two surviving manuscripts was the original, so it is likely that more *Bracton* manuscripts contained these treatises than survived today. Another canon law treatise, *Quia tractare intendimus*, which was probably written by Raymón of Penyafort c.1235, is similarly adapted in a couple of small statute books copied in the early fourteenth century (BL MS Hargrave 433, fos. 99r–100r and OB MS Douce 17, fos. 161v–163r).[18] The adaptations by common lawyers reduce these treatises, which as a genre are relatively short, even further: the adaptation that occurs in some statute books reduces *Quia tractare intendimus* from 184 lines on consanguinity (in a word processed transcription) to 26, from approximately 2220 words to 296. We are left with only a few definitions, guides to how to count in degrees, and guides to how to draw the tree. The adaptors remove most commonplaces, most examples and most marriage law; they remove all the references to canon law authorities and citations from the *Decretum* and *Decretals* (this is like removing all the footnotes from a modern academic article); they remove all the affinity material that true canon law kinship treatises typically included. Common lawyers were interested in the skeleton of the canon law kinship system; in the structures, the visual images and the underlying ideas; they were not really interested in marriage law. This movement was impulsive, non-systematic, and based on personal interest; yet the fact that these canon law kinship treatises are the most consistent genre of non-common law material to be copied into *Bracton* manuscripts, and the fact that this material was adapted, apparently by common lawyers, suggests that it had practical uses.[19]

16 St Raymundus de Peniafort, *Summa*, pp 533–6.
17 Compare 'Et qualiter gradus cognationis computetur, in quoto gradu quis distet ab alio in linea descendente vel ascendente, in figura inferius depicta manifestius ad oculum apparebit' from BL MS Harley 653, fo.41v, with the last line from the section 'Of those who ought to succeed others and the order of succession' in *Bracton* ii, 200.
18 On *Quia tractare intendimus* see Stephen Kuttner, 'The Barcelona edition of St Raymond's First Treatise on Canon Law' *Seminar*, 8 (1950), 52–67 at 54–6. The short common law adaptation can be compared with the full version as copied into another common law statute book: Winchester Cathedral Library MS 18, fos. 190v–194v.
19 The treatises copied into *Bracton* manuscripts are an eclectic collection by canon law standards; this suggests that the common lawyers copied whatever was near at hand. On additional material in *Bracton* manuscripts see Woodbine's summaries: *Bracton*, i, 5–20.

WHY THEY WERE COPIED INTO COMMON LAW MANUSCRIPTS

So why did common lawyers copy this canon law material? The position of the treatises and trees in *Bracton* manuscripts suggests a partial reason. They are copied into the text of *De Legibus*, beside its difficult and somewhat confusing section on common law kinship where the author explained the parentelic system, but blended and ornamented it with the idea of the tree of consanguinity and with civil law kinship.[20] They are copied after it, as if in answer to it. *Bracton* had offered an ambiguous understanding of degrees of kinship that complicated the discussion of parentelic inheritance.[21] The author had frequently changed the perspective of his discussion, while at the same time talking as if a definite visual structure was being followed.[22] He had used wrong terminology.[23] He had promised a tree that did not occur in the majority of the manuscript tradition (it is impossible to tell if it occurred in his original).[24] All these problems are addressed in the consanguinity treatises where the issues are explained clearly; however, in those treatises the issues are explained clearly in the context of the dominant learned law system – the canon law (which actually operated and affected people's lives and marriages) – rather than the ancillary civil law.

Bracton manuscripts are not alone among common law texts in revealing the influence of canon law kinship. Adapted treatises were copied into statute books; trees were drawn in *Britton* manuscripts; and there are various other small hints of canon law kinship in common law treatises. *Britton* itself quotes a canon law commonplace, that the tree is like a standard, and teaches how to draw two trees adapted from canon law models.[25] The peculiar *Mirror of Justices*, written between 1285 and 1290, also quotes a canon law kinship treatise and refers to the dominant canon law imagery.[26] Even smaller treatises such as *Modus Componendi Brevia* (c.1285) contain hints of such material; when the author is discussing pleas brought on the seisin of a dead ancestor he says that pleas can be arranged by degrees of consanguinity.[27] These canon law

---

20 After *Bracton*, ii, 195–200; except the treatise in CUL MS Dd.vii.6 which occurs before the start of *Bracton*, at the end of a section containing various short common law treatises.

21 For example, *Bracton*, ii, 196, 199.

22 *Bracton*, ii, 195–200.

23 The *tripatruus magnus* is an example; this term appears to have been created by the author to signify the brother of the great-great-great-great-grandfather. The author also made mistakes: for example he used the term *proavunculus magnus* for the great-grandmother's brother who would usually be called *proavunculus*: *Bracton*, ii, 199–200.

24 *Bracton*, ii, 200.

25 *Britton* ii, 326 and ii, 164–5, 323–4.

26 W.J. Whittaker (ed.), *The mirror of justices*, with an introduction by F.W. Maitland, Selden Society vol. 7 (London, 1895), pp 21, 50.

27 George E. Woodbine, *Four thirteenth century law tracts* (New Haven, 1910), pp 147–8.

treatises and trees were part of a broader movement and wider interest in learned law kinship among common lawyers. But why were they interested? What uses did common lawyers have for this canon law material?

The operation of the canon law could have an impact on the common law. Recent studies of the canon law of marriage have shown that the system operated in England, more or less, though 'divorces' on the grounds of consanguinity and affinity were actually very rare.[28] There are a few more examples of *ex officio* prosecutions of 'incestuous' unions, with some sense of scandal for unions between kinsmen as distant as the third and fourth degrees.[29] There are also examples of people purchasing dispensations to be able to marry within the degrees.[30] The mechanism of the banns,[31] and the repetitions of the rules in synodal legislation suggest that the canon law kinship rules could have been fairly well known.[32] The church's kinship system, operating in the field of marriage law, could affect land at common law. A 'divorce' could have an impact on whether the wife got her dower and the son his inheritance: there was an action for dower and of entry *cui ante divortium*;[33] and a mnemonic on the seven types of 'divorce' and the consequences for dower and inheritance occurs in the short thirteenth century *Summa on Bastardy*

---

28 On the operation of the canon law on marriage and 'divorce' (and thus consanguinity and affinity) in England see R.H. Helmholz, *Oxford history*, chapter 10. There was a remarkably low level of 'divorces' on the grounds of consanguinity and affinity, in fact of 'divorces' as such: R.H. Helmholz, *Marriage litigation in medieval England* (Cambridge, 1974), pp 77–87; Norma Adams and Charles Donahue Jr. (eds), *Select cases from the ecclesiastical courts of the province of Canterbury c.1200–1301*, Selden Society vol. 95 (London, 1981), pp 81–4; Frederik Pedersen, *Marriage disputes in medieval England* (London, 2000), p. 137; D. L. d'Avray, *Medieval marriage: symbolism and society* (Oxford, 2005), pp 112–16.

29 Charles Donahue Jr., 'The monastic judge: social practice, formal rule and the medieval law of incest' in Peter Landau and Martin Petzolt (eds), *De iure canonico medii aevi: Festschrift für Rudolf Weigand*, Studia Gratiana 27 (Rome, 1996), pp 49–69; L.R. Poos (ed.), *Lower ecclesiastical jurisdiction in late-medieval England: the courts of the dean and chapter of Lincoln, 1336–1349, and the deanery of Wisbech, 1458–1484* (Oxford, 2001), p. 32.

30 R.N. Swanson (ed.), *The register of John Catterick, bishop of Coventry and Lichfield, 1415–1419*, Canterbury and York Society vol. 77 (Woodbridge, 1990), pp 24–33.

31 X 4.3.3 in A. Friedberg (ed.), *Corpus iuris canonici: editio Lipsiensis secunda post Aemilii Ludouici Richteri, II, decretalium collectiones* (Graz, 1959). Conciliar legislation from England repeated the need for the banns and marriage at the church door: Michael M. Sheehan, 'Marriage theory and practice in the conciliar legislation and diocesan statutes of medieval England', in James K. Farge (ed.), *Marriage, family, and law in medieval Europe: collected studies* (Toronto, 1996), pp 118–76 at pp 145–54.

32 F.M. Powicke and C.R. Cheney (eds), *Councils and synods with other documents relating to the English church: II. A.D. 1205–1313*, 2 vols (Oxford, 1964) pp 34, 88, 89 190, 197, 234, 377, 636, 644.

33 For examples see: G.J. Turner (ed.), *YB 4 Edward II*, Selden Society vol. 42 (London, 1926), pp 47–50; *EELR*, ii, 309–10; and Luke Owen Pike (ed.), *YB 20 Edward III*, vol. 2 (London, 1911), pp 72–81.

and also circulates alone in various statute books and other manuscripts.³⁴ This could be useful material for a common lawyer to know.

But 'divorces' were relatively rare. And 'divorces' on the ground of consanguinity were extremely rare. They cannot explain the interest common lawyers showed in canon law kinship. It seems rather that the canon law kinship system, which was the dominant pan-European kinship system, and which operated more or less in England, was part of the background against which the common law operated. In this period some common lawyers had a university education, some owned canon law books, some obviously copied and took an interest in canon law kinship.³⁵ The material was generally interesting and possibly particularly useful; and the mnemonic about claims for dower after 'divorce' shows one small instance of this.

This material could be theoretically useful too. Trees like that in figure 2 are associated with the action of cosinage (in Latin the writ was a *breve de consanguinitate*).³⁶ The title of one of the adapted canon law treatises copied into statute books was *Des degrez de cosinage* despite the fact that most of the material on degrees that occurred in the original canon law treatise had been removed.³⁷ It is possible that this material was useful in sorting out the kinsmen who could use an action of cosinage.

There are intriguing hints that this material could be associated with teaching. One of the adapted treatises that occur in *Bracton* manuscripts contains a collection of 'items' that the reader is commanded to note. These expand upon and explain the kinship material that had come before, for example, there is a discussion of a problem that appears to have been caused by an occasional common law adaptation of the *arbor consanguinitatis* that can be seen in figure 2, in *Bracton* and in several adapted trees – omitting the *ego* to make the ascending and descending lines one (a necessity for a common law conception of kinship which did not put *ego* at the centre of its calculations but rather detailed the different lines through which land might descend from the dead landowning *propositus* to the claimant):³⁸

---

34 For a transcription of the mnemonic on 'divorce' see Wilfred Hooper, *The law of illegitimacy: a treatise on the law affecting persons of illegitimate birth, with the rules of evidence in proof of legitimacy and illegitimacy; and an historical account of the bastard in mediæval law* (London, 1911), pp 227–33. For further references to this mnemonic see: J.H. Baker, *Catalogue*, p. 354, art.78 a.

35 On lawyers with a university education see: Paul Brand, *Origins of the English legal profession* (Oxford, 1992), p. 155. For the book collection of Matthew of the Exchequer see: R.J. Whitwell, 'The libraries of a civilian and canonist and of a common lawyer, an. 1294', *Law Quarterly Review* 21 (1905), 393–400 at 399–400.

36 Such trees occur in *Britton*, beside the section 'Of the writs of Cosinage, Ael, and Besael': *Britton*, ii, 165.

37 BL MS Hargrave 433, fo.99r.

38 *Bracton*, ii, 196–7, 199 and, among others, in MS CUL Dd.vii.6, Part III, fo. 47v or MS BL Harley 493A, fo.11r.

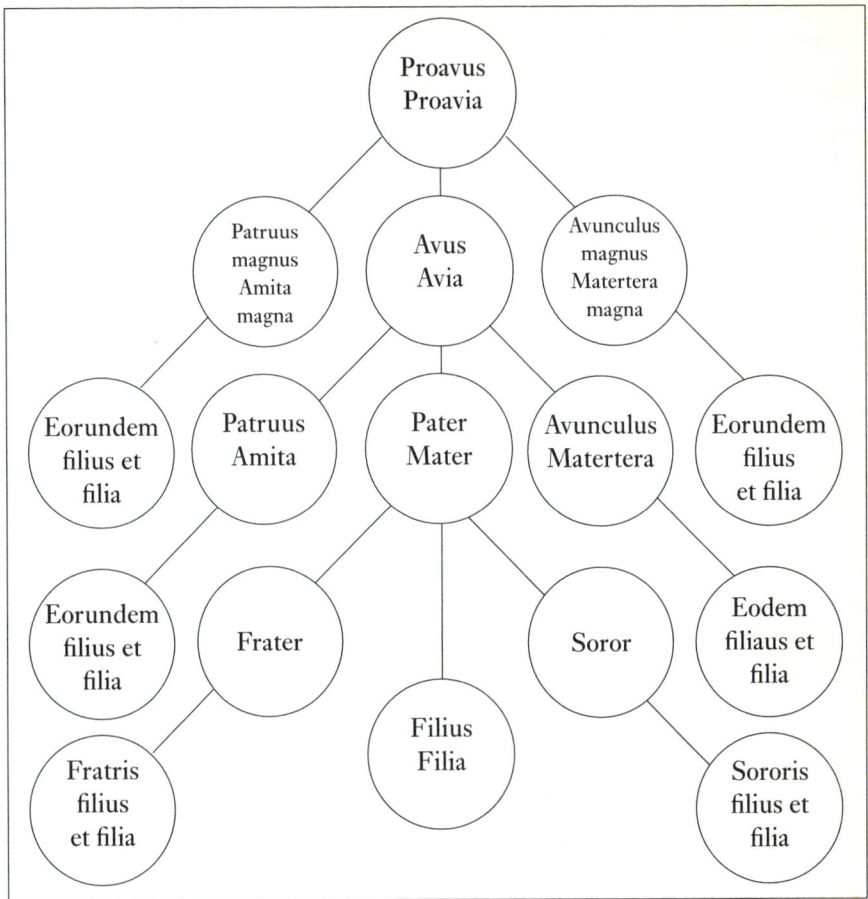

Figure 2: A 'cosinage tree', based on a tree drawn beside the section on the actions of aiel, besaiel and cosinage in a *Britton* manuscript: BL MS Harley 3644, fo.132v.

> Note that the same line is called ascending and descending, being made higher or lower, in relation to different computations. But if only one line were to be put in the tree, which would be ascending, on account of the changing of people's names, something would be lacking, and it could not be called ascending and descending in respect of the *truncus* [that is, *ego*]. Two lines are therefore put so that the defect might be avoided and so that this one might be called ascending, and that one descending in respect of the *truncus*.[39]

[39] At the end of *Quibus modis*: 'Non [*correctly* Nota] quod eadem linea dicitur ascendens et descendens, superiori [*correctly* superior] et inferiori [*correctly* inferior] facta relatione ad diversam computationem. Set si tantum una linea poneretur in arbore, que esset ascendens propter mutationem nominum personarum, esset ibi defectus, nec posset dici ascendens et

It is tempting to speculate that such 'items' could be associated with teaching. Elsewhere, the adapted canon law trees that occur in *Britton* manuscripts are explicitly given *en eyde des prentiz*.[40] In the British Library, a manuscript that was probably a teacher or student's collection (BL MS Harley 493A) contains an adapted canon law tree.[41] We know that some common law lectures used handouts and visual images.[42] If there ever was a common law lecture on the degrees of cosinage, might it not have used one of the trees that common lawyers copied instructions to draw? It is an interesting idea, but is impossible to prove.

CANON LAW KINSHIP AND COMMON LAW PRACTICE

This interaction between the common and canon laws was not merely a matter of cultural interest, limited to texts and manuscripts; it occurred in practice too and some elements of the canon law kinship rules had an impact on cases in the common law courts.

This conclusion is based on the year books, the records of common lawyers' pleas and arguments, where we are most likely to find evidence of their thinking about canon law kinship. The three case studies examined below reveal the possible influence of canon law kinship ideas on common law cases: in the choice of four degrees as a limit on kinship; in the fact that common lawyers sometimes counted in degrees of kinship; and in the confusion over who could be called a 'cousin' at common law. A case can be made for a modest but important influence of this material. It is often not explicit. However, explicit references to the learned laws in the year books are rare.[43]

THE FOUR-DEGREE LIMIT ON KINSHIP

The strongest case for influence seems to be the number of times common lawyers chose four degrees (or four generations, or the great-great-grandfather) as a limit for kinship.

Four degrees was the canon law limit.[44] *Britton*, who had clearly read some canon law treatises (since he quoted one), occasionally used four degrees or

descendens respectu trunci. Posite ergo sunt due linee ibi, ut vitaretur defectus et ut diceretur [iste] ascendens, et ille descendens, respectu trunci.' BL MS Harley 653, fos. 40v–41r corrected against Worcester Cathedral Library MS F 87, fo.29r.

40 *Britton*, ii, 323.
41 BL MS Harley 493A, fo. 11r. On the probability that this is a teacher's or student's collection see: *EELR*, i, p. lxxxi.
42 Paul Brand, 'Courtroom and schoolroom: the education of lawyers in England prior to 1400', in his *The making of the common law* (London, 1992), pp 57–75 at p. 62, n.21.
43 David Seipp found between one and seven references to the civil and canon laws per decade during the fourteenth century: David J. Seipp, 'The reception of canon law and civil law in the common law courts before 1600', *Oxford Journal of Legal Studies*, 13:3 (1993), 388–420 at 392.
44 X 4.14.8.

the equivalent as a limit on common law kinship.⁴⁵ Sometimes common lawyers made the canon law parallel explicit. There is a thirteenth century lecture on *De Donis* (part of which has been published by Paul Brand) which makes it plain that some common lawyers drew analogies with the canon law limit on kinship; it says:

> according to some in conditional gifts the blood of the feoffees is not made pure and the estate does not return to its first nature until marriage could take place between the issue of the feoffor and the issue of the brother or sister to whom the tenements are thus given.⁴⁶

Common lawyers could draw on the underlying rules of the canon law when they wanted to limit the extended family. Not all common lawyers drew on these rules to find a limit; but a number did. This limit, the great-great-grandfather, was used in a cosinage case from 1278.⁴⁷ In the 1340s, the four-generation limit was confirmed when the great-great-grandfather (the *tresaiel*) was allowed to be called a cousin.⁴⁸ According to *Bracton*, and in various cases, four degrees was the limit at which homage and services had to be done in frankmarriage and other *maritagia*.⁴⁹ Four degrees was the limit some people put on parceners who could draw other more distant relatives into an action: Justice Brunton (interpreting chapter 6 of the Statute of Gloucester) added a four-degree limit, where the original clause had just said that the heirs who could claim by mort d'ancestor could draw parceners 'of a further degree' into the action;⁵⁰ and in *Robert de Lascelles and Others v. Thomas of Moulton and Others* it was said that 'the fourth degree of lineal descent can and ought to attract the other degrees even though they are more remote'.⁵¹ Four degrees was the limit some people put on an ascending resort in a possessory action, that is, how many generations a claimant could count upwards from the person who had died seised in making a resort to a collateral line connecting themselves to that last seised person, as in the 1286

---

45 For him a plea of *rationabili parte* extended as far as the great-great-grandfather (*Britton*, ii, 82) and the great-great-grandfather was his ascending limit for cosinage (*Britton*, ii, 163).
46 Paul Brand, 'Legal education in England before the inns of court' in Jonathan A. Bush and Alain Wijffels (eds), *Learning the law: teaching and the transmission of law in England, 1150–1900* (London, 1999), pp 51–84 at pp 66–7.
47 Paul Brand, *Kings, barons and justices: the making and enforcement of legislation in thirteenth-century England* (Cambridge, 2003), p. 54, n.45.
48 Luke Owen Pike (ed.), *YB 15 Edward III* (London, 1891), pp 370–3; and Luke Owen Pike (ed.), *YB 19 Edward III* (London, 1906), pp 332–5.
49 *Bracton*, ii, 77. This is discussed in detail in Joseph Biancalana, *The fee tail and the common recovery in medieval England, 1176–1502* (Cambridge, 2001), pp 43–51.
50 Alfred J. Horwood (ed.), *YB 30 & 31 Edward I* (London, 1863), pp 104–7; cf. 6 Edward I, Statute of Gloucester, c.6 in *Stat Realm*, vol. 1 (1810).
51 *EELR*, ii, 264.

case *Robert de Lascelles and Others v. Thomas of Moulton and Others*, where it was said: 'In the ascent in making a resort it is only possible to go up to the fourth degree.'[52] The four-degree limit was also, famously, used as the limit on inalienability of entails that Chief Justice Bereford implied into the statute *De Donis* in *Belyng v. Anon:* 'He that made the statute meant to bind the issue in fee tail as well as the feoffees until the tail had reached the fourth degree; and it was only through negligence that he omitted to insert express words to that effect in the statute.'[53]

When a limit on kinship was necessary and the common law did not offer an obvious one, some common lawyers turned to the limit of the canon law; after all, this would have operated in wider society, or at least people, with mechanisms like the banns reminding them of the impediments to marriage, would have been aware of it as if it operated.

COUNTING IN DEGREES OF KINSHIP

Common lawyers quite often counted in degrees of kinship, sometimes on learned law models. The author of *Bracton* had used degrees, as had *Britton* and various other authors of short common law treatises, though their understanding of degrees was not always the same as those of the canon or civil lawyers.[54] The man who copied an adapted and abbreviated canon law treatise into a small statute book called it *Des degrez de cosinage*, linking it to that action, despite the fact that it retained virtually none of the canon law learning on degrees that had occurred in the original.[55] Obviously the concept was important to common lawyers. This adapted treatise suggests a common law context for degrees of kinship: it changes the original canon law reading and says that the calculation of degrees is made *ad mortem*.[56] Now, there is no point calculating canon law degrees (for the purposes of marriage)

---

52 *EELR*, ii, 262–4 at 262; however, one justice says that 'one can only make resort to the fifth degree in ascending'.

53 William Craddock Bolland (ed.), *YB 5 Edward II*, Selden Society vol. 31 (1915), p. 177.

54 For example, *Bracton*, ii, 77, 196, 199. *Britton*, ii, 57, 322, 324 treated degrees like cells on a tree and discussed 'vacant degrees'. Various short common law treatises also speak of degrees, for example William Huse Dunham Jr (ed.), *Casus placitorum and reports of cases in the king's courts, 1272–1278*, Selden Society vol. 69 (London, 1952), pp 23/6, 19/83; or *Fet Asaver*, in George E. Woodbine, *Four thirteenth century law tracts*, p. 100; or G.J. Turner (ed.), *Brevia placitata*, completed with additions by T.F.T. Plucknett, Selden Society vol. 66 (London, 1951), p. 179.

55 See note 37.

56 'Gradus est quedam habitudo sive distantia personarum, facta ad mortem, collectione ad communem parentem, qua cognoscitur qua generationis distantia due persone inter se defecerint.' BL MS Hargrave 433, fo. 99v. The canon law versions that I have seen merely read 'facta'.

at death. The addition suggests that this material was being thought about in the context of inheritance or a claim after death, a plausible common law context. Though not necessarily a useful one, since neither canon nor civil law degrees worked for calculating who was the nearer heir who should inherit according to the common law rules (for example, brothers and sisters were in the same degree in the learned law systems, while a grandchild by the eldest son would be in a more distant degree from his grandfather than a younger son).

This parallel between degrees of kinship as used by civil or canon lawyers and degrees of kinship as used by common lawyers is largely a feature of the common law texts. In common law cases degrees, in reference to kinship connections, are less obviously used under learned law parallels, although there was sometimes explicit reference to canon law degrees, for example, in cases mentioning 'divorces'.[57] There are various instances in the year books where we see common lawyers using the term degree: people are sometimes said to be 'in' a degree;[58] degrees are used to denote limits;[59] and other uses imply a series or line of degrees.[60] We might draw a parallel here with another sense in which common lawyers used 'degrees', that is with the degrees of entry. A writ of entry was aimed at tenants who had entered wrongly (for example, through a disseisin) and the degrees of entry were the hands the land had passed through. Degrees is the usual term to explain such a step-by-step progression. Yet some cases appear to show learned law influence, probably through the somewhat confused model offered by *Bracton*; some cases from the late thirteenth- and early fourteenth-century appear to use degrees of kinship in his manner, counting every person in a line as a degree, including ego.[61] These cases are less than clear, which suggests, perhaps, that the reporters or later copyists had problems with this system. Such parallels suggest that what influence degrees of kinship based on learned law sources had on common law cases, and texts, was a matter of parallel counting systems which could cause confusion. What sense of degrees of kinship there was may have come from the learned laws, probably through *Bracton*, or maybe through a synthetic law school that taught Roman and common law.[62]

---

57 For example, after a divorce for affinity in the fourth degree of blood: Alfred J. Horwood (ed.), with Preface and Index by Luke Owen Pike, *YB 11 & 12 Edward III* (London, 1883), p. 482.
58 *YB 30 & 31 Edward I*, p. 226; Luke Owen Pike (ed.), *YB 17 Edward III* (London, 1901), p. 560.
59 *EELR*, ii, p. 262; Alfred J. Horwood (ed.), *YB 30 & 31 Edward I* (London, 1863), p. 106.
60 Alfred J. Horwood (ed.), *YB 21 & 22 Edward I* (London, 1873), p. 364; *EELR*, ii, p. 262; William Craddock Bolland (ed.), *YB 5 Edward II*, Selden Society vol. 33 (1916), p. 226; Luke Owen Pike (ed.), *YB 13 & 14 Edward III* (London, 1886), p. 352.
61 Particularly in *Robert de Lascelles and others v. Thomas of Moulton and others*, in *EELR*, ii, pp 262–4 and possibly *YB 30 & 31 Edward I*, 104–7.
62 On the possibility of such a 'synthesis' school in Westminster see: Paul Brand, 'Westminster Hall and Europe: European aspects of the common law' in Julia Boffey and Pamela King

WHO COULD BE CALLED 'COUSIN'?

Canon law ideas about kinship seem likely to have contributed to the confusion over who could be called a 'cousin' (and thus be able to use cosinage, or be named a 'cousin' in a writ) at common law. From the late thirteenth century to the 1340s litigants kept trying to bring actions that named lineal ascendants, for example, great-great-grandparents (on whose possession of land a claim could not be asserted in possessory actions), as 'cousins'. These litigants (or their lawyers) kept arguing that beyond the besaiel (the great-grandfather) every relative was a 'cousin'. The justices kept rejecting that definition.[63] There is an element of convenience in the plaintiffs' arguments. They wanted to claim their land with the quicker, cheaper possessory action, rather than be driven to use their writ of right. But there is also a definitional argument. It seems that the Chancery, which issued the writs, defined 'cousin' differently than the justices in the courts did. When the justices finally allowed a great-great-grandfather to be called 'cousin' they conceded 'because there is no other form of writ, in as much as a great-great-grandfather is in Chancery made 'cousin' according to their custom'.[64] This does not seem to be merely a matter of litigants who used the canon law definition going to Chancery and requesting a writ to claim the land of their *consanguineus*. Senior Chancery clerks advised litigants on what writ to buy from the time of Edward I.[65] At least one case makes it clear that people were not merely asking for a writ based on the seisin of their *consanguineus*. This was a case of mort d'ancestor, where the land was claimed by two parceners, one of whom was the daughter of the *propositus* and the other of whom was a great-great-grandson (who descended from the other daughter of the *propositus*). Because of the structure of this mixed action, based on mort d'ancestor claiming on the 'father's' seisin, the Chancery must have knowingly issued a writ that made this direct ancestor to be a 'cousin' of his great-great-grandson.[66]

(eds), *London and Europe in the later Middle Ages* (London, 1995), pp 55–85 at pp 63–4; Paul Brand, 'Legal education', pp 57–8.

63 Alfred J. Horwood (ed.), *YB 20 & 21 Edward I* (London, 1866), pp 154–7 and pp 226–9; *YB 30 & 31 Edward I*, pp 104–7; Alfred J. Horwood (ed.), *YB 32 & 33 Edward I* (London, 1864), pp 16–21; G.J. Turner (ed.), completed with an Introduction by Theodore F.T. Plucknett, *YB 5 Edward II*, Selden Society vol. 63 (1947), pp 95–7; William Craddock Bolland, Frederic William Maitland and Leveson William Vernon Harcourt (eds), *YB of The Eyre of Kent 6 and 7 Edward II*, vol. 2, Selden Society vol. 27 (1912), pp 8–9; M. Dominica Legge and Sir William Holdsworth (eds), *YB 10 Edward II*, Selden Society vol. 54 (1935), pp 7–8; Luke Owen Pike (ed.), *YB 12 & 13 Edward III* (London, 1885), pp 360–1.

64 *YB 19 Edward III*, p. 332.

65 D.A. Carpenter, 'The English royal chancery in the thirteenth century' in Kouky Fianu and DeLloyd J. Guth (eds), *Écrit et pouvoir dans le chancelleries médiévales: espace français, espace anglais*, Textes et etudes du moyen age 6 (Louvain-la-Neuve, 1997), pp 25–53 at 35.

66 *YB 20 & 21 Edward I*, pp 154–7. The plea roll entry is JUST 1/303 (1292 Herefs eyre),

In fact, three definitions of 'cousin' appear from the cases. The first was the restrictive definition of the justices, who said that a 'cousin' had to be a collateral kinsman: 'My great-great-grandfather will never be named cousin to me, for cosinage is always in the collateral line.'[67] If the writ named someone a 'cousin' who, from the count, turned out to be a lineal ascendant, the plaintiff would lose because of this variation between their writ and count: 'you can not deny that he is great-great-grandfather. whereas your writ supposes that he is cousin'.[68] They were defeated by the rules of pleading. The second definition was advanced by Chief Justice Bereford in 1311, according to the report of *Latimer v. Clendon*. He would not allow ascendants to be called 'cousins', though he thought that 'the younger generation are strictly speaking "cousins" to their grandfathers, great-grandfathers and great-great-grandfathers'.[69] So 'cousins' could be blood-kinsmen descending from a common ancestor, but not ascendants. The third definition is that of the Chancery, which, 'according to their custom', allowed ascendants also to be called 'cousin', essentially using 'cousin' as a catch-all term for blood-kinsmen. The justices eventually accepted this definition in the 1340s.[70]

The potential for canon law influence comes from the fact that cosin in Anglo-French was translated as *consanguineus* in Latin.[71] Consanguinity (*consanguinitas*) was the canon law term for blood-kinship and the canon law definition of consanguinity was 'a bond of people descending from the same *stipes*, joined by propagation through the flesh'.[72] Canon lawyers thus defined a consanguine as someone descended from the same *stipes*, joined by fleshy propagation (limited to four degrees for the purposes of marriage), which appears similar to the third definition current from the common law cases, the one favoured by Chancery clerks. Even the second common law definition has canon law parallels; Kilwardby, in his treatise on canon law kinship, noted how the standard canon law definition can be read as if it excludes ascendants.[73]

If there was canon law influence it is hard to see directly. But, knowing as we do that some common lawyers read canon law treatises and were

m.26. My thanks to Paul Brand for providing me with a transcript of the plea roll entry for this case.
67 *YB 5 Edward II*, Selden Society vol. 63 (1947), p. 96.
68 *YB 20 & 21 Edward I*, p. 228.
69 *YB 5 Edward II*, Selden Society vol. 63 (1947), p. 96. There is a similar definition in *Britton*, ii, 163.
70 See note 64.
71 *YB 5 Edward II*, Selden Society vol. 63 (1947), pp xxxix–xl per Theodore F.T. Plucknett; *YB 5 Edward II*, Selden Society vol. 33 (1916), p. xl; *Brevia Placitata*, pp xxxvi, cxx–cxxi.
72 See note 13.
73 'Quia cum [*correctly* tamen] ista descriptio non continet nisi personas descendentes, excluso parente communi, et consanguinitas habeant [*correctly* haut] dubium est inter patrem et filios' CUL MS Dd.vii.6, Part III, fo.66r.

interested in the canon law definition of consanguinity, it seems likely that canon law ideas contributed to the intellectual confusion over who should be called a 'cousin' at common law. After all, a writ of cosinage was a *breve de consanguinitate*. If this was a matter of borrowing, or confusion, between the *consanguineus* at common and canon law, it was a selective borrowing: the writers of the year books and plea rolls do not appear to use the host of specific canon law terms for kinsmen.[74] Yet, most of the simple canon law beginners' treatises we find in common law manuscripts did not use that heavy terminology.

It seems likely that there was some school of thought that equated the cosin at common law with the *consanguineus* at canon law. Whether this usage was among the litigants themselves, who might have regarded lineal ascendants as consanguines, or the clerks and the lawyers is more difficult to tell, though context perhaps makes it seem likely that it may have been the Chancery clerks. Yet the fact that the common lawyers found their own tree (based on canon law trees) useful for depicting who could use the action of cosinage and the fact that one of the treatises is entitled *Des degrez de cosinage* suggests that at least some common lawyers made the analogy between the two.

CONCLUSION

Common lawyers had their own system for ordering the extended kindred, based on parentelic inheritance.[75] They did not co-opt canon or civil law kinship; nor did they take it as a model or borrow from it or use it consistently. Yet some common lawyers copied canon law kinship treatises and trees into *Bracton* manuscripts, and some adapted this material and included hints and quotations in other treatises at the end of the thirteenth and start of the fourteenth centuries. Some may have included this material in answer to *Bracton's* confusing synthesis with civil law kinship; others seem to have included it because canon law kinship was known (if not always followed) in society, and because the canon law way of thinking about kinship, as embodied in the many short kinship monographs copied and written by canon lawyers, was important intellectually. Common lawyers seem, judging by their adaptations, to have been most interested in canon law images of kinship and in their definitions and way of thinking about kin. They may even have used this material in a teaching context (though this is not certain, and this does not mean that there were lectures on the subject

---

74 Which can be seen in *Decretum* C.35 q. 5 c. 6 in A. Friedberg (ed.), *Corpus iuris canonici: editio Lipsiensis secunda post Aemilii Ludouici Richteri, I, Decretum Magistri Gratiani* (Graz, 1959).
75 Pollock and Maitland, *History of English law*, ii, 260–302.

since, after all, education can take place by reading). Some elements of canon law kinship appear to have had a modest but interesting influence on common law cases. Some common lawyers turned to canon law limits on kinship when the common law did not offer an immediate or necessary limit; some common lawyers counted in degrees of kinship, perhaps influenced or confused by learned law degrees; some common lawyers, or perhaps some clerks or some litigants at common law, seem to have drawn parallels between the *cosin* at common law and the canon law *consanguineus* (certainly there seems to be some link between the adapted canon law material and the action of cosinage). In many ways this borrowing is more of an indication of cultural interest than of practical cooption of rules or laws. Canon law ideas about how to structure the extended kindred, how to define and depict it, appear to have been culturally dominant. Some common lawyers took an interest in this, attempting to adapt some of these technical, structural ideas to suit their own needs – be it for a clear explanation of the extended kindred, an image, or a convenient limit for who counted as kin. Thus, this canon law material was not an 'idle ingenuity' for the common lawyers who copied, adapted, and occasionally borrowed from it.

The making of English thirteenth-century legislation: some new evidence

PAUL BRAND

THE PROVISIONS OF WESTMINSTER OF 1259 enjoyed only a brief period of full legal validity. Initially, they were superseded simply by the issuing of a revised and expanded version of the same Provisions in January 1263. These were in turn reissued later that same year and again in 1264. The 1263–4 revision of the Provisions was then itself in turn superseded in November 1267 by the Statute of Marlborough. This incorporated with only minor revisions almost all of the clauses contained in the original Provisions and in the revised versions of 1263–4, but prefaced the revised and reissued Provisions with eight new clauses. Quite deliberately, it made no acknowledgment of the extent of its indebtedness to the 1259 Provisions. It is hardly surprising then, that it was the Statute alone that was known to, and cited by, later generations of lawyers and justices; the Statute, and not the Provisions, that was copied into books of statutes and the subject of readings in the inns of court. The Provisions of Westminster then fell into a kind of historical limbo which lasted for almost five centuries. They do not seem to have been rediscovered by scholars until the second quarter of the eighteenth century. Serjeant William Hawkins must take the credit for being their first modern editor. He included a text of the Provisions in an Appendix to his edition of the *Statutes at Large* in 1735–6. This then led to the inclusion of a text of the Provisions (drawn unfortunately only from the inferior text on the Close Rolls) in its proper chronological place in volume I of the still standard *Statutes of the Realm* published in 1811. The Provisions of Westminster had at long last taken their proper, historical place in the English legislative canon.[1]

The Provisions of Westminster are of considerable interest in their own right as the first major legislation in England since Magna Carta. They gain additional interest from the fact that they are the one piece of English thirteenth century legislation other than Magna Carta for which we have multiple pieces of evidence to shed light on the process of their drafting. The

---

1 Paul Brand, *Kings, barons and justices: the making and enforcement of legislation in thirteenth century England* (Cambridge, 2003), pp 2–3.

rediscovery of these various pieces of evidence has been a much more gradual process; indeed, as this paper will show, it is one that is still continuing. The first stage in the process of drafting is that associated with the document known since the time of Bishop Stubbs (but somewhat misleadingly) as the 'Petition of the Barons'. This is a series of requests or demands in the form of petitions for legal and administrative changes, some of which clearly stimulated the drafting of certain clauses of the Provisions. These requests were submitted to the king at the Oxford parliament of the summer of 1258 and were perhaps channeled through the baronage, but they were certainly not all the work of the barons, nor did they represent only their demands.[2] One version of this document (that found in one of the two MSS containing the annals of Burton abbey) has been in print since 1684 and was re-edited by Luard in the Rolls Series in 1864 and included by Stubbs in his *Select Charters* of 1870. Two other versions with some significant variants, one in a second copy of the Burton Annals, a second in a seventeenth century transcript of material probably associated with Darley abbey, have only come to light since (in 1895 and 1933).[3]

A single text, which I discovered by lucky chance in a MS now in the Free Library of Philadelphia and published in 1990, provides our only evidence for the next stage in the drafting process, the first to produce any kind of draft of actual legislation. This is a French language first draft of just over one-third (nine) of the twenty-four clauses of the Provisions of Westminster as eventually enacted and published in October 1259, plus drafts of two other clauses, one of which was included in the revised and reissued Provisions of 1263, the other never enacted. It seems most likely that it was produced by a drafting sub-committee for discussion at the Candlemas parliament of February 1259.[4] Discussion and revision of this text at that parliament and translation of the revised text for formal publication produced the next document in the series, the *Providencia Baronum*, published in March 1259. This had been wholly unknown to scholars till edited by E.F. Jacob from two of the four surviving copies, in 1925. Denholm–Young drew attention to the existence of a third MS copy of the document in 1935, but did not print its text or even note its significant variants from other MSS. In 1990 I took the latter course and also noted for the first time the existence of a fourth (albeit only fragmentary) text.[5]

Until now, evidence was known to survive for only one other stage in the drafting process, the production of a penultimate draft version of the

---

2 For the relationship between the Petition and the eventual legislation see Paul Brand, *The making of the common law* (London, 1992), pp 328–33.
3 Brand, *Making of the common law*, pp 327–8.
4 Ibid., pp 337–44. The text is printed at pp 359–61.
5 Ibid., pp 335–7, 355–7.

Provisions as a whole for the Michaelmas parliament of 1259. This contained versions of all the clauses to be found in the eventual published text, though these are by no means identical in substance with those in the final version. It also contained versions of two clauses which were omitted from that published text. This penultimate draft survives in five different texts. Four are in French, evidently the languge of the original; in a fifth, the French text has been translated rather clumsily into Latin. The inclusion of two of these texts in the Burton annals ensured that they have been in print since the late seventeenth century, but it was not until 1990 that a proper edition using all five manuscripts was published. It was also only then that it was also recognized that these texts represented a late stage in the drafting process, not just a French version of the Latin official text of the Provisions.[6]

What was obviously still missing was any evidence of an earlier drafting stage than the penultimate draft for fifteen of the twenty-four clauses of the Provisions of Westminster. By the time I was working on the final revision of the text of my book *Kings, Barons and Justices* which discussed the evolution of this legislation and its subsequent interpretation and application for publication in 2003, I had become reconciled to what seemed to be the high probability that such evidence would never be found. I was wrong, and it was all the more galling that I discovered the evidence to the contrary while that book was still in the press, but too late to make any substantial changes to it. Equally galling was the fact that the evidence had been sitting all along in a library less than a mile from my London home in North Lambeth, in the library of Lambeth Palace. Lambeth Palace MS 499 is one of the Lambeth Palace MSS included in the *Descriptive Catalogue* published by M.R. James in 1932.[7] It is a very miscellaneous manuscript of just over three hundred folios associated with the Cistercian house of Whalley in Lancashire, which had transferred to Whalley from Stanlaw in Cheshire in 1296. The manuscript is divided into four separate sections. Only the fourth of these (beginning at fo. 217) contains any common law material, though it also contains canon law material as well. The common law material includes various statutory texts, including texts of Magna Carta and the Charter of the Forest, the Statute of Merton, the Statute of Marlborough, the Statute of Westminster I, the Statute of Acton Burnel and an incomplete text of the Statute of Wales, not in date order. There are curious features to several of these texts. What purports to be a text of the Statute of Westminster I begins on fo. 275v with the clear *incipit* 'Here begin the constitutions of the king Edward the son of king Henry, which he made for the amendment of the land on the advice of wise men two weeks after Easter in the year of our

---

6 Ibid., pp 349–52, 361–7.
7 M.R. James, *A descriptive catalogue of the manuscripts in the library of Lambeth Palace: the mediaeval manuscripts* (Cambridge, 1932), pp 691–701.

Lord's Incarnation 1275 and in the third year since his coronation'.[8] Slightly muddled maybe (for Edward had only just been crowned in 1275), but otherwise the date is right for the Statute of Westminster I. And there does indeed follow a text of that Statute, but beginning only on fo. 276v. What interests us here, however, is the intervening material (on fos. 275v–276v) between that *incipit* and the start of the Statute proper. And, to anticipate my conclusion, what it turns out to be is indeed part, and as it turns out perhaps all, of the missing evidence.

There is no original enumeration of the clauses in this section, but it comprises what I have divided for the purposes of analysis into eleven separate clauses. No less than seven out of these eleven are quite unmistakably draft versions of clauses that were to find their way into the eventual final text of the Provisions of Westminster of October 1259. One of them (clause 10 in my enumeration) is a draft of what was eventually to form clauses 1–3 of the Provisions. It is the only clause which covers a topic that had also been covered in the earlier French and Latin drafts of the *Providencia Baronum*.[9] Detailed analysis and comparison of this clause with the earlier clauses and the final text indicate that it almost certainly belongs to a later stage in the drafting process. Its statement of the general rules governing the obligation to perform suit of court represents a major revision of the rules in the earlier draft and is much closer to those of the final text; and the rules stated to apply on a division of an inheritance between parceners are also close to those of the final text. The only puzzling feature is the omission of the provisions relating to recovery by default in the tenant's action to redress the usurpation of suit of court, and to the creation of a lord's action to recover suit which are found in both the earlier draft and the final text. The more likely reason for this is scribal error or accidental omission, but it is possible that both were omitted deliberately but then reintroduced at a later stage.

The other six clauses (clauses 3–8 of this draft) are the earliest known surviving drafts of seven of the clauses of the eventual final text.[10] Clause 3 (the earliest known draft of what was to form clause 24 of the Provisions) exempts the sureties of a cleric accused of felony who then pleads his clerical status from amercement, provided they have produced him before the justices in eyre, even if he is then unwilling to stand trial.[11] This is close in substance to the eventual text but has an additional clause, which is not so much an explanation as an additional gloss, which is omitted from the final

8 The full text (and a translation) are given below in the Appendix.
9 For a discussion of the evolution of the drafting of these clauses see Brand, *Kings, barons and justices*, pp 51–3, and of the background to the legislation see ibid., pp 43–51.
10 They correspond to clauses 24, 12, 20, 14, 11 and 9–10 of the eventual final text.
11 For the context of this legislation and the penultimate draft version of the clause see Brand, *Kings, barons and justices*, pp 82–3.

text of that clause ('Which cleric, if he be wise, will [say that] he is not obliged to answer as he is a member of Holy Church, or he may say that the thing of which he is accused is not true and put himself on a jury on this, reserving his rights as a member of Holy Church. And what he says will be allowed if he is found tonsured'). The commission of waste by guardians in socage and the sale or gift of marriages of socage wards except for their own benefit was prohibited by clause 4 with a proviso requiring accounting for the profits of the wardship. This is the earliest known draft of what was to form clause 12 of the Provisions.[12] This, too, was close to the eventual final version, but with an additional reference to lands that were held in 'free farm' (this should perhaps have read 'fee farm') as also falling under the new rules that was eliminated from the final version.[13] Under clause 5 lessees were to be prohibited from making 'alienations' during their leases, unless the terms of their written lease allowed them to do this. This makes little sense as it stands, for alienations by lessees (in the sense of grants of any part of the lands they leased) were already prohibited, and the specific linking of the clause with the previous clause (on socage wardship) ('in the same manner, it is provided …') suggests that what was probably intended was the prohibition of waste and the sale of woods and buildings on the land, not sale of the land itself. This suggests that it is the earliest known draft of what was to form clause 20 of the final Provisions.[14] Clause 6 takes up one of the clauses of the Petition of the Barons and a decision made at the Oxford parliament of the summer of 1258 to prohibit any acquisition of real property into mortmain which was made without the consent of the lord of whom the property was held.[15] This makes even more explicit than does the final clause (clause 14 of the Provisions) the jurisprudential justification or logic for the proposed legislation by starting with the bald statement 'Moreover, it is provided that, since no one may sell or give his land unless he safeguards the rights of the chief lord …' and ending with the explanation 'since on the entry of the religious the chief lord loses two things, namely wardship, relief and escheats, and thus the chief lord never gets that which belongs to him'. Various kinds of distraint (distraint outside the lord's fee or in the king's highway), and certain behaviour after making a distraint (chasing animals

---

12 For the context of this legislation and the penultimate draft version of the clause see Brand, *Kings, barons and justices*, pp 66–9.
13 Legislation on socage wardships had been promised with other legislation by 1 November by the king's council and representative of the community of the realm in letters patent sealed on 22 February 1259, but not published till 29 March: Brand, *Kings, barons and justices*, p. 31 and references.
14 The final version also mentioned the payment of damages for any breach of its rules. This was almost certainly implicit in this draft version as well. For the context of this clause see Brand, *Kings, barons and justices*, pp 63–4.
15 Brand, *Kings, barons and justices*, p. 61.

which had been taken in distraint from one county to another, to a lord's chief manor) were prohibited by clause 7. This was evidently an earlier version of what became clause 11 of the final Provisions, though that omitted the provision against driving distresses out of one county into another.[16] This was, however, reintroduced into the final reissue of the Provisions as part of chapter 4 of the Statute of Marlborough. In this initial form the clause does not speak generally about 'lords', but more specifically about 'magnates'. This suggests that the original suggestion behind the legislation may have been royalist, rather than baronial, in origin; but it should be noted that it also omits the saving clause included in the final text that allowed the king and his officials to continue making distraints in the highway, which partly counts against that suggestion. Clause 8 took up and extended the concerns aired in clause 1 of the Petition of the Barons about lords not keeping underage heirs out of their land once they came of age nor taking more than a simple seisin if the heir was already of age and on the tenement. It constitutes an early draft of clauses 9–10 of the final Provisions.[17]

Four clauses are included in this document which did not form any part of the final Provisions. They are clauses 1, 2, 9 and 11. Clause 1 is about the redress of violence and wrongs against Holy Church and its personnel. It provides that the primary jurisdiction to correct such wrongs and violence is to lie with the bishops but, if they are unable to act, the chief justiciar is to take action at their request. This is to be without prejudice to the king's jurisdiction. This clause helps to confirm the date of the document as whole for a concern with the redress of grievances by the newly recreated chief justiciar was one of the features of the new baronial regime created in the summer of 1258.[18] This clause was perhaps the result of concerns voiced when the new role was created that this should not prejudice the existing jurisdiction of the church courts. Clause 2 is even more interesting. Its concern is with those taking vengeance against others for wrongs done to them and with those who resist the exercise of justice against themselves for wrongs they had done to others. This is a clear prefiguring of what was more fully developed in chapters 1–3 of the Statute of Marlborough and suggests that I (and others before me) may have been wrong to associate those chapters specifically (as they themselves seem to do) with the disorders of the period immediately preceding the enactment of that Statute.[19] Clause 9 is puzzling. It does not look like legislation at all, but to be merely a restatement of current law. It explains that a lease is suspended during wardship, but that a lease for life trumps the lord's right of wardship. It also explains that an heir

16 For the context of this legislation see Brand, *Kings, barons and justices*, pp 94–5.
17 For the context of this legislation see Brand, *Kings, barons and justices*, pp 54–7.
18 Ibid., pp 19, 24, 27, 39–40.
19 Ibid., pp 192–4.

on succeeding to his ancestor's inheritance inherits his debts. Clause 11, however, does again seem to be legislation, and legislation that is related to that in clause 10 on suit to seignorial courts. This legislation would, for the first time, have imposed clear criteria on who could hold seignorial courts (and thereby exercise seignorial jurisdiction) over free tenants in England. It would have restricted it to those who were barons and could show that they held their courts by charter (presumably a grant of 'sake and soke') or ancient usage. Otherwise, lords in future were only to be able to hold hallmoots (manorial courts) with jurisdiction over their villein tenants.

The coincidence of a major part of this draft legislation with what was eventually to form part of the Provisions of Westminster suggests strongly that it is to be identified as a hitherto unknown draft of the Provisions; and the reference to the chief justiciar in clause 1 of this document helps to confirm this identification. The fact that it did not form part of the draft legislation published in March 1259 strongly suggests that it belongs to a later stage in the drafting process. If it was prepared for discussion at a parliament, the most likely suggestion is perhaps that it was prepared for the June parliament of 1259.[20] This in turn suggests that the draft version of the remaining eight clauses found in the French penultimate version of the Provisions of Westminster (and of the two additional clauses omitted from the final version) were also the first version of those clauses. If that is so, the discovery of this draft version of these clauses in the Lambeth MS means that we now possess a full range of the preliminary texts produced for the Provisions of Westminster of October 1259.

It remains a puzzle why the monk of Whalley (or of Stanlaw) incorporated a text of the draft legislation possibly of June 1259 into his text of the Statute of Westminster I, making only minor changes in the text in order to do so.[21] The only reason that occurs to me is that both clause 1 of the draft legislation and clause 1 of the Statute of Westminster I dealt with (rather different) wrongs done to the Church, and that he may have confused the two pieces of legislation or thought that the earlier draft legislation was genuine legislation that constituted a useful addition to the legislation contained in Westminster I and, in the absence of anything that clearly identified its date and place of enactment, was best copied into his compilation at this point. His error has the fortunate side-effect of preserving an otherwise lost stage in the evolution of the text of the Provisions of Westminster and giving us a further, and precious, insight into that process.

---

20 Ibid., p. 34.
21 The only obvious change he has made to fit it to its supposed context is to amend the reference to Henry III's first voyage to Brittany in clause 10 to make it a reference to the first passage of Henry, the father of king Edward, the present king, to Brittany. This is said to have been 42 years ago, which would have been true of 1272, but not of 1275.

APPENDIX: LAMBETH PALACE LIBRARY MS 499, FOS. 275v–276r

Text

Si comencent les constituciouns le reis Edward fiz le reis Henri, le quels il fist pur lamendement de la terre par conseil de sage gent lan del incarnacion nostre [*seignur*][22] *1275 a la quinceine de Paske e lan de son coronement 3.*

[1] Purveu est par le rois et par son conseil ke violences ou toutes ke sunt fetes a Seinte Eglise ou a persones de Seinte Eglise par agard des prelaz seient amende. E, si poeir faut a prelaz de teu choses amender, le chef justice de la tere par requeste des prelaz imettra sa mein; issi nekedent ke nule chose ne seit turne a prejudice de la prohibicion nostre seignur le reis ke akune foyz est purchace pur defendre a demander dettes en christiene curt, sil ne seit de testament ou de matrimoigne, ne ke ren ne turne a prejudice del aunciene reau dignete avaunt ces houres usee.

[2] E si akun se vut memes venger de tort ke fet li seit e prenge vengaunce saunz forme de dreit lum li curra sur come sur celi kest encontre la pes. E ausi deit em sus celi ke ne vut pas justice suffrer pur tort kil a fet as autres.

[3] Si clerk seit rette de mort de houme ou de roberie ou de larcenie ou de autre crime ke apent a la coroune le reis e puis seit livere en bail par comaundement le rei a 12 prodes homes ou lesse seit par plegges saunz le comandement le reis e si les avaunt dit 12 ou les avaunt dit plegges eient son cors a premer jour devaunt justices ne seient pas desoremes amercie, tut ne voille le clerk respondre ne ester a dreit en la curt le reis, desicome il ne furent dautre chose plegges ou mainpornurs for ke daver le cors le clerk avaunt. Le quel clerk, sil est sage, la ne deit respondre pur co kil est membre de Seinte Eglise ou il purra dire ke co dunt il est acoupe nest pas veirs e de co se met il en son pais sauve a li kil est membre de Seinte Eglise. E co dit li serra alowe sil seit trove coronee.

[4] De garde de fraunc fermes e de socages est issi purveu ke si tere ke [*tenu*][23] seit en socage seit en garde par le plus prochein parent par la reison ke leir seit dedenz age ke le gardein ne puse wast fere ne vente ne exil de tenanz ne nule manere de destruccion de la terre ke il a en garde nel mariage vendre ne doner si a prou del enfaunt non, mes salvement les choses garde al hus lenfaunt, issi ke kaunt il vendra a son age ke le gardein le respoigne leaumment des issues, sauf a li ses renables mises.

[5] En meme la manere est purveu de fermers en tens de lur terme ke ren par eus ne seit aliene fors co kest especialment contenu en lescrit de lur covenaunt kil pusent fere.

---

22 MS *reads* seigur (*and so elsewhere also*)
23 MS *omits*

[6] Derechef, purveu est pur co ke nul ne put sa terre vendre ou doner sil ne salve al chef seignur co ke a li apent ke nul houme de religion puse tere achater ne entrer en fee saunz le gre le chef seignur, cest a saver celi seignur kest plus procein saunz le meen. Pur co ke al entre de gent de religion perd le chef seignur 2 choses [f. 276r] cest asaver garde, relef e eschettes. E issi nad il james le chef seignur co ke a li apent.

[7] Purveu est ensement ke nul haut houmes desoremes face destresces hors de son fee ne en le real chymin ou tote gent poent aler saunz chalenge ne enchace avers de un contee en autre a son chef maner kar co est encontre les poinz de la grand chartre.

[8] Derechef purveu est issi: ke si le chef seignur apres la mort son tenaunt seisist en sa mein ses teres par la raison ke leir seit dedenz age e puis kaunt leir seit de plein age ne li voille sa tere rendre saunz plai ke leir recovre sa tere par bref de mort de auncestre ensement od les damages kil avera eu puis son age. E si leir seit de age kaunt son auncestre morut le chef seignur nel deit pas boter hors, ne ren ne deit prendre for solement face une simple seisine, demoraunt leinz od leir sicome dreit est. E si issi seit ke le chef seignur leir tenge hors, par quei illi covenge purchacer bref de mort de auncestre ou de cosinage, recovera sa seisine ausi come par bref de novele disseisine. E co est asaver ke, coment kem entre en tenement deloure kom eit este en seisine peisible jours e nuz ne deit pas sanz jugement estre enjete ne saunz lei, kar sil seit par force oste taunt tost avera le bref de novele disseisine sil le voil le purchacer.

[9] Uncore fet asaver ke tere engage ou baille a ferme a terme de certeins aunz ne deivent pas garde toler a chef seignur, mes celi ke la prist a ferme perdra jeskes il puse recoverer ver le eir kaunt il vendra a son age, mes ferme a terme de vie tout garde pur co ke co est fraunc tenement e fee a vie. E kaunt un auncestre murt endette son eir, sil vut aver leritage, deit aquiter ses dettes totes, kar teu maner de dette ne mie solement leir oblige, mes enteimes tot leritage destret e departe fer es alienum et cetera.

[10] De sutes de curtz as seignurages issi est purveu: ke nul ne seit destreint desoremes a sute fere a la curt son seignur, si especialment ne seit contenu en sa chartre kil deive sa tere tenir par certain service e fesaunt sute a la court son seignur, si il ou ses auncestres ne eient la sute fet devaunt le premer passage le reis Henri le pere le rei Edward ke ore est en Bretaine, cest asaver 42 aunz est passe. E si heritage seit partie [entre]²⁴ plusurs parceneres dun heritage ke seient com un heir le einez des parceners face la sute pur tuz les parceners, mes tuz les autres parceneres deivent eider a la sute renablement e chever al einez. E si plusurs tenaunz seient feffez de memes leritage ja le plus ne purra le chef seignur demaunder fors une sute, sicome est devant dit. E si akun seignurage son tenaunt encontre ceste purveaunce

---

24 MS *reads* en

avera destreint dunk a la pleinte le tenaunt seit atache le seignur kil venge a un bref jour a la curt le reis a respondre. A quel jour il purra aver un essoigne. E meintenaunt seient les avers al pleintif delivres ke par cele acheson furent pris e issi remeignent dekes le plai entre eus seit chevi. E si celi ke avera la destresce fet al jour ke par son essoneur li est done ne veigne pas ou al premer jour, sil ne seit essonee, face defaute, kar a bref de trespas gisent 2 defautes, dunce maunde le reis al vesconte du pais kile face vener a un autre jour. E si dunke ne venge seit destreint par kaunt kil ad en sa baillie, issi quil respoigne au rei des issues, e kil destreigne son cors a un autre jour dekes il venge. E kaunt un tel seignurage vendra en la curt le reis a respondre e le pleintif sa querele par son pais puse averrer dunc par jugement de la court recovera ses damages ke par ceste occasion de son seignur avera suffert.

[11] Ne nul ne deit tel curt aver ne par delaie pleder for celi kad fraunche curt com baron par chartre ou par auncien usage, mes a son hallemot pura le seignur ses neifs a volunte maunder.

Translation

Here begin the constitutions of king Edward, the son of king Henry, which he made for the amendment of the land on the advice of wise men two weeks after Easter in the year of our Lord's incarnation 1275 and in the third year since his coronation.

[1] It is provided by the king and his council that violence or wrongs done to Holy Church or to persons belonging to Holy Church are to be remedied by the judgment of prelates. And if prelates are unable to remedy such matters the chief justiciar of the land is to intervene at the request of the prelates. On condition, nonetheless, that nothing be done to prejudice the prohibition of our lord the king that is sometimes obtained to stop the claiming of debts in court christian unless they are testamentary or matrimonial in origin, and that nothing prejudice the king's traditional position as hitherto maintained.

[2] And if anyone wishing to avenge himself for any wrong done to him takes vengeance outside the law he is to be dealt with as someone who is against the peace. The same is to be done in respect of anyone who is unwilling to have justice done on him for a wrong that he has done to others.

[3] If a cleric be accused of homicide or robbery or theft or any other crime which belongs to the king's crown and is then released on bail by the king's order to twelve men or is released on surety without the king's order and the said twelve men or the said sureties produce his body on the first day [of the eyre] before the justices, they are not in future to be amerced, even if the cleric is unwilling to answer or stand trial in the king's court, since they were not sureties or mainpernors for anything other than the production of

the body of the cleric. Which cleric, if he is wise, [will say that he] is not obliged to answer there because he is a member of Holy Church, or he may say that the thing of which he is accused is not true and put himself on a jury on this reserving his rights as a member of Holy Church. And what he says will be allowed him if he is found tonsured.

[4] Of the wardship of free farms and socages it is provided that, if land that is held in socage be in the wardship of the closest relative because the heir is under age, the guardian may not commit waste or sale or cause the dispersal of tenants or any other kind of destruction of the land which he holds in wardship nor sell nor give the marriage other than for the child's benefit, but is to keep the property in safe custody for the benefit of the child, and so that when he comes of age the guardian is to answer him honestly for the income received, less his reasonable expenses

[5] In similar manner it is provided that lessees during their leases are to alienate nothing unless it is specially contained in their written agreement that they may do this.

[6] Moreover, it is provided that, since no one may sell or give his land unless he safeguards the rights of the chief lord, no religious person may buy land or enter into a fee without the consent of the chief lord, namely that lord who is the closest and most immediate lord, since on the entry of the religious the chief lord loses two things, [f. 276r] namely wardship, relief and escheats, and thus the chief lord never gets that which belongs to him.

[7] It is also provided that no magnate henceforth make distraints outside his fee or in the king's highway where all men may travel without impediment, nor drive animals from one county into another to his main manor because this is contrary to the terms of Magna Carta.

[8] Moreover, it is provided that, if the chief lord after the death of his tenant seizes his lands into his hands because the heir is under age and then when the heir is of full age is unwilling to surrender his land without litigation, the heir is to recover his land by writ of mort d'ancestor together with the damages he has incurred since he came of age. And, if the heir is of age when his ancestor dies, the chief lord ought not to eject him or take anything but merely take a simple seisin by staying in with the heir, as is right. And if it be that the chief lord keeps the heir out and so he has to obtain a writ of mort d'ancestor or cosinage, he is to recover his seisin as through a writ of novel disseisin. It is to be noted that once someone has entered a tenement then, because he has been in peaceful seisin for days and nights, he ought not to be ejected without judgment or against the law for, as soon as he is ousted by force, he may have the writ of novel disseisin, if he wishes to obtain it.

[9] It is also to be known that the handing over of land as surety or on lease for a term of years does not remove the the chief lord's entitlement to wardship, but that he who has taken it on lease is to lose it until he can have

his recovery against the heir when he shall come of age, but a lease for a life term does displace wardship because it is free tenement and fee for life. And when an ancestor dies indebted his heir, if he wishes to have the inheritance, ought to acquit all his debts, for this kind of debt not only obliges the heir but even clogs and divides the whole inheritance to pay the debt etc.

[10] Concerning suits to the courts of lords it is provided that none is to be distrained in future to perform suit to the court of his lord unless it is specifically contained in his charter that he is to hold his land for a certain service and for the performance of suit to the court of his lord, unless he or his ancestors have performed the suit before the first voyage of king Henry, the father of the present king Edward, into Brittany, namely 42 years ago. And if an inheritance is divided between several parceners of a single inheritance who are, as it were, a single heir, the eldest of the parceners is to perform the suit for all the parceners, but all the other parceners ought to assist reasonably with the performance of the suit and attorn to the eldest. And if several tenants are enfeoffed of the same inheritance the chief lord cannot even so claim more than a single suit, as aforesaid. And if any lord shall have distrained his tenant contrary to this provision then the lord is to be attached on the complaint of the tenant to come quickly to the court of the king to answer. On that day he may have one essoin and the animals which were taken for this reason are to be immediately released to the plaintiff and so to remain until the plea between them is determined. And, if he who made the distraint does not come on the day which is given him by his essoiner or makes default on the first day, if he is not essoined, the king is then to order the local sheriff to secure his appearance on another day (since two defaults lie in the writ of trespass). And, if he does not then come, he is to be distrained by all he has within his jurisdiction, so that he answer the king for the profits, and that he distrain his body for another day until he comes. And when such a lord comes to the king's court to answer and the plaintiff can prove his complaint by a jury then he is to recover his damages that he has suffered for this reason from his lord by the judgment of the court.

[11] No one is entitled to have such a court nor to plead by delay except one who has a free court as a baron by charter or ancient usage, but a lord can require the attendance of his villeins at his hallmoot.

Thirteenth-century legislation on mortmain alienations in Flanders and its influence upon France and England

DIRK HEIRBAUT

ALTHOUGH THERE WAS NOT as much legislation in the Middle Ages as in our time, statutes restricting alienations of land into mortmain were quite popular.[1] This should come as no surprise, for a gift or sale of land or any other form of real property to the church threatened the foundations of feudal power. Property acquired by the church was lost to the world, or at least to its lay lords, forever because church law did not allow any religious institution to alienate its property in turn.[2]

Understandably, this was of great concern to lay lords and led to legislation being issued to counteract this. Both in France, in 1275,[3] and in England, in 1279,[4] statutes were issued about alienations in mortmain. This chronology in itself suggests that the king of England may have been inspired by his French colleague,[5] which is not to say that this was his only source of inspiration, as

---

I would like to thank Dr P. Brand for his very helpful comments. Needless to say any remaing errors are entirely my own.
1   Cf. for France, G. Giordanengo, 'Consuetudo constituta a domino rege. Coutumes rédigées et législation féodale. France: XIIe et XIIIe s.' in *El dret comú i Catalunya* (Barcelona, 1996), p. 62.
2   D. Heirbaut, *Over heren, vazallen en graven. Het persoonlijk leenrecht in Vlaanderen, ca. 1000–1305* (Brussels, 1997), pp 321–5; P. Brand, *Kings, barons and justices.: the making and enforcement of legislation in thirteenth century England* (Cambridge, 2003), pp 58–9.
3   C.V. Langlois, *Le règne de Philippe III le Hardi* (Paris, 1887), nr. 5, pp 422–3 (French version); E. De Laurière, *Ordonnances des roys de France de la troisième race* (Paris, 1723), i, 303–5; F. Isambert and A. Jourdan, *Recueil général des anciennes lois françaises* (Paris, 1822), ii, 657–60 (Latin version).
4   7 Edw. I, De viris religiosis: 'quod nullus religiosus aut alius quicunque terras aut tenementa aliqua emere vel vendere, aut sub colore donationis aut termini vel alterius tituli cuiuscunque ab aliquo recipere aut alio quovis modo, arte, vel ingenio sibi appropiare presumat': F.M. Powicke and C.R. Cheney (eds), *Councils and synods with other documents relating to the English church*, ii/ii (Oxford, 1964), pp 864–5.
5   Cf. G. Giordanengo, 'La difficile interprétation des données négatives. Les ordonnances sur le droit féodal' in A. Gouron and E. Rigaudière (eds), *Renaissance du pouvoir législatif et genèse de l'état* (Montpellier, 1988), p. 103.

the fight of lay lords and the crown against the dead hand had a long history in England before 1279.[6] Nevertheless, it is remarkable that English historians mention the French example for the 1279 statute on mortmain alienations (De viris religiosis) only in passing or not at all.[7]

Yet, even on the continent, the answer may not lie in France, as the French legislation itself may not have been original. In fact, Gérard Giordanengo, the expert on feudal legislation in medieval France, suggested in 1988 that France might have followed the example of one of its neighbours, but he could not elaborate upon this, because the state of research did not allow it at that time.[8] His suggestion turns out to be right for there was an earlier ordinance against mortmain alienations, issued by Countess Margaret of Flanders and her son Count Guy, which has remained unknown outside the circle of specialists in medieval Flemish history and even to them it has been a rather obscure text. Thus, any study of the possible influence of this Flemish statute outside Flanders, has to start with a detailed analysis of the Flemish legislation itself.

A LOST TEXT

That the Flemish statute is not so well-known is in part due to the fact that its original text has not been preserved. We know of it only because it was quoted in charters a generation later of the years 1295–1297, which contain settlements made between the count and religious houses which had acquired real property in contravention of the statute. There are also similar charters from 1294 relating to cities, because the Flemish statute also forbade burgesses to acquire fiefs. Of these charters only a few were mentioned in the older literature,[9] but more recent research has discovered sixteen of them.[10] This larger number of charters indicates that the statute was more important than has hitherto been thought.

---

6   J.M.W. Bean, *The decline of English feudalism, 1215–1540* (Manchester, 1968), pp 49–52; P. Brand, 'The control of mortmain alienation in England 1200–1300' in J. Baker (ed.), *Legal records and the historian* (London, 1978), pp 29–36 (also published in P. Brand, *The making of the common law*, London, 1992, pp 233–40).

7   S. Raban, *Mortmain legislation and the English church, 1279–1500* (Cambridge, 1982), pp 21–2.

8   Giordanengo, 'La difficile interprétation', p. 103.

9   One charter was quite well known because it had become part of a collection of Flemish statutes in the seventeenth century: *Tweeden druck van den eersten bouc der ordonnancien, statuten, edicten ende placcaerten van Vlaenderen* (Ghent, 1639), pp 47–8. R. Koerperich, *Les lois sur la mainmorte dans les Pays-Bas catholiques. Étude sur l'édit du 15 septembre 1753, ses précédents et son exécution* (Leuven, 1922), p. 21 n. 1 and 2 mentions five of these charters, including the one already printed in the seventeenth century, and two others were quoted by E. Warlop, *The Flemish nobility before 1300* (Courtrai, 1975), i/ii, p. 536, n. 413.

10 For these charters, see the Appendix.

The sixteen charters all follow the same pattern and always contain the following passage:

> As a long time ago for all our land of Flanders generally a command and a prohibition was made by the very noble and very high lady, the late our dearest and very loved lady and mother Margaret, of blessed memory, and by us, that no house of religion, cleric, burgess, nor non-noble to whom it is forbidden by law, shall acquire in our land of Flanders, fiefs, rents, lands, heritages, and other properties, subject to us ...[11]

With the exception of this group of sixteen charters and a 1298 charter,[12] there are no other direct references to this Flemish statute. This is not so amazing, as only a few traces of feudal legislation in Flanders can be found for the high Middle Ages. However, one should be very cautious here, because in a culture in which custom is dominant, the statutory origins of legal rules will soon be forgotten, either because the legislator was not successful and his measures were not generally accepted, or because the new rules were so successful that everyone forgot their legislative origins.[13] An example may be the right of the Flemish widow to a customary dower, consisting of the life tenancy of one half of her deceased husband's fiefs. It may well be that this 'customary' dower was introduced by a statute of Count Philip of Alsace in the 1160s, as in the 1150s there are charters establishing dower by agreement, in cases where later the widow had a customary dower, and these charters disappear in the 1160s.[14] Would it then be too presumptuous to suggest that they disappeared because new legislation had rendered them unnecessary, keeping in mind that Philip was a very active legislator, especially in criminal law, and that in neighbouring principalities feudal and criminal legislation went hand in hand?[15] Unfortunately, one can only

---

[11] For this translation the text of the Douai charter, which is the best-known, thanks to the edition by Thomas, was used: 'ke comme grant tans a fust par toute nostre terre de Flandres fais génèralment uns commandemens et une deffense de par très noble et très haute dame, jadis no très chière et très amée dame et mère, Margharite de bone mémoire, contesse de Flandres et de Haynau, et de par nous, ke nule maisons de religion, clers, bourgois, no gens nonoble deffensavle a le loy, acquissisent en no terre de Flandres fiès, rentes, terres, hyretages et autres choses ki meuscent de nous': P. Thomas, *Textes historiques sur Lille et le Nord de la France avant 1789* (Lille, 1931–6), ii, nr. 80, pp 253–4 (1294).

[12] State archives Ghent, Boudelo abbey, 8 (nr. 379), fos. 63 r–64 r (1298).

[13] Cf. J.Gilissen, 'Loi et coutume. Quelques aspects de l'interpénétration des sources du droit dans l'ancien droit belge', *Legal History Review*, 11 (1953), 270–9.

[14] D. Heirbaut, *Over lenen en families. Het zakelijk leenrecht in Vlaanderen, ca. 1000–1305. Een studie over de vroegste geschiedenis van het leenrecht in het graafschap Vlaanderen* (Brussels, 2000), pp 124–7.

[15] In 1200 Baldwin, count of Hainault, issued both a criminal and a feudal charter: L. Devillers, *Chartes du comté de Hainaut de l'an 1200: reproduction des originaux avec introduction, traduction et notes* (Mons, 1898).

indicate the high probability of a statutory origin of the 'customary' dower of one half in Flanders, without being able to give this suggestion more substance. Even so, this makes one wonder how many other 'customary' rules may also be statutory in origin and how many statutes are lost to us.

THE DATE OF THE LEGISLATION

Count Guy's citation of the statute he and his mother had issued offers only scanty information about its date. We are informed only that Guy had acted together with his mother, which narrows the period down to the years between 1252 (when Guy became the titular count of Flanders) and 1278 (when his mother retired from affairs of state and relinquished all power in Flanders to him). More precise dates are given by Verbruggen (1249),[16] Britz (1263),[17] Des Marez (1266)[18] and Nicholas (1268),[19] though none of them has offered convincing arguments for these dates. The date given by Verbruggen even ignores the fact that in 1249 Guy had not yet become count of Flanders. As consensus about a precise date is lacking, some authors just cautiously mention that the statute was issued in Margaret and Guy's time.[20]

Nevertheless, it is possible to be more precise about the date since there is evidence that Margaret may already have been applying this legislation in 1261. In that year she confirmed the acquisitions of allods in her county by St Martin's abbey in Tournai.[21] That the countess only refers to allods is in line with our more extensive information about the application of the statute in the 1290s, when the count generally insisted on confirming only acquisitions of non-feudal property. The countess also made a distinction between allods acquired more than thirty years earlier and later acquisitions. The countess made no difficulties about confirming the former, but as to the the latter agreed only to some acquisitions. For the remainder she made a separate settlement with the abbey.[22] Once again, this conforms to the

16 J. Verbruggen, *Het leger en de vloot van de graven van Vlaanderen vanaf het ontstaan tot in 1305* (Brussels, 1960), p. 41.
17 J. Britz, *Code de l'ancien droit belgique, ou histoire de la jurisprudence et de la législation, suivie de l'exposé de droit civil des provinces belgiques* (Brussels, 1847), i,. 522.
18 G. Des Marez, 'Le droit privé à Ypres au XIIIe siècle', *Handelingen van de koninklijke commissie voor de uitgave van de oude wetten en verordeningen van België*, 12 (1926–7), 279.
19 D. Nicholas, *Town and countryside: social, economic and political tensions in fourteenth-century Flanders* (Bruges, 1971), p. 280.
20 Warlop, *Flemish nobility*, i/i, p. 292; R. Opsommer, 'Leenwetgeving en overdrachtsoctrooien in het graafschap Vlaanderen (13de–15de eeuw)' in F. Stevens and D. Van den Auweele (eds), *Uuytwysens d'archiven. Handelingen van de XIe Belgisch-Nederlandse rechtshistorische dagen* (Leuven, 1992), pp 157–83.
21 A. d'Herbomez, *Chartes de l'abbaye de Saint-Martin de Tournai* (Brussels 1898–1901), ii, nr. 736, pp 191–7.
22 A. d'Herbomez, *Chartes*, ii, nr. 755, pp 221–4 (1261).

practice of the 1290s, when there was also a thirty year limitation on the inspections undertaken by the count's administration.[23] There are later documents than the 1261 charter for St Martin's which can also be seen as applying the statute on mortmain alienations,[24] but no earlier ones. Thus, one may presume that the legislation was issued after 1252, but no later than 1261. The latter date may be the closest to the mark, as Guy had been in captivity from July 1253 until September/October 1256.[25] Moreover, probably around 1262,[26] Margaret reorganized her financial administration by making Philip of Bourbourg her receiver-general. If the statute had been issued as late as 1261, it might have been part of a more general reform, in which a reorganization of the financial administration was caused by the new revenues which fines for evasion of the statute prohibiting mortmain alienations would bring.

The statute also has to be seen in the light of earlier reforms made by Margaret. When she came to power in December 1244, she completely changed the central and local administration of Flanders. Until then, the central *curia* had retained competence over feudal cases. The jurisdiction over these was now handed over to local comital feudal courts, which ensured that the *curia* could henceforth deal exclusively with the administration of the county, a change which became visible in the new name given to the *curia*, the council.[27] This must have happened by 1245, and by 1246 at the latest the countess had instituted stricter measures against the religious houses in her county. Their charters were inspected,[28] and, if they could not prove their title to a piece of land, it was seized by the countess.[29] Margaret even had

23 Cf. M. Vanhaeck, *Cartulaire de l'abbaye de Marquette* (Lille, 1937–40), i, nr. 321, pp 305–6 (1297); State archives Ghent, Boudelo abbey, 8 (nr. 379), fos. 63r–64r (1298; this charter mentions a term of 32 years, but that is because it refers to a lost 1295 charter; 1298 minus 1295 is not two, but three years, but the 1298 charter was issued in January, and thus, for contemporaries, in 1297).
24 See e.g. E. Feys and A. Nelis, *Les cartulaires de la prévôté ou abbaye de Saint-Martin à Ypres (1102–1543)* (Bruges, 1880), nr. 230, p. 155 (1264).
25 T. Luykx, *Het grafelijk geslacht Dampierre en zijn strijd tegen Filips de Schone* (Leuven, 1952), pp 55, 59.
26 T. Luykx, *De grafelijke financiële bestuursinstellingen en het grafelijk patrimonium in Vlaanderen tijdens de regering van Margareta van Constantinopel (1244–1278)* (Brussels, 1961), pp 62–3; E. Kittel, *From ad hoc to routine: a case study in medieval bureaucracy* (Philadelphia, 1991), p. 15.
27 D. Heirbaut, *Over heren, vazallen en graven. Het persoonlijk leenrecht in Vlaanderen, ca. 1000–1305* (Brussels, 1997), p. 155; D. Heirbaut, 'Le cadre juridique. Institutions et droit en Flandre vers 1302', in R.C. Van Caenegem, *1302. Le désastre de Courtrai* (Antwerp, 2002), p. 136.
28 J. Kruisheer, *Oorkondenboek van Holland en Zeeland tot 1299* (Assen, 1986), ii, nr. 699, pp 328–9; nr. 701, pp 330–1.
29 T. Luykx, *Johanna van Constantinopel. Gravin van Vlaanderen en Henegouwen. Haar leven (1199/1200–1244). Haar regering (1205–1244), vooral in Vlaanderen* (Brussels, 1946), nr. 86, pp 619–20 (1252).

sworn surveyors (instead of the knights on horseback who had served her predecessors) to make measurements of church lands. Any surplus which they found was also seized by the countess.[30] Eventually these lands were returned by the countess, but on her conditions.[31] These actions from the start of Margaret's reign concerned only land held by the church without a title (or at least, without a title acceptable to her), but it is easy to see the 1252x1261 statute forbidding mortmain alienations, which ensured that the countess could apply her strong arm tactics to any real property acquired by a church, as a next step.

THE SCOPE OF THE 1252X1261 STATUTE

Although only the bare bones of the 1252x1261 statute are known, its contents are clear. Religious houses and clerics on the one hand, burgesses and others forbidden by law on the other,[32] could not acquire real property. However, there is a distinction between these two groups which is not immediately clear from the quotation from the statute in the sixteen charters which refer to it. Burgesses and other non-noble persons forbidden by law seem, at first sight, to have been unable to acquire any real property at all, but the charters for the cities of Douai and Courtrai make it clear that in this case they were only barred from acquiring fiefs.[33] Thus, there is a distinction. The church could not acquire any real property at all, whereas burgesses and other non-noble laymen forbidden by law were only banned from buying fiefs. (In reality, the statute was aimed only at burgesses, for there is no sign of it ever having been applied to other non-nobles.)

The words '*fiefs, rents, lands, heritages, and other property, subject to us*' have to be taken as meaning any real property, situated in the county of Flanders, as the counts of Flanders claimed to have dominion over all lands in their county.[34] Margaret and Guy acted as sovereigns of Flanders, not as feudal lords.[35] In fact, if the statute had only applied to tenures held from the count it would have been useless, as in Flemish thirteenth century feudal law all

30 De Smet, *Codex*, nr. 213, p. 905 (1249).
31 De Smet, *Codex*, nr. 213, p. 905 (1249); Luykx, *Johanna*, nr. 86, pp 619–20 (1252).
32 By this were meant the inhabitants of certain territories who had privileges like those of citizens: cf. R. Opsommer, '*Omme dat leengoed es thoochste dinc van der weerelt.' Het leenrecht in Vlaanderen in de 14de en 15de eeuw* (Brussels, 1995), ii, . 518.
33 Thomas, *Textes*, ii, nr. 80, pp 253–4 (1294)); T. De Limburg-Stirum, *Coutumes de la ville et de la châtellenie de Courtrai* (Brussels, 1905), nr. 6, pp 149–50 (1294).
34 Cf. State archives Ghent, Charters of the counts of Flanders, collection Saint-Genois, 401 (*c.*1280).
35 For the distinction see N. Didier, 'Les origines du droit souverain d'amortissement dans le comté de Hainaut', *Revue d'histoire ecclésiastique*, 34 (1938), 488–9. For the meaning of the word sovereign, especially in medieval Flanders, see Heirbaut, *Over heren*, pp 106–27.

lords could still refuse their permission to any transfer of fiefs held from them, whether by tenants in chief or by mesne tenants, which endangered their rights, and like rules applied to non-feudal tenure.[36] Thus, the count himself sometimes gave his permission for a certain sale, but in those cases in which the land was held from another lord he made it clear that he did so respecting the rights of others, whose permission had still to be requested.[37]

As this makes clear, the count's prohibition was not meant to be absolute. In fact, it seems that from the start Margaret and her son had a licensing system in mind, as already in 1261 Margaret was confirming acquisitions made in contravention of the 1252x1261 ordinance. The count might give permission for a particular sale or gift, but sometimes religious houses or clerics received a blank licence to acquire real property up to a certain value.[38] The count's license was almost never given unconditionally. The count could stipulate that the status of a piece of land acquired by a church remain unchanged,[39] that the rents it was charged with would still be paid in the future,[40] that its fiscal status should not change,[41] and so on. The most common requirement was that his rights should not suffer.[42] In this case the count was thinking principally about his jurisdiction,[43] but that was not really to the disadvantage of the church because in return the count would, as prince of Flanders, promise to warrant the church's newly acquired property.[44]

One condition seems to have been almost universal. Most of the time the count required that only non-feudal property should be acquired, though this might be either allods or non-feudal tenancies.[45] The count's insistence on this is easy to explain. In Flanders, there was something like a 'big deal' between the count and the noble families, by which the property aspects of feudalism (the rules concerning inheritance, matrimonial property and transactions) served the family's interests by keeping as much of the feudal inheritance in the hands of the eldest son as possible, whereas the personal

---

36 Heirbaut, *Over lenen*, pp 142–54.
37 F. Van De Putte and C. Carton, *Chronique et cartulaire de l'abbaye de Hemelsdaele* (Bruges, 1858), nr. 27, p. 65 (1292); L. Van Hollebeke, *L'abbaye de Nonnenbosche de l'ordre de Saint Benoit près d'Ypres (1101–1796), suivi du cartulaire de cette maison* (Bruges, 1865), nr. 57, p. 127 (1289).
38 Archives départementales du Nord (Lille), Series B, 1561, nr. 589, fo. 162r; E. Hautcoeur, *Cartulaire de l'abbaye de Flines* (Lille, 1873), i, nr. 311, p. 361 (1295).
39 J. De Smet, *Cartulaire de l'abbaye de Cambron*, Brussels, 1869, nr. 14, p. 519 (1274).
40 Hautcoeur, *Abbaye*, i, nr. 331, p. 361 (1295).
41 State archives Ghent, Doornzele abbey, charter dated 26 June 1296.
42 E.g. Thomas, *Textes*, ii, nr. 71b, pp 224–5 (1295).
43 Tournai, Saint Mary's church, cartulary D, fo. 282v (1289).
44 State archives Ronse, Abbey of Saint Adrian at Geraardsbergen, 641 (1281); I. De Coussemaker, *Documents relatifs à la ville de Bailleul en Flandre* (Lille, 1877–8), i, nr. 34, pp 39–40.
45 Archives départementales du Nord (Lille), Series B, 1562, nr. 589, fo. 126r (1293); Bruges, Diocesan archives, Monastery of the Urbanists, charter dated 24 January 1272.

aspects of feudalism, the vassals' services, benefited the count. The most striking example of this is military service. The only person Flemish vassals could serve militarily was their count. They could not fight for anyone else without his leave. Moreover, all vassals had to serve the count. A Flemish lord had to bring all his vassals to the count's army, if asked to do so. A quota-system, fixing the number of vassals a lord had to bring to the count's army, did not exist, as it would have meant that, if a lord had a surplus of knights, he would have been free to leave these at home. It did not matter whether these vassals had been enfeoffed out of lands held of the count or out of the lord's allods; all without exception had to serve the count.[46] Thus, the main beneficiary of feudal service in Flanders was the count. The downside of this was that he had the most to lose if feudal service was endangered. Alienations of fiefs into mortmain eroded his military power, and so the count tried to stop them through the 1251x1261 statute.

Even with all these conditions, a license was never issued for free. Although there were a few exceptions, most churches and clerics had to pay. The normal price seems to have been the fifth penny,[47] that is, the value of the land for a two-year period.[48] No distinction was made between allods, fiefs and non-feudal tenancies.

ENSURING COMPLIANCE WITH THE STATUTE

For churches the 1252x1261 statute provided few advantages. In return for the count's warranty of their new acquisitions, they had, in most cases, to refrain from buying fiefs, and other property could only be bought at a higher price and with new strings attached. Needless to say, they tried to evade the new legislation as much as possible, but this was not easy. As has been mentioned, even before Margaret and Guy had issued their mortmain ordinance, Margaret had started started inspecting the property of Flemish churches, seizing those lands to which they were not entitled, and this

---

46 D. Heirbaut, 'Flanders: a pioneer of state-oriented feudalism? Feudalism as an instrument of comital power in Flanders during the high Middle Ages (1000–1300)', in A. Musson (ed.), *Expectations of the law in the Middle Ages* (Woodbridge 2001), pp 23–34.

47 Cf. I. De Coussemaker, *Un cartulaire de l'abbaye de Notre-Dame de Bourbourg (1104–1793)* (Lille, 1882–1891), i, nr. 156–7, pp 167–8; M. Vanhaeck, Cartulaire, i, nr. 321, pp 305–6 (1297). An exception was made for the abbey of Flines, which only had to pay the tenth penny: Hautcoeur, *Abbaye*, i, nr. 263–4, pp 284–7 (1288); nr. 290, pp 315–19 (1290); but Count Guy had his reasons for doing so. This abbey had been founded by his mother and several members of his family were nuns in this abbey or were buried there: Luykx, *Het grafelijk geslacht Dampierre*, pp 26–7, 30–1, 104.

48 The profits from one year were considered to be 10% of the land's value: M. Gysseling, *Corpus van Middelnederlandse teksten (tot en met het jaar 1300)* (The Hague, 1977), i/ii, nr. 609, pp 1028–9 (1285).

continued after 1261. However, these inspections were neither general nor systematic, nor were they undertaken by specialized officials.[49]

This changed in 1292 (or perhaps a year later), when Count Guy charged one of his clerks, Jan Calward, to inquire into acquisitions made in contravention of the 1252x1261 statute, to seize any of the property concerned and to make a settlement in the count's name, which confirmed a church's acquisitions in return for the payment of a fine. Again, Jan's commission is not preserved, but it is quoted verbatim in a later charter.[50] The first evidence of Jan's work comes from the towns. In 1294 several settlements were made with them.[51] Jan could work fast here because he was not really concerned with individual acquisitions.[52] Towns paid a collective fine for their citizens, and had to arrange to recover the money from them. They, on the other hand, had only two years to ask for a regularization of their situation.[53] Thereafter, it was too late. It is not insignificant that, whereas big cities like Ypres, Lille and Douai had to pay, Ghent and Bruges, the most powerful and the most rebellious of them, never did so. In 1294 Ghent even received additional privileges from the count.[54]

For religious houses and clerics Jan had to investigate individual acquisitions, which took more time, though he was helped by the thirty years limit, which meant that he did not have to look at any charters more than thirty years old. He may have had at least one assistant,[55] but it is unclear whether there were other people assisting him. As soon as he had gone through the charters, he could seize the property concerned, but it seems that this was

---

49 E.g. in 1271 Margaret had had the charters of Rozenberg abbey inspected by two Franciscans: F. De Potter and D. Broeckaert, *Geschiedenis van de gemeenten van de provincie Oost-Vlaanderen* (Ghent, 1864–1900), series 4, ii, p.114 n. 3.

50 Jan Calward's letter of appointment is quoted in State archives Ghent, Boudelo abbey, 8 (nr. 379), fos. 63r–64r (1298). The wording echoes that used in the letter of appointment of Jakemon of Deinze, the new receiver-general of Flanders in 1292 (Kittel, *Ad hoc to routine*, nr. 1, p. 217), who was the first to receive a formal written appointment to this position: Kittel, *Ad hoc to routine*, p. 62. Kittel wonders why the count wanted a new receiver in 1292, but this can easily be explained by a reform, of which the new letter of appointment is only part. If there was an administrative shake-up in 1292, it becomes very likely that Jan Calward was also appointed at that time, keeping in mind that his letter of appointment was modelled on Jakemon's. Moreover, Jan was certainly in action by 1293: State archives Ghent, Charters of the counts of Flanders, Collection Saint-Genois, 704.

51 See the Appendix.

52 Unlike the charters for religious houses, those for the cities do not contain lists of acquisitions.

53 M. Brun-Lavainne, *Roisin. Franchises, lois et coutumes de la ville de Lille* (Lille, 1842), pp 331–2 (1294).

54 R.C. Van Caenegem, 'Het charter van Graaf Gwijde van Dampierre over de Gentse rechtspraak (10 juli 1294)', in *Handelingen van de koninklijke commissie voor geschiedenis*, 150 (1984), 415–36.

55 State Archives Ghent, Charters of the counts of Flanders, Collection Saint-Genois, 704 (1293).

only by way of distraint, because, according to the sources we now have, Jan always reached an agreement.[56] The settlement meant that, after payment, the religious house would receive a charter, in which the count listed and confirmed its individual acquisitions, renouncing any further claims, but expressly reserving all his other rights and the rights of other parties.

THE LONG TERM FAILURE OF THE STATUTE

The 1252x1261 statute was enforced to the full from 1293 onward. Its effects were undeniable then. Whereas before 1293 religious houses had only sometimes asked prior permission for the acquisition of real property, this now became the rule. Blank licences were solicited from the count in greater numbers than before and in at least one case an abbey did not wait for Jan Calward to arrive, but drew up its own list of transgressions and made its own settlement with the count.[57] For fiefs the change was even more dramatic. A drop in the acquisition of fiefs is visible already in the second half of the thirteenth century. After 1295 they dwindle to almost nothing. Thus, although the statute was only a moderate success at first, it achieved its aim once there was a specialized official to enforce it. The religious institutions of Flanders may have liked this less and it may be wondered how far the enforcement of the 1252x1261 statute may have contributed to their financial difficulties at the end of the thirteenth and the beginning of the fourteenth century. Strange as this may sound, none of the historians studying the finances of abbeys and chapters in Flanders has ever really considered the impact of the legislation on mortmain alienations.[58]

The count's success was far from complete. He had wanted, by banning the sale of fiefs to the church, to stop the erosion of the military strength of the county, but he was already too late to prevent this by the mid thirteenth century.[59] In practice, the statute was no more than a valiant, though lost, rearguard operation. Financially, it was more successful. There is no doubt that it helped Countess Margaret and her son fill their treasury. Similar legislation is found in the latter Middle Ages, but it never referred to the ordinance of Margaret and Guy,[60] which seems to have been forgotten, and

---

56 This may be misleading, as Jan's failures are nowhere recorded.
57 De Potter and Broeckaert, *Geschiedenis*, series 4, ii, p. 114, n. 3 (1271).
58 See, for example, the very detailed A. d'Haenens, *L'abbaye Saint-Martin de Tournai de 1290 à 1350. Origines, évolution et dénouement d'une crise* (Leuven, 1961).
59 It is telling enough that in 1297 and 1300 the Flemish knights were beaten by the French, but that in 1302 the Flemish cities could successfully revolt against the king of France and beat his troops in the battle of Courtrai. On this battle, see for example R. Van Caenegem (ed.), *1302. Le désastre de Courtrai* (Antwerp, 2002).
60 For this later legislation see Opsommer, *Leenwetgeving*, pp 157–83; E. De Moreau, 'La législation des ducs de Bourgogne sur l'accroissement des établissements ecclésiastiques', *Revue d'histoire ecclésiastique* 41 (1946), 43–65.

it followed other principles (for example a forty, instead of a thirty, years term and a much more elaborate system of fines).[61]

The explanation is to be found in the events of 1297 and later. In 1297 Count Guy revolted against his French overlord, but in order to do so had to surmount some formidable obstacles. From 1196 onwards the vassals and cities of the count of Flanders had to stand surety for their lord when he did homage to the French king for 'Crown Flanders', the part of his county he held from France. This meant that if the count were to fight against the king, the vassals and cities had to chose the king's side against the count, unless the king had refused the count the justice of the peers of France. In addition the count had to concede the French king the right to have him excommunicated in case of a revolt. Of course, the king had him excommunicated in 1297 and called on the Flemings for support against him. Count Guy, however, appealed against the excommunication to Rome and had his appeal made public in several cities of his county. That way, the excommunication was suspended and Guy had a venue for publicizing and explaining his complaints against the French king. All this resulted in the Flemings remaining faithful to him.[62] However, this also tied up some of the best and brightest of Guy's servants, one being Jan Calward, who was sent to Rome to plead the count's case there.[63] With Jan being occupied elsewhere from 1297 and Flanders long being plagued by war and internal troubles, Margaret and Guy's ordinance and the idea of a special official for enforcing it, was forgotten. However, the idea that the count's license was needed for all acquisitions by religious houses lived on in new legislation in 1366 enacted by count Louis de Male,[64] and most of all in 1396, by his son in law and successor, Philip the Bold, duke of Burgundy.[65]

THE POSSIBLE FLEMISH INFLUENCE ON FRANCE

There was one person who did not immediately forget Margaret and Guy's legislation: the king of France. In 1300–2 when Flanders[66] was occupied by

---

61 See, for example, the 1396 ordinances of Philip the Bold: A. Van Nieuwenhuysen, *Ordonnances de Philippe le Hardi, de Marguerite de Mâle et de Jean sans Peur, 1381–1419*, ii (Brussels, 1974), pp 171–6.
62 Heirbaut, *Over heren*, pp 229–31, 300–3; Heirbaut, *Le cadre juridique*, pp 137–9.
63 Archives départementales du Nord (Lille), Series B, 1264/3897 and 3902, 1512/3909 (1297).
64 *Tweeden druck van den eersten bouc der ... placcaerten van Vlaenderen*, pp 724–5.
65 De Moreau, *La législation*, nr. 1–2, pp 60–4. Philip's successors did not add much to his legislation: ibid., pp 49–59.
66 The whole county, not just the part held from France: D. Heirbaut, 'Vlaanderen in 1302: alleen Kroon-Vlaanderen? De Romeinsrechtelijke regel "de bijzaak volgt de hoofdzaak" toegepast op Rijks-Vlaanderen', *Legal History Review*, 71 (2003), 65–77.

the French, the French administration simply continued the policies of the dispossessed count of Flanders.[67]

However, the Flemish example had also influenced the kings of France at an earlier date. In 1275 King Philip III issued an ordinance about mortmain alienations and, as already has been mentioned, Giordanengo suggests that the French king may have been following the example of one his neighbours here. There are, however, too many differences between the Flemish statute and its French counterpart for the contents of the latter to have been influenced by the former. For example, whereas in Flanders a very simple tariff for licences prevailed, the French statute is very elaborate, making all kinds of distinctions which were ignored in Flanders; and the French statute concerned itself only with regularizing past acquisitions, not with forbidding future ones. That a thirty years limitation[68] was applied, just as in Flanders, does not prove much, since in both cases it did not apply to non-nobles, but only to the church.[69] This shows the origins of the rule in the learned law. Thus, the contents of the 1275 French statute did not follow the Flemish model. In fact, it has been shown that the 1275 statute of Philip III was influenced by the policies of Alphonse of Poitiers, Philip's uncle, whose possessions had escheated to the crown in 1270.[70]

There is nonetheless a link between the 1275 statute and the older Flemish legislation. The French statute was almost revolutionary, as the French king now assumed the right to authorize the amortization of all lands in his kingdom, even those not belonging to his domain, such as allods or fiefs not held directly of him.[71] This sounds more like the count of Flanders, who already enjoyed a similar right within his principality, than Alphonse of Poitiers. The king of France was, moreover, aware that this change was too great to be enforced completely at once. Thus, those of his barons who already had the right to authorize amortizations were able to continue doing so without any royal interference.[72] A list of these has been preserved. It is very short, as only the peers of France, and five counts, the greatest princes after the peers, are mentioned.[73] It is remarkable that the first of the peers

---

67 Bruges, Grand seminary, Eeckhoutabbey, cartulary A, fo. 72v (1300).
68 Some manuscripts of the Latin text have 29 years (De Laurière, *Ordonnances*, i, 304 n. d) and this version was chosen by the editors of the Latin text. However, the French version has 30 years (Langlois, *Philippe le Hardi*, nr. 5, pp 422–3) and thirty years counting from 1275 is also used in a 1291 ordinance (De Laurière, *Ordonnances*, i, 322–4, art. 3).
69 For Flanders, cf. State Archives Ghent, Charters of the counts of Flanders, collection Saint-Genois, 66 (1271), 775, 780 (1295). For France, see art. 3 of the 1275 ordinance.
70 P. Guébin, 'Les amortissements d'Alphonse de Poitiers', *Revue Mabillon. Archives de la France monastique*, 16 (1926), 41.
71 G. Sautel, 'Note sur le droit royal d'amortissement (XIIIe-XVe siècles)' in *Études d'histoire du droit canonique dédiées à Gabriel Le Bras* (Paris, 1965), i, 695.
72 Art. 1.
73 Latin version: De Laurière, *Ordonnances*, i, 305, n. e; French version: Langlois, *Philippe le Hardi*, pp 423–4 (1275).

named in this list is the count of Flanders and not one of the dukes, not even the duke of Guyenne, who was, after all, also king of England.[74] This can, however, easily be explained by the count of Flanders's foremost position in France not as a peer, but as a prince who controlled mortmain alienations within his territories and was the main source of inspiration for the royal statute, not in respect of its contents, but for the very idea of securing through legislation the right to control all mortmain alienations, even where those not did not belong to one's domain.

That the counts of Flanders had a well established position in this respect also becomes clear from events after 1275. The French king had been willing to privilege a few of his highest tenants in chiefs by allowing their control over amortizations to go on undisturbed. However, they could only authorize amortizations, not ask for anything in return.[75] The counts of Flanders did not comply with this, though they must have been well aware of it, as the Parliament of Paris in 1290 decided that the count of Nevers, the grandson of count Guy of Flanders, could ask no money for an amortization.[76] Moreover, in 1291 Philip the Fair issued a new statute, again excluding the barons privileged in 1275. This time the king did so reserving his future rights. In practice, licences for amortizations issued by the king's barons, even the peers of France, were later to disappear. In 1320 a new ordinance failed to mention the right of barons to authorize amortizations without royal intervention. A French historian has claimed that even the peers of France no longer pretended to have a right to autonomously control all mortmain alienations in their territories.[77] However, the counts of Flanders never stopped doing so, authorizing amortizations and legislating about mortmain alienations without French intervention.

The Flemish example may also have inspired the French king and others in the 1290s when count Guy of Flanders stepped up his controls over mortmain alienations by appointing Jan Calward to enquire into them from 1292. It is no coincidence that in exactly the same years (1294–97) as Guy of Flanders made settlements with the cities and religious houses who had acquired land in his county, the French king did likewise in Picardy.[78] The count of Artois had officials investigating acquisitions by churches in 1293,[79] also leading to an extensive documentation of such acquisitions dating from 1294.[80]

---

74 This is clearest in the French version.
75 De Laurière, *Ordonnances*, i, 305, n. e; Langlois, *Philippe le Hardi*, nr. 6, pp 423–4 (1275).
76 O. Beugnot, *Les Olim ou registres des arrêts rendus par la cour du roi* (Paris, 1839–48), ii, nr. 30, p. 309.
77 Sautel, 'Note', pp 697–8.
78 R. Fossier, *La terre et les hommes en Picardie jusqu'à la fin du XIIIe siècle* (Paris, 1968), ii, p. 626.
79 C. Wood, *The French apanages and the Capetian monarchy, 1224–1328* (Cambridge, MA 1966), p. 99.
80 See M. Flament, 'L'Artois à la fin du XIIIe siècle. Étude de la mobilité de la propriété

It may be that both the count of Artois and the French king were only imitating Guy, though this is not completely sure, as new research about Artois or the French king's activity in Northern France, may alter our chronology.

POSSIBLE FRENCH AND FLEMISH INFLUENCE ON ENGLAND

Continental historians can only envy their English colleagues. The 1279 Statute of Mortmain has been well studied, in particular in several publications of Paul Brand[81] and in a book by Sandra Raban. Raban even mentions that it was in line with developments abroad, most of all the 1275 statute of King Philip III of France,[82] though this is more to prove that action against mortmain alienations was in the air than because she sees any direct link between the English and French legislation. However, the French king had already been encroaching upon the duke of Guyenne's power to control mortmain alienations within his territories before 1275,[83] which must have put the duke of Guyenne under pressure. In fact, one year after the 1275 statute, Edward I ordered his officials to investigate alienations of fiefs in Guyenne, and during the 1280s he referred several times to the 1275 statute.[84] It is strange that English historians have ignored this. True, the problem of alienations into mortmain had already led to legislation in England in 1259 through clause 14 of the Provisions of Westminster, which required the consent of the immediate lord for mortmain alienations,[85] and in all likelihood a 1279 Yorkshire case concerning this clause was the direct occasion for issuing the Statute of Mortmain.[86] Nevertheless, even though there were enough English reasons for doing so, the French 1275 ordinance was not without its importance for England. In the Yorkshire case already

---

féodale d'après les rôles de franc-fiefs et de nouveaux-acquets du trésor des chartes d'Artois' (unpublished *doctorat de l'université*, Paris IX, 1977)).

81 See the following publications of Paul Brand: *Control of mortmain alienation*, pp 29–40 (also in Brand, *Common law*, pp 233–44; *Kings, barons and justices*, pp 57–62, 122–3, 126, 146–7, 162, 183–4, 191, 277–81; 'Rhetorics and realities: the making of medieval English legislation' in P. Chassaigne and J.-P. Genet (eds), *Droit et société en France et en Grande-Bretagne (XIIe-XXe siècles). Fonctions, usages et représentations* (Paris, 2003), pp 39–49; 'The mortmain licensing system, 1280–1307' in A. Jobson (ed.), *English government in the thirteenth century* (Woodbridge, 2004), pp 87–96; 'King, church and property: the enforcement of restrictions on alienations into mortmain in the lordship of Ireland in the later Middle Ages' in *The making of the common law* (London, 1992), pp 245–66.
82 Raban, *Mortmain legislation*, pp 21–2.
83 Beugnot, *Olim*, i, nr. 33, p. 891 (1272).
84 P. Chaplais, 'La souveraineté du roi de France et le pouvoir législatif en Guyenne au début du XIVe siècle', *Le moyen âge*, 69 (1963), 455–6.
85 Brand, *Kings, barons and justices*, pp 59–62.
86 Ibid., pp 277–80.

mentioned the dispute was not about a minor detail concerning clause 14 of the Provisions of Westminster, but about whether it was still the law of the land. In fact, clause 14 had been repealed in 1263, undoubtedly under pressure from the clergy, and it had never been reinstated.[87] The French example offered the king an argument against the clergy when he wanted once again to place stricter controls on mortmain alienations and thus may be more important than has hitherto been thought, as one of several factors contributing to the Statute of Mortmain.

However, the French influence in this case was only minor. The 1275 French ordinance does not resemble the Statute of Mortmain, which contains no detailed tariff for licences, but is primarily a ban on all future mortmain alienations. In this, it resembles the Flemish statute of 1252x1261, and the latter should perhaps be taken into account, when studying the Statute of Mortmain. For example, two questions have bothered English historians and have remained largely unanswered. First of all, why was there a total prohibition of mortmain alienations in 1279? The king himself did not need it, as land held in chief could not be granted to the church without his permission. The barons who wanted a better protection of their rights since lands held of them could be alienated into mortmain without their permission, would have been satisfied if, as in 1259, their consent had been required, when a church wanted to acquire lands held from them. Also puzzling is why, when under the 1279 statute the king imposed a ban on mortmain alienations, he acted against its terms by licensing some of them after all.[88]

A possible answer can be found by looking at Guy and Margaret's ordinance. They too put an absolute ban on mortmain alienations into their ordinance, although they were quite willing to lift the prohibition in certain cases, so that in practice the ban provided the basis for a licensing system. Because of the close relationship between Flanders and England, the chances are great that this may have inspired the Statute of Mortmain. If so, it is easy to see why King Edward I by this piece of 'disingenuous' legislation[89] forbade in theory what he was willing to allow in practice. The counts of Flanders had shown him the way. However, nowhere a clear link can be proven and, for the present the hypothesis of Flemish legislation having influenced England must remain a possibility which needs further investigation. Even if future research does not find the 'smoking gun' proving Flemish influence beyond any doubt, the Flemish statute still remains a useful basis for comparison, for it shows that an absolute ban on

---

87 Ibid., pp 146–7, 162, 191.
88 Raban, *Mortmain legislation*, pp 1, 16–18; Brand, 'Rhetorics and realities', p. 47; Brand, 'Mortmain licensing system', p. 95. Cf. T. Plucknett, *Legislation of Edward I* (Oxford, 1949), p. 101: 'the actual application of the statute is very different from its tenor.'
89 Brand, 'Rhetorics and realities', p. 49.

mortmain alienations which conceals a licensing system was not that unusual and, as such, is less in need of an explanation.

It is has to be stressed here that the comparison should not be a one way and that Flemish historians might learn a lot from what their English counterparts have written on this subject.[90] For example, Flemish historians have never wondered why the count of Flanders organized a licensing system by prohibiting all alienations into mortmain. Paul Brand has, convincingly, argued that in this way the details of the licensing system could be worked out later.[91] If this was the logic for the legislation of Countess Margareth and Count Guy in 1252x1261, it would help to explain why only a few lines of their ordinance have been preserved. The rest has not been lost. This was all there was, the rest having to be developed over time. This also explains why a systematic control of compliance with the Flemish ordinance came into existence only some decades after its promulgation.

Another interesting element of comparison, is with the more systematic exploitation of the licensing system by the English kings from 1299 onwards. Fines for licenses were exceptional before 1299, whereas they became a regular feature of licences on the patent rolls after that date.[92] Again, the coincidence of the chronology with that of events on the continent is striking. In 1292 Guy of Flanders commissioned Jan Calward to ensure the stricter application of the 1252x1261 statute. Within two years or less he was followed by the king of France and the count of Artois. The exact chronology and order of events has not yet ascertained with complete certainty, but there can be no doubt that there was a boom in fines from religious houses and cities in the years 1294–7, both in Picardy and in Flanders. This windfall for his continental colleagues may have made the English king's administration more aware of the potential of the licensing system for generating significant revenue. It may even be that King Edward himself had witnessed Flemish practices by the time he started to fully exploit the financial potential of the licenses for future alienations in 1299. In the autumn of 1297 and the winter of 1298 he was in Flanders at the head of an English army supporting the count of Flanders in his revolt against the French king,[93] and Jakemon of

---

90 Which they have, to be fair, neglected as much as their English colleagues have neglected their publications about the Flemish mortmain ordinance. In general, it is a bit strange, that although many continental legal historians read lots of articles in English, some English literature is completely neglected because it does not fit into the framework of contemporary civil law. An example is tenurial warranty, which was very important in feudal law anywhere in Europe wherever fiefs were to be found. However, continental authors do not study it, whereas there is an extensive literature about it by English legal historians: Heirbaut, *Over heren*, p. 31 n. 89.

91 Brand, 'Rhetorics and realities', p. 47; Brand, 'Mortmain licensing system', p. 95.

92 Raban, *Mortmain legislation*, pp 23–5; Brand, 'Mortmain licensing system', pp 94–5.

93 B. and M. Lyon, 'The logistics for Edward I's ill-fated campaign in Flanders (1297–1298)' *Handelingen van de maatschappij voor geschiedenis en oudheidkunde van Gent*, 55 (2001),

Deinze, the receiver-general of Flanders, and a close colleague of Jan Calward, had been instrumental in bringing about this alliance.[94] Moreover, the Flemish expedition caused great financial troubles for King Edward,[95] which must have given him an additional incentive for following the example of his Flemish colleague. Thus, Flanders may have contributed in more than one way to the systematic exploitation of the licensing system from 1299 in England.

CONCLUSION

The preceding pages sometimes contain speculations about matters which cannot always be proved beyond reasonable doubt. Even so, the hypothesis that a Flemish statute of 1252×1261, which was later forgotten, might have influenced both the French and the English legislation on mortmain alienations, should prove intriguing to any student of thirteenth-century legislation. This article hopes, at the least, to have shown that any future discussion of the French and English thirteenth-century legislation on mortmain alienations should also take Margaret and Guy's ordinance into account, and that comparisons between continental and English legal developments may lead to interesting results.[96]

APPENDIX

List of 1294–1297 charters containing a settlement made between the count and religious houses or cities which had acquired real property in contravention of the statute

Religious houses
abbey of Eversam: State Archives Bruges, Aanwinsten, 3904 (cartulary of Eversam), fo. 42r–v (1295)

> 77–89; B. and M. Lyon, 'An account of the provisions received by Robert de Segre, clerk of Edward I of England, in Flanders and Brabant in the autumn of 1297' *Handelingen van de koninklijke commissie voor geschiedenis,* 169 (2003), 37–49; B. and M. Lyon, *Wardrobe (the) book of 1296–1297: a financial and logistical record of Edward I's 1297 autumn campaign in Flanders against Philip IV of France* (Brussels, 2004); B. Lyon, 'The failed Flemish campaign of Edward I in 1297: a case study of efficient logistics and inadequate military planning', *Handelingen van de maatschappij voor geschiedenis en oudheidkunde van Gent* (forthcoming).

94 State archives Ghent, Charters of the counts of Flanders, collection Saint-Genois, 1040 (1296; for this date see F. Funck-Brentano, *Les origines de la guerre de cent ans. Philippe Le Bel en Flandre* (Paris, 1897), p. 191, n. 5).
95 Lyon, 'Logistics', p. 78.
96 For other examples, see e.g. P. Hyams, 'The common law and the French connection', *Proceedings of the Battle conference on Anglo-Norman Studies,* 4 (1981), 77–92. See also Giordanengo, *Consuetudo,* p. 62 about the 1181 Assize of arms of Henry II, which inspired like measures in France and Flanders.

abbey of Oudenburg: L. Gilliodts-Van Severen, *Coutumes des petites villes et seigneuries enclavées* (Brussels, 1890–3), iv, nr. 3, pp 314–16 (1296)

abbey of St Andrew near Bruges:State Archives Bruges, Découvertes, 2501 (cartulary of St Andrew), fos. 21v–23r (1295)

abbey of Ter Doest: F. Van De Putte and C. Carton, *Chronique de l'abbaye de Ter Doest*, (Bruges, 1845), nr. 40, pp 64–5 (1295)

abbey of Vicoigne: Archives départementales du Nord (Lille), 59 H, 96, nr. 299, fo. 138 r–v (1295)

abbey of Zonnebeke: C. Callewaert, *Chartes anciennes de l'abbaye de Zonnebeke* (Bruges, 1925), nr. 128, p. 140 (1295)

abbey of Ter Duinen at Koksijde: F. Van De Putte, *Cronica et cartularium monasterii de Dunis* (Bruges, 1864), ii, nr. 593, pp 654–5 (1295)

Eeckhoutabbey near Bruges: Bruges, Grand seminary, Eeckhoutabbey, Charters, p. 49 (1295)

Saint Mary's church at Bruges: State archives Bruges, Saint Mary's church, charters, provisional nr. 230 (1297)

Saint Mary's hospital at Oudenaarde: Oudenaarde, O.C.M.W. (Social Welfare Centre) Saint Mary's hospital, 80 bis (cartulary of Saint Mary's hospital), nr. 191, fo. 49 r–v (1295)

Rozenbergabbey at Waasmunster: F. De Potter and D. Broeckaert, *Geschiedenis van de gemeenten van de provincie Oost-Vlaanderen* (Ghent, 1864–1900), series 4, ii, p. 117 n. 1 (1295)

Towns
Douai: P. Thomas, *Textes historiques sur Lille et le Nord de la France avant 1789* (Lille, 1931–6), ii, nr. 80, pp 253–4 (1294)

Ypres: L. Gilliodts-Van Severen, *Sources et développement de la coutume d'Ypres* (Brussels, 1908), nr. 31, pp 45–6 (1294)

Courtrai (T. De Limburg-Stirum, *Coutumes de la ville et de la châtellenie de Courtrai*, i (Brussels, 1905), nr. 6, pp 149–50 (1294)

Nieuwpoort: L. Gilliodts-Van Severen, *Coutume de la ville et du port de Nieuport* (Brussels, 1901), nr. 20, pp 168–9 (1294)

Lille: M. Brun-Lavainne, *Roisin. Franchises, lois et coutumes de la ville de Lille* (Lille, 1842), pp 331–2 (1294)

Feodo de Compedibus Vocato le Sewet: the medieval prison 'oeconomy'

JONATHAN ROSE[1]

THE FEES IMPOSED ON MEDIEVAL prisoners have not received much recent scholarly attention. Ralph Pugh's *Imprisonment in Medieval England*, the seminal work in the field, lays the foundation and starting point for this paper, which discusses a mid-fifteenth-century payment by a prisoner in the King's Bench Marshalsea. An entry in an account in the Fastolf Papers says:

> Item paid by Thomas Howes ... for the fee of shackles called the sewet (*feodo de compedibus vocato le sewet*) both for himself and for John Porter until the jurors impaneled in the attaint might appear before the justices of the King at Westminster[2]

This appears in a section listing expenditures relating to an attaint challenging the outcome of a 1454 conspiracy suit brought against Thomas Howes, Fastolf's servant and chaplain, and John Porter, another Fastolf servant, by John Andrew, an associate of Fastolf's East Anglian foes, the supporters of the duke of Suffolk.[3]

---

1 The author wishes to express appreciation to Sir John Baker, Paul Brand, Robin Darwall-Smith, Jean Dunbabin, Richard Helmholz, Susanne Jenks, Wendy Rose, and Henry Summerson. I am particularly grateful to Henry Summerson and Susanne Jenks for their detailed comments and for providing numerous plea roll references. As usual, the author bears full responsibility for the article's analysis and conclusions as well as all errors.

2 *Item soluta per Thomam Howes in curia banci regis coram Johanne Fortescue justiciario ... feodo de compedibus vocato le sewet tam pro ipso quam pro Johanne Porter dummodo juratores impanellati in attincta comparerent coram justiciariis Regis Westmonasterium:* Fastolf Paper 42. The entry is one of several appearing under the heading *Custus in Attincta ac pro judicio querele conspiracionis Johannis Andrews.*

3 Fastolf Paper 42, Archives of Magdalen College, University of Oxford, a long account of payments made during ten years of litigation, 1448–59. It lists the expenses that Sir John Fastolf incurred in five major legal disputes. I want to express my appreciation to the officers and fellows of Magdalen College for their support and hospitality in giving me access to the College Archives and, in particular, to Robin Darwall-Smith, the College Archivist, and to Christine Ferdinand, the Fellow Librarian.

This entry raises two interesting questions: what was the 'fee of shackles', and why was it called *le sewet*?[4] The answer lies in the financial characteristics of the medieval prison system, its 'oeconomy'.[5] As the discussion will reveal, sewet was a payment by a prisoner to the keeper of a jail to make the conditions of custody less uncomfortable. Understanding its meaning does not, however, by itself answer the substantive question regarding the legality and rationale of its imposition. The purpose of this paper is to explore these questions.

OVERVIEW OF PRISON FEES

Imprisonment in medieval England was not used solely as a means of punishment and was initially used for certain offences such as interference with the administration of justice.[6] Prisons were also used to hold defendants in both civil and criminal actions until trial, and also to retain debtors until they had paid their debts to the crown,[7] and (after 1283) their debts to others.[8] By the end of the thirteenth century, imprisonment for trespass and misdemeanors was common.[9] Such imprisonment could be terminated by paying ransom to the crown, though after 1275 statutes began to require specific terms of imprisonment before ransom could be paid.[10] In London, there were five main prisons: the Tower of London, Newgate, Ludgate, the Fleet, and the King's Bench Marshalsea.[11] The Tower held a variety of prisoners, including state prisoners and prisoners of war and both royalty

---

4 I am grateful to Dr Henry Summerson and Dr Jean Dunbabin for putting me on the right track to unravel these questions and to Dr Michael Clanchy for suggesting that I contact them.

5 A. Jessop (ed.), *The oeconomy of the Fleete* (London, 1879).

6 Ralph Pugh, *Imprisonment in medieval England* (Cambridge, 1968), pp 9–25.

7 Pugh denominated these 'custodial' and 'coercive' imprisonment: Pugh, *Imprisonment in medieval England*, pp 1–25. These three different types of imprisonment – coercive, custodial, and punitive – tended to merge in the Middle Ages. Ireland has questioned the utility of this categorization and argued that imprisonment as a form of punishment was common: Richard Ireland, 'Theory and practice with the medieval prison', *Am. J. Leg. Hist.*, 31 (1987), 56–67 at 1 n. 4, 56–7, 62–7.

8 The statute of Acton Burnell extended imprisonment to debtors of private creditors: Statute of Merchants, 11 Edw. I, *Statutes of the realm*, i, 53. Two years later the Statutes of Merchants repeated and superseded the earlier statute: Statute of Merchants, 13 Edw. I (*Stat. realm*, i, 98). In 1352, further legislation providing for imprisonment of private debtors was enacted: 25 Edw. III, st. v, c. 17 (*Stat. realm*, i, 322).

9 Pugh, *Imprisonment in medieval England*, pp 26–47.

10 Ibid., pp 15, 30–1.

11 There were also other prisons as well such as the Counters, the jails of the London and Middlesex sheriffs. Most felons were held in the Tower and Newgate: Pugh, *Imprisonment in medieval England*, pp 114–39; Caroline Barron, *London in the Middle Ages* (Oxford, 2004), pp 164–8.

and nobility as well as some, although not many, common felons. Newgate was the official prison of the City of London, but also became a national prison, holding those charged with serious crimes from all over England as well as violators of municipal ordinances and debtors. Ludgate held the freemen of London imprisoned for trespass, debt, and contempt. The Fleet, connected to the courts of Common Pleas and the Exchequer, held crown and private debtors and those convicted of more minor offenses, including wealthier prisoners who could pay for more comfortable accommodation. The Marshalsea of King's Bench contained felons and debtors as well as outlaws and those awaiting trial in King's Bench.

In medieval English prisons, there was a well established practice of jailers collecting a variety of fees from prisoners,[12] which were an important source of income for them.[13] The fees included entry and release fees as well as fees collected for all the basic amenities within the prison such as heat, light, food and drink, bedding, and lodging.[14] These fees varied in amount and from place to place as well as according to the prisoner's social status.[15] Because such fees provided opportunities for soliciting bribes and extortion against a vulnerable group, their imposition caused controversy. Two late thirteenth-century commentators questioned their propriety. *The Mirror of Justices* stated that 'it is an abuse that prisoners or others on their behalf should pay anything on entering or leaving gaol.'[16] *Britton* also criticized these fees.[17] Fees might, however, be viewed more favourably as life for prisoners depended heavily on the ability to pay,[18] a particular problem for paupers, a

12 Pugh has a very detailed discussion of all aspects of the various fees that jailers imposed on prisoners: Pugh, *Imprisonment in medieval England*, pp 166–77. Jailers preferred prisoners whose ability to pay fees made them more profitable and might refuse to take others lacking that ability as they would displace the former: Helen Cam, *The hundred and the hundred rolls* (New York, 1930), p. 68. The payment of such fees was not confined to England: Jean Dunbabin, *Captivity and imprisonment in medieval Europe, 1000–1300* (New York, 2002), pp 141–3.
13 *The oeconomy of the Fleete*, pp ix, xvii; *Select cases in the court of King's Bench*, i, ed. G.O. Sayles, Selden Society vol. 55 (London, 1936), p. xc; M. Bassett, 'The Fleet prison in the Middle Ages', *U. Toronto Law Journal*, 5 (1944), 383–402 at 384, 401.
14 Pugh, *Imprisonment in medieval England*, pp 175–6; J.G. Bellamy, *Crime and public order in England in the Middle Ages* (London, 1973), pp 171–2.
15 Pugh has identified many fees and the amounts charged in various different locations: Pugh, *Imprisonment in medieval England*, pp 167–8. Although these fees were most commonly paid to the jailer, they were on occasion paid directly to the crown: ibid., pp 172–3.
16 *The mirror of justices*, ed. W.J. Whittaker, Selden Society vol. 7 (London, 1895), p. 160.
17 He said, 'We forbid any one to take money, or the value thereof, for receiving prisoners ... or to take for the keeping any prisoner more than four pence, on pain of ransom and fine. Of the poor let nothing be taken, and let no prisoner be longer detained for the default in payment of such fees': *Britton*, ed. F.M. Nichols (London, 1865), i, 46–7.
18 Bassett, 'The Fleet prison in the Middle Ages', 402. She stated further that 'every prisoner was a source of income as long as he had anything in his pockets or even a coat on his back': ibid., p. 384. In one instance, it was noted that a prisoner 'had chattels, but he ate them in

significant proportion of those incarcerated. Absent charity obtained through begging outside the prison,[19] they faced starvation, which not uncommonly caused death.[20] Perhaps payment of fees offered brief relief from this subsequent fate.[21]

Although there was no effort to prohibit fees, there were a number of measures aimed at regulating them. In 1307, the king limited the fees charged prisoners by the earl marshal.[22] In 1319, the Barons of the Exchequer investigated fees charged by jailers;[23] and the keeper of Newgate was removed from office for charging excessive fees and extortion against prisoners.[24] The 1356 regulation of Newgate prison limited the fee for custody of each prisoner to four pence and expressly prohibited charging an entry fee.[25] A 1393 London ordinance limited the jailers at Newgate and Ludgate prisons to four pence for each prisoner delivered to the jail and prohibited any further fees except for treason or felony (*iiii deniers, sanz plus, pur fee de gaoler pur toutes causes, tresoun et felonie exceptes*).[26] A 1401 Commons petition expressed concern

prison': *Rolls of the justices in eyre, being the rolls of the pleas and assizes for Yorkshire in 3 Hen. III (1218–19)*, ed. D.M. Stenton, Selden Society vol. 56 (London, 1937), p. 203. Basset noted, quoting the London Lickpenny, that 'money paved the way for all transactions in Westminster Hall "for he that lack'd money myght not spede"': Bassett, 'The Fleet prison in the Middle Ages', 385. Bassett said further that 'if he was poor when he came to prison, he was likely to be destitute before he left' and once prisoners 'had exhausted their private resources they were faced with life imprisonment and, unless they could find some employment within the prison, starvation': ibid., 399, 402.

19 Pugh, *Imprisonment in medieval England*, pp 327–8, 336–7. Although Pugh suggested that begging outside the prison did not begin until 1373–4, Henry Summerson has found evidence of its existence as early as 1243 in Somerset and that it was customary in Canterbury by 1259. TNA:PRO, KB 26/167, m. 18d; e-mail from Dr Henry Summerson to Jonathan Rose, Feb. 15, 2005.

20 The London Coroners' Rolls record many deaths in Newgate, presumably often due to starvation during the early fourteenth-century famine: E-mail from Dr Henry Summerson to Jonathan Rose, Feb. 15, 2005.

21 I am grateful to Dr Henry Summerson for this suggestion.

22 *Select cases in the King's Bench*, i, pp cxlix–cl.

23 *Chronicles of the reigns of Edward I and Edward II: annales Londoniensis and annales Paulini*, i, ed. William Stubbs (London, 1862), p. 285; M. Bassett, 'Newgate prison in the Middle Ages', *Speculum* 18 (1943), 233–46 at 233, 236; *YB Eyre of Kent, 6–7 Edward II 1313–4*, ii, ed. William Bolland and others, Selden Society vol. 27 (London, 1912), pp xxvi–vii.

24 Bassett, 'Newgate prison in the Middle Ages', 236.

25 *Munimenta Gildhallae Londoniensis*, i, ed. Henry Riley (London, 1859) , p. 47. The penalty for violating the regulation was forfeiture of office. For the dating, see *Letter book G, calendar of letter-books of the city of London*, ed. Reginald Sharpe (London, 1905), pp 71–4.

26 *Munimenta Gildhallae Londoniensis*, i, 524. Paul Brand has suggested that the ordinance language (*a lour deliverance*) is unclear and may mean when delivered from the jail. In 1431, extensive regulations forbidding the sale of certain items to prisoners and governing the prices charged Newgate prisoners for various items were promulgated and the use of fees as a form of punishment was forbidden: *Letter book K, calendar of letter-books of the city of London*, ed. Reginald Sharp (London, 1911), pp 124–7.

about the fees of the marshals, including the King's Bench marshal, and asked that the jailers be limited to taking such fees as were set by the present Parliament ('*serroit limite en ceste present Parlement*').[27] In response, the king ordered the council to investigate fees generally. Although parliament enacted a statute, it covered only the fees of the marshalsea of the king's household, limiting fees to the standard four pence.[28] A 1445 statute prohibited jailers from charging fees for any reason other than the four pence for a prisoner committed to their custody.[29] Generally, four pence was the well established fee for each prisoner in custody, described in 1356 as '*iiii deniers pur soun fee, come auncienement ad este usee*.[30] Regulation of the fees charged in Newgate and Ludgate prisons continued into the fifteenth century.[31]

Although the 1445 statute exempted the warden of Fleet,[32] similar fee practices were longstanding in that prison.[33] During the fourteenth century, the warden of the Fleet was collecting 2s. 4d. for prisoners in the Fleet, the only jailer permitted to exceed the standard four pence fee.[34] A 1401 Commons petition expressed concern with the fee charging practices of the Fleet warden and requested that his fees be specified ('*soient mys en certein*').[35] But no regulation resulted. Perhaps the reason for the different treatment of fees in the Fleet was that most prisoners were held there for debt or payment of a fine to the king, and not for serious criminal offences.

27 *Rotuli Parliamentorum*, iii, 469, no. 55, 2 Hen. IV (1767).
28 2 Hen. IV, c. 23, *Statutes of the realm*, ii, 130–1, adopting the remedy requested by the Commons petition of forfeiture of office and treble damages for the aggrieved party.
29 23 Hen. VI, c. 9, *Statutes of the realm*, ii, 334–5. The statute provided treble damages for aggrieved victims as well as a £40 penalty for each violation, half going to king and the other half to the plaintiff.
30 This statement appeared in a regulation of the Newgate jail: *Munimenta Gildhallae Londoniensis*, i, 47; *Letter book G, calendar of letter-books of the city of London*, ed. Reginald Sharpe, p. 74. In 1283, a 4*d*. release fee was described as being paid 'according to custom': *Select cases in King's Bench*, i, p. 126.
31 In 1463 and 1488, more ordinances regulating fees charged in both Ludgate and Newgate prisons were adopted. *Letter book L, calendar of the letter-books of the city of London*, ed. Reginald Sharpe (London, 1912), pp 40–3; Bassett, 'Newgate prison in the Middle Ages', 242. A primary objective of this ordinance was to extend the 1431 regulation of Newgate prison to Ludgate prison.
32 Pugh, *Imprisonment in medieval England*, p. 336; Bassett, 'The Fleet prison in the Middle Ages', 397.
33 Bassett, 'The Fleet prison in the Middle Ages', 394.
34 Ibid., p. 384. The wardenship of the Fleet was apparently a very valuable office, likely probably worth much more than comparable positions in the other prisons: ibid., 386; Pugh, *Imprisonment in medieval England*, pp 156–8. In the fourteenth and fifteenth centuries, it produced high annual values and was sold by its last hereditary owner in 1559 for £4,000: *The oeconomy of the Fleete*, 16–17; Bassett, 'The Fleet prison in the Middle Ages', 386–93.
35 *Rotuli Parliamentorum*, iii, 469, no. 55.

Several factors may explain why none of this regulation was very effective. First, the leverage the jailers had was too one-sided to police effectively. Also, conditions in prison were so miserable that those with money were willing to pay to alleviate them. Second, the attempt to regulate fees in itself gave them a certain legitimacy. While there were complaints, no one other than the author of *The Mirror* suggested prohibiting them altogether, but only suggested limiting them to prevent overcharging. The common complaint was extortionate fees.[36] Legitimate fees were recognized. Third, jailers, wardens, and other officials depended on the fees, which were their primary source of income. Permitting the charging of fees was a more acceptable alternative than raising wages,[37] and was in keeping with the fee system common to the entire judicial system. Finally, the level of fees set by statute seems unrealistically low. The common four pence fee per prisoner appeared as early as the late thirteenth century and was still the one set by statute as late as 1445. Given all these considerations, the widespread use of additional fees is not surprising.[38] However, the recognition of the legitimacy of fees did not sanction all and any fees, only reasonable ones. High fees might still be considered extortionate and, therefore, unacceptable, but drawing the line between 'an illegal act' and 'a tolerated irregularity' is most difficult.[39]

'FEODO DE COMPEDIBUS'

Among the fees charged prisoners was one for 'irons'. This fee was either for attaching irons to the prisoner or for removing them, although the latter was more common. *Compes* and *compedio* were among the Latin words used to designate leg-irons and shackling.[40] Thus, *feodo de compedibus* likely referred to this practice. Although irons were expressly required by statute for certain prisoners,[41] the use of shackles or fetters on the legs of prisoners was a

---

36 The City of London attempted to diminish extortion against prisoners by reducing the financial pressure on keepers by 'forbidding sheriffs taking money from ... the gaolers of Newgate and Ludgate, for exercising their several offices, inasmuch as it induced these officers to practise extortion on their poor prisoners': *Letter book I, calendar of letter-books of the city of London*, ed. Reginald Sharpe (London, 1909), p. 262.
37 Their wages varied over time and geographically: Pugh, *Imprisonment in medieval England*, pp 165–6.
38 The impact of the inspection system instituted to monitor compliance with the jail regulation is apparently unknown: ibid., pp 186–8.
39 Ibid., pp 176–7.
40 *Bracton on the laws and customs of England*, ed. G.E. Woodbine & Samuel E. Thorne (Buffalo, NY, 1997), ii, 385. The word *vinculum* was also used, as was *ferrum*. Ibid., 394, 410. The law french equivalents were *fiergers, defirger*, and *a fere*: *The mirror of justices*, pp 52, 160; *Britton*, ii, 35, 44.
41 Statute of Westminster II, c. 11, 13 Edw. I: *Stat. realm*, i, 80 (auditors and receivers).

controversial practice. In 1234, the mayor and sheriffs of London were ordered to remove the irons from two prisoners in Newgate jail.[42] Among the misconduct for which the warden of the Fleet was convicted and removed from office in 1319 was the excessive use of irons.[43] *Britton* would have permitted irons for felons and those imprisoned for certain trespasses or account arrears.[44] *Bracton's* attitude is less clear. In one passage, he condemned the use of chains as 'forbidden by law' and a form of punishment inconsistent with the purpose of prison as detention, criticizing 'the custom of authorities to injure those detained in prisons by keeping them in chains'.[45] But the precise practice to which he was objecting is unclear, as the word 'chains' (*vinculis*) may have referred to some more extensive form of shackling.[46] Moreover, *Bracton* seems to endorse the use of irons for felons and to prevent escape.[47]

Nonetheless, shackling prisoners was a long-standing practice and every jailer's equipment included shackles.[48] Felons were commonly shackled.[49]

---

42 *Close Rolls 1231–4* (London, 1905), p. 423.

43 Bassett, 'Newgate prison in the Middle Ages', 236–7. In 1388, a prisoner complained about the use of irons as punishment in retaliation for complaining: Barron, *London in the later Middle Ages*, p. 166.

44 *Britton*, ii, 44. The Statute of Westminster II explicitly required irons in the third case: Statute of Westminster II, c. 11, 13 Edw. I.

45 *Bracton*, ii, 299. Although relying on Justinian's Digest, *Bracton* may have expanded on Justinian, albeit the latter's position is not clear. There is one statement almost identical to that in *Bracton*: *The digest of Justinian*, ed. Theodor Mommsen, Paul Krueger & Alan Watson (Philadelphia, 1985), iv, book 48, ch. 8.9. However, just preceding that passage is another sanctioning chains of different weights as punishment for criminals condemned to the mines or *opus metali*. Moreover, in an earlier passage, Justinian generally prohibited the use of chains for an accused prepared to give sureties, but makes exceptions for crimes sufficiently serious to warrant the rejection of sureties and justifying imprisonment prior to conviction: ibid., ch. 3.3.

46 In several references to shackling, *Bracton* uses the words, *in vinculis, compeditus,* and *in ferro*, translated respectively as 'chains' and 'fetters,' 'leg-irons,' and 'irons.' *Bracton* also uses *vinxerit*, translated as 'put in irons': *Bracton*, ii, 299, 346, 350, 385, 394, 410; ibid., iii, 20, 30; ibid., iv, 236. Pugh stated that '"irons" [is] a comprehensive term used to cover chains, fetters, manacles, rings, and collars': Pugh, *Imprisonment in medieval England*, pp 177, 370–3. Others have agreed: Christopher Harding, Bill Hines, Richard Ireland & Philip Rawlings, *Imprisonment in England and Wales: a concise history* (London, 1985), p. 22. Thus, in these various passages, it is not clear whether these different words were used to differentiate different forms of shackling or just used generically and interchangeably.

47 *Bracton*, ii, 350, 385. He sanctioned the use of more severe punishment, 'the supreme penalty,' greater than that imposed for the original crime, for those who conspired to escape from prison by 'breaking their chains' (*conspiraverint ut ruptis vinculis ... evadant*): ibid., p. 350. His view reflected the fact that death remained the penalty for prison breach until 1295. His position was identical to that taken in Justinian's Digest: ibid., nn. 13–14; *The digest of Justinian*, iv, book 48, ch. 3.13.

48 Pugh, *Imprisonment in medieval England*, pp 177–8.

49 H.R.T. Summerson, 'The early development of the *peine forte et dure*', in E.W. Ives & A.H. Manchester (eds), *Law, litigants, and the legal profession* (London, 1983), pp 116–25 at 119.

Not only were prisoners shackled while in prison, but it was the custom of the realm for accused felons to appear before the justices in irons.[50] Nevertheless, Britton criticized this practice, saying that felons ought to appear in court 'without irons', so that they 'not be deprived of reason by pain', impairing their ability to defend themselves.[51] Placing incarcerated prisoners in irons continued throughout the fourteenth and fifteenth centuries.[52]

Several rationales were advanced to justify the use of irons. The primary justification was to prevent prisoners from escaping.[53] The 1431 prohibition on the use of irons for minor offenses because Newgate prison was 'sufficiently strong' illustrated the linkage to escape.[54] Also, serious crimes like felonies warranted shackling.[55] Finally, the use of irons was thought to be appropriate for difficult prisoners. The warden of the Fleet so justified his shackling of some prisoners, stating that he had shackled one prisoner 'for wounding the Warden and attempting to beate out his braynes with a hammer and stabbing three officers of speciall trust'.[56]

Since irons were regularly used, it is not surprising that prisoners paid fees to have them removed and that there were complaints about these fees. It was apparently quite common for prisoners with sufficient means to pay jailers to remove their irons.[57] In 1299, a writ alleging false imprisonment by the mayor of the city of York and others alleged the charging of six pence to remove irons.[58] In the 1292 Shropshire Eyre, prisoners paid to have their irons removed when coming to court.[59] In the sixteenth century, Fleet

50 In 1293, a parliamentary plea complained that Stephen de Rabaz, sheriff of Warwickshire and Leicestershire, had brought Ralph de Cokehull, who had been indicted for murder, before the justices without irons (*sine ferris*) contrary to the custom of the realm (*contra consuetudinem regni*): *Rotuli Parliamentorum*, i, 95. For this and many other forms of misconduct, the sheriff was imprisoned: ibid., 96. Officials bringing prisoners to court without irons might be penalized: TNA: PRO, JUST 3/99, m. 7; TNA: PRO, JUST 1/877, m. 63d.; TNA: PRO, JUST 3/69, m. 3.
51 *Britton*, ii, 35. Another version of the text would only have prohibited irons if they were very heavy (*trop gros fers*): ibid., p. 35, n. 8.
52 Pugh, *Imprisonment in medieval England*, pp 178–80.
53 Transferring prisoners without first putting them in irons facilitated escape by the prisoner: *Select cases in the court of King's Bench*, ii, ed. G.O. Sayles, Selden Society vol. 57 (London, 1938), pp 149, 150. Thus, prisoners were fettered when being moved between prisons or when being brought to jail after initial arrest: TNA: PRO, JUST 1/943, m. 21.
54 *Letter book K, calendar of letter-books of the city of London*, ed. Reginald Sharpe, p. 126.
55 Pugh, *Imprisonment in medieval England*, p. 179; Basset, 'The Fleet prison in the Middle Ages', 400.
56 *The oeconomy of the Fleete*, pp 58, 59, 60, 88. He said further, 'And why doe they in Bedlam binde men, in Newgate iron them, in other prisons shutt them up? But because some are madd or crackt braynd, some are full of villany, others drunken and refractory': ibid., p. 8.
57 Pugh, *Imprisonment in medieval England*, pp 178–9.
58 *Select cases in the court of King's Bench*, iii, ed. G.O. Sayles, Selden Society vol. 58 (London, 1939), p. 87.
59 TNA: PRO, JUST 1/736, mm. 37d, 43.

prisoners paid such a fee as part of the entry fee, denominated as 'The Warden's fyne for liberte of the Howse and irons at first cominge'.[60]

Because of the potential for abuse, these fees were regulated. In 1356, the warden of Newgate had to swear personally to take no fine or extortion from any prisoner to put on or remove irons (*ne prendra fyn ne extorcioun dascun prisoun pur mettre ou oustier ferres*).[61] Nevertheless, most Newgate prisoners were put in irons.[62] A 1393 regulation governing Newgate and Ludgate prison authorized reasonable *suwette* for removing the irons of prisoners in custody for debts of 100s. or higher (*maes bien lise ditz gaolers de prendre suwette resonablement, pur la somme de c soultz, et paramount, pur ouster lour ferres*).[63] A 1431 regulation of Newgate prison prohibited the use of irons for debts under 100s. if the prisoner gave a bond, but permitted their use and a 'reasonable fee' for removing them for serious offenses.[64] The other major prisons were subjected to these regulations in 1488.[65] A 1445 statute prohibited such fees altogether.[66]

'LE SEWET'

Sewet and its various Law French and Latin variants appear frequently during the fourteenth century, but perhaps appear first in 1262.[67] The most common form was *suete* and the most common phrase, *suete de prisone*. However, a dozen or more Law French, Latin, and English variants appear in legal documents: *suete de prisone, sueta de indicatis de transgressionibus, sueta indicatatorum, sueta prisonum indicatorum de transgressionibus, denarii pro sueta prisone, pur greynour suete, pur greindre suite, suete et aise de prisone, suete ou eese de prisone, pro sueta prisone, suyte of prison, sewet de prison, for suavity of the prison,* and *pro suavitate prisone.* The entry in the Fastolf papers,[68] and the

---

60 This fee ranged from £10 for an archbishop, duke or duchess to 13s. 4d. for yeoman or other commoner (with nothing for a 'poore man'): 'Forme of the table that shall hang in the hall of the Fleet' in *The oeconomy of the Fleete*, following p. 152.
61 *Munimenta Gildhallae Londoniensis*, i, p. 47.
62 Bassett, 'Newgate prison in the Middle Ages', 245.
63 *Munimenta Gildhallae Londoniensis*, i, p. 524. Bassett noted that the customary fee at the end of the fourteenth century was '100s or more.' She recounts the case of prisoner who paid only 40s. 'for a fyne for irons which they said they showed me great favour in, I shuld else have paid £4 or £5': Bassett, 'Newgate prison in the Middle Ages', 245 & n.2.
64 *Letter book K, calendar of letter-books of the city of London*, p. 126.
65 Ibid.
66 23 Hen. VI, c. 9:9, *Stat. realm*, ii, 334–5.
67 An official charged with misconduct in the 1262 Warwickshire Eyre paid the beadle 16*d*. for *suete de prison*: TNA: PRO, JUST 1/954, m. 55 (e-mail from Dr Henry Summerson to Jonathan Rose, 15 February, 2005).
68 See above, pp 72–3.

prior discussion indicate that primary meaning of *sewet* was a payment of money associated with the imposition or removal of the shackles of prisoners. However, they do not explain fully why it was called *sewet*, the possible existence of additional meanings, and the implications of that explanation for the rationale for its imposition. Exploring those further questions is the focus of this section.

In the early twentieth century, the use and meaning of these words and phrases puzzled historians,[69] and later scholars, building on that initial work, have clarified them.[70] In 1909, Stewart-Brown made the first, and still most detailed, study.[71] Despite some confusion with the Latin word *secta* ('suit'), the evidence suggested that the words were not connected.[72] He concluded that '*suete* or *sueta* [was] simply good classical Latin for "customary [payments,]" in this case bail or gaol fees levied by sheriffs and their officers,' suggesting that the words derived from *suetus*, classical Latin for customary.[73] Although Stewart-Brown captures the core meaning of the term, a payment of money in connection with imprisonment, it does not seem to be the only one. There is a considerable variation both in contemporary usage and in later translation,[74] suggesting some confusion about the precise meaning of *suete* and *sueta*, as Bertha Putnam pointed out.[75] Several statutes used *sewet* and its variants in connection with the payment of money, but others not so.[76] Another usage of these words related to allowing Fleet prisoners the privilege of going at large to attend to their business.[77] Here there was no connection

---

69 R. Stewart-Brown, '*Suete de prisone*', *EHR*, 24 (1909), 506–10; B.H. Putnam, '*Suete de prisone*', *EHR*, 25 (1910), 307–8.
70 R.E. Latham, 'Minor enigmas from medieval records: second series', EHR, 76 (1961), 633–6.
71 Stewart-Brown, '*Suete de prisone*', 506–09.
72 Stewart-Brown, '*Suete de prisone*', 509; Latham, 'Minor enigmas from medieval records', 634. Bertha Putnam was less sure, stating that the difference between *suete* and *secta* was 'not clearly understood': Putnam, '*Suete de prisone*', 305.
73 Ibid., 510. In 1862, the *Liber Albus* editor translated *suetz* as 'customary fees': *Munimenta Gildhallae Londoniensis*, iii, p. 362.
74 It is difficult to date the English translations of *sueta*, *suete*, and other similar words used in the various statutes to get some idea a contemporary understanding of those words. Although the *Statutes of Realm* compilation occurred between 1810 and 1825, the translations are often earlier in date and represent earlier compilations of translations that themselves incorporated even earlier versions.
75 She identified four examples where, in Exchequer enrollments, contemporary translators had used three different words, '*sectis*,' '*pro feodis suis vel aisaimentis prisonum*,'and '*sueta prisone.*' for the Law French, '*suete de prisone,*' which appeared in the 1351 Statute of Labourers to which the enrollments pertained: Putnam,' *Suete de prisone*', 308.
76 1 Edw. III, c. 7, *Stat. realm*, i, 253 (*pur aver raunceons des tieux appellez pur [suete] de prisone, ou pur autre cause*); 3 Edw. III, st. 2, c. 6, *Stat. realm*, i, 313 ('*pur fees, suete de prisone, nen autre manere*); 23 Hen. VI, c. 9, *Stat. realm*, ii, 334–5 (*pur fyn fee sewet de prison maympris lessance a baille ou monstraunce ascun ease ou favour a ascun tiel persone issint arrestuz* ...).
77 1 Rich. II, c. 12, *Stat. realm*, ii, 4 (*pur greynour suete y avoir de prisone qe aillors*).

with the payment of money and 'liberty' captures its sense, as the Fleet prison permitted excursions outside the prison ('going at large'),[78] used leg irons less, and generally had less harsh conditions.[79] This additional meaning is also consistent with the use of such phrases as *suete et aise de prisone, suete ou eese de prisone,* and *pro aisiamentis prisonum*.[80] Thus, while Stewart-Brown's conclusions pointed in the right direction, equating sewet simply with customary prison payments minimized the range of its contemporary usage.

Half a century later, R.E. Latham again explored the meaning of *suete de prison*.[81] Although he generally corroborated Stewart-Brown's research,[82] he disagreed with some of his conclusions. In particular, he doubted that *suetus* was the correct Latin source of the word due to its rarity, the failure to replace it with a more common word, and its inconsistency with *aise* and *aisiamentum*.[83] Latham felt that Stewart-Brown had given insufficient attention to the use of *suavitate*, finding five additional uses of *suavitate*. He concluded that the 'origin of the expression is probably to be found in the use of the word *suavitas*,' which was 'now well attested as an alternative to *sueta*'.[84] Thus, he determined that the Old French equivalents were '*soeveté* or '*soueveté*.'

Now almost a half century later again, the Fastolf Paper 42 entry provides an occasion to build on this earlier research and to further understand why this payment was called *sewet* and to explore further the rationale for its imposition on prisoners. In so doing, it is important to identify the language in which the term first appeared, and to be less literal-minded about its ultimate derivation. The term appears in Law French, Latin, and English, but much less frequently in the latter. Since the most frequent initial appearances were in fourteenth century legal documents, Law French (rather than Latin or English) seems to be the primary language.[85] The most common Law French word is *suete* although *seute* and *sewet*, likely a later variant, also appear.[86]

---

78 In 1388, after paying *aisiamentum prisone*, the marshal of the king's house permitted John Wareyn 'to go at large' (*ipsum dimisit ire ad largum*): TNA: PRO, KB 27/510, m. 67.
79 Bassett, 'The Fleet prison in the Middle Ages', 400; Bassett, 'Newgate prison in the Middle Ages', 245, 246; Pugh, *Imprisonment in medieval England*, p. 118.
80 Other words were also used to convey this same sense. An order in 1234 to a jailer *de alleviatione prisonum* mandated the removal of a prisoner's irons (*faciant alleviari de oneratione ferramentis*): *Close Rolls 1231–4*, p. 423.
81 Latham, 'Minor enigmas from medieval records', 633–6.
82 Latham found several more examples linking *sueta* to the payment of money: ibid., pp 634–5.
83 Ibid., p. 635.
84 Ibid., pp 635–6.
85 Latham's definitions in *Revised Latin medieval word-list*, which focus on *suete de prisone* may indicate that he also considered Law French and not Latin as the primary source.
86 It is possible that *sewet*, used in Fastolf Paper 42 and 23 Hen. VI, c. 9 was a fifteenth-century spelling, although there is evidence of its earlier use. The *Medieval Latin word-list* also indicates a Latin variation, *sewettum prisone* appearing before 1564: Latham, *Revised Latin medieval word-list* (London, 1980), p. 462.

However, Stewart-Brown and perhaps Latham approached an understanding of the meaning of the term by treating Latin as the original language. Thus, the former identified *suetus*, customary, and the latter, *suavitas*, sweetness or attractiveness, both classical Latin words, as the primary source words. Stewart-Brown concluded that it meant customary payments by a prisoner to a custodian. Latham equated *suavitas* with 'Anglo-Norman ... *suete*, possibly influenced by Middle English *swete*, "sweet."' He concluded that '*suete de prison*' meant 'amenity' or 'alleviation' of imprisonment and was consistent with the Latin, *suavitas* or *aisiamentum*.[87] Sayles translated the *pro suavitate prisone* in a 1299 plea roll as 'for alleviating his imprisonment.[88] In the *Medieval Latin Word-List*, Latham defined *suavitas* and *sueta* as '*suete de prisone*, (payment for) relaxation of prison conditions or freedom from detention before trial',[89] which seems to be the most accurate of all the meanings.[90] However, focusing on Latin may not give sufficient weight to the different contexts in which *sewet* was used and may fail to capture fully the rationale for its payment..

The most important refinement to these earlier understandings of the term is the suggestion that charging *sewet* may have been linked to the escape of prisoners and its consequence for the keeper. The primary justification for the use of irons was to reduce the chance of escape. The critics of their use recognized the legitimacy of this justification. Even the *The Mirror of the Justices* relented a bit, stating that 'it is lawful for gaolers to put fetters upon those whom they suspect (of trying to escape).'[91] *Fleta* concurred that their use to curb escape was legitimate.[92] *Bracton* accepted bringing prisoners into court 'sometimes in leg-irons because of the danger of escape'.[93] The Fleet warden stated that 'who doth mutiny, conspire, or breake the prison, it is an offence against the King, State, and the Office, and they have ever beene put in irons, as may be mayntened both by Lawe, custome, and discretion ... '.[94]

---

87 Latham, 'Minor enigmas from medieval records', 636. *Suavitas* has also been understood to mean 'gentle keeping': E. Peters, 'Prison before the prison: the ancient and medieval worlds' in Norval Morris & David Rothman (eds), *The Oxford history of the prison* (New York, 1995), p. 35.
88 *Select cases in King's Bench*, iii, 87. There was a separate charge of six pence to remove the prisoner's irons (*pro ferris quibus vinctus fuit sex denarios*). Others have also understood *suete* of prison to mean 'more comfortable accomodation': Harding, Hines, Ireland & Rawlings, *Imprisonment in England: a concise history*, p. 27.
89 Latham, *Revised Latin medieval word-list*, pp 456, 462.
90 The statute used 'ease or favor' as well as *sewet*: 23 Hen. VI, c. 9, *Stat. realm*, ii, 335.
91 *The mirror of justices*, p. 52.
92 *Fleta*, ii, ed. H.G. Richardson & G.O. Sayles, Selden Society, vol. 72 (London, 1955), p. 68. Medieval prisons were vulnerable to escape and some prisoners escaped despite being in irons: Harding, Hines, Ireland & Rawlings, *Imprisonment in England and Wales: a concise history*, p. 22.
93 *Bracton*, ii, 385.
94 *The oeconomy of the Fleete*, p. 62.

The absence or removal of irons increased the possibility of escape. Since the escape of a prisoner had adverse consequences for a jailer, there was a rationale for charging money for removing the shackles.[95]

The escape of prisoners from jail was a matter of significant concern to the crown.[96] The punishment of jailers for the escape of their prisoners has a 'long and complex history' and could involve significant financial liability and even imprisonment.[97] The most common sanction was a £5 fine.[98] With imprisonment for debt, liability for the debt was imposed on the jailer if the prisoner escaped.[99] Jailers were conscious of these penalties and liabilities and they undertook measures to deal with this problem. One common measure was the requirement that the prisoner pay a fee to the keeper upon entering the prison, which regulations formally sanctioned.[1] Such fees may have evolved from the provision of a surety upon entering prison with a forfeiture by the surety in the event of escape, a time-honored practice appearing as early as the *Leis Willelme*.[2] In 1350, sureties gave the jailer a conditional bond to produce prisoners for trial.[3] At some point, the use of such personal surety was reinforced by the prisoner also giving a bond. A 1431 regulation of Newgate prison twice used the word, *suerte*, referred to both as a bond and as surety.[4] By the sixteenth century, a personal bond,

---

95 Pugh, *Imprisonment in medieval England*, pp 232–54; Harding, et al., *Imprisonment in England and Wales*, pp 23–5.

96 In 1324, the marshal of the King's Bench Marshalsea was dismissed because of the large number of prisoners he permitted to escape. But preventing escape was a difficult problem and solving it was not met with great success. In one instance, it was claimed that nine pairs of fetters, two chains, one mallet and two puncheons provided to prevent escapes from the King's Bench Marshalsea were inadequate: *Select cases in the court of King's Bench*, v, ed. G.O. Sayles, Selden Society vol. 76 (London, 1957), pp xxiv–xxviii.

97 Pugh, *Imprisonment in medieval England*, 232, 235; Bassett, 'Newgate prison in the Middle Ages', 234. As to persons indicted for 'Felonies, Robberies, and Theft,' marshals of the King's Bench were to be imprisoned for six months 'if any such prisoner be found wandering out of prison, by bail or without bail': 5 Edw. III, c. 8, *Stat. realm*, i, 267. Pardons and other forms of mitigation existed for jailers and others subjected to liability for escapes: Pugh, *Imprisonment in medieval England*, pp 245–8.

98 Pugh, *Imprisonment in medieval England*, p. 236. A charter of Edward III amerced the sheriffs of London 100s. for the escape of thieves: *Munimenta Gildhallae Londiensis*, i, 145, no. 182.

99 J.H. Baker, *The Oxford history of the laws of England*, vi (Oxford, 2003), pp 383–4; Pugh, *Imprisonment in medieval England*, pp 242–5; Bassett, 'Newgate prison in the Middle Ages', 234.

1 *Letter book K, calendar of letter-books of the city of London*, ed. Reginald Sharpe, pp 126–7; 'Constitutions and orders newlie renewed and to be established in the Fleete anno dni. 1562' in *The oeconomy of the Fleete* at p. 157; 'Presidents of his majesties prerogative' (June 3, 1561) in *The oeconomy of the Fleete* at p. 111.

2 Pugh, *Imprisonment in medieval England*, pp 166–7.

3 *Select cases in the court of the King's Bench*, vi, ed. G.O. Sayles, Selden Society vol. 82, (London, 1965), p. 74.

4 *Letter book K, calendar of letter-books of the City of London*, pp 126–7; Bassett, 'Newgate prison in the Middle Ages', 240.

perhaps also a conditional one, was used.[5] The most common justification for sureties and bonds was 'for good behaviour'.[6] But they may have also have been aimed at the consequences of escape.[7] In addition to these forms of security and fees, the prisoner also paid fees for *suete de prison* or *sewet*, most commonly for the removal of irons and secondarily for the privilege of 'going at large' to tend to business outside the prison. A 1455 action defined *aisiamentum prisone*, a synonymous term, as 'loosening of chains, irons, and shackles by which the same prisoners were bound'.[8]

It is not surprising that keepers would charge these additional fees. First, they were granting special privileges to the prisoner, each of whom posed the risk of escape and liability for the keeper. In one action where the keeper received *sewet*, the prisoners escaped.[9] In another action where a prisoner was permitted to go at large after paying sewet, he fled to sanctuary.[10] Second, the other fees were small relative to the keeper's much larger liability for escape. The entry fee was customarily four pence, perhaps the same amount forfeited by the surety to the jailer. Also, the bond put the risk of the prisoner's insolvency on the jailer.[11] Moreover, some prisoners, for whose escape the jailer would be liable, would have been unable to pay these fees or provide bonds. For these reasons, jailers were likely to maximize their fees. Thus, *suete de prisone* was normally charged in addition to a bond or entry fee.[12] However, in the sixteenth century, they were combined and the prisoner paid a fee 'for libertie of the Howse and irons at the first cominge'.[13] The explicit legal approval and customary acceptance of *suete de prisone* for the removal of

5   *The oeconomy of the Fleete*, pp 9–60; 'Constitutions and orders newlie renewed and to be established in the Fleete anno dni. 1562' in *The oeconomy of the Fleete* at p. 157.
6   See the sources cited above p. 84 in notes 3 & 4.
7   Bellamy, *Crime and public order in England in the Middle Ages*, p. 171.
8   '*videlicet laxando vincula, ferrea et compedes quibus iidem prisones vinciebantur*': TNA: PRO, CP 40/779, m. 675.
9   In this action, it appears to be a result of removing the two prisoners' irons. After doing so, the record states that prisoners escaped (*per que quidem aisiamentum et favorem dicti prisones extra prisonam predictam evaserunt*): TNA: PRO, CP 40/779. Later in the same action there were further complaints about the keeper: TNA: PRO, CP 40/781, m. 130.
10 '*ipsum dimisit ire ad largum postea fugiit ad abbatiam Westmonasterium in sanctuaria ejusdem abbatis*': TNA: PRO, KB 27/510, m. 67.
11 The warden of the Fleet noted that 'he hath given his owne bond onely to the Warden for true imprisonment which is nothing worth (being non solvent) neither to Creditor nor Warden': *The oeconomy of the Fleet*, p. 147.
12 After recognizing the propriety of surety, the 1431 regulation of Newgate prison said that 'in graver cases the keeper may take a reasonable fee (*suette*) for removing irons as accustomed in other prisons of the King and prohibited *fees* or *suettes* in certain circumstances': *Letter book K, calendar of letter-books of the city of London*, p. 126. The 1356 and 1393 regulations also seemed to permit charging *suete de prisone* as an additional charge.
13 'Forme of the table that shall hang in the hall of the Fleet': *The oeconomy of the Fleete*, following p. 152.

chains and outside visits reflected this need for additional money.[14] Thus, it legitimated the generality of its use, but not in an extortionate and unjustified manner.[15]

A 1393 regulation of the fees charged by the Newgate and Ludgate jailers raises an additional possibility for the meaning of *sewet*. It provided that they could take reasonable sewet (*prendre suwette resonablement*) for removing prisoners' irons.[16] The *Anglo-Norman Dictionary* says that *suwette* is an alternative to *seurté*, which is defined as 'security'.[17] The *Liber Albus* editor translated *suwette* as 'surety'.[18] Several additional circumstances link *sewet* or *suete de prisone* to security. First, contemporary usage occasionally tied it to 'going at large', one of the meanings or purposes of *sewet*. In 1388, a prisoner was granted *aisiamentum prisone* ('to go at large') after he provided pledges and security to the marshal ('*invenit dicto marescallo plegios et securitatem habendi aisiamentum prisone*').[19] It was also connected to the removal of irons upon entry, another meaning of *sewet*. The warden of the Fleet said that 'if

14 Bassett said that 'whatever its precise meaning, *suwette* gave the jailer a means of answering all accusations except for the most flagrant extortion': Bassett, 'Newgate prison in the Middle Ages', 238.
15 A 1376 commons complaint charged that sheriffs, under-sheriffs, and jailers were abusing their positions as justices of the peace to indict persons wrongfully in order to charge them numerous fees: 'a fine for entry in the jail, then for *suete de prison*, and after for mainprise, then to have an inquest procured to know their lives (*vies*); and when they were acquitted to pay a fine to the gaolers for their irons, and then for their exit from the gate': *Rotuli Parliamentorum*, ii, 335. It was not uncommon for sheriffs and keepers to extort increased fees. Tactics included coercing prisoners to appeal innocent persons or unlawfully arresting people in order to benefit economically by the resulting fees charged: Harding, Hines, Ireland & Rawlings, *Imprisonment in England: a concise history*, p. 27. Pugh identified several cases in the thirteenth century: Pugh, *Imprisonment in medieval England*, p. 181. Parliament acted against some of these efforts: 1 Edw. III, st. 1, c. 7, *Stat. realm*, i, 253–4; 14 Edw. III, st. 1, c. 10, *Stat. realm*, i, 284. But complaints continued that jailers and others caused persons to be indicted to produce fines for the jailers and to have *suete*: *Rotuli Parliamentorum*, ii, 265.
16 '*ditz gaolers de prendre suwette resonablement de les prionsers esteantz dessouz lour garde, pur la somme de c soultz, et paramount, pur ouster lour ferres*': *Munimenta Gildhallae Londiensis*, i, 524.
17 W. Rothwell, L.W. Stone, & T.B.W. Reid (eds), *Anglo-Norman dictionary* (London, 1992), p. 705 (citing only one instance). The *Manual of law French* defines *seurte* as surety or security and its Latin equivalent as *securitas*: J.H. Baker, *The manual of law French* (2nd ed. Aldershot & Brookfield, vt, 1990), p. 195.
18 *Munimenta Gildhallae Londiensis*, iii, 217. Another late fourteenth-century London ordinance provided that prisoners in the Counters '*ne paierent rien pur lour suetz as porters, ne as Viscountes, pur une noet, par cause de demoer en la dit Countour*': ibid., i, 523. The *Liber Albus* editor translated this plural of *suete* as 'customary fees': ibid., iii, 362. The City of London Calendar of Letter-Books editor questioned this distinction in the translation of *suwette* and *suetz*, stating that the *Liber Albus* editor's translation of *suwette* as 'surety' was incorrect in light of the more common usage of *seurte* for security: *Letter book K, calendar of the letter-books of the city of London*, p. 126, n.2.
19 TNA: PRO, KB 27/510, m. 67. It further stated that '*post securitatem predictam inventam idem marescallo ipsum dimisit ire ad largum*'.

he can give security for the good behaviour he shall have liberty of the howse, Or if he cannot give security, then if he will retorne to other prisons whence he came.'[20] Second, the 1352 accounts of the Cheshire hundreds used *sueta* with reference to money paid by indicted individuals. Stewart-Brown characterized these usages, *sueta de indicatis de transgressionibus, sueta indictatorum*, and *sueta prisonum indicatorum de transgressionibus*, as 'security for their appearance before the court, and to be allowed to find bail'.[21] Although the meaning of *sueta* in this context clearly carries an aspect of security, neither he nor others connected it with the other uses of *sueta*. Finally, the practice of sheriffs requiring keepers to give them bonds or enter indemnity provisions for the formers' liability in the event of escape linked the notion of security to problem of escape, another notion connected with the use of *sewet*. The 1431 regulation of Newgate prison required that the jailer 'find *seurte* for Sheriffs for safeguarding the prisoners'.[22]

However, there are several problems with this suggested meaning. First, the payment is not a security in the traditional sense. It is not the provision of money, property, or third party surety that is returned when the condition of the security is performed. Instead, it is a nonrefundable cash payment. Another weakness is the failure of the Law French word *seurté* and the Latin word *securitas* to appear in any of the passages describing the payments made by the prisoners to the jailers. Moreover, *seurté* was a word used more commonly to mean surety.[23] Finally, as John Baker and Paul Brand have both noted, all the different words for security contain an 'r' not present in any of the forms of *sewet*.[24] Thus, this additional meaning for *sewet*, while interesting, should be rejected.

In conclusion, the most complete understanding of *suete de prisone* and *sewet* is as a payment of money by a prisoner for less stringent conditions of imprisonment, most commonly the removal of irons, but that it also provided revenue to offset the substantial financial burdens on the keeper for escape, as removing the irons or going at large increased that possibility.[25]

---

20 *The oeconomy of the Fleete*, p. 134.
21 Stewart-Brown, *'Suete de prisone'*, 506.
22 *Letter book K, calendar of the letter-books of the city of London*, p. 127.
23 *Letter book K, calendar of the letter-books of the city of London*, p. 126, n. 2. The 1431 Newgate and Ludgate regulation used both words, *suerte* and *suette*, translated respectively as 'surety' and 'reasonable fee,' with the latter referring both the fee for removing irons and entry and discharge fees: ibid., p. 126.
24 E-mail from Prof. John Baker to Jonathan Rose, 2 August 2004; e-mail from Dr Paul Brand to Jonathan Rose, 10 August 2004.
25 In 1351, it was determined that while Thomas of Ketteringham, deputy to Walter de Mauny, was keeper of the King's Bench Marshalsea, £289 10s. had become due to the king for escaped prisoners, but that as deputy he was not liable for this sum. He had not been made responsible for the escape of prisoners and had therefore proved no security to Mauny for this: *Select cases in the court of the King's Bench*, v, p. xxvii.

FASTOLF PAPER 42, 'FEODO DE COMPEDIBUS VOCATO LE SEWET'

A more complete understanding of this entry increases our knowledge of fifteenth-century prison fees. Although it is only one instance, it provides further evidence that sewet was the more common term by this date for *suete de prisone*.[26] In 1529, the word, 'suet' was used as the English word.[27] Almost all the instances of *suete de prisone* appear in the fourteenth and early fifteenth century. *Sewet* appears in the statute, 23 Hen. VI, c. 9 (1444)[28] and in the 1457 entry in Fastolf Paper 42. Moreover, the addition of the explanatory words *feodo de compedibus* is not found in any of the numerous earlier usages.[29] It is difficult to know whether these words were a contemporary term or just inserted in the entry to make sure that Fastolf understood how his money was being spent. The need for a further explanation may have a social significance. Shackling may have been more common in a lower social stratum and have been strange to a knight like Fastolf.[30] Their inclusion also helps understanding of the use of *sewet* and the rationale for charging it. More importantly, this entry seems to be the only evidence so far discovered of jailers imposing such a fee for removing irons in the King's Bench prison. The original sources and scholarship on fees charged by keepers provide abundant evidence of practices in the Fleet, Newgate, and Ludgate, but contain only a few references to the practices in the King's Bench Marshalsea. However, these bits of new information leave unanswered whether it was lawful or acceptable to impose this fee on Thomas Howes and John Porter.

Answering this question is not easy, as it must be determined both whether it was appropriate to put irons on Howes and Porter, and also whether the amount then charged to remove the irons was reasonable. Uncertainty clouds both inquiries. An answer requires an understanding of why Howes and Porter were in the King's Bench prison as well as some knowledge of the normal practice of the King's Bench jail. It seems most likely that Howes and Porter were in the King's Bench prison because,

---

26 Clerks continued to struggle with appropriate Latin or official word and variants such as *suecto* and *sawetto* continue to appear. TNA: PRO, KB 146/6/34/2 (1456); TNA: PRO, KB 27/841, m. 14d.

27 Ordinance of the city of London, 13 J. Ct Common Council, 19 May 1527–4 May 1536, fo. 212b (April 2, 1529).

28 *Stat. realm*, ii, 335. A variant spelling *sewette* appeared as early as 1393: Latham, *Revised medieval word-list*, p. 462. In the same 1393 regulation another variation *suetz* appeared as well: *Munimenta Gildhallae Londiensis*, i, 523, 524.

29 As noted, a 1455 Common Bench record did define *pro aisaimento prisone*.

30 I am grateful to Dr Henry Summerson for this insight: e-mail from Dr Henry Summerson to Jonathan Rose, 15 February 2005.

although damages under the judgment in the conspiracy action had been paid to Andrew,[31] Howes and Porter both still owed a fine to the king,[32] which the king had made numerous efforts to collect.[33] It was finally paid during Hilary term 1457.[34] It is likely that Howes and Porter were also in the King's Bench prison awaiting the appearance of the jurors impanelled in the attaint, as mentioned in the Fastolf Paper 42 entry.[35]

Would imprisonment for failure to pay their fine have justified putting them in irons? In Newgate, Ludgate, and the Fleet, the use of irons was not limited to felons and was used for misdemeanants, debtors, and other non-felonious prisoners. However, among the various complaints were charges that irons were used when not warranted.[36] Pugh observed that there was unjustified use of irons to obtain fees for removing them, a 'practice, however much it may have been disliked, [which] was incapable of prohibition'.[37] Wardens had considerable discretion about whether or not to use irons. The marshal of the King's Bench Marshalsea, like other keepers, charged prisoners fees and imposed the standard four pence release fee.[38] The profits of

---

31 The Fastolf Paper 42 entries reveal that the court awarded Andrew £73 6s. 8d and that Howes paid one portion of the judgment and another Fastolf servant paid the balance. (*Item soluta per Thomam Howes in curia banci regis coram Johanne Fortescue justiciario cum £46 13s 4d ad complendam summam £73 6s 8d adiudicatam Johanni Andrews super conspiracione; Item solut' per manus Christofori Hansson ad complendam summam £73 6s 8d adiudicatam Johanni Andrews ultra £46 13s 4d solut' per manus Thome Howys £26 8s 4d*.) Of course, it was actually Fastolf who paid, as the entries account for the expenditure of Fastolf's money by his receiver to those who had incurred expenses, and, in some cases, submitted bills.

32 About this time, the sheriff was order to have both Howes and Porter before the king 'to make satisfaction to us of his ransom by reason of certain trespass and contempt both to us and to John Andrew of Beylom gentleman' as a result of John Andrew's successful conspiracy suit against them: TNA: PRO, KB 27/782, m. 12d (14)(rex)(Howes); TNA: PRO, KB 27/783, m. 8 (rex)(Porter).

33 TNA: PRO, KB 27/782, m. 12d (rex); TNA: PRO, KB 27/783, m. 8 (rex); TNA: PRO, KB 29/84, m. 35d; TNA: PRO, KB 145/6/33.

34 Howes paid 20s. and Porter one mark. It was probably paid at the end of Hilary term, as it is entered at the end of the list: TNA: PRO KB 27/ 783, *Fines, etc*. (dorse).

35 Howes and Porter were probably arrested initially in Trin. 33 Hen. VI (1454). They appeared on an exigent on 28 April 1455 and were sent to the king's prison in Norwich where they remained until Thomas Howes was taken into the King's Bench by a writ of a *habeas corpus cum causa* on 3 November 1456 and committed to the Marshalsea. TNA: PRO, KB 29/84, m.35d; TNA: PRO, KB 27/782, m. 12d. The records are less clear and more complicated for John Porter as he was mainprised and did not appear and the sheriff pursued his pledges. TNA: PRO, KB 27/783, mm.8, 12 (rex); TNA: PRO, KB 27/785, m. 90, Trin. But the outlawry writ *ad satisfaciendum* in the latter action was issued to John Clopton, sheriff for Norfolk-Suffolk, 4 Nov. 1455–17 Nov. 1456. The Fastolf Paper 42 entry makes clear, however, that Howes paid *sewet* both for himself and Porter (*pro ipso quam pro Johanne Porter*).

36 *The oeconomy of the Fleete*, p. 58.   37 Pugh, *Imprisonment in medieval England*, p. 179.

38 *Select cases in the court of King's Bench*, i, p. xc. There was some doubt, however, whether the schedule of fees applicable to other prisons applied to the King's Bench Marshalsea: Pugh, *Imprisonment in medieval England*, p. 171.

the keeper were substantial and caused frequent, but ineffective, investigations.[39] Since the conditions in the King's Bench prison were probably harsher than those in the Fleet, although not as oppressive as those in Newgate,[40] the use of irons in the Marshalsea is not unexpected. In one case, the justices said that prevailing custom permitted the use of irons.[41] In the mid-fourteenth century, the Marshalsea equipment regularly included irons and chains.[42]

The marshal of the King's Bench Marshalsea had the same incentives to use irons and to require payment for their removal as other keepers. Although the number of prisoners in his custody was limited,[43] the King's Bench prison had historically been considered vulnerable to escape, perhaps due to its initial lack of a permanent structure and facilities that were insufficiently secure.[44] However, the use of such facilities continued well into the fourteenth century and escapes from the Marshalsea remained relatively common.[45] In the fourteenth century, the coroner made regular reports on escapes from the custody of the marshal, indicating significant numbers of missing prisoners.[46] The normal £5 fine for the escape of each prisoner was

---

39 *Select cases in the court of the King's Bench*, v p. xxviii. The fees of the King's Bench marshal as well as others were the subject of a 1401 Commons Petition: *Rotuli Parliamentorum*, iii, p. 469.
40 *The oeconomy of the Fleete*, p. 9; Bassett, 'Newgate prison in the Middle Ages', 245, 246; Pugh, *Imprisonment in medieval England*, p. 388.
41 In 1293, the marshal said that the need to remove a prisoner's irons so that he could walk while being transferred from London to Kent resulted in his escape. The justices noted that the use of irons was 'proper according to the law and custom of the realm of England hitherto used for such a prisoner to be more strictly and better guarded': *Select cases in the court of King's Bench*, ii, 149–51.
42 In 1350, it included four iron chains, 21 pairs of fetters, and two pairs of iron manacles; in 1352, nine pairs of fetters and two chains; and in 1361 the keeper had two iron chains, nine pairs of foot irons, and one pair of 'well-worn iron manacles': *Select cases in the court of the King's Bench*, vi, p. xliv. Sayles noted a 1347 record that stated that prisoners were *inter ceteros prisones eiusdem marescallie ferris et anulis firmiter ligatos*. After indictment, the prisoners had escaped and a jailer was charged with their escape. He explained that he had put them in secure custody and was not responsible for their escape, as the jury confirmed: *Select cases in the court of King's Bench*, v, p. cxxii.
43 *Select cases in the Court of King's Bench*, v, p. xxvi; Pugh, *Imprisonment in medieval England*, p. 368.
44 Throughout the fourteenth century, King's Bench prisoners were kept in a variety of locations, including the keeper's houses. By the end of the century, this prison had become relatively fixed in Southwark: Pugh, *Imprisonmentin medieval England*, pp 119–21, 207–8.
45 *Select cases in the court of King's Bench*, v, pp xxv–vii. The king made Thomas de Mauny keeper of the marshalsea in 1331 on condition that he take complete responsibility for the escape of prisoners, but in 1334 pardoned him for all escapes since he had become the keeper of the Marshalsea. In 1349, the king again forgave Mauny all escapes; by 1351 the debt owed the king for escapes had escalated to £289 10s.: ibid., pp xxv & n.5, xxvii & n.3.
46 In 1342, ninety-one indicted prisoners were missing from the Marshalsea and in 1350, twenty-two were missing: *Select cases in the court of King's Bench*, vi, pp xliv–xl.

commonly imposed on the King's Bench marshal.⁴⁷ His willingness to grant bail even to felons aggravated the concern with escape.⁴⁸

This escape problem produced special measures aimed at the King's Bench prison. A 1331 statute provided that if any prisoner was 'found wandering out of prison, by bail or without bail, ... the marshals shall have half a year's imprisonment and be ransomed at the king's will'.⁴⁹ Concern with escapes from the Marshalsea appeared again in 1351 as the king was concerned with his profit from escapes.⁵⁰ Despite these measures, the problem of escapes from the King's Bench Marshalsea persisted into the fifteenth century.⁵¹ Escapes continued to create economic burdens on the marshal,⁵² and the fines for escape sometimes exceeded the normal £5.⁵³ In 1455, another statute imposed a £400 fine on King's Bench jailers who had permitted certain prisoners to go at large without proper authorization.⁵⁴ About 1472, the duke of Norfolk, the marshal of the King's Bench Marshalsea (although his deputy was responsible), successfully sought 'to be discharged, released and quieted of almaner of eschapes, fynes, paynes, amerciamentes, all thynges that may growe to your highnes by cause of' the escape of 99 prisoners resulting from an attack on the Southwark prison by 300 rioters in October 1470.⁵⁵ Thus, given the customary practices of the King's Bench, the longstanding concern with escape from that prison, and

47 Pugh, *Imprisonment in medieval England*, p. 236.
48 In 1320, complainants, victimized by released prisoners, were given an action against these prisoners: *Rotuli Parliamentorum* i, 372. In 1331 a statute prohibited bail for felons: Statute of Westminster, 5 Edw. III, c. 8, *Stat. realm*, i, 267.
49 Statute of Westminster, 5 Edw. III, c. 8, *Stat. realm*, i, 267. The statute eliminated bail for those indicted or appealed of a felony. Even before the statute, it had been the custom for a jailer, guilty of permitting prisoners charged with felonies to escape, to be jailed indefinitely at the will of the king: *Rotuli Parliamentorum*, i, 365.
50 The King's Bench justices informed him that he was entitled to 100s. and also said that a prisoner without an adequate explanation for being at large should be put to death: *Select cases in the court of King's Bench*, v, p. cxxii.
51 *Select cases in the court of King's Bench*, vii, p. xxi.
52 In 1409, the marshal was required to pay the escapees' debts and damages and in 1408 the coroner found that six prisoners had escaped, which the marshal admitted and he was assessed 10s. for each escapee: ibid., pp xxi, 184.
53 In 1411, the marshal was fined £30 for each of six escapees: ibid., p. xxi. In 1405, the coroner found that five prisoners were missing. The justices imposed a twenty mark penalty on the marshal for the escape of one outlawed for a death and an unidentified amount to the use of the king for the other four escapees: ibid., pp 163–4. A creditor sued the marshal in 1406, alleging that the latter had permitted the debtor to go at large, but the marshal prevailed when the creditor failed to appear and later appeared indicating payment in full by the debtor: ibid., pp 165–6.
54 33 Hen. VI, c. 2, *Stat. realm*, ii, 370. The statute concerned household servants who had embezzled their masters' goods after the latters' decease. The fine was payable to their executors.
55 *Rotuli Parliamentorum*, vi, 49–50.

the consequences for the marshal, it is not surprising that Howes and Porter found themselves in irons in the King's Bench Marshalsea.

Nor is it clear that the use of irons in the King's Bench was legally impermissible. The 1445 statute limiting fees to four pence and prohibiting all other charges seemed to apply to the King's Bench prison.[56] Moreover, this statute specifically prohibited collecting any fee for *sewet de prison* or for showing 'ease or favor' to any prisoner, other than the permissible four pence.[57] Nevertheless, it remained customary to charge *sewet* for removing irons in Newgate, Ludgate, and the Fleet after 1445 and it is likely that these charges were an accepted custom in all these prisons. In addition, in 1488 the 1431 regulation authorizing *sewet* was extended to the King's Bench.[58]

The second question is whether the amount charged Howes and Porter to remove their irons was reasonable or abusive. Not surprisingly, charging *sewet* was claimed to be extortionate. In 1349, the king sued a York man who was charged by a jury with extorting (*pro extorsione*) five shillings for *suavitate de prisone*.[59] But it is difficult to know whether the amount charged Howes and Porter was reasonable, as it is part of an entry with three components. The unallocated payment in the entry, £16 4s. 5d.,[60] was divided between two items, 'the fee of shackles called *le sewet*' and 'certain expenses and costs while the same Thomas was personally detained in the King's Bench for [not indicated] weeks'.[61] There is no way to determine how to allocate the £16 4s. 5d. as between the two items, but the amount for *sewet* could have been several pounds.

Such an allocation may, however, be unnecessary, as the 1445 statute contained a complete prohibition on taking any fee for *sewet* or ease or favor.[62] Several actions suggest that, despite past practices permitting *sewet* that conflicted with applicable regulations, there was some attempt to enforce this statute during the middle of the fifteenth century.[63] In 1455, an Essex keeper

---

56 This statute specifically exempted the warden of the Fleet, but otherwise applied to all sheriffs, keepers and prisons: 23 Hen. VI, c. 9, *Stat. realm*, ii, 334–5.

57 Ibid., p. 335.

58 Pugh said that in 1488 the 1431 Newgate regulation was 'extended to the other three prisons,' which may have included the King's Bench prison: Pugh, *Imprisonment in medieval England*, p. 179 (citing the Journals of the court of the common Council of the city of London, 4, fo. 170b ff.).

59 TNA: PRO, KB 27/354, m. 31. The record does not reveal whether the objection was to the amount or the mere fact of charging anything.

60 The total of expenses in the entry is £62 17s. 9d., from which must be subtracted £46 13s. 4d., the remaining damages paid to John Andrew in the conspiracy action, the only one of the three items specifically quantified.

61 Ibid.

62 23 Hen. VI, c. 9, *Stat. realm*, ii, 334–5. It applied to all jails except the Fleet.

63 This increased stringency regarding abuses in the judicial systems parallels Bean's view that concern with other abuses such as maintenance increased in the fifteenth century: J.M.W. Bean, *From lordship to patron* (Manchester, 1989), pp 200–30.

was sued for violating the statute in taking 13*s*. 4*d*. *pro aisiamento prisone* from each of two women for two prisoners in his custody.[64] In 1456, the Norfolk and Suffolk undersheriff was sued for violating the statute by taking 20*s*. in *sewet*.[65] In 1471, an Ipswich keeper was indicted for taking 18d. for *suete de prisone*.[66] The following year another keeper was indicted for violating the statute.[67] There were also complaints to the Chancellor about extorting money for the release of prisoners.[68] Further, in 1468, the King's Bench justices warned the marshal of the Marshalsea about extortionate fee practices.[69] These actions all occurred in the exact time period in which Howes and Porter paid *sewet*, and therefore, raise considerable doubt regarding the legality of its imposition in their case.[70]

CONCLUSIONS

Prisoners, including those in the King's Bench prison, were charged various fees and often put in irons, practices that caused controversy. Although statutes governed the imposition of fees, there is doubt concerning the efficacy of the statutes and the fees seem often to exceed the statutory maximums, but their acceptability had the approval of custom. The use of irons was also regulated to some extent by statute. Again the practices seem to exceed what was formally authorized but were also customary. Thus, existing norms seem to have endorsed these practices and to do so more generously than the positive law. One accepted fee included payment for the release from irons. Both norms and positive law endorsed the charging of *suete de prisone*. Such fees were imposed in some cases, perhaps until 1488 in the King's Bench Marshalsea, without statutory authorization and, even

64 One woman was a wife of one of the prisoners. The keeper imparled and then denied taking the money and violating the statute: TNA: PRO, CP 40/779, m. 675; TNA: PRO, CP 40/781, m. 130.
65 TNA: PRO, KB 146/6/34/2.
66 TNA: PRO, KB 27/840, m. 3d (rex).
67 TNA: PRO, KB 27/841, m. 14d (rex).
68 TNA:PRO, C1/19/27; TNA:PRO, C1/19/468; TNA:PRO, C1/27/454; TNA:PRO, C1/31/121; TNA:PRO, C1/71/18; TNA:PRO,TNA: PRO, C1/19/27; TNA: PRO, C1/19/468; TNA: PRO, C1/27/454; TNA: PRO, C1/31/121; TNA: PRO, C1/71/18; TNA: PRO, C1/64/1040. In one action, the petitioner complained that the keeper had imprisoned him in a deep pit and extorted a fine from him. TNA: PRO, C1/22/192.
69 YB Mich. 8 Edw. IV, pl. 27, fol. 18b. Justices Markham and Yelverton said to the marshal that 'il ne purra deteigne ascun person apres cest que il fuit discharge del court, pur nul rien forsque per les fees del court, & nemy pur maunger & boier, & auters choses queux il ad achate de vous esteant en prison, &c. pur que veies que ne faits auterment, ne forte vous soies endictes de extorcion.' I am grateful to David Seipp for giving me this reference.
70 I am grateful to Susanne Jenks for the King's Bench and Common Bench plea roll entries and to Henry Summerson for TNA: PRO, C1/31/121.

when authorization existed, prevailing norms blessed amounts exceeding the statutory maximum. Thus, *sewet* was not, on its face, a form of extortion or bribery. But the mid-fifteenth century may reveal a stiffening of attitudes against *sewet* and abuse may have existed in individual cases. Unfortunately, it is difficult to conclude whether prevailing norms sanctioned the payment of *sewet* for Thomas Howes and John Porter or whether its imposition illustrated an instance of abuse or was within the acceptable range. Supporting permissibility are the widespread acceptance of putting prisoners in irons, charging them to remove them, and the concern with escape from the King's Bench Marshalsea, and its financial consequences for the marshal.

On the other hand, several factors make the imposition of *sewet* in this instance suspect. Its imposition certainly violated the 1445 statute. Also, the nature of Porter's and Howes's offence raises some question about the propriety of putting them in irons; nor is it clear that they presented a significant likelihood of escape. It is also possible that the amount charged was excessive. Most importantly, all this must be considered in the context of the involvement of Sir John Fastolf, who footed the bill for these expenses. He was viewed as (and probably was) an ambitious and wealthy parvenu. Fastolf had long been adverse to the controlling forces in East Anglia, the Suffolk affinity. After Suffolk's death, he still seems to have been on the losing end of the continuing conflict, as the Suffolk adherents continued to hold the balance of power,[71] and his land holdings continued to be subject to attack.[72] Given all his legal and political battles, several pounds for *sewet* might have added a little more insult but not much injury. Fastolf was a relatively convenient, and perhaps easy, target for abuse. Thus, overall requiring the payment of *sewet* by Howes and Porter in this case seems to have been of dubious legality.

---

71 Helen Castor, *The king, the crown, and the duchy of Lancaster* (Oxford, 2000), pp 156–89.
72 Anthony Smith, '"*My Confessors have exorted me gretely ther too* …": Sir John Fastolf's dispute with Hickling Priory' in Colin Richmond & Eileen Scharff (eds), *St George's Chapel Windsor in the late Middle Ages* (Windsor, 2001), pp 57–69; Anthony Smith, 'Litigation and politics: Sir John Fastolf's defence of his English property' in Tony Pollard (ed.), *Property and politics: essays in later medieval English history* (Gloucester, 1984), pp 59–75; Anthony Smith, 'Aspects of the career of Sir John Fastolf, 1380–1459' (D. Phil., University of Oxford, 1982), pp 126–218; Peter S. Lewis, 'Sir John Fastolf's lawsuit over Titchwell 1448–55', *Historical Journal*, 1 (1958), 1–20.

The trust beneficiary's interest before *R. v. Holland* (1648)

N.G. JONES

SOME FORTY YEARS AGO D.E.C. YALE observed that Rolle J's assertion in *R. v. Holland* (1648) that 'a trust is not a thing in action, but may be an inheritance or a chattel as the case falls out'[1] was the opening of the way for Lord Nottingham's work, for the development of the trust beneficiary's interest as an interest in the land, marking the beginning of the departure from the influence of medieval uses and presaging Nottingham's policy of modelling equitable interests upon their legal counterparts.[2]

The influence of the learning of medieval uses upon trusts after the Statute of Uses 1536 could hardly have been avoided: while the question of whether uses and post-1536 trusts were identical was not easily answered,[3] similarity encouraged reasoning by analogy, if no more. As Mr Yale observed,

> [a]s soon as the Chancery had decided to protect the second use or trust, it found itself with a new and formless mass of justiciable

---

I am grateful to Professor David Ibbetson and Professor Joseph Biancalana for their comments upon previous versions of this paper. Unless otherwise indicated, manuscripts are in the National Archives: Public Record Office. Transcriptions from manuscripts have been rendered into modern orthography. The year is taken to begin on 1 January.

1 Style 20, at 21. See also Style 40, 75, 84, 90, 94; Aleyn 14; D.E.C. Yale (ed.), *Lord Nottingham's 'Manual of Chancery Practice' and 'Prolegomena of Chancery and Equity'* (Cambridge, 1965), p. 279. *Holland's Case* concerned a copyhold granted to Holland and his heirs in trust for Margaret Taylor, an alien, and her heirs. Upon Margaret Taylor's death commissioners for the crown seised the land as that of an alien. The questions were whether the king should have the trust; if so, whether he might seize the land; and whether the case was special because concerning copyhold. Mountague argued that the alien had no estate in the land, and that therefore the king could not have it as he might had the alien had an estate; further, the trust was 'a thing only in action, and lies in privity, and not to be seised upon by another', and was analogous to a trust of copyhold land for a villein, which the lord 'should not have seised'. Mathew Hale responded that 'the trust was not a thing merely in action, but an hereditament; and partly in possession'; moreover, though a *chose* in action was not transferable to a common person it was transferable to the king, and here *a fortiori* there was not 'a thing merely in action but mixed with an interest'. Judgment was ultimately given against the king.
2 D.E.C. Yale (ed.), *Lord Nottingham's Chancery cases*, ii, Selden Soc. vol. 79 (London, 1961), p. 90.
3 For discussion of distinctions between uses and trusts see N.G. Jones, 'Uses, trusts, and a path to privity', *Cambridge Law Journal*, 56 (1997), 175, at 176–82.

interests in equity. Though these interests are called trusts, there is no magic in the word to distinguish them in their operation from the old use. But though the trust turned out to be a different product and was put to very different ends from the use, it was of the same raw material from the same source. It was inevitable, therefore, that the rules of the use should be applied to the new trust. The learning of the law of uses had been kept alive in Chancery and an attempt at an adaptation was altogether natural and understandable, [though] it was very far from being beneficial.[4]

But the learning of the law of uses did not speak with one voice: in the decades before 1536 it had developed both in Chancery and at common law;[5] and in different aspects the use might be no more than a personal trust and confidence reposed by one in another, or an hereditament.[6] Within the period of this paper the trust beneficiary's interest was hardly the latter. But it need not follow that it was therefore in all contexts no more than the former. In the light of the Chancery record, and of reports in manuscript or recently published, this paper begins the process of recovering the trust beneficiary's interest in the period from the shadows cast by comparison with medieval uses, and by the dicta of Edward Coke.

USES AS HEREDITAMENTS

An aspect of the question of the nature of the trust beneficiary's interest arose for the common law judges in the context of the application of rules of forfeiture to trust beneficiaries convicted of treason or felony,[7] where

---

[4] Yale (ed.), *Lord Nottingham's Chancery cases*, ii, *88*. The question of the extent to which trusts after the Statute of Uses should be identified with the 'second use', that is, the use upon a use, is outside the scope of this paper; see N.G. Jones, 'The use upon a use in equity revisited', *Cambrian Law Review*, 33 (2002), 67. The question of distinction in operation between uses and trusts is an aspect of the present question, though trusts, that is, uses not executed by the Statute of Uses 1536, may have differed from executed uses in more than name: see Jones, 'Uses, trusts and a path to privity', 175 at 176–82.

[5] The statute 1 Ric. III, c. 1 (1484) enabled legal title to be traced from a grant by the beneficiary of a use. 'The use was [now] no longer merely an interest in conscience, nor even a mere power, but a form of property or ownership governed by legal rules noticed by the courts of common law', Sir John Baker, *Oxford history of the laws of England*, vi, *1483–1558* (Oxford, 2004), p. 658.

[6] The extremities of the personal trust and confidence view have eased over time, but the tension, which has come to be expressed as a question as to whether the beneficiary of a trust has a right *in rem* or *in personam*, remains familiar, and may be inherent in the nature of modern trusts: '[a] beneficial interest under a trust is a package of constituent elements, some of which can consistently be viewed as matters of property, others of which can consistently be viewed as matters of obligation', R.C. Nolan, 'Equitable property', *Law Quarterly Review*, 122 (2006), 232, at 254.

[7] At common law those convicted of treason forfeited their land to the crown, while those

comparison with medieval uses, bolstered as they were by the statute 1 Richard III, c. 1 (1484) and the Statute of Uses 1536,[8] while capable of supporting the preservation of trust beneficiaries' interests against forfeiture, did little to increase their substance. As Davenport put it in argument in *Attorney-General v. Abington* (1613–19) – seeking to show that Abington's beneficial interests in freehold and leasehold land should not be forfeited upon his attainder of treason – 'the statutes have taken great notice of uses ... 1 Ric. III [c. 1] gives *cestui que use* the power of his feoffees to dispose at his pleasure. And 27 Hen. VIII [c. 10] unites the possession to them. But the law does not have such regard or esteem for a trust, which is but a voluntary agreement not issuing out of land.'[9]

The same comparison had appeared a few years earlier in *Ford and Sheldon's Case* (1606), where counsel had argued in Exchequer Chamber that the beneficial interest under a trust of recognisances should not be forfeited under the statutory penalties for recusancy, since

> at the common law, in a far stronger case, if *cestuy que use* had been attaint of treason[,] this use forasmuch as it was but a trust and confidence, of which the law did not take notice, it was not forfeited to the King, and could not be granted:[10] and if an use shall not be for-

---

convicted of felony forfeited it to their immediate feudal lord (though described as forfeiture the latter process was strictly an escheat). As Mr Yale has said, '[t]here is much interesting material indicative of the nature of the equitable interest in the mazes of Crown law over forfeiture and royal escheats', Yale (ed.), *Lord Nottingham's Chancery cases*, ii, p. 100. This complex material, the detail of which is beyond the scope of this paper, awaits a thorough examination.

8   27 Hen. VIII, c. 10. The Statute of Uses had the effect of executing uses, passing legal title from the feoffees to the beneficiary, and thus recognized uses as engendering legal interests in former *cestuis que use*.

9   W.H. Bryson (ed.), *Cases concerning equity and the courts of equity, 1550–1660*, 2 vols (London, 2001), ii, Selden Soc. vol. 118, p. 408 no. 210, at 410. In contrast, Sir Henry Hobart A-G, on the other side, sought to turn the Statute of Uses to his advantage, arguing that 'even though the purview of the statute [of uses] does not extend to a trust ... still the preamble is sufficient to direct a trust to be all one with a use in equity, so that according to equity they can decree the same thing of a trust that they could do of a use', ibid., at 419.

10 The forfeiture cases are not unanimous as to whether uses could be granted. An emphasis upon the element of trust and confidence, as here, led to the conclusion that they could not. But a distinction might be drawn between uses of chattels and uses of freehold. It was said in Chancery in the time of Elizabeth that 'a use of a term of one attainted for treason or who is outlawed for felony or for another offence ... by the better opinion ... may not be forfeited inasmuch as it cannot be given, because if a man has a use in a term for years, he cannot give it. [It is] otherwise [for lands] of inheritance or freeholds, by which etc.', Bryson (ed.), *Cases concerning equity*, i, 168 no. 109. It seems likely that this distinction turns upon doubt as to whether there might be a use of a term of years in the same sense that there might be a use of freehold (see Jones, 'Trusts in England after the Statute of Uses', pp 180–1), with the conclusion that only freehold uses could be 'given'. The distinction

feited, of which there shall be a *possessio fratris* ... and which shall descend to the heir; *a multo fortiori*, a mere trust and confidence shall not be forfeited.[11]

That the doctrine of *possessio fratris*, characteristic of the legal title in fee simple, applied also to uses as a rule in Chancery, and not merely in consequence of the chancellor consulting the rules of law where the parties' intention was unclear, was not universally accepted.[12] But uses might nonetheless be spoken of within the period as hereditaments. Mountague CJCP had said as much in 1550 in *Wimbish v. Tailbois*: 'for a use is an hereditament, and such an hereditament, whereof [the possession of the brother in fee simple shall make the sister an heir]'.[13]

between chattels and freehold was drawn again in a dictum in Jenkins's report of *Coningesby v. Throkmorton* (1558–60), 2 Dyer 174b: 'at this day uses being abolished and ordained to be united to the possessions if land is conveyed to one and his heirs, to the use of him and his heirs, in trust for the feoffor and his heirs, the king in this case shall not, upon the death of such feoffor, have the wardship, neither shall he have the forfeiture of such land for treason or felony. An use was not forfeitable at common law, but it was grantable. A trust at this day (except of chattels) is neither forfeitable nor grantable by law', Jenk. 219 (the reference to 'this day' seems to be to the date of Jenkins's report, decades after the decision). Here discussion is in terms of trusts of freehold in the form of a use upon a use, which, being seen as distinct from pre-statute uses of freehold are said not to be grantable, while uses of chattels, being un-affected by the Statute of Uses are said to be grantable.

11   12 Rep. 1, at 1–2. The *possessio fratris* doctrine applied where a man, seised of land in fee simple, had a son and a daughter by one wife, and a son by a second wife. If the elder son entered the land after his father's death and then died without issue, the daughter would have the land and not the younger son: 'possessio fratris de feodo simplici facit sororem esse haeredem'. Since the elder son was the person last seised and had no lineal heir, a collateral heir inherited, but only a collateral of the whole blood. See *Coke upon Littleton* (Co. Litt.), pp 14bff; W. Blackstone, *Commentaries on the laws of England*, ii (Oxford, 1766), pp 227ff; and A.W.B. Simpson, *A history of the land law* (2nd ed. Oxford, 1986), p. 60.

12   It appeared from a note in YB Mich. 5 Ed. IV, fo. 7v, pl. 17, perhaps of 1465, that there might be *possessio fratris* of a use, for example: *Abbot of Bury v. Bokenham* (1536), 1 Dyer 7b at 10b–11a *per* Willoughby, sjt., 'So if *cestui que use* have issue a son and a daughter by the same *ventre*, and a son by another *ventre*, and die, the eldest son takes the profits, and dies without issue, the use shall descend to the daughter, as sister and heir to him, and not to the younger son: and this is holden in 5 Edw. 4'; *Brown's Case* (1581) 4 Rep. 21a at 22a: 'As 5 E. 4. 7.b. when uses had gained the reputation of inheritances descendible, the common law directed the descent of them, and that there should be *possessio fratris* of an use, as well as of other inheritances at the common law'; *Chudleigh's Case* (1594) 1 Rep. 113b, at 121b: 'These uses and confidences to some respect were reputed as chattels and therefore they were devisable; and to other respects they were esteemed as hereditaments of which there should be *possessio fratris etc.* as 5 Edw. 4. 7b is'. See also Co. Litt., p. 14b: 'there shall be *possessio fratris* of an use'. Francis Bacon spurned the 'vulgar opinion collected upon 5 E. IV. that there might be *possessio fratris* of an use', observing that Anderson CJCP had said in *Chudleigh's Case* 'that it was no more but the chancellor would consult with the rules of law, where the intention of the parties did not specially appear', W.H. Rowe (ed.), *The reading upon the Statute of Uses of Francis Bacon* [Gray's Inn, 1600] (London, 1804), p. 11.

13   1 Plowd. 38, at 58 (referring to YB Mich. 5 Ed. IV, fo. 7v, pl. 17).

The point was agreed in the King's Bench in 1583 in *The Marquess of Winchester's Case*, in course of considering the scope of forfeiture under an act of attainder:[14] 'an use were an hereditament (for there shall be *possessio fratris* of it)', albeit uses were not comprehended within general statutory words 'of all hereditaments'.[15] In *Attorney-General v. Abington* (1613–19) Davenport in argument in the equity side of the Exchequer asserted that uses 'are in the nature of inheritance, of which there will be *possessio fratris*', which Attorney-General Hobart, echoing the words of Mounson J in *Brent's Case* (1575),[16] conceded, to the extent that 'after uses were frequent in the commonwealth they gained the reputation of a fictionary hereditament similar to copyholds, which at first were feeble and at the will of the lord, but after custom has made them common and vulgar, the law gives more reputation to them'.[17]

THE DESCENT OF TRUST BENEFICARIES' INTERESTS

If the use was an hereditament, it should descend to the heir: as Coke put it, 'whatsoever may be inherited is an hereditament'.[18] It had been said late in the time of Elizabeth, that 'a use was but a trust at first, and no remedy lies for it but a subpoena. And time made it descendible as the land was, and yet

---

14 The attainder was that of Henry Norris in 1536, for alleged adultery with Anne Boleyn. The act provided for forfeiture of 'all [Norris'] manors, messuages, lands, tenements, rents, reversions, remainders, uses, possessions, offices, rights, conditions, and all other his hereditaments', 3 Rep. 1a–1b.

15 3 Rep. 1, at 2b–3a. The same was true, it was said, of conditions, though 'without question a condition is an hereditament'. Francis Bacon sought to explain the rule that a use upon a use is void on the ground that the Statute of Uses spoke of seisin of 'honours, castles, manors, lands, tenements, rents, services, reversions, remainders *or other hereditaments*' (emphasis added), and that the reference to hereditaments 'excludes ... uses themselves; so that an use cannot be to an use', Rowe (ed.), *The reading upon the Statute of Uses of Francis Bacon*, p. 44.

16 'These uses at the first were of no value, but afterwards by continuance communis error facit jus, so as they were taken and esteemed as inheritances: and they cannot be more fitly resembled to any thing, as to copyholds, which at beginning were but tenures at will, and were not known at the common law, but now they are in the same reputation in law as inheritances', 2 Leo. 14, at 16.

17 Bryson (ed.), *Cases concerning equity*, ii, 410–14. Hobart asserted that it had been observed in *The Marquess of Winchester's Case* that 'a use is not forfeited by the common law because it is not a hereditament known to the common law', but this does not appear to represent the sense of the case as reported by Coke. The judges were agreed that even an undoubted hereditament (a condition) was not given to the king by general words 'of all hereditaments' in an act of attainder. That the same was true of uses therefore need not indicate that uses were not hereditaments, and indeed, as has been seen, it was agreed that 'an use were an hereditament' of which there was *possessio fratris*.

18 Co. Litt., p. 6a.

till 27 Hen. VIII [the Statute of Uses], it was not *jus*, either in *re* or *ad rem*.[19] Shortly thereafter was considered the case of a purchase in the name of another, to hold upon trust for the purchaser, an arrangement not uncommon in this period:[20]

> if I purchase lands in fee simple in the name of J.S. and this upon trust and confidence, and I die and this trust descends to my heir, he may exhibit his bill in Chancery to have his land estated in him and his heirs as I might have done. And if I in my lifetime say that I will that this land shall be to J.D. and his heirs, this notwithstanding works no translation of [the] use to J.D. and his heirs because it was by parol only 37 Hen. VIII, 1.[21]

The distinction between the descent of the trust interest, and the descent of the subpoena supporting it is elusive: while 'this trust' descends, the manifestation of that descent is in the availability of the subpoena to the heir. But the tendency in Chancery was towards a view of the trust beneficiary's interest as descendible.

In *Billson v. Wroughton* (1618) it was found in Chancery that lands had been conveyed in trust only to the use of Sir Richard Mill and his heirs 'so as in equity the trust and use of these ... lands ought to descend to the complainants being heirs of ... Sir Richard',[22] notwithstanding a claim by Sir Richard's widow, one of the defendants, that the lands 'appertained' to her under Sir Richard's will.[23] And in *Calton v. Newton* (1630) it was possible for

---

19 Bryson (ed.), *Cases concerning equity*, i, Selden Soc. vol. 117, p. 212 no. 117–[251], from Richard Powle's reports for 1596.
20 On purchases in the name of another see N.G. Jones, 'Estate planning in early-modern England: "having" in the Statute of Wills 1540' in J. Tiley (ed.), *Studies in the history of tax law* (Oxford, 2004), p. 227. A similar arrangement gave rise to the observation in Chancery before 1594 that 'If I give money to one to purchase lands therewith to him and his heirs, and to permit me to take the profits thereof during my life, and he withholdeth the profits, he shall be compelled by subpoena', Cary 10 (and further references in Jones, 'Estate planning in early-modern England', at p. 234 fn. 44).
21 Bryson (ed.), *Cases concerning equity*, i, 329 no. 120–64, from reports of cases *c.* 1599–*c.* 1604. The reference to '37 Hen. VIII, 1' seems intended as a reference to YB Trin. 37 Hen. VI, fos. 35–6 (1459), where one who had four feoffees to his use sold 'his land' to H, and directed two of the feoffees to enfeoff H. It was held in Exchequer Chamber that the feoffees were not bound to make a feoffment 'without specialty proving his will'. See also Cary 10: 'if the feoffor [to uses] require [the feoffee] to make an estate to any other, he ought to do it; but thereof he ought to have request in writing, for he is not to do it upon a bare message, or upon desire by word only (37 Hen. 6 35, 36)'.
22 C 78/225, no. 3.
23 On the facts, for reasons not clearly apparent from the enrolled decree, one half of the lands was decreed to the plaintiffs. This does not appear to affect the generality of the proposition that the trust ought to descend to the heirs.

the plaintiff in Chancery, claiming as heir of one of three sisters holding as coparceners, to assert that 'the ... trust for and concerning the third part of the ... lands and premises in three parts to be divided did descend and come to the complainant as cousin and heir' of the dead beneficiary.[24] The descent of the trust interest, and, it seems, descent according to common law rules, was established in Chancery before *Jones v. Lady Reasby* (1634), to which Lord Nottingham referred in his *Prolegomena* for the proposition that 'if there be [a] custom that land shall descend to eldest daughter only, [the] trust of such land shall descend accordingly'.[25]

THE DOCTRINE OF NOTICE

In forfeiture cases, as has been seen, comparison with medieval uses tended to the diminution of the trust interest: 'if an use shall not be forfeited, of which there shall be *possessio fratris* ... and which shall descend to the heir; a *multo fortiori*, a mere trust and confidence shall not be forfeited'.[26]

The tendency of the application of the old rules concerning notice, which allowed the enforcement of uses not only against the feoffee but against a purchaser from him,[27] was in the opposite direction. An early example in Chancery after the Statute of Uses is provided by *Rooke v. Staples*, where it was decreed in 1577 that the plaintiff should enjoy the lease in question against the defendant trustee, and against 'any other person or persons ... having notice or understanding of the ... trust and confidence at such time as he or they did obtain the ... lease of the defendant'.[28]

Little development of constructive notice is apparent in this period, except insofar as it may be represented by notice derived from pending

---

24 C 78/406, no. 8. The plaintiff was dismissed without remedy on the grounds that he had failed to prove the trust; that the defendant had alleged that his father had obtained the land for good consideration; and that the defendant and those under whom he claimed had had forty years possession. The common law doctrine of tenancy in coparcenary gave rise to an equal division of the inheritance among all the daughters where a freehold tenant died with more than one daughter but no sons.

25 Yale (ed.), *Lord Nottingham's 'Manual of Chancery Practice' and 'Prolegomena of Chancery and Equity'*, pp 202 and 245. See also H. Rolle, *Un Abridgment des Plusieurs Cases et Resolutions del Common Ley* (London, 1668), bk 2, p. 780 D(7).

26 *Arguendo* in *Ford and Sheldon's Case* (1606), 12 Rep. 1, at 1–2.

27 See the note in YB Mich. 5 Edw. IV, fo. 7v, pl. 16, perhaps of 1465, printed in J.H. Baker and S.F.C. Milsom, *Sources of English legal history: private law to 1750* (London, 1986), p. 97: 'If J. enfeoffs A. to [J.']s use and A. enfeoffs R., even though [A.] sells to [R.] if A. gives notice to R. of the intent of the first feoffment, [R.] is bound by writ of *subpoena* to carry out [J.'s] will.'

28 C 33/53, fo. 259. For further discussion see N.G. Jones, 'Trusts in England after the Statute of Uses: a view from the 16th century' in R. Helmholz and R. Zimmermann (eds), *Itinera Fiduciae: Trust and Treuhand in historical perspective* (Berlin, 1998), p. 173 at 196–9.

litigation: it was said in Chancery in *Diggs v. Boys* (1598) that a suit depending for a trust constituted sufficient notice to anyone who bought the land 'hanging that suit',[29] though in *Ford v. Pomery* (1587), where a manor was found to be subject to a trust in favour of the plaintiff, two persons taking interests in the manor after the exhibition of the bill were ordered to exhibit a bill against the plaintiff on the point of knowledge of the trust or suit: the matter was not as yet automatic.[30]

In the realm of actual notice, Egerton LK observed in *Cornwallis's Case* (1595) that where there was a conveyance absolute in words but a 'bruit of a trust, but doubtful whether there be a trust or not', a purchaser hearing the rumour would not be concluded by it, neither was the buyer to believe one who would not have him buy if he told him there was a trust.[31] And in the following year in *Ragland v. Wilgosse* he said, '[i]f a man will say to one "take heed you buy not such land of such a man for he has it but upon a trust", a man is not forced to believe it. But if the feoffee in trust tell it him, then he is to believe it',[32] or, as another report has it, 'flying reports are more often fables than true; and if [contradictory stories as to the existence of a trust] were sufficient notice, then any man's inheritance might easily be slandered'.[33] This latter dictum has been taken as illustrating Egerton's 'narrow view' of trusts,[34] but it was repeated by Nottingham,[35] and has accompanied trusts into maturity: as the Rt. Hon. Thomas Pemberton Leigh put it in the Privy

---

29 That is, *pendente lite*. Bryson (ed.), *Cases concerning equity*, i, 266 no. 118–[276]. It appears from the record that the action concerned a purchase of land by Thomas Diggs in trust in the name of his brother: C 33/9, fo. 749, though nothing is revealed as to the question of notice.

30 C 33/79, fo. 19. The case is briefly reported, but not on this point: see Tothill 18, and Bryson (ed.), *Cases concerning equity*, i, 232 no. 118–[341], p. 272 no. 118–[322], and p. 275 no. 118–[341]. In the 1670s Lord Nottingham took it as a rule that 'the filing of a bill in Chancery is legal notice to all men', Yale (ed.), *Lord Nottingham's 'Manual of Chancery Practice' and 'Prolegomena of Chancery and Equity'*, p. 253; and see Yale (ed.), *Lord Nottingham's Chancery cases*, i, 444: resolved in *Culpeper v. Austin* (1673) before Lord Shaftesbury LC that '*lis pendens* was legal notice to all purchasers'; see also *Yeaveley v. Yeaveley* (1638–9) Tothill 161: 'purchasers coming in *pendente lite* bound'.

31 Tothill 186, BL MS Hargrave 281, fo. 225v.

32 Bryson (ed.), *Cases concerning equity*, i, 258 no. 118–[199].

33 Baker and Milsom (eds), *Sources of English legal history*, p. 125, from Gouldsb. 147, pl. 67 and CUL MS Gg.3.25, fo. 92v. The record of the long-running litigation in this case (which had appeared in Chancery by the early 1580s) reveals no details of discussion of the substantive meaning of notice.

34 J.H. Baker, *An introduction to English legal history* (4th ed. London, 2002), p. 309; Jones, 'Trusts in England after the Statute of Uses', pp 198–9.

35 'Therefore if a man purchases under a conveyance, which is absolute in words, but under doubtful report of the country of a trust, he is not concluded under such report; for the buyer is not bound to believe him who would not have him buy the land', Yale (ed.), *Lord Nottingham's 'Manual of Chancery Practice' and 'Prolegomena of Chancery and Equity'*, p. 254, referring to *Cornwallis's Case* and Gouldsborough's report of *Ragland v. Wilgosse* (sub nom. *Wildgoose v. Wayland*). See further Jones, 'Trusts in England after the Statute of Uses', p. 198.

Council in *Barnhart v. Greenshields* (1853), 'the rule is settled, that a purchaser is not bound to attend to vague rumours – to statements by mere strangers, but that a notice, in order to be binding, must proceed from some person interested in the property'.[36]

PRIVITY

If the availability of principles of notice tended to support the trust beneficiary's interest, enabling its assertion against third parties, 'the greatest dangers', as Mr Yale put it, 'were connected with the notion of privity between feoffee and beneficiary ... To confine the equitable obligation to those who were in privity would have put the trust in crippling fetters.'[37]

Privity was in one aspect an element of notice: as Fenner J put it in the 1590s 'Uses ... are created by confidence; [and] preserved by privity, which is nothing else but a continuance of the confidence, without interruption.'[38] But it was not only the purchaser without notice who lacked privity and was hence free of the trust: '[o]n the side of the feoffee, the doctrine of privity prevented a use being enforced against tenant by the curtesy, tenant in dower, tenant by elegit, disseisors, abators, lords taking by escheat, those taking by title paramount, purchasers without notice, in short, making it a somewhat precarious and ephemeral interest'.[39] So, as Nottingham put it in the 1670s, 'he who comes in in the *post*, as lord by escheat, disseisor, etc., is never subject to the former uses. And this is the standing rule for trusts at this day, as appears by common experience.'[40]

In the law of uses the heir of *cestui que use*, being, like his ancestor, in privity with the feoffee, had the subpoena against the feoffee. But the judgment creditor of *cestui que use*, or his widow claiming dower, lacked privity and were left to the common law.[41] There was a tendency to apply these rules to trusts: '[s]oon after the Restoration', as Mr Yale has observed,

---

36 (1853) 9 Moo. P.C. 18, at 36. See also E.B Sugden, *A practical treatise of the law of vendors and purchasers of estates* (5th ed. London, 1818), pp 636–7, and J. McGhee, *Snell's Equity* (31st ed. London, 2005), para. 4–32: 'It has been said of actual notice that to make it binding it must be given by a person interested in the property and in the course of the negotiations, that it must be clear and distinct, and that vague reports from persons not interested in the property will not affect the purchaser's conscience. It seems, however, that a purchaser cannot safely disregard information from any source if it is of such a nature that a reasonable man or a man of business would act upon the information.'
37 Yale (ed.), *Lord Nottingham's Chancery cases*, ii, *88*.
38 Rowe (ed.), *The reading upon the Statute of Uses of Francis Bacon*, p. 11.
39 Yale (ed.), *Lord Nottingham's Chancery cases*, ii, *88*.
40 Yale (ed.), *Lord Nottingham's 'Manual of Chancery Practice' and 'Prolegomena of Chancery and Equity'*, p. 244.
41 See Yale (ed.), *Lord Nottingham's Chancery cases*, ii, *88*. The exclusion of the widow from

there are decisions to the effect that the trust of the fee descended to the heir free from debts, that the widow [of the beneficiary] could not have dower of the trust estate, and that the judgment creditor of the beneficiary should not be allowed to go against the trust estate. The total result was that heirs took free in the ordinary devolution of settled property from specialty debts and incumbrances ... No doubt the new trust was made easier of digestion by attributing to it familiar properties.[42]

Little may yet be said as to these questions within the period, though denial of dower out of the trust estate was not new at the Restoration. In *Lady Kempe v. Risby* (1626) it was alleged in Chancery 'that the substance of the plaintiff's bill is to have a decree for dower out of the lands purchased by her husband in the names of friends in trust, wherein this court declared that a woman is not dowable of a trust'.[43]

And if a beneficiary's widow was not dowable of a trust, it was said in the King's Bench in *Nash v. Preston* (1631) that equity would not relieve a mortgagor against dower in the mortgagee's widow: 'when she is dowable by act or rule in law, a Court of Equity shall not bar her claim for dower'.[44]

Lord Nottingham in due course disagreed, holding that equity would relieve as a matter of course against the assertion of a right of dower at law by a trustee's widow,[45] and in the same year as *Nash v. Preston* the plaintiff in

dower in the case of lands subject to a feoffment to uses was an element in the medieval practice of jointure provision upon marriage. For the position of the creditor of *cestui que use* at common law in the fifteenth century see J. Biancalana, 'Medieval uses' in Helmholz and Zimmermann (eds), *Itinera Fiduciae*, pp 145ff.

42 Yale (ed.), *Lord Nottingham's Chancery cases*, ii, *89* referring to *Bennet v. Box* (1662) 1 Ch. Cas. 12, 2 Freeman 184; *Colt v. Colt* (1664/5) 1 Ch. Rep. 254; and *Prat v. Colt* (or *Holt*) 1 Ch. Cas. 128.

43 C 33/151, fo. 5v. This being so, it was 'held not fit to retain the bill', though the defendant was required to amend his answer by 'setting down who is the true tenant to the *precipe*, and in case the plaintiff have laid an agreement and promise in the bill that her husband would make her a jointure out of those lands ... then this court will not dismiss the cause but the plaintiff is to go on in ordinary course to prove the ... promise or agreement'. The case is reported as *Kempe v. Lady Reresby*: 'a woman cannot have dower of a trust ... but compels the defendant to answer who is tenant to the land to enable her to bring her writ of dower', Tothill 99, BL MS Hargrave 281, fo. 166v, BL MS Lansdowne 640, fo. 61. The record does not appear to support the assertion that the defendant's answer as to the identity of the tenant to the land was ordered to enable a writ of dower to be brought at common law: the point seems to have turned rather upon the possibility of proving an agreement or promise by the husband (as trust beneficiary) to make a jointure.

44 Cro. Car. 190, *per* Croke and Jones JJ on a reference from Chancery. See Yale (ed.), *Lord Nottingham's Chancery cases*, ii, *92* and Yale (ed.), *Lord Nottingham's 'Manual of Chancery Practice' and 'Prolegomena of Chancery and Equity'*, pp 201 and 329.

45 Yale (ed.), *Lord Nottingham's Chancery cases*, ii, p. 92, referring to *Tassel v. Hare* (1675), case no. 339, and *Noel v. Jevon* (1678) 2 Freem. 43, where the rule was said to be the 'constant practice of the court now'.

Chancery in *Petty v. Styward*, claiming 'a widow's estate in certain copyhold lands', which had been held by her husband as trustee, was denied relief:

> forasmuch as it appeared that the defendant always received the profits thereof to his own use, and as was conceived the defendant granted the same lands to his son [the plaintiff's late husband] in trust, and it appeared not that his son paid anything for the same, this court therefore could not give the plaintiff any relief therein.[46]

Nothing may yet be said in the period of the judgment creditor, though in the case of debt on an obligation it was found in Chancery in *Stone v. Lyndsey* (1631) that Edward Lindsey, deceased, being beneficiary of a trust of a lease, and becoming indebted to the plaintiffs, had devised the lease to his daughter. The plaintiffs failing to find a sufficiency in the hands of the executor to satisfy the debt, it was declared that 'the testator's debts were to be preferred before legacies', and ordered that the trustee, being saved harmless, should assign the lease to the plaintiffs 'towards the satisfaction of their debts'.[47] The conclusion in the equity side of the Exchequer in *Attorney-General v. Sands* (1669) that 'clearly the trust of a lease for years is assets to charge an executor in equity' may be taken back into the 1630s.[48]

Absence of privity had also prevented a use being enforced against the feoffee's husband, claiming upon his wife's death as tenant by the curtesy of England. As Mr Yale observes, 'women were so infrequently made trustees that the ... question over tenants by the curtesy does not seem to have arisen directly; but the answer [that the husband as tenant by the curtesy took subject to the trust] appears to have been a matter of assumption since Lord Nottingham's time'.[49] Little may yet be seen of this question within the period, but in *Reynell v. Peacock* (1619), Walter, arguing in Chancery, found it possible to assert that: 'a trust is more strong and does more nearly fix and

---

46 C 33/162, fo. 93. The bill appears not to refer to this aspect of the case, the main burden of which concerned a mortgage: C 3/412/117. The case was reported as *Pettit v. Steward*: 'whether the wife of a feoffee shall have dower or not?', BL MS Lansdowne 640, fo. 41. The defendant, Nicholas Styward, or Steward (d. 1634) was a Cambridge LLD, admitted as an advocate in 1573, and MP for Cambridge University 1604–11, J. Venn and J.A. Venn, *Alumni Cantabrigienses*, pt I, iv (Cambridge, 1927).

47 C 78/513, no. 2. It was well established that a beneficial interest under a trust was subject to debts owed to the king: see *Sir Edward Coke's Case* (1623), Godbolt 289, and *Attorney-General v. Bindloes* (1628), Bryson (ed.), *Cases concerning equity*, ii, p. 556 no. 301.

48 2 Freem. 219.

49 Yale (ed.), *Lord Nottingham's Chancery cases*, ii, p. 93, referring to Edward Sugden's assumption in his edition of Gilbert that the dower cases carried the point on curtesy: E.B. Sugden (ed.), *The Law of Uses and Trusts by the late Lord Chief Baron Gilbert* (London, 1811), p. 18 fn. 1: 'An estate in a trustee is not now subject to dower ... , nor of course to curtesy', referring *inter alia* to *Noel v. Jevon* (1678).

bind the land than a use at the common law ... A tenant by the curtesy shall not be seised to a use at common law but still he will be seised and subject to a trust, and thus all others, if no valuable consideration.'[50]

TRUST BENEFICIARIES' INTERESTS AS UNASSIGNABLE CHOSES IN ACTION

While the old rules concerning uses were applied in the case of trusts to questions of dower and debts in the years following the Restoration, 'fortunately', Mr Yale has said,

> a particularly vital proposition had been settled a generation earlier. The trust would have been crippled from the start had there been any considerable check upon its assignability. Had there been it would have been impossible for Maitland to have selected elasticity and generality as the leading features of 'the most distinctive achievement of English lawyers'. Indeed, there would have been very little achievement at all if the trust had continued to be regarded as a mere chose in action. Lord Coke's celebrated definition of a trust,[51] though a milestone in its day, was a millstone round the neck of later generations. His resolute refusal to contemplate the trust as conferring on the beneficiary an interest in the land encouraged the opinion that the trust was a mere chose in action and so attracted the notorious sentiment of the common law against the assignment of such rights.[52]

---

50 Bryson (ed.), *Cases concerning equity and the Courts of Equity*, ii, 479 no. 254.
51 Referring to Co. Litt., p. 272b: 'an use is a trust or confidence reposed in some other, which is not issuing out of the land, but as a thing collaterall, annexed in privitie to the estate of the land, and to the person touching the land, *scilicet*, that *cestuy que use* shall take the profit, and that the terre-tenant shall make an estate according to his direction. So as *cestuy que use* had neither *jus in re*, nor *jus ad rem*, but only a confidence and trust, for which he had no remedy by the common law, but for breach of trust, his remedie was only by *subpoena* in chancerie.' See also *Chudleigh's Case* (1594), 1 Rep. 120, at 121a–121b. Compare *Hopkins v. Hodylo* (1591) where 'Chief Baron Peryam puts a distinction between a trust and a promise concerning land, because the trust is united and goes with the land whereas a promise is collateral. And on account of this ... the infant heir will not be bound by the promise of the father to assure land as he would be if the father had it in trust', Bryson (ed.), *Cases concerning Equity*, i, 248 no. 118–[123], and 193 no. 117–118.
52 Yale (ed.), *Lord Nottingham's Chancery cases*, ii, 89. Compare Maitland's observation in respect of the medieval use: 'There is one strong reason against treating it as a contract, the feoffor (who is *cestui que use*) has then a chose in action and this would be inalienable. But our landowner did not mean to exchange ownership of land for the (inalienable) benefit of a promise', F.W. Maitland, *Equity* (Cambridge, 1909), p. 31. On the non-assignability of *choses* in action at common law see *Lampet's Case* (1612) 10 Rep. 46b, at 48a: 'no possibility, right, title nor thing in action shall be granted or assigned to strangers, for that would be

Perhaps the most well-known example of the view that trust beneficiaries' interests were mere *choses* in action is the case of *Wytham v. Waterhowse* (1596)[53] which, as Mr Yale puts it, 'illustrates the prevailing way of judicial thought at that time'.[54] Anne Waterhowse married one Johnson, who assigned a lease to the plaintiffs, Anne's brothers, to the use of Anne. After Johnson's death Anne married Wytham. After Anne's death her brothers took the administration of her goods, and 'the sole question was whether the husband [Wytham] shall have the lease or the profits of it, or the administrators of … Anne'.[55] An English bill against Wytham was exhibited by the administrators in the Council of the North, which referred the question to the justices of assize, Beaumont JCP and Ewens B, who 'gave their resolutions that neither by the law nor by equity the defendant did not have any right to the lease or to the profits of it',[56] whereupon Wytham exhibited a bill in Chancery.

Attorney-General Coke, for the administrators, based his argument upon a distinction between things in possession and things in action. A use of a lease was not, he said, 'transferred by the statute [of uses] in possession'; by the 1590s it was orthodox learning that such a use was un-executed by the statute, and the wife therefore did not have the lease in possession.[57] A husband would have a lease which his wife had in possession and not in use only; yet even if the wife had once had possession, but had been unlawfully evicted before the marriage (and the husband had not entered during her life), the wife's administrator or executor, and not the husband, would have the term after the wife's death, 'as of obligations and other choses in action, and thus here'.[58] Puckering LK 'was of the same opinion',[59] but referred the case for further consideration, and, at last, 'by the opinion of all the justices,

the occasion of multiplying contentions and suits', and see generally W.S. Holdsworth, 'The history of the treatment of *choses* in action by the common law', *Harvard Law Review*, 33 (1920), 997 ('in the sixteenth century the conception of a *chose* in action was beginning to expand. Therefore the common lawyers of that period had no hesitation in asserting that at common law an equitable trust, consisted only "in privity", was unassignable on account of the risk of encouraging maintenance, and was therefore in the nature of a *chose* in action … But inasmuch as the incidents of such interests are shaped by equity, the fact that they are at law classed as *choses* in action has had very little influence on their development', p. 1015).

53 Bryson (ed.), *Cases concerning equity*, i, 148 no. 80; see also Cro. Eliz. 466, Popham 106, Tothill 91, Coke, *Fourth Institute*, p. 87.
54 Yale, *Lord Nottingham's Chancery cases*, ii, 90. Questions as to assignability of the beneficiary's interest did not arise on the facts.
55 Bryson (ed.), *Cases concerning equity*, i, 148, from the report in BL MS Lansdowne 1084, fo. 111v.
56 Ibid.
57 See Jones, 'Trusts in England after the Statute of Uses', pp 178–9.
58 Bryson (ed.), *Cases concerning equity*, i, 149, from the report in BL MS Lansdowne 1084, fo. 111v.
59 Ibid.

decrees the term to the brothers, administrators of the wife, because the confidence was *quasi* a chose in action'.[60] This was 'against the opinion of Egerton, master of the rolls',[61] but when the suit was revived before him as Lord Keeper after Puckering's death Egerton changed his mind, 'because of the opinions of the justices to whom it was referred anew'.[62]

Coke is not reported in *Wytham's Case* as having directly asserted that a trust beneficiary's interest was a *chose* in action, but rather that it behaved in that case 'as of obligations and other choses in action', and a note of caution may appear in the report of Puckering LK having said that the 'confidence was *quasi* a chose in action'. As Mr Yale has observed, the analogy between trusts and *choses* in action 'was not a very accurate one',[63] and the decision in *Wytham v. Waterhowse* may have been driven more by policy and the settlor's intention than by a characterization of the trust beneficiary's interest as a *chose* in action:

> Sir Thomas Egerton, keeper of the great seal, says openly that he has conferred with the lords Popham and Anderson, lords chief justices, and that they agree in opinion that the second husband, who survives, should not have [it], but the administrator of the wife, because inasmuch as it was conveyed by her first husband in special trust to the use of the wife, it will go to the benefit of the wife after her death as well as in her life.[64]

The married woman's separate use, finding its feet in Chancery in the later sixteenth century, would have been a more precarious interest had *Wytham's Case* gone the other way.[65]

Two years before *Wytham v. Waterhowse* it was said in Chancery in *Flecton v. Dennys* of a married woman who was the beneficiary of a separate use of a lease, that 'the disposition of so much of the ... term which shall be to come after her death rests now in her power during her life though she be covert, and the ... assignees or grantees ought by the ... trust to convey and assure the same according to her appointment and disposition',[66] or, as a reporter put it, 'a married woman, [who] has conveyed a lease before marriage to her

---

60 Bryson (ed.), *Cases concerning equity*, i, 150, from the report in Inner Temple MS Misc. 46, fo. 60v.
61 Ibid.
62 Ibid.
63 Yale (ed.), *Lord Nottingham's Chancery cases*, ii, p. *89*.
64 Bryson (ed.), *Cases concerning equity*, i, 151, from the report in Folger Shakespeare Library MS V.b.48, fo. 313v.
65 For the married woman's separate use at this time see Jones, 'Trusts in England after the Statute of Uses', pp 186–9.
66 C 33/87, fo. 304v.

[own] use, can during coverture appoint the remainder of the lease and the use will go'.[67]

The same approach was taken in the year after *Wytham v. Waterhowse* in *Fitzjames v. Hipsley* (1597).[68] Before her marriage Dorothy Morgan had assigned a lease to one Younge upon trust for her use. Younge had subsequently assigned the lease to trustees upon trust for Dorothy's use and 'to the intent that ... Morgan who was to marry her should not have any power to convey the same away'. The trustees then assigned the lease to the defendant to his own use, until he was satisfied from the profits of the land for money disbursed for the debts of Dorothy and her husband, and thereafter to the use of Dorothy. The trustees subsequently purported to assign the lease to the plaintiff to the use of Dorothy. Dorothy and her husband having separated, it was decreed that the defendant should pay a portion of the profits of the land to Dorothy during the coverture, and the remainder to her husband.

> And after the coverture dissolved then all the remnant of the term then to come shall be enjoyed by ... Dorothy if she be living and by her assigns, but if she die then the same shall go and be enjoyed to the use of such persons or person to whom she shall dispose or appoint the same as this court conceives it was truly meant to be.

If the married woman was to appoint the remnant of the lease to come after her death, that remnant could hardly fall by operation of law into the hands of her husband.

The devolution of the interest under a trust of a lease for the use of a married woman, as in *Wytham v. Waterhowse*, may thus not have been a matter of the consequences of a rule that it must behave as a *chose* in action (though the behaviour of *choses* in action provided a helpful analogy in excluding the husband), but rather a question of the nature and purpose of the trust: as it was put in *Flecton's Case*, the woman had assigned the lease upon trust in part 'to the intent ... that her second husband if she married again should have no power to make away or incumber the said lease'.[69] In a different context the interest might behave differently: as Egerton said while lord chancellor, 'a lease assigned in trust to the intent that it will not merge by the purchase of the reversion will go to the heir and not to the executor or administrator'.[70] The lease being assigned in trust to keep it on foot

---

67 Bryson (ed.), *Cases concerning equity*, i, 200 no. 117–[162].
68 C 33/93, fo. 465. See also Tothill 43; BL MS Lansdowne 640, fo. 37; BL MS Hargrave 281, fo. 133.
69 C 33/87, fo. 304v.
70 Bryson (ed.), *Cases concerning equity*, i, 381 no. 165–664. See also *Leman v. Walter* (1583–4) where an annuity had been assigned in trust to the use of one Sercher, his executors and

notwithstanding a purchase of the reversion, the beneficiary's interest would behave as if it were freehold, descending to the heir upon the beneficiary's death.[71] Similarly, as Egerton LK put it in *Haskett v. Hastings* (1601), where leases were in the hands of trustees to prevent merger, estates granted by the beneficiary out of the reversion 'should stand good', and the tenants' possession would be 'maintained and established' by the court, notwithstanding the trust.[72]

TRUST BENEFICIARIES' INTERESTS AS UN-DEVISABLE CHOSES IN ACTION

From a characterization of the trust beneficiary's interest as a *chose* in action, it was a short step to the conclusion that it could not be devised. Coke is reported to have said in Chancery as attorney-general that

> if a man conveys his lands to one upon special trust and confidence to reconvey the same to him whensoever he shall require the same, [and] the feoffor does not in all his life require any reconveyance, but by his last will he does devise that he whom he trusted shall convey these lands to J.D. and [dies], [and] the party trusted refuses so to do, it is plain ... he shall never have [a] subpoena to compel the party trusted to convey the lands unto him, for this trust is but [a] chose in action, which he cannot devise, and so the subpoena descends to the heir of the feoffor as the land should have done.[73]

---

assigns. Upon Sercher's death the defendant trustee was ordered to grant his interest in the annuity to Sercher's widow, who was also his administratrix, and his daughter. This was put on the basis that the widow 'is administrator to ... her late husband and so ought as assignee to have the same annuity', and on the basis that 'the ... annuity was intended to the said Sercher his wife and child': C 33/67, fos. 147, 473.

71 In the practice of keeping the lease on foot by means of a trust, examples of which are known from the later sixteenth century (e.g. *Losse v. West* (1587) C 33/74, fo. 360; *Glascocke v. Savell* (1598) C 33/96, fo. 81), lay the seeds of the later doctrine of the attendancy of satisfied terms: 'by construction of equity ... when a term was carved out of the inheritance for some purpose and that purpose later fulfilled, the term was not extinguished or drowned in the inheritance but was attached to it, devolving with it into the hands of the heir and not into the hands of the executors, as did ordinary leases on the holder's death', Yale (ed.), *Lord Nottingham's Chancery cases*, ii, 150–1.

72 C 78/113, no. 24.

73 Bryson (ed.), *Cases concerning equity*, i, 306 no. 119–15, from CUL MS Gg.2.31, fos. 437–78v (Coke was attorney-general 1594–1606). The manuscript report ends 'descends to the heir of the *feoffee* as the land should have done' (emphasis added). This appears to be an error. Compare the late Elizabethan note above at note 20, where it was said that an *inter vivos* direction to a trustee as to disposition would be effective, provided it was in writing.

It may be that here, too, the nature and purpose of the trust was in question. Coke's dictum was carefully linked to a conveyance upon trust to reconvey as required, and the report is expressed in particular terms of the trust in question: 'for *this* trust is but [a] chose in action, which he cannot devise'.[74] It thus seems possible that Coke was referring specifically to a trust to reconvey during the settlor's life. Such a trust was not a trust to perform a last will, but was rather a trust to reconvey as directed during the settlor's life and, implicitly, in the absence of a direction to reconvey, to hold upon trust for the settlor's heir (to whom the land would have descended had there been no trust). As in the case of trusts of leases for the separate use of married women or to prevent merger, it may be misleading to suppose that all trust beneficiaries' interests must behave in the same fashion, irrespective of the intention with which they were created.

But even if Coke himself did take the *chose* in action analogy to be generally applicable, rendering trust beneficiaries' interests as a whole, and the subpoena supporting them, undevisable and unassignable, his approach did not reflect contemporary Chancery practice.

ASSIGNMENT AND DEVISE OF TRUST BENEFICIARIES' INTERESTS IN CHANCERY

In *Weston v. Ratcliff* it was found in Chancery in 1586 that a lease had been made to the plaintiff in trust for Sir Edmond Traford, 'who sold his interest therein to ... Sir John Ratcliff', whereupon the plaintiff was ordered to 'convey his trust and interest thereby in the ... lease' to Sir John.[75]

In *Williams v. Fane* (1590) it was asserted in Chancery by Serjeant Puckering, counsel for the plaintiff, that the lease in question had been 'made in trust by one Barker to the use of one Fysher', and had been 'assigned to ... the ... plaintiff by ... Fysher'.[76]

In 1597 it appeared in Chancery in *Kedeward v. Baker*, upon the reading of the masters' report that

---

74 Emphasis added.
75 C 33/71, fo. 499. The suit arose from the plaintiff's complaint that he had had to pay rent due on the lease and other charges (see C 33/69, fo. 642). Upon the plaintiff's argument that he had promised the lease to Sir Edmond Traford's son, the order to convey to Sir John Ratcliff was suspended to enable Sir John to take out a subpoena against the son to show cause why the promise should not be discharged.
76 C 33/79, fo. 762v. The plaintiff went on to allege that Henry Fane, one of the defendants, a relative, and perhaps the son of the original trustee (also Henry Fane), claiming title to the lease under the original trustee had 'assigned the same lease to ... Thomas Fane, who assigned it to ... Balam [the other defendant] to the intent to defraud or avoid the trust'. An injunction was issued against the defendants to permit the plaintiff to occupy the land until the matter was heard.

it was without question of law that the assignment made by John Tyler and his wife to the plaintiff's father of the moiety of the lands in question is void in law, and yet that the trust and equity for that moiety was in ... Tyler and his wife and ought in true meaning as it seemed to pass by their assignment to the plaintiff's father, and so from him to the plaintiff according to the assignment thereof from the plaintiff's father to the plaintiff.[77]

Three years later in *Smythe v. Goodman* the trustee of a lease to the 'use of the dean of Westminster and of such as he the said dean should dispose or appoint the same' was ordered to assign the lease to the plaintiff, to whom it was found that the dean had 'bargained and sold all his right, interest, estate, trust, and demand of and to the said lease', the dean having confessed the receipt of £300 which he meant to employ for the maintenance of poor scholars.[78]

The question of assignment arose also in the context of assignment of possibilities. So in *Warmestrey v. Tanfield* (1628) it was found in Chancery that William Freeman had assigned a term of years in trust for himself and his wife for their lives, and then to the use of such issue male of their two bodies as William appointed by his last will. William appointed the use of a third part of the land to Richard Freeman, who, during his mother's life, made 'an assignment of the said third part unto the ... complainant for the consideration therein expressed and with covenant to make further assurance'. The trustee's 'interest in law' having passed by mesne conveyances to John and Robert Palmer they 'assured all their interest in law' to the plaintiff. This being so,

> the Lord Keeper and also Mr Justice Jones were of opinion and did so declare that howbeit that agreement of a future possibility is not good in law yet a possibility of a trust in equity might be assigned. And ... Richard Freeman's assignment of his trust unto the complainant is also confirmed by the assignment of the ... Palmers, who had the interest in law.[79]

The mechanism of these assignments is not commonly spelt-out in the record, but an indication is provided by *Stydolf v. Byrche* (1590–1) where the plaintiff's mother had assigned a lease to the defendants upon trust for herself for life, and after her death or marriage to the use of the plaintiff. The

---

[77] C 33/93, fo. 457. See also the same point at C 33/93, fo. 404. The case concerned a trust of a lease.
[78] C 33/97, fo. 468.
[79] C 78/237, no. 4.

plaintiff asserted in Chancery that in respect of money which he had paid for his mother's debts, she had 'assigned all her use and interest' in the lease to him, or, as the master subsequently put it, had 'by conveyance declared her mind to be that the plaintiff should presently have the lease assigned to him'.[80] The distinction reflected here between a direction to the trustee to hold the trust property to the use of or to convey to a third party, and an assignment of the beneficiary's interest directly from the beneficiary to a third party is fine, and no doubt not invariably clearly drawn by contemporaries. But there is no suggestion that the assignees here proceeded under letters of attorney, or in the name of the assignor.

If trust beneficiaries' interests were assignable in Chancery at this period, they were also devisable. In *Isabell, countess of Rutland v. Constable* (1587) it was noted in Chancery that by a former order 'the defendant was to show cause wherefore he should not assign a lease unto the plaintiff (whereof he was possessed in trust to the use of [Edward Manners, earl of Rutland,] her late husband) according to the true meaning of [the earl's] devise thereof made to the plaintiff'. Rejecting an argument that the assent of the earl's executor was necessary, it was ordered that unless he should show cause to the contrary, the defendant should assign the lease to the plaintiff.[81] Similarly, in *University College, Oxford v. Nuttall* (1596) it was found proved in Chancery that the late earl of Leicester had conveyed lands and tenements within a certain manor to trustees upon trust for the earl and his heirs, and in his last will had devised to the college the fee farm lands within the manor for the maintenance of two poor scholars. Difficulties arose as to whether the lands conveyed in trust were the same as those devised, and because the heir of the last surviving trustee, to whom the lands had descended, was in ward to the crown. But the devise itself was found proved without comment.[82]

In this context an analogy with the old use might strengthen the trust beneficiary's interest. In *Cole v. Moore* (1607) it was found in Chancery that Elizabeth Pollard had devised a term of years to the defendant James Moore, and if James Moore died before the expiry of the term, then to Philip Cole. After Elizabeth's death, but while James Moore was alive, Philip Cole devised his interest in the lease to his son Richard, the plaintiff, who exhibited a bill complaining that the defendant had attempted to defraud his possibility by conveying the term away in trust for his own use. It was doubted whether the plaintiff's interest, being a possibility, was capable of being devised. Ellesmere LC held that the possibility was devisable: it was

> founded upon a trust of executorship ... and therefore Philip Cole to whom the possibility is limited of the years to come at the death of

80 C 33/81, fos. 24 and 465.
81 C 33/75, fos. 29v and 226v.
82 C 33/89, fo. 907.

James Moore, is for that purpose cestuy que trust, and although the possibility be not grantable nor devisable by rules of law, yet of the trust, cestuy que trust may declare his will as cestuy que use might of lands before the statute of 1 R. 3 [c. 1].[83]

As was noted in Ellesmere's time, 'a trust at this day can be devised by parol, but then his intent must appear clearly'.[84]

Most of the examples above of assignments and devises of trust beneficiaries' interests concern trusts of leases, and Chancery litigation involving such questions in the period appears most often to have concerned trusts of leases. It is possible that such trusts were taken to behave differently to trusts of freehold, perhaps on the ground that trusts of leases, being unexecuted by the Statute of Uses, might be assimilated to pre-statute uses, of which, as Davenport put it in argument in *Attorney-General v. Abington* (1613–19), 'statutes have taken great notice',[85] while unexecuted trusts of freehold, in the form of a use upon a use, or where the trustees had active duties, being necessarily distinct from uses executed by the statute, might be regarded as giving rise to more ephemeral interests.[86] But, as has been seen, it was said in *Ford and Sheldon's Case* (1606) that the pre-statute use was 'but a trust and confidence' which 'could not be granted':[87] an analogy with pre-statute uses would not lead straightforwardly to the conclusion that trust beneficiaries' interests so treated were assignable. Moreover, while in the 1590s it could still be asked 'whether a use of a [lease] was possible at all',[88] trusts of leases had been appearing in Chancery since the 1550s, if not before.[89] Had post-statute trusts of leases been treated as analogous to pre-statute uses, the question in the 1590s as to whether uses of leases could be would not have arisen.

---

83 Moo. K.B. 806 and 806–7; C 78/113, no. 7.
84 Bryson (ed.), *Cases concerning equity*, i, 381 no. 665.
85 Bryson (ed.), *Cases concerning equity*, ii, 408 at 410.
86 The observation in Jenk. 219 that 'A trust at this day (except of chattels) is neither forfeitable nor grantable by law' (see note 10 above) might be taken to support this approach, though the reference seems to be to the position at law, rather than in equity. Compare Mountague's argument in *R. v. Holland* (1648), in support of his view that 'this trust [of copyhold land] was a thing only in action', that 'this is but a trust not executed, which is in the nature of a use at the common law, and not as it is now by the statute', Style 21.
87 12 Rep. 1, at 1–2.
88 Simpson, *A history of the land law*, p. 194, referring to the discussion in Serjeants' Inn in the time when Francis Beaumont was a justice of the Common Pleas (that is, 1593–8) reported in 1 Anderson 293. See Jones, 'Trusts in England after the Statute of Uses', pp 180–1.
89 Ibid.

CONCLUSION

It seems clear, therefore, that caution is required in supposing, as it has been put, that 'in Coke's time trusts had been regarded as mere unassignable personal rights of action'.[90] Mr Yale observed in 1961 that 'the trust would have been crippled from the start had there been any considerable check upon its assignability', referring to *R. v. Holland* (1648) for the demise of the 'prejudice against assignability'. It is now clear that the 'start' of the post-1536 trust was earlier than was supposed in 1961,[91] and in the light of the frequency with which trusts were created in the sixteenth century, assignability and devisability of trust beneficiaries' interests in Chancery may not be surprising, though doubt seems to have remained possible: in *Plasted v. Algood* it was asked in Chancery in the late 1620s 'whether a conveyance in trust a man may dispose of the same by will or otherwise',[92] and a different view may have been taken in the equity side of the Exchequer, where in *Ogle v. Lady Shrewsbury* (1632) 'the question was whether a trust was assignable. And thought *prima facie* that a trust was not assignable and no subpoena lies for it',[93] though in a case drawn up before the chief baron in the course of the litigation it was asserted that Lady Shrewsbury's heir and executor had 'by her deed indented conveyed the said manor and *all her use and trust thereof* to the complainant'.[94]

---

90 Baker, *An introduction to English legal history*, p. 309.

91 See Jones, 'Trusts in England after the Statute of Uses', passim. See also N.G. Jones, 'The influence of revenue considerations upon the remedial practice of Chancery in trust cases, 1536–1660' in C.W. Brooks and M. Lobban (eds), *Communities and courts in Britain, 1150–1900* (London, 1997), p. 99.

92 BL MS Lansdowne 640, fo. 32v. Nothing of substance has yet been found in the record; there are procedural entries in *Playsted v. Algood* at C 33/152, fos. 221, 1496v, and C 33/153, fos. 74, 218v (1626–7).

93 Bryson (ed.), *Cases concerning equity*, ii, 636 no. 374a.

94 E 125/12, fo. 297v (also in E 128/80/2) (emphasis added). The report appears to relate to litigation in the Court of Exchequer between Sir William Lampton and Katherine his wife, and Thomas Ogle, concerning land demised by King James I to Jane (d. 1625 or 1626), daughter of Cuthbert, Lord Ogle, wife of Edward Talbot, earl of Shrewsbury, for life, remainder to the plaintiff Katherine for life, which land was subsequently granted in fee farm to one Tomlinson and one Wells, who thereupon conveyed it to the defendant and one Urmeston in trust for the countess, whereafter the defendant and Urmeston granted it to the countess and her heirs, under whom the plaintiffs claimed, E 125/11, fos. 142v, 176, E 125/12, fos. 170v, 297v, E 125/11, fos. 386, 415, E 125/12, fo. 373. In the case directed to be drawn up before Davenport CB it was said that the defendant asserted in his answer that the grant of the land from himself and Urmeston to the countess and her heirs had been of no effect in law. It was further said (here without reference to the answer) that after the countess's death her sister, Lady Katherine Cavendish, being her heir and executor, had 'by her deed indented conveyed the said manor and all her use and trust thereof to the complainant Dame Katherine Lampton', E 125/12, fo. 297v (also in E 128/80/2). The summary of the case drawn up before the chief baron which accompanies the court's order

In his reading upon the Statute of Uses in 1600 Francis Bacon had pointed out that '[f]or the transferring of uses there is no case in law whereby an action is transferred, but the *subpoena* in case of use was always assignable'.[95] This, it seems, is the meaning of the assertion by the judges in *Sir Moyle Finch's Case* (1600), much concerned with the jurisdictional division between the Chancery and the courts of common law,[96] that

> admitting that Sir Thomas Heneage had a trust, yet could not he assign the same over to the plaintiff, because it was a matter in privity between them, and was in nature of a *chose* in action, for he had no power of the land, but only to seek remedy by *subpoena*, and not like to *cesti que use*, for thereof there should be *possessio fratris*, and he should be sworn on juries in respect of the use, and he had power over the land by the statute of 1 R. 3. cap. [1].[97]

A similar point had been made in 1580: the judges being asked by the lord chancellor whether a grant by the beneficiary of a trust of a term of years of 'such interest as he then had in the ... lands in lease', 'gave all the term' to the grantee, replied that 'the gift or grant of him, in trust for whom the Term was granted, was void, and out of the statute of *cestuy que uses*'.[98] That is, the beneficiary of a trust of a term could not pass a legal title under the statute 1 Richard III, c. 1: as another report has it, the beneficiary of a trust of a term 'cannot grant this land over within the provision of the statute of 1 Ric. III, c. [1]'.[99]

The trust beneficiary's interest was not yet an interest in the land, and was in some respects still very fragile: in *Yelverton v. Yelverton* (1599), where

> may assume, contrary to the defendant's contention, that Ogle and Urmeston's grant to the countess was effective in law: 'the defendant and the said Urmeston afterwards granted the same unto the said countess and heir heirs under whom the complainants entitle themselves', E 125/11, fo. 386. Possession was ultimately decreed for the plaintiffs. The question of the assignability of a trust does not appear directly in the record. Thomas Ogle, the defendant, was perhaps Thomas Ogle of Lorbottle, brother of Jane Talbot's father: see the pedigree of Ogle in Sir Henry A. Ogle, *Ogle and Bothal: or a history of the baronies of Ogle, Bothal, and Hepple* (Newcastle-upon-Tyne, 1902), between pp 82 and 83.

95 Rowe (ed.), *The reading upon the Statute of Uses of Francis Bacon*, p. 16.
96 Another aspect of the same dispute gave rise to the decision of the judges in Exchequer Chamber in 1598 in *Finch v. Throgmorton* that the Chancery could not re-examine matters after judgment at law. See J.H. Baker, *The legal profession and the common law* (London, 1986), pp 208–9.
97 Coke, *Fourth Institute*, p. 85.
98 3 Dyer 369a, pl. 50.
99 Bryson (ed.), *Cases concerning equity*, i, 107 no. 23. See also Jones, 'Trusts in England after the Statute of Uses', p. 178. The reason given for the exclusion of a beneficiary of a trust of a lease from 1 Ric. III, c. 1 was that the language of the statute indicated that it applied only to uses of hereditaments.

William Yelverton 'did of his own good will covenant with and trust Sir Thomas Cornwallis with [an] indenture to the use of William's children', a subsequent redelivery of the indenture at William's request was said to be no breach of trust, for, as Egerton LK put it:

> it is no breach of trust if any man of his own accord, minding to do good to another, do put one in trust with assurance and the party trusted do re-deliver it at the request of him which did trust him without the privity of him to whom the good was meant, for the party to whom the good was meant did not trust him but the party which did mean to do good.[1]

In similar fashion, outside the sphere of charity, little can be seen in the period of corporations as trustees,[2] perhaps because they were, as it was said in *Chudleigh's Case* (1594), dead bodies in which 'a confidence cannot be put'.[3] And little may be said of the duties of trustees, though in *Godderd v. Swayne* (1591) it was said that the defendant trustee of a lease to the use of children had failed to let the lands at the best possible rent, whereupon it was ordered that steps be taken to find a tenant 'as will give most for the said land', and that in the meantime the defendant should continue in possession 'he accounting truly upon his oath to the uttermost value for the same'.[4] There was no question here of merely accounting for what the trustee had in fact received.

---

1   Bryson (ed.), *Cases concerning equity*, i, 270 no. 118–[308].
2   Corporations are not infrequently found as charity trustees in the later sixteenth century, e.g. *Ramsforde v. Neale* (1598) C 78/117, no. 6 (mayor and chamberlains of Northampton and their successors trustees for the poor); *Mayor, Sheriffs and Commonalty of Norwich v. Pettus* (1589) C 33/77, fo. 611v (complaint that executors have failed to purchase land and deliver it to the plaintiffs for the use of the poor as directed); *Ormeston v. Palmer* (1587/88) C 33/75, fo. 315v (devise to the company of clothworkers for the use of the poor).
3   Popham 70, at 71 *per* Ewens B, Owen and Fenner JJ, and 'Bateman' (perhaps Beaumont J). See also Bryson (ed.), *Cases concerning equity*, i, 290 no. 119–123. It was noted in the early seventeenth century that 'Where a corporation has offended in a matter of equity, though they can answer under their common seal, yet they will not be sworn because they do not have a soul', to which Coke's solution was to 'take a subpoena against them or those particular persons of the corporation who have committed the actual wrong', ibid. p. 380 no. 165–576. Obstacles arose also from difficulty in imprisoning a corporation (see argument in *Croft v. Howell* (1579) 2 Plowd. 530, at 538), which Nottingham was prepared to overcome: 'Though a corporation could not stand seised to an use, yet they may stand seised to a trust, for the old reason fails and there are other ways to enforce the execution of a trust besides the imprisonment of the trustee', Yale (ed.), *Lord Nottingham's Chancery cases*, ii, 91 and 447.
4   C 33/81, fo. 520v. For the duties of trustees in the later seventeenth century and earlier eighteenth century see M. Macnair, 'The conceptual basis of trusts in the later 17th and early 18th centuries' in Helmholz and Zimmermann (eds), *Itinera Fiduciae*, p. 207 at pp

The shift, as Mr Yale put it, 'from the relationship to the equitable right, from power to property'[5] was by no means complete within the period.[6] But insofar as trust beneficiaries' interests within the period may be brought out from the shadow of the learning of medieval uses and the dicta of Edward Coke, they prove somewhat more substantial than has been supposed. The trust beneficiary's interest was descendible in Chancery; rules concerning notice were applicable, and, in the case of express notice at least, no narrower than in later periods when trust beneficiaries' interests had come to maturity; trust beneficiaries' interests in leases could behave as assets in equity; it could at least be said that trust beneficiaries' interests were not subject to curtesy; and in appropriate cases trust beneficiaries' interests were assignable and devisable in Chancery. *R. v. Holland* may have marked a turning point, but Lord Nottingham's work had roots in the period before 1648, at which time in Chancery the trust beneficiary had had something more than a mere unassignable chose in action.

224ff: 'Modern trustee liability points in the direction of a proprietary conception of the trust in three ways', one aspect of this being the rule that 'the trustee who fails to invest properly may be liable to account for income he has not received' (p. 224).

5   Yale (ed.), *Lord Nottingham's Chancery cases*, ii, 90.
6   Though language of ownership might be used of trust beneficiaries: in *Inhabitants of Woodford v. Parkhurst* (1640) it was held by Finch LK that Sir Henry Leigh, having bought copyhold land in the names of two of his younger sons, being infants, and having devised a rent charge out of the land for the relief of the poor, had had power to do so, for although he had 'nothing in the land in strictness of law, for that the estate in law was in the children, yet Sir Henry making the purchase and enjoying the land as owner and receiving the profits of it, he shall be said in equity to have power to dispose to a charitable use', W.H. Bryson (ed.), *The Chancery reports of John Herne and of George Duke* (Buffalo, 2002), p. 91 no. 47. I am grateful to Professor Bryson for drawing my attention to this report.

Localism v. centralism: tensions in the administration of tax in nineteenth-century England and America

CHANTAL STEBBINGS[1]

FROM THE SEVENTEENTH CENTURY, and indeed earlier, the principle of localism permeated the administration of taxes in England. With few exceptions, taxes were to be assessed and collected in the communities of the taxpayers by commissioners who were themselves local laymen. The purpose of the principle was to safeguard the taxpayer against illegal encroachment in taxation by the crown. It was regarded as of great importance that the direct taxes should be assessed and collected by the representatives of the taxpayers, persons unconnected with and totally independent of central government, and free from its control or influence. This status of the local commissioners as independent men without any personal pecuniary interest in the administration of the tax protected the individual and held the balance evenly between the crown and the taxpayer ensuring, in theory, that the former received and the latter paid no more and no less than each was bound to do by law. This method of administration accordingly ensured that taxation was not an uncontrolled arbitrary instrument in the hands of the state and as such constituted one of the principal safeguards of the taxpayer. As late as the 1920s the commissioners entrusted with the administration of income tax and their officials were variously described as trustees for their fellow taxpayers,[2] 'the bulwark and protection of the taxpayer against the executive',[3] and 'the sole guardians of the taxpayer's interests'.[4] The Royal Commission on the Income Tax in 1920 famously described them as 'a natural safeguard.'[5]

---

1 This research forms part of a wider project on the legal protection of taxpayers' rights, 1780–1914 funded by the Leverhulme Trust, which support is gratefully acknowledged.
2 *The Times*, 20 Apr. 1921.
3 *The Times*, letters to the editor, 28 May 1923.
4 *The Times*, letters to the editor, 1 July 1927.
5 'Report of the Royal Commission on the Income Tax', *House of Commons Parliamentary Papers* 1920 xviii (615) 97 para. 344.

The object of this paper is to examine the reasons why the principle of localism in tax administration was valued in England, why it was adopted by the legislature and why it was robustly defended and maintained through much of the nineteenth century despite a powerful and national movement for centralization in most areas of public life and government. The decline in its effectiveness, the challenge of centralism and the response of the taxpaying public will be explored, with particular emphasis on how far the principle was able to meet the demands of the new and dynamic commercial world of the nineteenth century. In so doing, similarities and contrasts will be drawn with tax administration in the United States in the same period, reflecting the contemporary interest shown by politicians and others in the public finances of that country. The purpose is primarily to reveal the essential character of the English system and the impact of differing fiscal, constitutional and cultural conditions on the administration of taxes. The individual states of the union had a considerably better opportunity to establish satisfactory systems of taxation than did England, since the latter was constrained by powerful traditions and vested interests. Indeed they had no traditional institutions for the raising of public finance other than those that formed part of the legal culture the colonists brought with them. But the new social, economic and political conditions they faced enabled them to accept or reject elements of legal culture as they chose, and to mould a legal system – including a system of tax administration – that suited their particular and very different needs. The individual states thus possessed a degree of choice in their tax administration systems not available to England. And when the states declared their independence from Britain in 1776 and then formed a new federal constitution, the new political entity as such naturally possessed no infrastructure for the administration of tax. The culture of English tax administration, however, was common to all, and it was a culture which was imbued with a strong desire for local control and the possession of institutions which reflected it. Though the principal instruments of public finance diverged, with England preferring direct taxation as her main source of national revenue, and the United States adopting indirect taxation on a federal level and direct property taxation on an individual state level, both made use to some degree of the machinery of local tax administration. Despite common foundations, however, the differing fiscal demands in each country, along with differing emphases on the nature of individual taxes and differing cultural outlooks and political pressures, combined to make the administrative systems distinctive. Whether any jurisdiction adopted localism or centralism, or a combination of both, as the basis of its tax administration system, there was always an inherent tension between them that was of particular significance in the fiscal context. Localism embodied independent, and therefore variable, action, while centralism stood for uniformity and strong, focused control. It will be seen that in England localism was politically necessary to ensure the public acceptance of national direct taxation, while centralism became necessary to ensure the efficient collection of the public revenue. In their adherence to localism in tax administration, English governments and taxpayers were engaged in a conflict that came to a head in, and endured throughout, the nineteenth century. In America, on the other hand, although local tax administrative systems were employed, the same degree of conflict did not arise. In order to reveal the nature of the tensions in English tax administration, the factors that diffused potential tensions in the American systems will be identified.

THE PRINCIPLE OF LOCALISM

The principle of localism was so entrenched in the fiscal system of England that it was repeatedly claimed as a right and liberty of the English people. It could claim some constitutional provenance since the fundamental principle of English taxation, established beyond question by the civil war of the seventeenth century and lying at the heart of that conflict, was that taxation could only be levied with the consent of the people's representatives in Parliament. It was a principle that resonated beyond the narrow field of tax, for it was instrumental in destroying absolute kingship and imposing parliamentary rule and a constitutional monarchy. The great case of ship-money[6] had tested the fundamental principle of parliamentary consent. Though it ultimately found for the king on the facts, Sir George Croke's fearless judgment for John Hampden and his analysis of the statutes and the common law which from Magna Carta had required the consent of the people to the fiscal demands of the crown was a powerful affirmation of the principle.[7] It was ultimately confirmed in the Bill of Rights of 1689, which provided that 'levying money for or to the use of the Crown by pretence of prerogative, without grant of Parliament ... is illegal'.[8] This fundamental constitutional rule of consent to taxation through representation in Parliament served to promote and give legal integrity to four cognate canons of English taxation: that taxes should be voluntary in nature,[9] non-inquisitorial, necessary, and always be assessed and collected locally by the taxpayers' peers. The last was the principle of localism in tax administration.

These four principles gave English taxation its particular legal character and moulded popular responses to it. First, an involuntary tax, in the sense

---

6   *R. v. Hampden* (1637) 3 S.T. 825.
7   Ibid., at pp 1127–81.
8   Bill of Rights 1689 (1 Will. & Mary sess. 2 c. 2) s. 4.
9   See the speech of Sir William Pulteney in the debate on the income tax in 1798, *Parliamentary History*, vol. 34, 22 Dec. 1798, cols. 134–5; see too William Phillips, 'The origin of income tax', *British Tax Review* (1967), 113–26.

of a tax that could not be avoided, was regarded as conflicting with the right to dominion of property, which was inherent in a free constitution. It predisposed the English to favour taxation on luxury goods of consumption, for there an individual could choose whether or not to pay the tax simply by purchasing the item or taking the decision not to purchase it. So with the assessed taxes, which were taxes on various articles such as windows, inhabited houses, carriages, horses and servants, with other excise taxes and with customs duties, though they were unpopular, they were acceptable as they were submitted to through choice. Taxes that could not be avoided in this way were always fiercely resisted as an invasion of private rights. William Pitt's triple assessment of 1798[10] broke the principle of voluntaryism, since it was based entirely on past expenditure, and his income tax of the following year, though based on a bland general return, was nonetheless compulsory.[11] Secondly, an inquisitorial tax similarly challenged deeply held and peculiarly English notions of privacy. The eighteenth-century house and window taxes were regarded as excessively intrusive, with the government officers being permitted to enter houses and gardens for the purposes of taxation, and the principal focus of popular opposition to the income tax was its inquisitorial nature.[12]

Thirdly, it was felt that direct taxation, always distrusted and perceived as putting too much power in the hands of the central government and its officials, should be strictly necessitated by an extraordinary national emergency, and when it breached this principle it was the subject of vehement opposition. The imposition of ship-money in the seventeenth century stretched the concept of necessity, as did that of income tax in 1842. And fourthly, the administration of tax by the central government not only undermined the fundamental notion of taxation by consent, but challenged the sanctity of personal property, the profound attachment of the English people to local self-government and local institutions, and the common dislike of state interference in private affairs. Accordingly where a tax breached this principle, it was strongly opposed. The first to do so was the excise, for that tax was administered entirely by officers of the central government. The unpopularity of that tax, and of the excisemen who administered it, was notorious.[13] Of these four guiding principles, three were effectively undermined in the nineteenth century, with involuntary or inquisitorial or routine direct taxation giving rise to intense but relatively brief opposition and

---

10 38 Geo. III c. 16.
11 39 Geo. III c. 13.
12 But see William Phillips, 'The real objection to the income tax of 1799', *British Tax Review* (1967), 177–86.
13 It was equally unpopular in the United States. See Dall W. Forsythe, *Taxation and political change in the young nation 1781–1833* (New York, 1977), pp 38–51 for the failure of the unpopular whisky excise.

ultimately being accepted, however reluctantly, as part of the fiscal pattern in the relatively short term. Not to do so was understood to be economically unsustainable. The centralization of tax administration, however, was faced with unremitting resistance throughout the nineteenth century, and the challenge to localism proved remarkably intractable.

Though not expressed in terms of a principle in the Bill of Rights, the dominance of localism in tax administration was undoubtedly a well-established practice in English government. It was regarded as nothing less than an ideological, political, pragmatic and fiscal necessity. Traditionally there existed a powerful ideological allegiance of the English people to local interests and the influence of localism was still immensely strong in the nineteenth century.[14] They had always valued local self-government, and its institutions were perceived as enshrining their very liberties. From the earliest period of English taxation, therefore, legislative provision for the administration of direct national taxes was firmly based on local lay control, with some, though minimal, central professional supervision. It reflected the wider English tradition of amateur participation in both local government and the administration of justice. The use of lay adjudicators in the administration of the law had a long tradition, with the jury and the justices of the peace both being regarded as essential elements in the operation of the formal legal system. The jury was regarded as 'the constitutional tribunal for trying issues of fact',[15] and strengthened the traditional view that questions of fact could not only be decided by lay bodies, but indeed were best decided by them. The justices of the peace, unpaid local landowners with no formal legal knowledge, ultimately became the principal law enforcement agency in the provinces,[16] and constituted the face of the administration of justice in the eyes of the great proportion of the population. Arbitration, the private settlement of disputes by the appointment of arbitrators selected by the parties themselves, formed another aspect of lay adjudication. Jurymen, justices of the peace and, in general, arbitrators, were all locally appointed men. They formed the cultural bedrock of the administration of law, and, accordingly, the administration of tax at the beginning of the nineteenth century. Pre-eminent among these institutions to which the English were practically and emotionally attached were the justices of the peace, to whom the local tax commissioners were closely related. Since these local offices were almost invariably occupied by landowners, the Tories were committed to their defence. In that sense it was not surprising that the Tory Pitt should

14 See Derek Fraser, *The evolution of the British welfare state* (London, 1973), p. 109.
15 See the 'First report of the judicature commissioners', *House of Commons Parliamentary Papers*, 1868–9 xxv (4130) 12; W.R. Cornish and G. de N. Clark, *Law and society in England 1750–1950* (London, 1989), pp 19–21.
16 Elie Halevy, *A history of the English people in 1815* (Ark Paperbacks edition, London, 1987), pp 33–4.

retain justices of the peace as the basis for his fiscal tribunal to implement the income tax.

Attitudes to localism were brought sharply into relief in the nineteenth century when England saw an unprecedented political movement of centralization. From the 1830s practical issues of major social importance were demanding political and legislative attention, notably the need to provide for growing numbers of the poor, to promote public health, and to improve the appalling working conditions in mines and factories. Problems of such magnitude could only effectively be dealt with by direct state intervention, and there followed an extraordinary increase in central government control and an ever-growing bureaucracy to effect it. The Victorians were ambivalent in their attitude to such centralization, for in those instances where centralization was clearly the only option their firm adherence to localism was tempered by pragmatism. It has, however, been argued that the weight of localism triumphed in the wider national context in that it limited central state intervention by keeping a significant degree of power in local agencies.[17] The veneration of traditional institutions, the distrust of central government and state intervention, and the profound importance attached to private property interests all strengthened the principle of local tax administration.

This popular attachment to localism made the adoption of a locally based system of tax administration a political necessity. Taxes were invariably unpopular and yet they could not effectively be levied without the consent of the people. Formal consent was of course acquired through the absolute and fundamental constitutional rule that only Parliament, the collective representation of the people, had the power to impose a tax. Active consent was harder to achieve and yet essential to the successful levying of a tax. Examples abounded of legal levies failing when met with sustained and widespread popular opposition, a key instance being the excise taxes imposed by the British on the American colonies in the eighteenth century. Substantive national taxation was certainly an expression of centralism, of state interference with private property. That was disliked, but was accepted as an unpleasant necessity. What was far more difficult for taxpayers to accept were taxes that were involuntary, inquisitorial, and perceived as infringing private rights. The income tax was the prime example of such a tax. It was in its essential nature and substance inquisitorial, and its machinery was necessarily so. To use a traditional means of tax administration which was familiar and understood by all taxpayers, and which satisfied their desire for local control, was a powerful pacifier in view of widespread concern and distrust. The

---

[17] William C. Lubenow, *The politics of government growth* (Newton Abbot, 1971), pp 180–1, and see too pp 30–68. See Arthur J. Taylor, *Laissez–faire and state intervention in nineteenth-century Britain*, Studies in Economic History (London, 1972), pp 55–9.

political reasoning behind the adoption of the principle of localism in England was not lost on an American commentator, who perceptively observed that 'the institution of local commissioners was intended to render the tax less obnoxious to the taxpayer by protecting him against the possible rapacity of the Government and furnishing a guarantee that the assessment would not be conducted in an inconsiderate or unduly rigorous manner.'[18]

The constitutional provenance of the principle of localism in tax administration gave it considerable power, and few political leaders in the nineteenth century felt able to undermine it. William Pitt was acutely aware of the price he had to pay for the successful passage of his new income tax legislation, namely the closest adherence to the traditional principle of tax administration, leaving it formally and almost entirely in the hands of local laymen. Robert Peel acknowledged that the established policy of the law had always been

> not to make the collection depend on the will of the Government, because it was thought more consistent with constitutional law, to entrust the amount to local parties, and that those who may have the confidence of their neighbours shall be employed for this purpose.[19]

He saw the administration of taxation as a function primarily of local bodies, carefully selected for their integrity and local knowledge, and not an arbitrary act of the executive. It was, at most, a partnership of central government and local administration. He expressed this view repeatedly in the lengthy debates that culminated in the successful reintroduction of the income tax in 1842. Peel thus maintained localism in tax administration on the express basis of constitutionalism. Indeed he observed that he doubted whether he could 'constitutionally abolish altogether those privileges which the counties had of assessing themselves, and of collecting the tax by means of local authorities'.[20]

The local system of administration was fundamental to English taxation and was politically acknowledged as the only practicable means of ensuring an efficient and acceptable means of assessment to and collection of, tax. The importance of acceptable and efficient machinery was not to be underestimated in fiscal policy in any jurisdiction. It was the case in taxation that the machinery was almost as important as the substance. It was often the machinery that determined the popular response to a tax, that made it acceptable or unacceptable to the public, and in practice the success of a tax depended on whether taxpayers as a body were, in the last resort, prepared

---

18 Joseph A. Hill, *Economic Studies*, 4:4/5 (1899), 278.
19 *Parliamentary Debates* series 3, vol. 61, 18 Mar. 1842, HC, col. 912.
20 Ibid., vol. 62, 2 May 1842, HC, col. 1385 *per* Sir Robert Peel.

to pay it. As James Bayard observed in Congress in 1798, 'it was not so much the letter of a tax law which was offensive to the people, as the hand of the tax gatherer which compelled them to pay',[21] and in 1813 Charles Ingersoll remarked that the mode of collection was 'an article of the utmost delicacy and importance. It is collection,' he said, 'with all its domiciliary visits and examinations, that disgusts people more than the amount of their contributions.'[22] Where a tax depended on the willingness of taxpayers to make honest returns of their property or income, a fair, impartial and efficient machinery of taxation was essential, for it gave the public confidence that everyone was paying their due taxes and promoted public cooperation. The cost of machinery could determine whether the tax was worthwhile or not, for the ultimate success of a tax was judged entirely on its financial return. In the case of income tax, the whole tax was said to turn on the machinery,[23] a fact not lost on William Pitt, for it was the first issue he addressed in Parliament after announcing the introduction of his new and radical income tax.[24] That taxes failed for want of adequate administrative machinery was well known. In America one of the principal problems with the introduction of federal income taxes was the lack of machinery to administer them, the difficulty of creating a new infrastructure, and the need to have the machinery working for many years in order for problems to be revealed and addressed, and improvements made. Again, the reason why Ireland did not have to shoulder the burden of income tax until 1853 was the lack of existing machinery to implement it.[25] If new machinery had to be developed, the process was time-consuming and costly, with no guarantee of efficiency or success, and with the danger of further alienating the taxpaying public. Indeed, it was not a realistic possibility where, as in eighteenth-century England, the bureaucratic machinery of central government was virtually non-existent. The machinery of taxation had a further importance. Not only could it go far to ensure public acceptance of a tax, it also, once established, contributed significantly to its endurance. The establishment of the machinery possessed a momentum of its own. Once established and working, it had the effect of driving a tax on, partially because of an appreciation that once dismantled, it would be no easy task to re-establish it. So where a system of tax administration existed, or was introduced, the tax it serviced in practice would probably continue. This was recognized in Parliament, and fears were expressed that it was all very well for income tax

21 *Annals of Congress*, 5 Cong., 2 sess., 1231, 5 Mar. 1798.
22 Ibid., 13 Cong., 1 sess., 367, 29 June 1813.
23 *Parliamentary Debates* series 3, vol. 61, 21 Mar. 1842, HC, col. 1025 *per* Charles Buller.
24 *Parliamentary History*, vol. 34, 3 Dec. 1798, col. 6.
25 *Parliamentary Debates*, series 3, vol. 61, 11 Mar. 1842, HC, col. 445 *per* Sir Robert Peel. Gladstone introduced income tax into Ireland in 1853, and made use of the special commissioners to implement it.

to be a temporary tax in theory, in practice it would become permanent.[26] Those fears proved to be well founded.

England had the advantage of a long-established system of local administration which was thoroughly tested, familiar to the taxpaying public, developed to a considerable level of sophistication and found to be relatively efficient. It was therefore inevitable that when a new tax was introduced it would be, if at all possible, superimposed on the administrative machinery already in existence, and William Pitt did so when he introduced the income tax. One major reason why both he and Peel some forty years later felt able to promote that tax was precisely because the machinery to implement it was already available, and Peel admitted that one advantage of the income tax was that it could be introduced cheaply because 'the machinery is complete'.[27] It was also a strong response to the concerns about the cost of government, increasingly expressed throughout the nineteenth century.[28] A major reason, therefore, for the adoption of the traditional local system of tax administration was pragmatism.

Finally, the adoption of the traditional local system of tax administration was a fiscal necessity not only because it ensured public co-operation with the payment of tax, and hence determined the success or failure of the tax as a fiscal instrument, but because local knowledge was deemed crucial to the correct assessment of the tax in question. Local knowledge meant acquaintance with individual traders, knowledge of their methods of business and their profits, of local economic conditions, of local land values, and of everyday matters and problems in local commercial life. The placing of tax administration in men possessing such knowledge was central to tax policy.

Localism had its own importance to Americans. It was, however, a localism of a totally different order to England, in that there was an early and profound attachment to an individual's state. In his *History of the American Revolution*, David Ramsay observed that

> [f]rom the acquiescence of the parent state [in the growth of self-government], the spirit of her constitution and daily experience, the colonists grew up in a belief, that their local assemblies stood in the same relation to them, as the parliament of Great Britain, to the inhabitants of that island. The benefits of legislation were conferred on both, only through these constitutional channels.[29]

---

26 *Parliamentary Debates*, series 3, vol. 61, 21 Mar. 1842, HC, col. 1004 *per* Sir George Grey. And see Lord Beaumont at ibid., vol. 64, 21 June 1842, HL, cols 304–5.
27 Ibid., vol. 61, 11 Mar. 1842, HC, col. 445 *per* Sir Robert Peel.
28 Local tax commissioners were not remunerated, but their officials were, and there was a long-running debate as to whether administration by salaried civil servants was cheaper than by lay amateurs.
29 David Ramsay, *The history of the American revolution*, ed. Lester H. Cohen (Indianapolis, 1990), p. 18.

This included the principle reflected on a national scale in Britain that 'the people could not be compelled to pay any taxes, nor be bound by any laws, but such as had been granted or enacted with the consent of themselves, or of their representatives'.[30] The new federal government that emerged in the years after the Declaration of Independence in 1776 had to establish its place in relation to these powerful and independent sovereign states, whose status clearly challenged the very viability of federal taxation. The relationship between the central federal government and the individual states in terms of taxation was clearly reflected in the provisions of the American constitution. The nature of the constitutional structure of the United States was that the states retained all powers that they chose not to assign to the federal government. In that sense one major tension between localism and centralism was removed, in that the undoubtedly powerful allegiance felt by the people to their own state was recognized, and the powers of the central government strictly circumscribed. This found fiscal expression in the dominance of state property taxation over federal taxation. Each state raised its own public revenue, generally through a property tax that was broadly similar in substance and administration in all the states. The federal government, whose financial demands were relatively slight in its early years, was initially not permitted to tax at all, but subsequently was given the power, though a limited one.[31] In practice it raised the largest proportion of its required funding through a tariff on imported goods.[32] There would, therefore, be no administrative tension between central federal taxation and state taxation, no question of federal officers concerning themselves with state taxation, since constitutionally the two were quite distinct. The issue of localism did, however, present itself in the extent to which both federal taxes and state taxes depended on local laymen to administer them.

LOCALISM IN PRACTICE: PROPERTY TAXES

For the reasons discussed above, at the beginning of the nineteenth century localism was the accepted basis of tax administration in England. It domi-

---

30 Ibid., p.19.
31 Article 1, section 8, of the constitution stated that 'The Congress shall have power to lay and collect taxes, duties, imposts and excises, pay the debts and provide for the common defense and general welfare of the United States; but all duties, imposts and excises shall be uniform throughout the United States;' Article I, section 9 provided that 'No capitation, or other direct tax shall be laid, unless in proportion to the census.' For the ideological, political and pragmatic reasons for these provisions, see W. Elliot Brownlee, *Federal taxation in America*, (2nd edn Cambridge & Washington DC, 2004), pp 13–21; Forsythe, *Taxation and political change*.
32 For an overview of the different fiscal policies of the USA and Great Britain from a British perspective, see *Parliamentary Debates*, series 3, vol. 62, 22 Apr. 1842, HC, cols 1007ff.

nated the machinery of implementation and was highly developed so as to allow both in theory and practice an administration entirely on a local basis with central control being weak and largely ineffectual.[33] The principal direct tax prior to the introduction of income tax, the land tax,[34] which had been introduced as such at the end of the seventeenth century, though with far older roots, was assessed and collected by a body of local men known as the land tax commissioners. The sole authority to administer the tax lay in them, they were completely independent of the crown, and it was that body which formed the basis of tax administration of the modern age. The land tax in force in the nineteenth century[35] had shed its original character of a tax on real and personal property and incomes, and had in practice become a tax purely on land. Its governing legislation laid down a fixed global sum that had to be raised on land. The sum was divided among 128 counties and districts, and then divided again by the land tax commissioners so that each parish had a fixed quota to pay. Each district had to raise the apportioned amount charged on it by levying a pound rate on the annual value of the land, the maximum rate being 4s. in the £. The tax was in the nature of a perpetual charge on the land.

The land tax commissioners themselves were appointed for each district[36] through the mechanism of the Land Tax Commissioners Names Act, passed in the first session of each Parliament. That act appointed a number of men whose names were then printed in the London Gazette to act as commissioners for the places described. Other than the nominated commissioners, all justices of the peace were ex officio commissioners.[37] The legislation prescribed a local property qualification that was high[38] and which ensured the commissioners were generally members of the local gentry. The commissioners, who were unremunerated, appointed annually their own subordinate officers, including the assessors[39] and collectors[40] who worked entirely under their control and were paid for their work. The assessors, who were to be 'able and sufficient Inhabitants,' received their instructions from the

---

33 See E.V. Adams, 'The early history of surveyors of taxes', *Quarterly Record* (1956), 290–306 at 292–3.
34 See generally Pretor W. Chandler, *The land tax: its creation and management* (London, 1899). For its earlier history see W.R. Ward, *The English land tax in the eighteenth century* (London, 1953).
35 38 Geo. III c. 5; 38 Geo. III c. 60.
36 38 Geo. III c. 5 s. 8.
37 7 & 8 Geo. IV c. 75 ss 1, 2.
38 For a land tax commissioner for a county it was £100 p.a. landed estate in possession, or £300 p.a. in reversion, with half being within the county for which the commissioner was appointed: 38 Geo. III c. 48 s. 3. The qualifications differed for cities and boroughs and in London: see 38 Geo. III c. 48 s. 1; 38 Geo. III c. 5 ss 93, 94.
39 38 Geo. III c. 5 s. 8.
40 Ibid.

commissioners, as to how much they had to raise and how the assessments were to be made.

The assessment had to be made in a prescribed form,[41] with the names of owners and occupiers, and a description of each property. All forms of real property were subject to the tax, though there were some statutory exemptions. The most challenging element in the process was the fixing of the annual value of each property. The statute provided that the assessment should be made annually with as much equality as possible by a pound rate according to the annual value.[42] It was important to do this properly, in order to ensure that the taxpayers of the parish were fairly taxed, and the assessors had to ensure, for example, that new buildings were taken into account. However, in many parishes the assessments were simply copied each year, with no reassessment, and by the end of the nineteenth century the popular perception of the land tax was that it was a fixed charge upon the land. The basis of the assessment on which the assessors were to proceed was entirely within the discretion of the commissioners, though in practice they instructed the assessors to follow the rateable value from the poor rate assessment. Though by the end of the century, statute directed that in certain circumstances the annual value was to be taken as that determined by the general commissioners of income tax for the purpose of schedule A,[43] and this was a fair and convenient basis of valuation which could be adopted generally, the assessors in theory had to form their own opinion as to the annual value of the property to be taxed, namely the amount of rent that could be secured in the open market without any special conditions. Knowing the total sum that needed to be raised, and the total annual values of the property, the assessors could then determine the rate and the amount of each assessment calculated. The commissioners, if they agreed with the assessments, would formally 'allow' them, at which point duplicates would be delivered to the collectors, signed and sealed by the commissioners. The collectors too were local residents.

The land tax commissioners formed the purest example of localism in tax administration since virtually no interference from any official of the central government in the locality itself was permitted under the legislation. Having laid down in the Act the amount to be raised, central government was interested in its receipt rather than in the internal workings of the tax's administration. Even where the commissioners did not perform their duties, the crown found itself unable to control them effectively. In the eighteenth century they frequently asserted their independence and made it clear that it was the price of their cooperation and toleration of the tax itself. Local

---

41 Taxes Management Act 1880 (43 & 44 Vict. c. 19) s. 15.
42 38 Geo. III c. 5 s. 4.
43 Finance Act 1896 (59 & 60 Vict. c. 28) ss 31, 32, 35.

administration was then weak and inefficient, rife with factional disputes, vested interests, political squabbles, evasion, and a disregard for the law.[44] Beyond payment of the tax to the Receiver General, formal permitted crown intervention was minimal: the clerk and collectors had to produce the assessments to the government surveyor on demand.[45]

Through their own subordinate officials the commissioners controlled the assessing of the tax, and supervised the collection process. The strictest application of localism in tax administration left all administrative powers in the local institutions. The administration of tax was a process that comprised assessment and collection, but an essential element of that process was the right of appeal against assessment. It was important because it provided yet further protection to the taxpayer, and indeed was almost invariably the sole clear formal safeguard expressed in the legislation. The right of appeal for aggrieved taxpayers was regarded as a fundamental right of the individual. It constituted formal, controlled and overt protection against arbitrary fiscal action, and was material in ensuring the cooperation of taxpayers. The extent of the land tax commissioners' control of tax administration was emphasized by the provision that where a taxpayer felt he had been overcharged by the assessors he could appeal against his assessment, but the appeal was to be heard by the land tax commissioners themselves.[46] The commissioners would hear the evidence of the appellant, and would require the assessors to support their assessment, but the crown was not involved in the process. Furthermore, the determination of the commissioners on appeal was final. No further appeal, either to some other lay body or to the courts of the regular legal system, was permitted. The finality of their appellate determinations was a forcible expression of the principle of localism, though the denial or limitation of the right to appeal to the regular courts was itself not a positive expression of localism but rather a negative matter of public policy. The legislature wished to limit appeals from tax assessments beyond the local tribunals. Where a tax was unpopular, appeals would be numerous, and would severely impede the smooth and constant collection of revenue vital to any government. As Parke B. observed in 1848 in relation to a tax on horse dealers, '[a]ctions would be innumerable, juries would have to decide on facts without end, judges on law, and cases would be carried to the highest tribunal, when the exigencies of the state required a speedy determination'.[47] Undoubtedly the principle of localism in relation to tax disputes fitted in well with the demands of the state. As late as 1915, and speaking of the income tax, Lord Reading observed that the legislation showed that its object was

---

44 See Ward, *English land tax*, pp 22, 31, 38, 58–9, 65, 86–99.
45 53 Geo. III c. 123 s. 17.
46 38 Geo. III c. 5 s. 8.
47 *Allen v. Sharp* (1848) 2 Ex. 352 at 363.

to entrust the decision of the facts to a tribunal of persons specially selected for the locality, and who are often in a better position than the Courts to determine the questions of fact, sometimes very complicated, which may arise. The exigencies of the State require that there should be a tribunal to deal expeditiously, and at comparatively little expense with all such questions, and to decide them finally, reserving always to the individual the right to have the Commissioners' decisions of points of law reviewed by the Courts.[48]

Where a right of appeal beyond the local tribunal was permitted, it did remove the authority of finality from the local bodies, and as such weakened the principle of localism in tax administration.

When the overall sum to be raised by the land tax, and each quota, were fixed in 1798, the burden was assumed to be the same for all districts in England and Wales though in time it became unequal as property values fluctuated, and the tax itself unfair. The tax reduced in importance and effectiveness, and this was recognized when in 1798 provision was made for its redemption.[49] As the tax declined in England, however, a similar tax formed the mainstay of public revenue in the American states. During the whole of the nineteenth century the individual states raised money for their public expenditure primarily through the taxation of specific, visible property.[50] The state property taxes differed, often considerably, in their detail, reflecting the social, political and economic distinctiveness of the individual original colonies, but most followed the same general principles of administration.[51] To implement these state property taxes, which were to fund distinct town, county and state public expenditure,[52] most states employed one system that in some respects resembled the English tradition.

48 *R v. Commissioners of Taxes for St Giles and St George, Bloomsbury* (1915) 7 T.C. 59 at 65 *per* Lord Reading LCJ.
49 38 Geo. III c. 60. The object of the legislation was to make the land tax set in 1797 perpetual, to be raised by an equal pound rate, but subject to redemption and purchase. For contemporary debate as to Pitt's scheme, whereby the tax could be discharged by a single payment, see *Parliamentary History*, vol. 33, 9 May 1798, cols. 1434–54.
50 See generally Richard T. Ely, *Taxation in American states and cities* (New York, 1888); Sumner Benson, 'A history of the general property tax' in George C.S. Benson et al., *The American property tax: its history, administration, and economic impact* (Claremont, CA, 1965), pp 11–81; Brownlee, *Federal taxation*, pp 26–7.
51 See for example Charles J. Bullock, 'The taxation of property and income in Massachusetts', *Quarterly Journal of Economics*, 31:1 (November 1916), 1–61; *Laws of the general assembly of the commonwealth of Pennsylvania* (Harrisburg, 1885).
52 In the state of New York these were three distinct taxes for three distinct purposes, collected at the same time by the same machinery on the same basis of assessment: see the evidence of Dudley Selden of New York, sometime barrister and member of Congress, 'Minutes of evidence taken before the select committee on the income and property tax', *House of Commons Parliamentary Papers*, 1852 ix (354) 1 at q.1901 [hereafter 'Minutes, 1852'].

In 1796 the Secretary of the Treasury, Oliver Wolcott, conducted an exhaustive survey of the nature of the taxes levied in the individual states and their administrative machinery, and his report provides an invaluable insight into the nature and machinery of these taxes.[53] The differences between the states were striking, particularly between the northern states and those of the south, but the broadest generalization is possible. Most states taxed one or more of the following: land and buildings, farm stock, money, slaves, the stock in trade of merchants and personal property in general. Some imposed a poll tax and one a general income tax.[54] In the course of the nineteenth century in New York, for example, all real and personal property came to be subject to tax, though there were some exemptions for necessary personal property such as household furniture and linen.[55] In Texas, all real, personal and mixed property became taxable according to its selling value. In the northern states the state legislature determined a certain sum necessary to meet the expenditure of the state to be raised on certain property in the state and apportioned the sum among the counties, which then determined quotas for the towns, which were assessed on the property of the individual inhabitants. The towns were responsible to the counties, the counties to the state, for the amount of the assessments. The taxes were thus almost invariably collected using the town machinery and the stipulated sums remitted to the appropriate Treasury. In southern states the taxes were levied by the state directly upon the individual or his property.

The administrative machinery differed to some extent as between the northern and southern states. In the north, it almost invariably consisted of the annual election at a town meeting by the inhabitants, of a number of officers, variously called listers, selectmen or simply assessors. These officers were resident in the district and sworn to discharge their office faithfully, to undertake the duty of making the assessments to tax. In the southern states the appointment was by the state executive. In some the state legislature appointed county commissioners who appointed subordinate assessors for the districts in the county, or directly appointed the assessors, or again the county and corporation courts appointed commissioners of the revenue to

---

53 *American State Papers: Finance*, vol. 1, 4 Cong., 1 Sess, pp 413–41 (13 Dec. 1796).
54 See too 'Papers respecting the taxation of personal property in France, Germany, and the United States', *House of Commons Parliamentary Papers* 1886 lii (4909) 851 at 866–7; 'Reports as to the taxation of land and buildings in European countries and the United States of America', *House of Commons Parliamentary Papers* 1890–91 lxxxiii (6209) 555.
55 See the evidence of Colonel Benjamin P. Johnson from Albany, New York, in 'Minutes, 1852,' qq 1957–8; 'Papers bearing on land taxes and on income tax etc. in certain foreign countries, and on the working of taxation of site values in certain cities of the United States and in British colonies, together with extracts relative to land taxation and land valuation from reports of royal commissions and parliamentary committees', *House of Commons Parliamentary Papers* 1909 lxxi (4750) 365, 456–9 [hereafter, 'Papers bearing on land taxes, 1909'].

act as assessors, or justices of the peace. While the qualification for assessors was usually expressed to be residence or the status of freeholder, the character of respectability or suitability, or a property qualification were sometimes required. The assessors of the New York property tax were town officers, elected by the people of the district, and they had to be resident householders. Three were appointed, with each serving three years and one retiring at the end of every year, in order to ensure a measure of continuity and experience.[56] They were, it was said, 'a very respectable body of men',[57] 'the most elevated of any body of men'.[58] Though, as with English assessors, they were local residents, the possession of local knowledge of economic conditions was rarely mentioned as a reason for such appointments. Occasionally it is said that knowledge of local land values and of commercial conditions, particularly in rural areas, was helpful, but it did not form the principal justification for the use of local officers in the tax process. The assessors were invariably remunerated, at a fixed daily rate while in service or by a commission on the sums assessed. In New York in the mid nineteenth century they earned one dollar and a quarter a day.[59]

Election by the popular vote of the inhabitants was thus the usual method of appointment in the northern states, but it was the case that the local assessors, and the taxpayers who elected them, were perceived as favouring local interests against the interests of the state, and to attempt to ensure that their district did not pay too large a share of the tax. 'It may therefore be supposed,' it was later said of assessors in California, 'that candidates who are known to favour low assessment are generally the ones elected'.[60] An American commentator in 1899, looking into the practical workings of the English income tax system on behalf of the Massachusetts Commission on Taxation, noted the independence of the tax commissioners in England, and how they were neither responsible to any higher authority nor owing their offices to their fellow taxpayers, not being elected by them. It struck him forcibly that despite their being themselves property owners and taxpayers in the district for which they were appointed, they were not found to favour the taxpayer as against the crown, and defended the rights of both.[61]

The assessor was the key figure in the administration of state property taxes. His function was to ascertain all persons and property subject to taxation in his district.[62] He would call at each house and obtain a statement

---

56 See the evidence of Colonel Benjamin P. Johnson 'Minutes, 1852', qq. 1962–6.
57 Ibid., at q. 1924 *per* Dudley Selden.
58 Ibid., at q. 1925.
59 Ibid., at q. 2287.
60 'Papers bearing on land taxes, 1909' at 465. For a clear account of taxation in the state of California see ibid., pp 462–5.
61 Joseph A. Hill, *Economic Studies*, 4:4/5 (1899) 278.

or list, often under oath, setting out all the taxpayer's property, with a description and value.[63] The assessor would examine these lists, make inquiries and amend the assessments as he thought appropriate on the basis of his best information or judgment. As with the English land tax, the most challenging part of the assessor's duties was the valuation of land. In the District of Columbia this was undertaken by the assessor once every three years, from his actual viewing of the property and the best information he could obtain, taking additions and improvements to the land into account.[64] He had considerable freedom in his methods of ascertaining the value of real property, and he had to be diligent in his search for the best information. He would take into account the rents of the property, its use and its situation,[65] the sworn statements of the taxpayers, the examination of witnesses, and all plans, maps, and records pertaining to the valuation of the property. If a return was incorrect or not forthcoming, the assessor had the power not only to estimate the value of the property himself on the basis of the best information he could acquire,[66] but also to impose some kind of financial penalty.

Where individuals were aggrieved by the decisions of the assessing officers, maintaining their assessment was erroneous or excessive, provision was almost invariably made for appeal. The appeal was heard and determined by various bodies, for example justices of the peace, sometimes acting with men of the town, 'judicious freeholders', a county body, or the assessors themselves. The decision of this appellate body was usually final. In the nineteenth century, boards of appeal were common. In New York, appeal lay to the three assessors sitting as a board of appeal who would hear and determine the complaint.[67] In West Virginia, if a taxpayer was aggrieved by an entry in the land or personal property book, he could appeal to the county court on giving notice to the prosecuting attorney of the county who

---

62 For the process in West Virginia at the end of the nineteenth century, see J.S. Miller, *Laws of the state of West Virginia relating to assessments, taxes, licenses, collection of taxes, sales of delinquent lands and forfeited lands, in force in 1883* (Wheeling, 1883).

63 For the process in Texas in the mid nineteenth century, see the evidence of Ashbel Smith, secretary of state in Texas, in 'Minutes, 1852', qq 2149, 2152.

64 'Reports as to the taxation of land and buildings in European countries and the United States of America', *House of Commons Parliamentary Papers* 1890–91 lxxxiii (6209) 555 at 626–7.

65 'Papers bearing on land taxes, 1909', 458.

66 See generally 'Papers respecting the taxation of personal property in France, Germany, and the United States', *House of Commons Parliamentary Papers* 1886 lii (4909) 851 at 865–9.

67 See the evidence of Colonel Benjamin P. Johnson in 'Minutes, 1852', qq 1968–71. See too the evidence of Dudley Selden, though Johnson maintained that Selden was mistaken in some of his answers: ibid., at qq 1697–1929. For the board of appeal for the city of Philadelphia, see 'Reports as to the taxation of land and buildings in European countries and the United States of America', *House of Commons Parliamentary Papers* 1890–91 lxxxiii (6209) 555 at 622. See too 'Papers bearing on land taxes, 1909', 456.

represented the interest of the state, county and district. If he was not satisfied, he could appeal to the circuit court of the county.[68] Texas used arbitration to settle differences between the assessor and the taxpayer. If they could not agree as to the valuation of an item of property in the statement, then each would choose a freeholder from the district to arrive at an agreed value, and if they could not agree, they could choose a third, and his decision was final. This use of arbitration was seen in a number of state property tax systems, and reflected the common use of lay juries in valuation cases in England.[69] Taxpayers had the right not only to have their property assessed at no more than its value, but also not to have it assessed at a higher proportionate value than the other similar property on the roll. States and local districts thus made provision for some mechanism for equalization and in most there existed a board of equalization of real property.[70] In New York once the assessment roll had been corrected by the assessors, it went to the county board of supervisors who could correct any assessments to personal estate and would address any problems arising as to the valuation of a town's real estate so as to ensure that all districts were assessed equally.[71] By the end of the nineteenth century, the state of New York had considerably formalized its property tax machinery. It established a state board of tax commissioners consisting of three commissioners, whose duty it was to investigate and examine assessments, instruct local assessors, make rules and regulations, take evidence, and publish an annual report. They were the state equivalent of the English Commissioners of Inland Revenue, namely a branch of the executive government of the state.[72] It also established a state board of equalization, composed of the three tax commissioners and the commissioners of the land office. Their task was to examine and review the valuations of all property in the counties of the state.[73] Once the assessment was finalized, the tax was collected by collectors again appointed along the same principles as the assessors. Constables or the sheriff of the county were originally often used for this purpose. In some states the assessors and collectors were the same persons. The sum was then apportioned between the state, the counties and the towns to meet their public expenditure.[74]

68 See Miller, *Laws of the state of West Virginia*, para. 94.
69 See the evidence of Ashbel Smith in 'Minutes, 1852', q. 2149.
70 See for example the District of Columbia, 'Reports as to the taxation of land and buildings in European countries and the United States of America', *House of Commons Parliamentary Papers* 1890–91 lxxxiii (6209) 555 at 626–7.
71 See the evidence of Colonel Benjamin P. Johnson in 'Minutes, 1852', qq 1974–6, 1991–5; 2047.
72 'Papers bearing on land taxes, 1909', 457.
73 Ibid.
74 See the evidence of Colonel Benjamin P. Johnson in 'Minutes, 1852', q. 2013. The same was the case in Texas: see the evidence of Ashbel Smith, ibid., at q. 2154.

The administration of the property tax in the American states was considerably complicated by the multiplicity of jurisdictions involved. Although they looked to the English system as a model to some extent, and used local residents who were not always full-time nor necessarily properly trained to carry out the valuation and assessments, they differed markedly in that the assessing and collecting officers were directly responsible to the town authorities and indirectly to county and state authorities, or else directly to the state authorities. In West Virginia, for example, they were closely instructed and controlled by the state auditor[75] and supervised in the process by the county court. American state property tax officials were part of a clear hierarchy of local government officials, from the state fiscal officers of comptroller-general, the board of equalization and the treasurer, through the auditors, boards of supervisors, assessors, collectors and treasurers of the counties, cities and towns. They were not, as the English commissioners were, entirely independent of the control of the central tax authority.

ASSESSED TAXES AND INCOME TAX

The demands of Britain's war against France, and then of the long-term deficits it caused, placed successive political leaders under severe financial pressure. It led Pitt, Addington and Peel to look for new sources of finance from the close of the eighteenth century to the middle years of the nineteenth. The government introduced and extended the assessed taxes and, more radically, Pitt introduced the new income tax in 1799.[76] Addington refined the income tax to take its modern form, and Peel, after a suspension of some twenty-five years, reintroduced it in 1842.

All these new imposts made use of the principle of localism. The administration of the new taxes was placed in the hands of a local lay body of commissioners who appointed their own subordinate assessing and collecting officials. The assessed taxes were given to the land tax commissioners as additional duties. So, for example, they were to administer the window tax of 1747,[77] which imposed a fixed charge to tax on each inhabited house, and each window was subject to a further, progressive, charge, and appointed their own officers to do so. The assessors collected the necessary information, compiling lists of the occupiers of dwelling houses, the number of windows in each house and the sum to be paid in tax. The commissioners arrived at the assessments, prepared the necessary duplicates and issued the warrants for collection of the tax to the collectors.[78] Novel though Pitt's income tax

---

75 See Miller, *Laws of the state of West Virginia*, para. 5.
76 39 Geo. III c. 13.
77 20 Geo. II c. 3.
78 See generally, W.R. Ward, *The administration of the window and assessed taxes 1696–1798* (Canterbury, 1963).

was, its machinery of implementation was familiar. He placed the administration of this new 'general tax ... upon all the leading branches of income' in the hands of a lay and local body, the general commissioners of income tax.[79] It was a new body, though one appointed by and from the land tax commissioners themselves.[80] The general commissioners appointed assessors and collectors to undertake the practical work of distributing the tax returns, collecting the names of persons chargeable to tax and their statements of income, and ultimately collecting the tax itself, but the actual work of making the assessments to the income tax was in the hands of the commissioners themselves. They received the returns, examined them and made the assessments. Appreciating that these powers in the commissioners were necessarily wide and confidential, Pitt assured Parliament that they would be 'persons of a respectable situation in life; as far as possible removed from any suspicion of partiality, or any kind of undue influence; men of integrity and independence,'[81] qualities it was believed could be largely ensured through a high property qualification. They were in practice wealthy men of social standing in their country or mercantile communities. Pitt's system of commissioners was rearranged to some extent, with some amendment to the number and powers of bodies of commissioners, by Henry Addington in 1803, but these reforms were designed purely to make the administrative machinery simpler, and left the principle of localism untouched. Under that legislation the general commissioners became the supreme assessing and appellate body for income tax.[82] When Robert Peel's Tory government was forced to reintroduce the income tax in 1842, in order to meet a £5 million deficit inherited from the previous Whig administration, it was to be expected that he would adopt this traditional machinery of implementation. He did indeed do so, announcing[83] that he would adopt the machinery of the 1806 Income Tax Act[84] and the 1803 Taxes Management Act,[85] the latter applying to all taxes managed by the Commissioners of Stamps and Taxes. The Act of 1842 stated that the local commissioners were responsible for the execution of 'all Matters and Things relating to' income tax.[86]

There was, however, one development in the administration of the assessed taxes and the income tax that was of considerable significance for the future of localism. The assessed taxes legislation introduced an element of

---

79 So called because they were to carry out 'the general purposes of [the] Act'. Commercial commissioners were appointed to assess commercial income.
80 39 Geo. III c. 13 s.11.
81 *Parliamentary History*, vol. 34, 3 Dec. 1798, col. 6 *per* William Pitt.
82 43 Geo. III c. 122 s. 144.
83 *Parliamentary Debates* series 3, vol. 61, 18 Mar. 1842, HC, col. 910.
84 46 Geo. III c. 65.
85 43 Geo. III c. 99.
86 5 & 6 Vict. c. 35 s. 22.

active and effective central control and direction into the administrative process. The Treasury was to appoint salaried officers, called surveyors,[87] empowered to supervise the execution of the legislation by the local commissioners and acting under direct control and instruction of the tax office in London.[88] Under, for example, the window tax legislation of 1747,[89] that imposing a tax on male servants in 1777,[90] and that on inhabited houses in 1778[91] the surveyors could examine and challenge the assessments, and in order to ensure they were correct they were given the widest powers to inspect the properties themselves. They could amend the assessments if they found they were incorrect and could impose surcharges.[92] Their work in preventing evasion and abuse, and the extent of such practical central control over local administration of the taxes, is revealed by the reports of assessed tax cases published by the Tax Office. This official of central government constituted overt central control within the local administrative framework and thereby diminished the role of the local commissioners. This breach in the principle of localism was necessary for the effective administration of the tax, but paradoxically it enabled the system of local administration to continue. Without some central control and assistance the pressures that were emerging would have caused the local systems to collapse. Pitt had in earlier years expended much energy in overhauling the system of local amateur land tax administration with limited success. He had understood that its success required mutual cooperation between local and central agencies, and realized that professional surveyors were essential to the system's efficient working. He knew, however, that despite the many faults of the system and the undeniable need for increased central control, the traditional system of tax administration was the only possible system for his new income tax. He therefore declined to leave the full responsibility for ensuring correct taxation to the commissioners, and imposed on the government officer, the surveyor, the responsibility for bringing any doubts as to the correctness of the assessments to the attention of the commissioners, who could then call for further information from the taxpayer.[93] The surveyor accordingly had the power to inspect the returns and to object to them if he chose, while under the 1803 income tax legislation he retained the right to inspect the returns, and could make surcharges and appeal to the general commissioners in their appellate capacity. He attended all the meetings of the commissioners and

---

87 Surveyors had had more minor functions in early tax administration: see Adams, 'Early history of surveyors' at 294–5.
88 Ibid., at 296–300.
89 20 Geo. II c. 3 ss 30, 37.
90 17 Geo. III c. 39 s.15.
91 18 Geo. III c. 26 s. 23.
92 See Taxes Management Act 1803 (43 Geo. III c. 99) ss 20–1.
93 *Parliamentary History*, vol. 34, 3 Dec. 1798, col. 7.

was expected to provide full details of taxpayers on whom he had levied surcharges. He could, however, do nothing more. His power was limited to a somewhat detached observation; the ultimate authority and control remained with the commissioners. This limitation on the powers of central government was retained under Peel's income tax of 1842, for though the legislation provided that the Board of Inland Revenue had 'the Direction and Management' of the duties,[94] and there was a clear and public involvement of central government in the form of the retention of the surveyor, localism still dominated the process. The interference of the central government was limited to a 'general superintendence' by the Office of Stamps and Taxes.[95] While Pitt's adoption of a locally-based tax administration was essentially historical, based on the administration of the land tax, Peel's was a conscious and considered decision to retain it on its merits. He did not underestimate the popular importance of a familiar administrative machinery, nor the political importance of a relatively inexpensive system.

While the presence of the surveyor in the administration of the assessed taxes subjected the commissioners to an unprecedented degree of outside control, they lost yet a further degree of local control. Whereas in the case of the land tax, appeals beyond the commissioners themselves had been prohibited, in the case of the assessed taxes appeals to the courts of law from the appellate decisions of the commissioners were permitted from their inception. First appeals were heard and determined by the commissioners in the normal way. Both the aggrieved party and the surveyor could express his dissatisfaction with the outcome and demand that a case be stated to the superior courts of common law.[96] Under Pitt's income tax, by contrast, the local commissioners regained this element of control since the legislation permitted appeals to a lay and local body of commissioners of appeal,[97] that decision was final and any appeal to the regular courts was prohibited.[98] While it could be thought that opposition to the new income tax might be mitigated by giving a right of appeal to the courts of law, it was possibly precisely because the legislature knew the new tax would be very unpopular and foresaw excessive litigation if appeals were allowed to the courts of law that it denied this right and allowed only internal local appeal mechanisms.

94 5 & 6 Vict. c. 35 s. 3.
95 *Parliamentary Debates* series 3, vol. 61, 18 Mar. 1842, HC, col. 910.
96 21 Geo. II c.10 s. 10; 17 Geo. III c. 39 ss 21, 22 (servants); 18 Geo. III c. 26 ss 41, 42 (house duty); 25 Geo. III c. 43 ss 38, 39 (female servants); 25 Geo. III c. 47 ss 33, 34 (1785) (taxes management). See generally Ward, *Administration of the window and assessed taxes*.
97 39 Geo. III c. 13 ss 16, 64.
98 Appeals from the appellate decisions of the income tax commissioners was not permitted until 1874: Customs and Inland Revenue Act 1874 (37 Vict. c. 16) ss 9, 8, 10. The provision for an appeal to the courts by way of case stated was then included in the Taxes Management Act 1880 (43 & 44 Vict. c. 19), s. 59.

Possibly the legislature decided to err on the side of caution and forbid further appeal to the courts of law until it had ascertained the extent and nature of the demand. It foresaw unacceptable delays in the collection of the revenue. The same principle was adopted in relation to appeals under the income tax of 1803, with the appellate decisions of the commissioners still final and appeals to the regular courts prohibited.

FEDERAL TAXATION

At the same time as William Pitt was exploring all fiscal instruments in order to raise sufficient money to continue the war against France, so John Adams needed funds to prepare for a possible war with that country. Pitt's solution was a general income tax; Adams' was a direct federal tax on property. The federal government was limited in its ability to raise direct taxes by the constitution, and had traditionally preferred to rely on indirect taxation.[99] Any new direct tax had to be constitutionally sound, yet flexible so as to meet the differing circumstances of each state and engage sufficient popular support. Furthermore, while each state had its own fiscal machinery developed to meet its own particular customs, social circumstances and habits of the people and federal indirect taxation had an established machinery of its own, none existed for the administration of direct federal taxes. When Oliver Wolcott examined the state tax systems in 1796, it was precisely in order to see how far localism could be introduced into federal taxation. Like his contemporaries in England, he appreciated the importance of it both in ensuring the popular acceptance of a potentially highly unpopular tax, and in keeping the administrative costs to a minimum. While the British were not enamoured of taxation by central government, in imposing federal taxes on the American people Congress could expect particular resistance due to the constitutional structure of the country and the considerable attachment Americans felt towards their own particular state rather than the federal government. Wolcott agreed that if Congress could properly adopt the principles of the state systems to levy a direct federal tax, the dangers of experimentation and the delays inherent in establishing a new system would be avoided. Furthermore, he found the state systems quite efficient. '[H]abit,' he said, 'has rendered an acquiescence under the rules they impose, familiar.'[1] He appreciated that one reason for this success was that the state legislatures had 'a minute and particular knowledge of the circumstances and interests of the respective States'.[2] So diverse were they, however, that they

---

99 See generally Henry Carter Adams, 'Taxation in the United States 1789–1816' in Herbert B. Adams, *Institutions and economics*, ii (Baltimore, 1884), pp 5–45.
1 *American State Papers: Finance*, vol. 1, 4 Cong., 1 sess., pp 413–41 at p. 436 (13 Dec. 1796).
2 Ibid.

could not be used as machinery for the administration of federal tax. They were, he said, 'utterly discordant' and could not be reconciled.[3] Another major objection to adopting the laws of the states for a national tax was that there was a diversity of methods of collection. The southern states tended to appoint their tax officials through the state organs, while the northern states tended to appoint them through town elections. Lines of responsibility were unclear or weak, and tax officials open to public suspicion and personal temptation. The appointment of a single person as both assessor and collector equally led to abuse and an unclear responsibility. He felt it would be prohibitively expensive to establish officers in all districts to supervise collectors, and that it would be unsafe to allow assessors to be elected by the people and yet renounce the principle of local responsibility.

The difficulties inherent in establishing a new administrative structure for the assessment and collection of a federal direct tax led some members of Congress to oppose the imposition of a direct tax itself. It was felt that indirect taxation was by far preferable, since its machinery was already in place. To construct a new system of administration would, it was argued, be prohibitively expensive, even if a system could be agreed on. The systems of the states were so varied, that to adopt any one of them would mean the discontent of other states, for each had developed tax administration systems to suit their own circumstances and habits.[4] Nevertheless, it was clear that indirect taxation in time of war could not provide the necessary public revenue. A new direct tax would have to be imposed, and a new and independent administrative machinery would have to be established with the authority and control of the central federal government.

In 1798 Congress imposed a direct federal tax on land, slaves and houses. The administrative system supporting the new tax was found in two Acts of July 1798, the first providing for the valuation of the land and the enumeration of slaves[5] and the second for the apportionment and collection of the tax on houses, land and slaves.[6] The sum of two million dollars was to be raised, and was accordingly apportioned among the states. For the purposes of valuation, the country was to be divided into a number of divisions within the states. Sworn local resident commissioners were to be centrally appointed for each division, and empowered to appoint 'respectable freeholders' to act as principal and assistant assessors. All officers appointed under the legislation were to be remunerated. The commissioners were to establish all necessary regulations 'as ... shall appear suitable and necessary'

---

3   Ibid., at p. 43.
4   See *Annals of Congress*, 4 Cong., 2 sess., 1880–1881 (16 Jan.1797) *per* Joseph B. Varnum in the house of representatives.
5   Act of 9 July 1798, 5 Cong., 2 sess., ch. lxx.
6   Act of 14 July 1798, 5 Cong., 2 sess., ch. lxxv.

for the administration of the tax in their district and all instructions to the assessors. The assessors were to inquire into, enumerate and value all houses, lands and slaves in their division according to the provisions of the act and the instructions of the commissioners. The assessors were to obtain written lists of each taxpayer's property, and if a taxpayer refused to do so, or submitted a fraudulent list, the assessor would compile it himself according to the best information he could and the taxpayer would face financial penalties. Once the valuations and enumerations were made, the principal assessor would make the lists available for public inspection, and he would hear and determine appeals against any erroneous valuation or enumeration by the assessor. The lists would then be sent to the commissioners, who after correcting any errors, would transmit them to the Treasury. As to the subsequent assessment and collection, the legislation established a full federal administrative structure, making use of the existing machinery whereby the federal internal revenue duties[7] were raised, namely the supervisors of the internal revenue districts, and the inspectors of the surveys into which the districts were divided. These officers were to act under the direction of the Secretary of the Treasury. The supervisors made the assessments and were given the authority to appoint additional collectors if they found it necessary. While Congress could not directly employ state machinery to administer its new direct tax, the appointment of local boards of commissioners and their power to make the rules for assessment that would reflect local conditions and to appoint local assessors at the delicate valuation stage showed sensitivity to the importance of localism. Thus Congress, as Parliament, used local tax administration as a tool of political appeasement.

Congress did not lose sight of the importance of localism in subsequent direct federal taxation, though it adopted a different approach. Proposals for a substantial federal administrative structure were strongly criticised and the American resentment of tax administration by professional officers of central government was seen to be just as strong as that of the English. The American people had never liked centralized tax administration. Indeed, one of the objections to the imposition of new import duties by the British on America in 1767 was centred on the British establishment of customs commissioners in America itself to collect the duties, and equally after independence strong objection was taken to the implementation of the hated whisky excise in 1791 by federal officers. During the extensive debates on the civil war scheme of taxation, which comprised direct taxes[8] and for the first time a federal income tax,[9] Roscoe Conkling said that 'one of the most

---

7   Notably the duties on spirits, snuff, sugar, auction sales and carriages of the 1790s.
8   See generally, Charles F. Dunbar, 'The direct tax of 1861', *Quarterly Journal of Economics*, 3:4 (July 1889), 436–61.
9   See generally, Joseph A. Hill, 'The civil war income tax', *Quarterly Journal of Economics*, 8:4 (July 1894), 416–52.

obnoxious – perhaps the most obnoxious – of all [the bill's] features is that which creates an army of officers whose business it is to collect these taxes'.[10] 'It provides,' he said,

> oppressive modes of assessment and collection, ... It will deprive every State of the power to collect this tax by the mode known to its laws, out of all property taxable within its jurisdiction. It will supersede entirely the old-fashioned, economical system of laying and collecting taxes which our people are accustomed to and approve of, and puts in its place a system more unendurable than the tax itself.[11]

He said he was 'struggling for an arrangement by which that smaller army of office-seekers, and less odious one, provided by the States themselves, shall avoid the necessity of such a provision on the part of the Federal Government'.[12] He referred to the 'myriad of Federal emissaries',[13] 'this mammoth machine'.[14] Expense was an important factor of opposition.[15] One speaker referred to 'an army of twenty-five thousand office-holders'.[16] The only way the state machinery could legitimately be used for the administration of a federal tax was to adopt a quota system whereby each state would pay an allotted sum assessed and collected in the same way as state and local taxes were. That would save the considerable expense and delay of organizing the federal machinery for administering the tax. This method had been used in 1813 for the direct taxes on gold, silverware, jewellery and watches[17] necessary to fund the French war, and that legislation gave each state the option to raise and pay its own quota to the United States Treasury using its own rules and machinery. Only if a state chose not to do so would federal officers be used to assess and collect the tax. The granting of this option was political in motive, to placate the states and lessen the impact of a direct and centralized federal tax. In appreciating local values and customs the taxes gave rise to considerably less hostility, a fact clearly understood in 1813 and again in the 1860s.

A federal system was, however, necessary, and in this the American legislature faced a particular challenge. It was needed as a default system where states chose not to raise and pay their own quotas by their own

---

10 *Congressional Globe*, 37 Cong., 1 sess. 247 (July 1861) *per* Roscoe Conkling.
11 Ibid., at 272.
12 Ibid., at 284.
13 Ibid., at 285.
14 Ibid., at 286.
15 Ibid., at 299–300 *per* Messrs Shellabarger and Sedgwick.
16 Ibid., at 329 *per* Frederick Conkling.
17 Act of 22 July 1813, 13 Cong., 1 sess., ch. 16 (assessment and collection); Act of 2 Aug. 1813, 13 Cong., 1 sess., ch. 37 (apportionment).

machinery, and to administer the new federal income tax of 1861.[18] In view of the strength of feeling expressed in Congress, the system introduced in 1813 and adopted in its essentials during the civil war, though still a full bureaucratic structure, was considerably simpler, and therefore cheaper, than that of 1798. The office of supervisor was abolished, and each state was divided into collection districts, with a principal assessor and collector for each, who were to be respectable freeholders residing in the district and properly remunerated. The assessment process was similar to that for state property taxes, with the assessor or his assistant being the key official in the field, to make the assessments and frequently to hear appeals.[19] Where possible, for ease and economy, it was suggested that the lower grade officers in the field were to be drawn from those exercising similar functions under

18 Act of 5 Aug. 1861, 37 Cong., 1 sess., ch. 45 s. 49. It provided that the tax 'shall be levied, collected, and paid, upon annual income of every person residing in the U.S. whether derived from any kind of property, or from any professional trade, employment, or vocation carried on in the United States or elsewhere, or from any source whatever'. Rates under the Act were 3% on income above $800 and 5% on income of individuals living outside the U.S. The federal income tax was abolished in 1872, revived in 1894, and declared unconstitutional in 1895 on the basis that it was a direct tax which was not apportioned among the states on the basis of population in conformity with the Constitution (*Pollock v. Farmers' Loan and Trust Company* 157 U.S. 429 (1895); 158 U.S. 601 (1895). It was only securely reintroduced in 1913 after the passing of the Sixteenth Amendment to the Constitution which provided that 'The Congress shall have power to lay and collect taxes on incomes, from whatever source derived, without any apportionment among the several States, and without regard to any census or enumeration'. The literature is prodigious. See, for example, the contemporary comment of Gordon E. Sherman, 'The recent constitutional amendments', *Yale Law Journal*, 23 (Dec. 1913), 129–57; Dwight W. Morrow, 'The income tax amendment', *Columbia Law Review*, 10 (May 1910), 379–415; Joseph A. Hill, 'The income tax of 1913', *Quarterly Journal of Economics*, 28 (Nov. 1913), 46–68; Roy G. Blakey, 'The new income tax', *American Economic Review*, 4 (1914), 25–46; the modern analysis of Bruce Ackerman, 'Taxation and the constitution', *Columbia Law Review*, 99 (1999), 1–58. See too Arthur A. Ekirch Jr., 'The sixteenth amendment: the historical background', *Cato Journal*, 1 (Spring 1981), 161–82.

19 Act of 22 Jul. 1813, 13 Cong., 1 sess., ch. 16, ss 5–16; Act of 5 Aug. 1861, 37 Cong., 1 sess., ch. 45 ss 14, 50; Act of 1 Jul. 1862, 37 Cong., 2 sess., c. 119, ss 2–17; Act of 30 June 1864, 38 Cong., 1 sess., ch. 173 ss 11–24, 118. All subsequent federal income tax legislation made provision for aggrieved taxpayers to appeal from assessing decisions. In 1924 a board of tax appeals was created, which was based in Washington DC but heard appeals all over the country. The board, later known as the tax court, grew out of dissatisfaction with existing appeals provision, and while it was originally envisaged as an independent, informal and non-legalistic tribunal, it ultimately became a significantly more legalistic form of tribunal than was in use in England and is now a federal court of record staffed by judges experienced in tax law. See generally Anon., 'The tax court, the courts of appeals and pyramiding judicial review', *Stanford Law Review*, 9:4 (July 1957), 827–33, and the authorities there cited; Harold Dubroff, *The United States tax court* (Chicago, 1979); James O. Eaton, 'The legal battlefield of income tax administration', *Accounting Review*, 26:3 (July 1951), 371–83.

state authority.[20] The need for uniformity and strong central control was appreciated, and accordingly the Secretary of the Treasury was to establish the necessary binding regulations for implementing the legislation.[21] In 1813 a Commissioner of the Revenue was established in the department of the Treasury to superintend all officers employed in assessing and collecting federal taxation.[22] In this central office lay the origins of the Internal Revenue Service.[23] The entire scheme and its machinery consisted of a sensible and effective union of localism and centralism.

THE DECLINE OF LOCALISM

Though the principle of localism was, by statute, applied throughout the English fiscal system in the mid nineteenth century, it was already revealing profound social, economic and political tensions, caused primarily by the radical changes brought about by the industrial revolution. Commercial conditions had changed considerably in the forty years between Pitt's and Peel's income taxes. It was the particular nature of the income tax that exposed the frailties of the application of localism to tax administration. Where the tax was relatively non-inquisitorial, as with the land tax, local assessment and collection was an appropriate and welcome machinery of administration. The land tax had been inherently non-confrontational: a sum to be raised had been determined by Parliament, and subdivided among the different districts, and each landowner paid according to his property, not to his income. The disputes that arose in the course of the administration of the tax were not disputes between the taxpayer and the government, but between the taxpayers themselves. 'This', it was said, 'was a wise provision of our

---

20 *Congressional Globe*, 37 Cong., 2 sess. 1195 (Mar. 1862).
21 Act of 22 July 1813, 13 Cong., 1 sess., ch. 16, s. 4 ; Act of 5 Aug. 1861, 37 Cong., 1 sess., ch. 45, s. 12; Act of 1 July 1862, 37 Cong., 2 sess., ch. 119, s. 6; Act of 30 June 1864, 38 Cong., 1 sess., ch. 173, ss 8, 12.
22 Act of 24 July 1813, 13 Cong., 1 sess., ch. 22. See too Act of 5 Aug. 1861, 37 Cong., 1 sess., ch. 45, s.56; Act of 1 July 1862, 37 Cong., 2 sess., ch. 119, s.1; Act of 30 June 1864, 38 Cong., 1 sess., ch. 173, s. 1.
23 See Act of 1 July 1862, 37 Cong., 2 sess., ch. 119, s. 89; Act of 30 June 30 1864, 38 Cong., 1 sess., ch. 173. The federal income tax of 1913 was implemented by a professional federal Internal Revenue Service. The district collector would receive the sworn tax returns of individual taxpayers and the assessment would be made by the staff of the Internal Revenue Service. If the return was suspect or non-existent, the collector could summon the taxpayer and examine him and his books, and any other witnesses. See generally, Edwin R.A. Seligman, 'The federal income tax', *Political Science Quarterly*, 29:1 (March 1914), 1–27; James Coffield, *A popular history of taxation* (London, 1970), pp 221–34. For the history of the Internal Revenue Service, see generally Lillian Doris (ed.), *The American way in taxation: internal revenue, 1862–1963* (Englewood Cliffs, NJ, 1963).

ancestors, because they knew that such contests were not consistent with civil liberty.'[24] The income tax, on the other hand, by its nature potentially brought the taxpayer into direct conflict with the government.

The weaknesses of the localist system arose from its two essential characteristics, namely that it was lay and it was local. A lay body meant an amateur body. In order to meet the requirements of local commercial knowledge, and to satisfy the statutory property requirements, commissioners were generally landowners involved with the administration of their estates, or merchants, businessmen or bankers. Many were usually still working in some capacity, though often a reduced capacity if they were elderly or sufficiently wealthy. They all had other demands on their time and energies, and were, furthermore, unremunerated for their work in tax administration. This created tensions, particularly with the central government. The government wanted the tax administered efficiently, competently, promptly and uniformly, to ensure the greatest yield and a steady and predictable flow of revenue. As commerce increased in both scale and complexity, and the country generally became wealthier, so the income tax necessarily followed suit. The quantity of work grew, and part-time unremunerated commissioners with their own businesses or professions to tend to could not or would not devote sufficient time to the demands of their office. The Board of Inland Revenue increasingly complained that the local system was not administering the tax efficiently and that the local commissioners and their officials were not dedicated to their task. The board felt the local officials did not feel any sense of responsibility towards the Exchequer and complained that many assessors and collectors were illiterate, incapable and even corrupt.[25] In 1869, for example, an impatient board complained that the dog licence was being 'imperfectly levied by parochial assessors', and indeed was proved correct when the number of dogs licensed rose by half a million on the board taking responsibility for the tax.[26] In the same year the board reported that a local assessor, a butcher by trade, had declined to charge a taxpayer on his horse and carriage because if he had done so he would have lost his custom.[27] Though the legislation imposed a duty on the board to supervise the proceedings of local officials, it provided limited, dilatory and cumbersome remedies to use in the case of incompetent lay officials. The board was firm in its belief that if the assessed taxes were put under its own sole

24 *Parliamentary History*, vol. 34, 31 Dec. 1798, cols 143–4 *per* John Nicholls.
25 'Sixth annual report of the Commissioners of Inland Revenue 1862', *House of Commons Parliamentary Papers* 1862 xxvii (3047) 327 at 344–5, 350; 'Thirteenth annual report of the Commissioners of Inland Revenue 1870', *House of Commons Parliamentary Papers* 1870 xx (82) 193 at 207.
26 'Twelfth annual report of the Commissioners of Inland Revenue', *House of Commons Parliamentary Papers* 1869 xviii (4049) 607 at 617.
27 Ibid., at 635.

management and control, the tax yield would increase considerably. 'And we believe,' the report of 1869 continued, 'that since we first began to ventilate the subject, a great change has taken place in public opinion respecting the antiquated, cumbrous, and inefficient system absurdly named "self taxation", and that there will be no difficulty now in superseding it by a better arrangement'.[28] A surveyor writing to *The Times* in 1873 said the functions of the additional commissioners of income tax were in many districts poorly performed. In many instances their numbers had dwindled through death or resignation, 'or they shirk the odium and responsibility of their task till the tax becomes a mere voluntary payment at the discretion of the taxpayer ...'[29] He argued that either the additional commissioners should be strengthened or they should be abolished. He said the clerks were 'functionaries wholly useless' who often discharged their duties in a 'slipshod and irregular manner'.[30] The board also felt the law was not being administered uniformly, that the local system of administration both permitted and encouraged local variations.

The principal problem was one of time and, indirectly, expertise. The commissioners themselves were not entirely at fault. As laymen, any expert knowledge they had was acquired through reading or experience. They had no formal training, but had a general knowledge of business, finance and, what was viewed as most important, local conditions. While local knowledge may well have sufficed in Pitt's time, when trade and industry were relatively small scale, carried on in small geographical areas and largely self-contained, it was no longer adequate in a rapidly expanding commercial context. The making of income tax assessments was a technical and complex matter, requiring knowledge of tax law and accountancy, and an intimate knowledge of income tax practice. As income tax became more complex, so their mere local knowledge and any practical experience they had acquired became inadequate for their task. Taxpayers were equally concerned with this, and were aware that in many cases the local knowledge of the commissioners, which in theory was an important feature in arriving at an assessment to tax, was becoming little more than a general impression of the income of taxpayers, gleaned from gossip and outward appearances of their style of living.

While it was the amateur nature of the administrative system that caused tensions with central government, it was principally its local nature that caused tensions and considerable resentment among taxpayers. Commissioners and their officials, being local men resident in the tax district, were geographically and socially in constant and inevitable contact with the taxpayers. The main problems were the necessary invasion of privacy and the danger of commercial or social bias.

28 Ibid.
29 *The Times*, letters to the editor, 27 Jan. 1873.
30 Ibid.

By its very nature, the income tax was inquisitorial. Its administration necessitated a close investigation into the private financial affairs of individuals. The inevitable disclosure of personal property it entailed and the inquisitorial powers necessarily given to the implementing bodies to effect that disclosure were the main objections to the income tax.[31] It was presented as a constitutional argument, as an infringement of fundamental freedoms. 'I think it infinitely preferable,' said Sir John Sinclair in 1798, 'that we should lose some money, than run the risk of establishing principles abhorrent to that free constitution which this country has hitherto boasted of'.[32] Michael Taylor saw the inquisitorial nature of the tax as undermining the constitutional right of sanctity of private property. 'The genius of the constitution of England was,' he said, 'that a man's property was sacred. It was upon the strength of that principle that every man's house was called his castle'.[33] Under the income tax legislation, however, 'a spy comes, not only into the House, but opens the bureau of every man, and becomes acquainted with his most secret concerns. A man must show to this spy his bills, his notes, his bonds, and all his securities'.[34] Similarly, Sir William Pulteney believed the tax and its machinery undermined the individual's security of property, which was itself a fundamental freedom of the English people.[35] He thought the income tax bill was 'dangerous in its very nature' and that it 'encroached in an alarming degree, upon the principles of the constitution'.[36] Another speaker said the inquisitorial power the tax involved was 'not only unknown to the constitution, but totally subversive of it'.[37] The perception of an inquisitorial tax being unconstitutional persisted, for in 1806 'A Northern Freeholder' wrote that the disclosure of a man's private financial affairs to his neighbours made 'the principles of Magna Charta and the Bill of Rights; our ancient privileges; our birth-rights as Britons ... give way to the concerns of the tax-office',[38] and in the debate on the proposal to continue the income tax in 1816 despite the close of hostilities with France, Richard Preston called it 'the illegitimate offspring, the bastard of the constitution'.[39] When the income tax was reintroduced by Peel in 1842 the arguments against it were identical to those raised in 1798 and again in 1816, namely its inquisitorial

---

31 Though see Phillips, 'The real objection', 177–86.
32 *Parliamentary History*, vol. 34, 14 Dec. 1798, col. 84 *per* Sir John Sinclair.
33 Ibid., at col. 90 *per* Michael Taylor.
34 Ibid., at col. 91.
35 Ibid., 22 Dec.1798, col. 134 *per* Sir William Pulteney.
36 Ibid., at col. 138.
37 Ibid., col. 140 *per* Thomas Jones.
38 *Cobbett's Political Register*, vol. ix, 17 May 1806, col. 752.
39 *Parliamentary Debates*, series 1, vol. 33, 7 Mar. 1816, HC, col. 30 *per* Richard Preston. The tax was universally condemned and, to loud cheers, Parliament found against the proposal: ibid., 18 Mar. 1816, col. 451.

nature and machinery. Indeed Peel admitted, and had always admitted,[40] that the tax would require a close examination of a taxpayer's private financial affairs, and was accordingly inquisitorial, but thought nevertheless it was 'one of the best taxes that can be imposed'.[41] The adoption of the traditional machinery did little to quell the cries of inquisition,[42] and the strength of feeling against the income tax was apparent from the debates in Parliament in the spring of 1842.[43] To the cheers of the house Richard Sheil said that '[t]he evils of the Income-tax are so monstrous, that it is almost impossible to heighten them – they set hyperbole at defiance'. It was, he said, 'an impost ... which ... is the most prejudicial to the interests, offensive to the feelings, abhorrent to the religious sentiments, and revolting to the moral sense of the English people'.[44] Sir William Somerville said there was 'out of doors a general, not to say an universal, feeling prevalent against the inquisitorial nature of this tax',[45] while Percy Smythe called the tax 'repugnant to the practice of the constitution ... inimical to the common practice of the constitution ...'[46]

It was said that the English had particularly strong prejudice against disclosure of private financial affairs. At the end of the eighteenth century Charles Abbot maintained it was more pronounced in England than in any other country in Europe,[47] and called it 'a prejudice which universally existed'.[48] The French revolution had had a significant impact in this respect, as it had encouraged a measure of both national and personal insularity. The right to keep one's financial affairs a private matter was regarded as a civil liberty, particularly when their disclosure could have such a profound social or professional effect on the individual. Commercial men were particularly concerned, for disclosure of their business affairs might affect their very livelihood and certainly would affect their ability to attract credit. They also feared commercial espionage and misuse of the information by commissioners or officials who might be their rivals in trade. English taxpayers had

---

40 In the debate on the repeal of the house and window taxes and whether they should be replaced by a property and income tax in 1833, Sir Robert Peel had admitted that the latter would necessarily entail a 'rigorous inquisition,' a 'severe and unsparing scrutiny' into men's property:' *Parliamentary Debates* series 3, vol. 17, 30 Apr. 1833, HC, at col. 816.
41 Ibid., vol. 61, 18 Mar. 1842, col. 909.
42 Ibid., 21 Mar. 1842, col. 944 *per* Benjamin Hawes, at col. 980 *per* Lord Dalmeny; ibid., 23 Mar. 1842, col. 1229 *per* Charles Buller.
43 See for example the speech of Richard Sheil, *Parliamentary Debates* series 3, vol. 62, 8 Apr. 1842, HC, cols 142–53.
44 Ibid., cols 152–3.
45 Ibid.,col. 140 *per* Sir William Somerville.
46 Ibid., 22 Apr. 1842, col. 1039 *per* Percy S. Smythe.
47 *Parliamentary History*, vol. 34, 31 Dec. 1798 col. 146.
48 *The Times*, 1 Jan. 1799.

the strongest distaste for colleagues and equals becoming familiar with their private financial affairs.

Even if the state taxes had been inquisitorial, the Americans had, on the whole, a different attitude to the disclosure of private financial affairs. Their society was considerably more democratic than that of England, and accordingly less exercised by the question of appearances in society or commercial life. This profound social and cultural distinction considerably affected attitudes to tax administration. In general, therefore, a digest of the returns for state and local taxation, consisting usually of a list of the names of taxable individuals, the quantity and value of the real property of each and sums assessed upon individuals, was available in a convenient location for public inspection.[49] There were some sensitivities, however. It was said that in the state of New York, if a man considered that he had been over assessed on his personal estate, he might be reluctant to appeal against it to his local assessors, and would instead make his objection to the board of supervisors who were a local, but more remote, body.[50] Though not bound by an oath of secrecy,[51] assessors for the state property taxes were not to disclose the individual returns of personal property, as the damage to commercial men of the disclosure of their financial situation was understood as it was in England.[52] Only the final assessment roll was open for public inspection, not the details underlying it. Nevertheless, the exact amount of a taxpayer's property became public knowledge since it stated his real property and its value, and the amount of his personal property. However, the initial degree of disclosure required from commercial men was not as stringent as the authorities would have liked. An individual only had to make a general statement, albeit on oath, and he did not have to disclose full details of his business or his debtors and creditors. To demand such disclosure would, it was said, 'be a very hazardous and disastrous thing' for commercial men.[53] As to income tax, the civil war legislation did not prohibit the disclosure of the information in the returns and it seems that a custom developed of publishing the lists of taxpayers and their incomes.[54] Such was the public resistance to this publicity, however, that it was prohibited by later legislation, and when the first permanent income tax was introduced in 1913 it followed the English pattern and made it unlawful for any officer of the Internal Revenue to disclose any such information.

49 See, for example, Miller, *Laws of the state of West Virginia*, para. 79.
50 See the evidence of Colonel Benjamin P. Johnson in 'Minutes, 1852', q. 1995.
51 They were bound by a general oath of allegiance to the constitution of the United States and of the state of New York, and to faithfully discharge the duties of their office.
52 See the evidence of Colonel Benjamin P. Johnson in 'Minutes, 1852', qq 2040; 2065–7.
53 Ibid., at q. 2067
54 Joseph A. Hill, 'The civil war income tax', *Quarterly Journal of Economics*, 8:4 (July 1894), 416 at 436.

The English resentment as to the fact of inquisition was focussed on the machinery of the tax. The assessment and collection of the tax by local men of standing in the community exposed the private affairs of individuals to the scrutiny of their friends, neighbours, political opponents, commercial competitors or social rivals. This opened the way at worst to the danger of political bias and commercial espionage, and at least to embarrassment or humiliation. Those who carried out the tax were bound to be regarded as 'spies and informers'[55] and in 1842 the administrative system was referred to as the 'nefarious machinery'.[56] Even a commissioner under the old tax condemned the system as 'espionage' and the tax as 'burdensome ... inquisitorial ... odious'. He wished, he said 'to put the people on their guard as to the machinery employed...'[57] Charles Buller described the various bodies of commissioners as 'instruments of a very grinding tyranny' because of the extent of their inquisitorial and their judicial powers to fine.[58] In practice there was little if any evidence either of bias on the part of local commissioners against rivals in trade, nor of disclosure of private financial affairs. It is likely that there were some instances of both, but the evidence suggests that such occasions were rare. On the other hand, there is no doubt that taxpayers themselves felt uncomfortable at appearing before their colleagues in income tax appeals. The involvement of government officers, however, was no solution. Indeed, the fact that any inquisitorial powers were in the hands of an officer of central government exacerbated deeply felt objections. Although Pitt had said that he was persuaded that the role he had given to the surveyor would be 'most acceptable to the general feeling',[59] his opponents in the house were not convinced. George Tierney described the surveyor as an 'infamous informer',[60] and Michael Taylor said the government officers 'went around at random, and surcharged, without caring what they do'.[61] 'The mischief of this', he said, 'was in many cases monstrous.'[62] Pitt defended the surveyor and in so doing confirmed the traditional principle of localism by stressing the subordinate nature of that office. 'The surveyor is not to be a person on whose discretion any assessment is to depend: he is to assist the commissioners with information, and to discharge that duty which his oath prescribes, of preventing evasion where it might be within his knowledge that it was attempted'.[63] Any surcharge by the surveyor,

---

55 *Parliamentary Debates* series 3, vol. 61, 4 Apr. 1842, HC, col. 1267 *per* Milner Gibson.
56 Ibid., vol. 62, 18 Apr. 1842, HC, col. 694 *per* Thomas Duncombe.
57 Ibid., vol. 61, 4 Apr. 1842, HC, cols 1272–3 *per* Robert Wallace.
58 Ibid., vol. 62, 22 Apr. 1842, HC col. 1000 *per* Charles Buller.
59 *Parliamentary History*, vol. 34 , 3 Dec.1798, col. 7.
60 Ibid., col. 22 *per* George Tierney.
61 Ibid., 14 Dec. 1798, col. 90 *per* Michael Taylor.
62 Ibid.
63 Ibid., col. 102 *per* William Pitt.

he said, would have to be confirmed by the commissioners, and it was of course always open to the legislature to amend the powers of that officer.[64] This popular perception, and an increasing realization along with the central government authorities that local knowledge was becoming inadequate for the purpose of tax assessment, led to a certain lack of public confidence in the traditional local machinery of tax administration.

Public support for the local administration of taxes depended on maintaining a high quality of appointment, particularly in view of the considerable concerns as to disclosure. Most local communities were satisfied with their commissioners, but there was significant criticism as to their mode of appointment. Appointments of all tax commissioners were based on that of the land tax commissioners, and that was a process that was neither open nor understood. Once the Names Bill had been introduced to Parliament, the Board of Inland Revenue would request all clerks to local commissioners to instruct their commissioners to draw up a list of suitable persons to act as land tax commissioners, bearing in mind that an important duty would then be to choose general commissioners of income tax. The list would be sent to the local member of Parliament, who had complete discretion to approve, amend or reject it. Other than the justices of the peace, who were appointed ex officio, it was unknown how other individuals came to be included in the list, though there is evidence to suggest the system was highly localised and new commissioners were chosen by existing commissioners from among their own social and professional circles.[65] In the budget debate of 1853 John Bright condemned the process as nothing short of 'hocus-pocus'.[66] There was support for the adoption of the American system of electing assessors in order to prevent the appointment of commissioners who might be prone to bias.[67] Richard Cobden praised the election by American taxpayers of 'experienced, able, discreet men, of the town and neighbourhood'[68] who made the assessments upon their neighbours. If a man there felt he had been overcharged, he could take an oath or produce his books. In that country, he said, there were no complaints as to the system, and he could see no reason why this should not be adopted in England.[69] The chancellor of the Exchequer argued that the plan was impracticable since it was not possible to ascertain by name all those who had paid tax under all the schedules, and it would also entail the identification of taxpayers who had been exempted from

64 Ibid., cols 101–2.
65 See 'Sixth annual report of the Commissioners of Inland Revenue 1862', *House of Commons Parliamentary Papers* 1862 xxvii (3047) 327 at 343.
66 *Parliamentary Debates*, series 3, vol. 127, 27 May 1853, HC, at col. 717.
67 Ibid., 23 May 1853, HC, at col. 536, *per* John Blackett; ibid., 27 May 1853, HC, at cols 717–18 *per* John Bright.
68 Ibid., vol. 126, 28 Apr. 1853, HC, col. 689 *per* Richard Cobden.
69 Ibid., at col. 690.

payment through low incomes, breaching the tradition of secrecy in income taxation. Though he did agree the machinery needed some reform, and called it 'an old and somewhat crude system',[70] any reform was complicated because of the time needed to introduce new machinery and the fact that the machinery dealt with many taxes and not just income tax.[71] Generally speaking there were no serious difficulties in appointing commissioners of a sufficiently high calibre, though in industrial centres the residency requirement caused recruitment difficulties as increasingly businessmen did not live at their places of business.

It is clear that increased central control would have eased most of the tensions caused by the decline in the efficacy and appropriateness of the principle of localism in tax administration and provided efficient workable solutions for both government and public. The central government had an expert, professional, full-time, salaried, dedicated and detached staff who would undertake the work of tax assessment and collection efficiently and effectively. It would ensure that each taxpayer in every part of the country paid his due taxes promptly so that the government could receive a constant, predictable, prompt and secure flow of public revenue to finance its activities. Such central control would, however, evidently undermine the traditional local system. Taxpayers were ambivalent in their views, in that they criticized the system for its invasive nature and the danger of disclosure, but valued it highly as a constitutional principle which asserted their independence and protected them from the rapacity of the crown and were always suspicious of the centralization which was dominating all aspects of their lives. The executive despised it as inefficient and wasteful, and yet appreciated the protection it gave its officials from public odium and the emphasis it gave to the consensual nature of taxation. However, views on the value of localism in tax administration began to polarize. Taxpayers wanted this buffer between themselves and the crown, and were vociferous in their determination to retain the system, while the Inland Revenue wanted efficiency and made repeated attempts to extend their jurisdiction at the expense of the local institutions.

As a result, the nineteenth century saw a continuous struggle between the taxpaying public and the central government as to which system of tax administration to adopt. So entrenched was the principle of localism in tax administration, both ideologically and practically, that there was no question of outright abolition. When in 1853 the question came up in Parliament as to the revision of the entire machinery, it was recognized that such a time-consuming and complex task could not be achieved without endangering the smooth and constant collection of the public revenue. Earlier fears as to the

---

70 Ibid., vol. 127, 30 May 1853, HC, col. 813 *per* the chancellor of the Exchequer.
71 Ibid., 27 May 1853, cols 720–2.

momentum of tax administration machinery once established were thus seen to have been well founded. Instead the struggle took the form of rare formal and express legislative inroads into the principle, numerous attempts by the executive to assume some of the local bodies' duties supported by official recommendations to that effect, and the public resistance to them, some local abdication of responsibility and a significant degree of insidious growth of central authority within the orthodox system.

An early inroad into the principle of localism was made by Peel himself in response to the very real public fears of local publicity. Pitt had fully appreciated the problem and had gone to considerable lengths in his legislation to ensure the secrecy of individual fiscal affairs was maintained, particularly in the commercial sphere where the concerns were the greatest.[72] The popular feeling was undiminished when Peel proposed the reintroduction of the tax, and his approach was, despite his protestations to the contrary, one that undermined the principle of localism. In maintaining the traditional principle, he had found a weakness that could only be addressed by its breach. He extended the powers of the special commissioners, a tribunal of officials appointed by central government and introduced by Pitt in 1805[73] so as to enable them to assess commercial income and to hear appeals against assessments on such income if the taxpayer chose to do so.[74] Peel admitted that it was 'more consistent with former usage to employ local parties in each neighbourhood to collect the tax',[75] but was pragmatic in his approach and unequivocal in the status of the tribunal. He said the special commissioners would be 'under the control of the Government, and appointed by the Tax-office'.[76] They were, in effect, salaried civil servants. While this was undoubtedly a breach of the traditional principle, it was a very circumscribed breach. It applied in the specific and limited field of commercial income, and was intended to meet a real practical problem that undermined not only the potential yield of the tax, but its very acceptance by Parliament. However, he wanted the breach of the principle to go no further. He determined to keep the local and government commissioners quite distinct and each under their own governance.[77] Such formal inroads into the principle of localism were rare. The extension of the powers of the special

---

72 See Chantal Stebbings, 'The budget of 1798: legislative provision for secrecy in income taxation', *British Tax Review* (1998), 651–65.
73 45 Geo. III c. 49 s. 30.
74 5 & 6 Vict. c. 35 s. 131; 'Minutes, 1852', qq 1036ff, q.1311; 'Minutes of evidence before the royal commission on the income tax', *House of Commons Parliamentary Papers* 1919–20 xxiii, (288–4) qq 13,781–83.
75 *Parliamentary Debates*, series 3, vol. 61, 18 Mar. 1842, HC, col. 912.
76 Ibid.
77 Ibid., vol. 62, 2 May 1842, HC, col. 1384 *per* Sir Robert Peel; see too ibid., 18 Apr. 1842, HC, col. 657 *per* Sir Robert Peel where he proposes the creation of special commissioners.

commissioners gave rise to remarkably little comment in Parliament, and their full significance passed almost unnoticed. Only Charles Buller observed that the inquisitorial, penal and secretive machinery of the income tax was unconstitutional, and was made even more so because it now included commissioners appointed by the crown.[78] The paucity of comment was the first evidence that the principle of localism in tax administration was not going to endure.

The popular perception was clearly that the Board of Inland Revenue was hostile to this traditional division of function and the protection which assessment by independent local commissioners afforded to the taxpayer.[79] Numerous attempts were made by the board to assume the duties of the local administrative bodies and to take complete control of the assessment and collection of income tax. Notably there were periodic attempts to remove the right of the local commissioners to appoint their own officials. Though these were strongly resisted, and the right jealously guarded,[80] there was an unrelenting and to some degree successful movement to allow collectors to be appointed by the Board of Inland Revenue. While this was optional, in that the board only appointed a collector when the commissioners failed to do so, in 1883 the government attempted to ensure that the board filled all vacancies arising in the future in relation to collection of commercial and employment income, areas where disclosure to government officials was still sensitive.[81] The reform had been proposed by the Associated Chambers of Commerce, and it had the added advantage of saving money, since it was shown to be cheaper to collect the tax by government collectors earning a salary than local collectors remunerated by poundage.

This ostensibly sensible reform narrowly failed, unsurprisingly perhaps in the current climate of opposition to increasing centralization. The member for Manchester called it a 'striking change, which really aimed at the alteration of ... the Constitutional collection of the Income Tax', and one that tended towards 'compulsory centralization'.[82] William Smith said it undermined 'one of the ancient safeguards which were thought to be necessary in raising the tax originally',[83] and recalling the words of Sir Robert Peel in 1842, he observed that the constitutional principle of localism in tax administration was 'a sound principle of human nature'.[84] The prevailing

---

78 Ibid., 22 Apr. 1842, HC, col. 1001 *per* Charles Buller.
79 See for example the leader in *The Times*, 'Income-tax administration', 12 Sept. 1928, p.13 col.c.
80 This had been resisted as early as 1842: *Parliamentary Debates*, series 3 vol. 62, 2 May 1842, HC, col. 1384 *per* Sir Robert Peel.
81 Ibid., vol. 279, 10 May 1883, HC, cols 488–506. See too B.E.V. Sabine, 'The general commissioners', *British Tax Review* (1968) 18–42 at 30–31.
82 *Parliamentary Debates*, series 3, vol. 279, 10 May 1883, HC, col. 492 *per* John Slagg.
83 Ibid., col. 500 *per* William Smith.
84 Ibid., col. 501.

opinion in Parliament was that the popular preference was still for local collectors, that the measure would neither increase efficiency nor save expense, and that such a fundamental amendment to the underlying principles of tax administration was not warranted. A further attempt in 1887 failed, the bill being withdrawn when the constitutional right of taxpayers to assess themselves was strongly and widely asserted. The bill was opposed in the press[85] and a large meeting of commercial taxpayers in London formally protested against it as depriving the taxpaying public of some measure of legislative protection.[86]

The formal legislative undermining of the principle of localism in tax administration was vigorously resisted well into the twentieth century. In 1906, when the potential for commercial bias among local assessors and collectors was raised with concern in Parliament, the profound implications of any changes in local administration were appreciated.[87] *The Times* called assessment by independent local commissioners representing the taxpayer 'the cardinal principle of income-tax assessment'.[88] In 1915 the issue was discussed in Parliament when it was proposed that certain weekly wage earners should be assessed not by local commissioners but by the surveyor of taxes, and their tax collected by a collector appointed by the Board of Inland Revenue.[89] The proposal was opposed as undermining a system of tax administration that not only was 'in accordance with the constitutional usage of this country', but had worked well for over seventy years and was both trusted and economic.[90] The principal concern was that the taxpayers in question would, under the proposed scheme, be denied that protection available to all other taxpayers, namely an impartial and independent local body standing between them and the crown to ensure that the crown did not take more tax than was legally due – the very raison d'être of the principle of localism in tax administration. These taxpayers were in need of the traditional safeguards since they were particularly vulnerable and generally unable to obtain or afford expert technical advice.[91] Others saw the proposal as a clear extension of bureaucratic control at the expense of local control.[92] The chancellor of the Exchequer disarmed the opponents of the proposal by

85 See *The Times*, letters to the editor, 15 Aug. 1887.
86 *The Times*, 'The inland revenue bill', 19 Aug. 1887.
87 *Parliamentary Debates*, series 4, vol. 155, 25 Apr. 1906, HC, cols 1476–7; ibid., vol. 158, 14 June 1906, HC, cols 1146–8; ibid., vol. 163, 30 Oct. 1906, HC, cols 861–2.
88 *The Times*, leader, 'More bureaucratic finance', 29 Oct. 1915, complaining about the increased power of the Inland Revenue in relation to the excess profits tax. See too *The Times*, 29 June 1927.
89 *Parliamentary Debates*, series 5, vol. 76, 6 Dec. 1915, HC, cols 1098–129.
90 Ibid., col. 1101 *per* John Butcher. See too *The Times*, letters to the editor, 25 Oct. 1915.
91 *Parliamentary Debates*, series 5, vol.76, 6 Dec. 1915, HC, col. 1104 *per* John Butcher. See too *The Times*, letters to the editor, 30 Oct. 1915.
92 *Parliamentary Debates*, series 5, vol. 76, 6 Dec. 1915, HC, col. 1118 *per* George Barnes.

announcing that it was the outcome of an agreement with the representatives of the general commissioners,[93] and pointing out that taxpayers would continue to be protected through their right of appeal to the general commissioners.[94] Despite popular opposition,[95] the proposal was accepted because it was clear that it was essential in order to make a large number of new assessments immediately.[96] Thereafter the instances where assessments were made by the central authorities grew. By the early twentieth century super-tax, the income of railway companies, the salaries of railway officials, crown employees and civil servants, and all dividends paid in the United Kingdom were assessed and collected by officials of the Board of Inland Revenue. In all, in 1915, 36% of the income tax was assessed by Inland Revenue officials and 64% of the income tax was collected by them.[97]

Such attempts were overt efforts by the Board of Inland Revenue to acquire the powers of the local administrative bodies. The board was also accused of a long-term policy of 'peaceful penetration'[98] and more covert attempts to gain jurisdiction, by denying improvements to those elements of the local system with which the board had some influence. So, for example, they were accused of starving the local system of resources in order to reduce its efficiency, by denying the reorganization that assessors and collectors had long demanded, permanent appointments, fixed salaries and superannuation. It was said that the board had offered assessors and collectors better terms if they agreed to the transfer of their functions to officers of the board.[99] The president of the national association of assessors and collectors was reported as having accused the board of adopting a 'policy of attrition', to strengthen their claim that the work of the assessors was of such 'minor quality and quantity that in the interests of efficiency and economy their office should be abolished'.[1] While such accusations owed not a little to journalistic license and vested interests, they clearly illustrate the popular opposition to the undermining of the principle of localism. While there were undoubtedly shortcomings in the system of local administration, of which the public were aware, an entirely central administration was clearly still unacceptable.

While clearly in the face of such popular support and with the principle of localism so firmly entrenched in English tax law, any significant and formal

---

93 Ibid., col. 1110 *per* the chancellor of the Exchequer, Reginald McKenna.
94 This was thought to be unrealistic in relation to 'the simple working man who is being taxed for the first time': ibid., col. 1118 *per* George Barnes.
95 See *The Times*, letters to the editor, 25 Oct. 1915 and 26 Oct. 1915.
96 The Inland Revenue had felt confident of success since they had already, albeit provisionally, advertised for extra staff: see *The Times*, letters to the editor, 26 Oct. 1915.
97 The figures are those of the financial secretary to the treasury, in the debate on the Finance (No. 3) Bill in 1915: *Parliamentary Debates*, series 5, vol. 76, 6 Dec. 1915, HC, cols. 1123–4.
98 *The Times*, 29 June 1927.
99 *The Times*, leader, 'Income-tax administration', 12 Sept. 1928.
1 Ibid.

breaches were bound to fail. Throughout the century the most effective and potent erosion of the principle was achieved not through a number of minor formal infractions, but by informal, unplanned, and naturally occurring changes in practice. Much of this erosion was due to the development of tax law and practice, and its inevitable increase in complexity and technicality reflecting a rapidly expanding commercial life of ever-growing sophistication. The part-time, amateur, unpaid lay commissioners who were motivated by their belief in and commitment to civic duty and entirely dependent on their sometimes imperfect and anecdotal local knowledge, were no match for the professional and expert tax official. In practice the system of tax administration was working only because the surveyor was, necessarily but informally, taking over work which had hitherto been left in the hands of the local commissioners. Increasingly the assessment work and some appellate work of the general commissioners was merely nominal; the real work was often undertaken by the surveyor. He came to dominate the general commissioners, and therefore the administrative process itself, through his knowledge and expertise. Then as always knowledge meant power, and the surveyor possessed technical and arcane knowledge in abundance. The assessment and appeals process was dominated by the expert, articulate and informed surveyor whose superior knowledge pre-empted any serious contention by the commissioners themselves.

By the early years of the twentieth century, formal and informal breaches in the principle of localism had eroded it to the extent that the chancellor of the Exchequer could respond to objectors to the proposal of 1915 by saying that '[i]t is not unconstitutional; it is not a novelty'.[2] Though the principle had been considerably undermined in practice, however, in theory it was largely untouched. The legal structure of the machinery embodying the principle of localism remained essentially the same as it had been in 1803, and yet the practical administrative process reflected very little of it since the administration of income tax was no longer in the hands of the local commissioners and their own appointed officers, with the surveyor playing an insignificant role. Their roles had been reversed, with the surveyor now being the 'pivotal figure' in the income tax administration.[3] The Royal Commission on the Income Tax in 1920 acknowledged this dislocation between theory and practice, but admitted that had this not happened, the machinery of tax administration would have been 'hopelessly inadequate'.[4]

With the collapse of the principle of localism in all but name, the Royal Commission recommended that the situation in practice be formalized.

2 *Parliamentary Debates*, series 5, vol. 76, 6 Dec. 1915, HC, col. 1112 *per* the chancellor of the Exchequer, Reginald McKenna.
3 'Report of the royal commission on the income tax', *House of Commons Parliamentary Papers* 1920 xviii (615) 97 para.375.
4 Ibid., para. 331

While it did not propose the complete abolition of the local commissioners, it did recommend the restriction of their jurisdiction to the hearing appeals, with the placing of all assessing functions in the surveyor[5] and all collecting functions in Inland Revenue staff. Only a vestige of the principle of localism was to be retained, though a not insignificant one, in the form of the appellate jurisdiction of the general commissioners. Indeed, the removal of the appellate power of the general commissioners was never proposed, and was accepted as the ultimate protection of the taxpayer against possible injustice. The proposals of the royal commission were embodied in the Revenue Bill of 1921 but the bill aroused such intense opposition in the country that it had to be abandoned.[6] The opposition to it, and to similar repeated attempts to abolish the local offices of assessor and collector, was vehement, and conducted largely through the medium of *The Times*. The proposed alterations to the traditional system were seen as fundamental, vicious,[7] and unequivocally promoting an increased control by the Inland Revenue. Headlines such as 'Hunting the Taxpayer: Safeguards to be Withdrawn',[8] and 'A Principle at Stake',[9] were typical of the popular rhetoric of the time. However much the principle had declined in practice, it was clearly still immensely important to some sections of the public. Understandably perhaps, the general commissioners themselves feared being reduced to mere figureheads and alarmed the public by suggesting that all elasticity[10] and personal attention to individual taxpayers would be lost if the Inland Revenue took over their functions.[11] Taxpayers were urged not to surrender the protection afforded to them by the system.[12] So fiercely were the proposals opposed that it led to the founding of the Income Taxpayers' Society. At the time of its formation its object was stated to be 'the protection of the liberties and rights of the taxpaying public'.[13] It was to 'hold a permanent watching brief on behalf of the taxpayers, one of its chief principles being to defend what is regarded as the constitutional issue – assessment independent of the bureaucracy – against further attacks'.[14] Led by its director, Lord Decies, an advocate of decentralization and a critic of an

---

5 Now renamed the inspector of taxes.
6 *The Times*, leader, 'Protection for the taxpayer', 28 July 1921.
7 So called in *The Times*, 'A principle at stake', 18 Mar. 1920.
8 Ibid., 20 Apr. 1921.
9 Ibid., 18 Mar. 1920.
10 For example, the leniency shown by local collectors in allowing further time to pay in certain cases.
11 *The Times*, 'Hunting the taxpayer', 20 Apr. 1921.
12 For later opposition, see *The Times*, letters to the editor, 19 May 1931. See too the opposition of the Law Society in *The Times*, letters to the editor, 25 Apr. 1931.
13 Ibid., leader, 'Protection for the taxpayer', 28 July 1921.
14 Ibid., leader, 'Income-tax administration', 1 Apr. 1931.

expanding bureaucracy, it was to prove an organ of immense energy in the following decade in matters of income tax reform.

While the formal and informal erosion of the principle was vigorously resented, it could not be resisted since the inadequacy of the principle of localism in tax administration was undeniable. Over the next thirty years the local commissioners were directly and indirectly stripped of all their administrative powers and their officials abolished. This clear yet delicate balance of localism and centralism that had been a central feature of the administration of all taxes and had been so highly valued by Pitt, Peel and Gladstone was upset in the relentless tide of centralism. It had had a wider influence in that it had been adopted to implement most of the new regulatory legislation of the new industrial age, and in that sense the taxing statutes provided a model for much of the new administrative state in Victorian England. For the purposes of taxation, however, it was no longer appropriate or effective. The principle had failed not because it was inherently misguided, but because it had proved inadequate to administer taxes in a new sophisticated commercial society. The fiscal and administrative demands of central government, the difficulties in appointing suitable commissioners, and a change in public opinion towards the handling of private affairs by civil servants all contributed to the triumph of centralism over localism. Economic forces drove the movement while social forces allowed it to happen. The retention of an appellate jurisdiction in the lay local commissioners recognized the importance of decentralisation to the popular acceptance of the income tax and the protection of the regular courts of law from litigation of a nature and quantity they could not and would not entertain. It also recognized to some degree the importance of an independent safeguard to the taxpayer. That safeguard was now to consist solely of the right of appeal to the taxpayers' peers.

CONCLUSION

The English system was plagued by internal conflicts and tensions throughout the nineteenth century, which it was able to resolve only with difficulty and discord. It achieved a workable system through the development of an administrative practice that diverged considerably from the legal theory. Not only did this dislocation obscure the true legal position of the administrative machinery, it caused practical confusion to the taxpaying public. Furthermore, it burdened the English fiscal machinery with features, often major ones, which caused problems in modern tax tribunal structure and process enduring to the present day. The legislative provisions which gave the local general commissioners the sole responsibility for making assessments to income tax remained unaltered in their fundamental principles, even when the practical responsibility had been removed and given to the surveyor, thus making that body uncertain and ambivalent in role and jurisdiction, particularly when it became a purely adjudicatory body. Its original conception as a local body of tax administration resulted in a jurisdiction neither clearly inquisitorial nor adversarial, a continued insistence on appointing only commissioners with local knowledge, a cultural reluctance to give reasons for its decisions, and the secrecy of its hearings, all of which became increasingly inappropriate in a modern, accountable and cost-conscious society sensitive to the upholding of human rights. The informal dominance of the surveyor led to the most damaging modern legacy, namely a perceived lack of independence of the tribunal from the Inland Revenue. Ironically it was this very quality of independence from the executive which had been the reason behind the adoption of, and popular support for, the principle of localism in tax administration. Localism did have some successful historical legacies. That of geographical location, with sittings occurring within easy reach of most taxpayers, was particularly valuable, though it is a degree of physical accessibility to justice that is soon to end.[15] The local provenance of the tribunal also resulted in a simplicity of procedure that equally gave a high degree of accessibility to unrepresented taxpayers.

Tensions between localism and centralism in tax administration existed in both England and America. Though faced with more complex and radical fiscal questions, the Americans addressed them with success. The different jurisdictions in that country, though more complex, were more clearly defined. Furthermore the states and the federal government were not inhibited by established practices and traditions, and vested interests were less tenacious, and so they had a greater degree of choice in the systems they adopted. Culturally too a degree of localism was satisfied to some extent by the constitutional structure of the country. Added to that, America was not to experience a permanent federal income tax until 1913, and until then most taxation was property-based and so relatively benign. These factors enabled America to succeed in establishing a system of tax administration at the state level that combined localism and centralism in a sensible and effective way, ensuring popular involvement in the process and yet sufficient central control. Federal taxation bowed to state machinery whenever it could, but when that was impossible it established a simple, accessible and efficient system.

---

15 At the time of writing the divisions of general commissioners within each district are being required to amalgamate.

The will theory of contract in the nineteenth century: its influence and its limitations

WARREN SWAIN

IN 1826 JOSEPH CHITTY remarked that 'Perhaps no branch of the jurisprudence of the country has of late years been more subject of judicial inquiry and decision than the Law of Contracts'.[1] Chitty was writing in the preface of his new book on the law of contract and so hardly counts as an impartial witness but his observation was an astute one. The law of contract in England did undergo some fundamental changes in the early nineteenth century. But at the same time there was much that remained fundamentally the same. Some legal historians have attributed these developments to the economic growth prompted by industrialization and political change.[2] Others have sought explanations from an internal perspective – from within the law itself.[3] These writers have stressed the influence of new ideas[4] and the rise of the legal treatise.[5]

In 1800 English law was still dominated by the forms of action which were descended from the original writs by which medieval plaintiffs instigated their suits.[6] In place of a law of contract there were a series of contractual actions: assumpsit, debt, covenant and account.[7] Sir William Blackstone

---

1 J. Chitty, *A practical treatise on the law of contracts not under seal* (London, 1826), p. iii.
2 The best known examples are P. Atiyah, *The rise and fall of freedom of contract* (Oxford, 1979) and M. Horwitz, *The transformation of American law 1780–1860* (Cambridge, MA, 1977).
3 On the internal point of view more generally see D. Ibbetson, 'What is legal history a history of ?' in A.D.E. Lewis & M. Lobban (eds), *Law and history* (Oxford, 2003), p. 33.
4 A.W.B. Simpson, 'Innovation in nineteenth century contract law', *LQR*, 91 (1975), 247; J. Gordley, *The philosophical origins of modern contract doctrine* (Oxford, 1992); D.J. Ibbetson, *A historical introduction to the law of obligations* (Oxford, 1999), pp 220–44.
5 A.W.B. Simpson, 'The rise and fall of the legal treatise: legal principles and the forms of legal literature', *Univ Chicago Law Rev*, 48 (1983), 632.
6 A.H. Chaytor & W.J. Whittaker (eds), F.W. Maitland, *The forms of action at common law* (Cambridge, 1948).
7 This was reflected in the arrangement of the abridgments for example C. Viner, *A general abridgement of law and equity*, 24 vols (Aldershot, 1741–56).

bravely tried to impose a different structure but a marriage of natural law and civil law with the common law was never going to be a very harmonious one.[8] One of his successors as Vinerian Professor, Richard Wooddesson, abandoned Blackstone's project. His lectures consisted of little more than a simple description of the forms of action.[9] Other writers at this time were more innovative and began to toy with the idea that there might be a substantive legal category called contract.[10] This intellectual shift took place against the backdrop of reforms of legal procedure. The boundary between the function of judge and jury, which had always been murky, began to sharpen.[11] The process quickened as a result of reforms which precipitated the rise in special pleading and exposed what had previously been hidden behind a blank jury verdict.[12] Where once English contract law had relied on the good sense of jurors – which was why specialist juries had become so important –[13] questions of law now began to be separated from issues of fact.[14] The long retreat of the civil jury had begun.[15] It had always been possible to bring questions before the bench in *banc*, but regular use of the motion for new trial[16] alongside devices like the reservation of points of law[17] and case stated[18] made the process easier. As a result of these changes judges

8 W. Blackstone, *Commentaries on the laws of England*, 4 vols (Oxford, 1765–69).
9 R. Wooddesson, *A systematical view of the laws of England, as treated of in a course of Vinerian lectures*, 3 vols (London, 1792–93).
10 J. Powell, *Essay upon the law of contracts and agreements*, 2 vols (London, 1790).
11 Anon, 'Of the function of the judge as distinguished from those of the jury', *Law Rev* 2 (1845), 27.
12 *Second report of his majesty's commissioners appointed to inquire into the practice and procedure of the superior courts of common law* (1830) [123] PP vol xi 48; Reg Gen HT (1834). The Hilary Rules are reproduced in (1834) LJ Repts KB 5.
13 J. Oldham, 'The origin of the special jury', *Univ Chicago Law Rev*, 50 (1983), 137; J. Oldham, 'Special juries in England in the nineteenth century usage and reform', *Jour Leg His* 8 (1987), 148.
14 W. Forsyth, *History of trial by jury* (London, 1852), p. 282; Anon, 'Of the distinction between law and fact', *Law Rev*, 1 (1844) 37. On the earlier position see S.F.C. Milsom, *Studies in the history of the common law* (London, 1985), pp 171–89; M.S. Arnold, 'Law and fact in the medieval jury trial: out of sight, out of mind', *Am Jour Leg His* 18 (1974), 267.
15 J. Getzler, 'The fate of the civil jury in late Victorian England: malicious prosecution as a test case' in J. Cairns & G. McLeod (eds), *The dearest birth right of the people of England: the jury in the history of the common law* (Oxford, 2002), pp 218–24; C. Hanly, 'The decline of civil jury trial in nineteenth-century England', *Jour Leg Hist*, 26 (2005), 253.
16 The grounds for a motion were set out in J. Morgan, *Essays upon the law of evidence, new trials, special verdicts, trials at bar and repleaders*, 2 vols (London, 1789), ii, p.1. On the motion for new trial generally see J. Mitnick, 'From neighbor-witness to judge of proofs: the transformation of the English civil juror', *Am Jour Leg Hist*, 32 (1988), 201.
17 M.J. Pritchard, 'Non-Suit: a premature obituary', *CLJ* [1960], 18; *Baskerville v. Brown* (1761) 2 Burr 1229, 97 ER 804; *Dally v. Smith* (1771) 4 Burr 2148, 98 ER 120; *Clay v. Willan* (1789) 1 H Bla 298, 126 ER 174.
18 B.J. Sellon, *The practice of the Courts of King's Bench and Common Pleas*, 2 vols (London,

sitting in Westminster were left with greater control over the direction of legal doctrines than ever before.

Once impediments to change, both practical and intellectual, were removed, judges and legal writers were left with a problem. If they were going to build a substantive law of contract – and it was very much a joint venture – then they needed the raw materials to complete the job. The emerging body of treatise writers turned to Robert-Joseph Pothier for inspiration.[19] Although Pothier was not the only civilian will theorist to influence English lawyers, he was the first.[20] He was not short of eminent admirers who included Lord Campbell[21] and Sir William Jones.[22] His most influential book, *Traité des obligations*, originally published in the 1760s, appeared in a translation by Sir William Evans in 1806.[23] Pothier's work was particularly attractive because he mapped out an escape route for legal writers keen to get away from the intellectual cul-de-sac represented by the alphabetical abridgments.[24] His basic premise that contracts were formed out of a meeting of wills was easy to grasp.[25] It also had echoes in contemporary

---

1792), i, 489–91; J. Oldham, 'The seventh amendment right to jury trial: late eighteenth century practice reconsidered' in K. O'Donovan & G. Rubin (eds), *Human rights and legal history essays in honour of Brian Simpson* (Oxford, 2000), p. 235.

19 For the influence of Pothier see: Simpson, 'The rise and fall of the legal treatise', p. 255; Atiyah, *Rise and fall*, pp 399–400; W. Cornish & G. de N Clarke, *Law and society in England 1750–1950* (London, 1989), p. 200; Ibbetson, *A historical introduction*, pp 220–44; J.H. Baker, *An introduction to English legal history* (4th ed. London, 2002), p. 352; K. Teevan, *A history of the Anglo-American common law of contract* (New York, 1990), p. 179; B. Rudden, 'Pothier et la common law' in J. Monéger (ed.), *Robert-Joseph Pothier, d'hier à aujourd'hui* (Paris, 2001), p. 91.

20 Savigny was also important. On his wider influence see M. Hoeflich, 'Savigny and his anglo-american disciples', *Am Jnl Comp Law*, 37 (1989), 17. He was a favourite of Frederick Pollock on which see N. Duxbury, *Frederick Pollock and the English juristic tradition* (Oxford, 2004), pp 190–2.

21 *Hall v. Wright* (1858) El, Black & El 746, 760, 120 ER 688. Lord Campbell was not the only judge who admired Pothier: *Hoare v. Cazenove* (1812) 16 East 391, 398, 104 ER 1137 (Lord Ellenborough); *Cox v. Troy* (1822) 5 B & Ald 474, 480, 106 ER 1264. Rudden, 'Pothier et la common law', p. 97 demonstrates that Pothier was cited in the courts on more than four hundred occasions in the nineteenth century.

22 *An essay on bailment* (London, 1781), pp 29–30.

23 R. Pothier, *A treatise on the law of obligations or contracts*, trans. Sir William Evans, 2 vols (London, 1806). His best known work apart from his *Traité des obligations* (1761) was probably his *Traité du contrat de vente* (1762).

24 W. Holdsworth, *Sources and literature of English law* (Oxford, 1925), pp 104–11. In addition to Viner other popular abridgments included M. Bacon, *A new abridgment of the law*, 5 vols (London, 1736–66); J. Comyns, *A digest of the laws of England*, 5 vols (London, 1762–76). The last abridgment was C. Petersdorff, *A practical and elementary abridgment of the common law*, 5 vols (London, 1841–44).

25 Pothier, *Obligations*, 1.1.1§1. For examples of judges referring to will in their definitions of contract see *Haynes v. Haynes* (1861) 1 D & S 426, 433, 62 ER 442; *Dickinson v. Dodds* (1876) 2 Ch D 463, 472.

philosophy.[26] In so far as Pothier put forward a promissory theory of contract, his version of the will theory shared some features with natural law writing on contract, although the roots of the idea went much deeper.[27] The attraction of Pothier's work was not wholly theoretical. He had also succeeded in creating a complete framework into which nineteenth-century writers could, albeit with some modifications, slot English law. His writings were also full of examples for lawyers and judges looking for quick solutions to practical problems.

It would be a mistake to assume that the English had no interest in legal theory before the nineteenth century. Roman law cast a long shadow.[28] English civilians were not short on the ground.[29] Natural law also began to attract attention.[30] An English translation of Samuel Pufendorf's *Of the law of nature and nations* appeared in 1703.[31] Writers like Hobbes[32] and Blackstone[33] were prepared to take what they wanted from natural law and adapt the principles for their own purposes. A few writers even tried to work natural law into a body of rules suitable for describing the common law of contract. The impact of this group was relatively slight. They were very much ahead of their times. Sir Jeffrey Gilbert's treatise on contract remained in manuscript.[34] Significantly Henry Ballow called his book, which drew heavily on

---

26 M. Gregor (ed.), I. Kant, *The metaphysics of morals* (Cambridge, 1996), p. 57; A. Wood (ed.), G.W.F. Hegel, *Elements of the philosophy of right* (Cambridge, 1991), § 75.

27 These themes are explored in Gordley, *The philosophical origins*.

28 P. Stein, *The character and influence of the Roman law: historical essays* (London, 1988), p. 208.

29 H. Jolowicz, 'Some English civilians', *CLP* 2 (1949), 139. Well known examples of writers who were influenced by civilian learning from the eighteenth century included R. Eden, *Jurisprudentia philologica sive elementa juris civilis secundum methodum et seriem Institutionum Justiniani* (Oxford, 1744); T. Wood, *A new institute of the imperial or civil law* (London, 1704).

30 For an overview of some natural law writers see P. Stein, *Legal evolution the story of an idea* (Cambridge, 1980), pp 1–22. For the influence of natural law on English private law see D. Ibbetson, 'Natural law and common law' *Edinburgh Law Rev*, 5 (2001), 4.

31 It was translated by Basil Kennet.

32 Hobbes' interest in contract went beyond the 'social contract' which was the basis of his great work *Leviathan* first published in 1651 see F. Tönnies (ed.), T. Hobbes, *The elements of law, natural and politic* (London, 1889). On the influence of the common law of contract on Hobbes see R.A. Glover, 'The legal origin of Thomas Hobbes's Doctrine of Contract', *Journal of the History of Philosophy*, 18 (1980), 177.

33 G. Jones, *The sovereignty of law* (London, 1973), pp xxiii–xlvii; M. Lobban, *The common law and English jurisprudence 1760–1850* (Oxford, 1991), pp 18–19, 27–33; M. Lobban, 'Blackstone and the science of law', *Historical Journal,* 30 (1987), 311; H.L.A. Hart, 'Blackstone's use of the law of nature' *Butterworth's South African Law Review* (1956), 169; J.M. Finnis, 'Blackstone's theoretical intentions', *Natural Law Forum*, 12 (1967), 163; P. Lucas, 'Ex parte Sir William Blackstone "plagiarist": a note on Blackstone and natural law', *Am Jour Leg His*, 7 (1963), 142.

34 BL MS Hargrave 265, 266. For a discussion of Gilbert's work see M. Macnair, 'Sir Jeffrey Gilbert and his treatises' *Jour Leg Hist*, 15 (1994), 252.

Pufendorf, a *treatise on equity* rather than a Treatise on contract.[35] If English law remained isolated it was not completely insular. Continental literature was already having some influence on the common law.[36] Closer to home, Scots law may have provided inspiration.[37] Judges occasionally referred to Roman and even natural law.[38] In the nineteenth century these early shoots would blossom into something more substantial.

THE WILL THEORY AND EXISTING CONTRACT DOCTRINE

Discussions of substantive doctrine in litigation before the nineteenth century are relatively unusual though not unknown.[39] The silence was not unique to the law of contract. It was a product of the way that litigation was built around pleading and the jury.[40] That did not mean that the law of contract lacked any substantive coherence. An earlier opportunity to create a law of contract based on promises was only wasted when deeds became mandatory in the action of covenant.[41] Informal contracts on the other hand derived their binding force from an exchange. In debt on a contract, exchange was expressed through the doctrine of *quid pro quo*;[42] assumpsit used consideration.[43]

---

35 (London, 1737). A second edition appeared in 1756. Subsequent editions were edited by John Fonblanque in 1793–94. The fifth and last edition appeared in 1820.
36 C. Rogers, 'Continental literature and the development of the common law by the King's Bench: c.1750–1800' in V. Piergiovanni (ed.), *Courts and the development of commercial law* (Berlin, 1987), p. 161; Stein, *Character and influence*.
37 Hard evidence is difficult to come by but Lord Kames's *Principles of equity* (1760) may have influenced Lord Mansfield: see M. Lobban, 'The ambition of Lord Kames's Equity' in Lewis & Lobban (eds), *Law and history*, p. 97. The doctrine of offer and acceptance was also a long standing feature of the Institutional works: see D. Walker (ed.), Viscount Stair, *The institutions of the law of Scotland* (Edinburgh, 1981) 1.10.3; Lord Bankton, *An institute of the laws of Scotland 1751*', Stair Society 41 (1993) 1.11.5. Stair's book was first published in 1681 and Bankton's in 1751.
38 A good example of both is provided by Wilmot J.'s judgment in *Pillans v. Van Mierop* (1765) 3 Burr 1663, 97 ER 1035.
39 *Reninger v. Fogossa* (1550) Plo 1, 17, 75 ER 1.
40 For similar trends in the law of tort see J.H. Baker, 'Trespass, case, and the common law of negligence 1500–1700' in E. Schrage (ed.), *Negligence: the comparative legal history of the law of torts* (Berlin, 2001), p. 47.
41 Ibbetson, *A historical introduction*, pp 25–8; for a statement on the nature of covenant see Herle J. in the Eyre of London *Anon* (1321) 86 Selden Soc 286.
42 Ibbetson, *A historical introduction*, pp 80–3.
43 For the importance of the principle of exchange in consideration see D.J. Ibbetson, 'Consideration and the theory of contract in sixteenth-century common law' in J. Barton (ed.), *Towards a general law of contract* (Berlin, 1990), p. 67; Ibbetson, *A historical introduction*, pp 141–5.

In Sir William Jones's opinion, 'the greatest portion' of Pothier's writing 'is law at Westminster as well as Orleans'.[44] Jones was keen to emphasize that Pothier, a writer that he admired, was worth the attention of an English audience. But his remarks also serve to introduce an important but often overlooked fact: the will theory worked best when it coincided with existing common law rules.[45] In the will theory the doctrine of offer and acceptance is crucial because it shows that a meeting of wills has taken place.[46] A similar idea can be found as a way of determining consent to marriage.[47] Under the influence of natural law, offer and acceptance had already entered English legal writing in the eighteenth century.[48] By the time of *Payne v. Cave*,[49] English judges were familiar with the terminology but it was not yet a universal requirement for all valid contracts. With a doctrine like offer and acceptance, the role of the will theory lay in the way in which it helped to bring about a change in emphasis, so that what was once peripheral became central. By the middle of the century, offer and acceptance was a staple of judicial reasoning[50] and contract textbooks.[51]

The rule that a non-party could not enforce a right under a contract to which he was not a party was much more well established than the doctrine of offer and acceptance.[52] In the period when the action of assumpsit was dominated by the idea of exchange, it was expressed in the formula that consideration must move from the promisee.[53] The effects of the restriction could be ameliorated where mercantile instruments were involved, where equity intervened or where the pleading rules could be manipulated.[54] By the

44 Jones, *Bailment*, p. 29.
45 P. Hamburger, 'The development of the nineteenth-century consensus theory of contract', *Law and Hist Rev*, 7 (1989), 241 argues that consensus theory was a well established feature of the common law long before the nineteenth century. This is probably an overstatement but the point that nineteenth-century developments had roots in the earlier common law is a valuable one.
46 Pothier, *Obligations*, 1.1.1§§1–2.
47 [T Salmon], *A critical essay concerning marriage* (London, 1794), pp 180–213. On the similarities see Ibbetson, *A historical introduction*, p. 222.
48 Ballow, *Equity*, 1.3§12.
49 (1789) 3 TR 148, 100 ER 502.
50 *Dunlop v. Higgins* (1848) 1 HLC 38, 9 ER 805. For a detailed discussion see S. Gardner, 'Trashing with Trollope: a deconstruction of the postal rules in contract', *OJLS*, 12 (1992), 170 at 172–5.
51 S.M. Leake, *The elements of the law of contract* (London, 1867), pp 12–23; F. Pollock, *Principles of contract at law and in equity* (London, 1876), pp 4–24; W. Anson, *Principles of the English law of contract* (Oxford, 1879), pp 10–28. For a discussion of offer and acceptance see Duxbury, *Frederick Pollock*, pp 201–2.
52 For a history of the rule see V. Palmer, *The paths to privity: a history of third party beneficiary contracts at English law* (San Francisco, 1992).
53 J.H. Baker, 'Privity of contract in the common law before 1680' in D. Ibbetson & E. Schrage (eds), *Ius quaesitum tertio* (Berlin, forthcoming).
54 D. Ibbetson & W. Swain 'Third party beneficiaries in English law 1680–1861' in Ibbetson & Schrage (eds), *Ius quaesitum tertio*.

late eighteenth century some judges were inclined to wonder whether the rule existed at all.[55] But a solution to what the law reporters Bonsanquet and Puller called the 'great contradiction in the older cases' was not yet seen as a priority.[56] The issue was ignored by Joseph Chitty in the first edition of *A practical treatise on the law of contracts not under seal*.[57] But by the 1830s new life was breathed into the old restriction. In *Price v. Easton*,[58] Lord Denman remarked that 'I think the declaration cannot be supported, as it does not shew any consideration for the promise moving from the plaintiff to the defendant'.[59] Littledale J. expressed himself differently. In his view, 'No privity is shewn between the plaintiff and defendant. This case is precisely like Crow v. Rogers and must be governed by it.'[60]

The parties only rule had never gone away but it was largely seen as a rule about deeds.[61] For Littledale J. it had a wider application alongside the consideration formula. Both versions also found their way into *Tweddle v. Atkinson*.[62] In less than a decade, the textbook writers began treating *Tweddle v. Atkinson* as a leading, and unequivocal, authority on the parties only rule.[63] The consideration version largely dropped out of the picture.[64] Pothier's views may have played a part in the process early on. In his *Traité des obligations* he wrote that:

> When I stipulate something for you in favour of a third person, the agreement is void: for by this agreement you do not contract any obligation in favour of such third person or myself. It is evident that you do not contract any in favour of the third person: for it is a principle that agreements can have no effect except between contracting parties, and consequently that they cannot acquire any right to a third person who is not a party to them.[65]

---

55 Buller was a leading advocate of a more relaxed approach: F. Buller, *An introduction to the law relative to trials at nisi prius* (London, 1767), p. 125; *Martyn v. Hind* (1779) Cowp 437, 439, 99 ER 142; *Marchington v. Vernon* (London, 1787) 1 B & P 101 note c, 126 ER 801. Buller J was not alone in this view Lord Alvanley CJ made similar comments see *Pigott v. Thompson* (1802) 3 B & P 147, 127 ER 80.
56 3 B & P 149 note a.
57 Chitty, *Contracts*. The issue was discussed in the 2nd edition of 1834.
58 (1834) 4 B & Ad 433, N & M 303, LJKB 51, 101 ER 518.
59 (1834) 4 B & Ad 433, 434.
60 (1834) 4 B & Ad 433, 434.
61 C.G. Addison, *A treatise on the law of contracts and liabilities ex-contractu* (London, 1847), p. 238.
62 (1861) 1 B & S 393, 30 LJQB 265, 4 LT 468, 9 WR 781, 121 ER 762.
63 Leake, *Contract*, p. 221; Pollock, *Contract*, pp 190–1; Anson, *Contract*, p. 200.
64 Largely but not totally: see the speeches of Lords Dunedin and Parker in *Dunlop Pneumatic Tyre Co. Ltd. v. Selfridge & Co. Ltd.* [1915] AC 847, 855, 859; W. Swain, 'Third party beneficiaries in English law 1880–2004' in Ibbetson & Schrage (eds), *Ius quaesitum tertio*.
65 Pothier, *Obligations*, 1.1.5§1.

That doctrines of offer and acceptance and privity became so important to the English law of contract in the nineteenth century was due, in no small part, to the efforts of textbook writers. One of the reasons that the process was so successful was the way in which writers were able to combine Pothier's views with home grown rules. Reconciling the will theory with the doctrine of consideration was a more difficult task. Over time the edges of reciprocal consideration had become frayed but the extent to which it had begun to unravel is usually exaggerated.[66] As consideration stood in 1800, it was impossible to reconcile with the basic premise of the will theory. If contracts were binding because of a meeting of wills, then any element of exchange should have been superfluous.[67]

Despite attempts to re-structure contract law, consideration remained firm. Any efforts to undermine the doctrine by introducing moral consideration had been soundly trounced by the 1840s.[68] English writers were left facing a dilemma. One of the defects in a contract described by Pothier was the absence of causa – a phrase significantly translated by Evans as 'Want of a good consideration'.[69] Causa and consideration were very different but in the minds of some writers the distinction became blurred.[70] Consideration continued to be described as a benefit and detriment but it also began to be bound up with intention.[71]

Judges also began to see consideration in a new light. The number of situations in which the presence of consideration was difficult to reconcile with reciprocity began to increase. As benefit and detriment began to become stretched, forbearance consideration was extended to include agreements to curtail questionable suits.[72] By the late 1830s, provided a contract was seriously intended, there was little danger that it would not be enforced, whether or not there was genuine reciprocity between the parties.[73]

Pollock, who later became sceptical about the value of consideration, stressed the historical foundations of the doctrine.[74] Even if English writers

---

66 This debate is considered in greater depth in W. Swain, 'The changing nature of the doctrine of consideration 1750–1850', *Jour Leg Hist*, 26 (2005), 47. The exaggerated but orthodox analysis can be traced to Sir William Holdsworth, *A history of English law*, 17 vols (London, 1925), viii, 26–9, 31.
67 On this tension see Ibbetson, *A historical introduction*, p. 238.
68 *Eastwood v. Kenyon* (1840) 11 Ad & E 438, 3 P & D 276, 113 ER 482.
69 Pothier, *Obligations*, 1.1.3§6. In the original French the title of this passage is 'Du défaut de cause dans le contrat'.
70 Simpson, 'Innovation', 262; 'Our next requirement is consideration, a doctrine thought in the early nineteenth century to be a local version of the civilian *causa promissionis*'.
71 Chitty, *Contracts*, pp 6–7; Addison, *Contracts*, p. 17; Leake, *Contract*, p. 310.
72 *Longridge v. Dorville* (1821) 5 B & Ald 117, 106 ER 1136.
73 *Haigh v. Brooks* (1839) 10 Ad & E 309, 113 ER 119; *Bainbridge v. Firmstone* (1838) 8 Ad & E 743, 1 P & D 2, 1 W, W & H 600, 112 ER 1019; *Westlake v. Adams* (1858) 5 CBNS 248, 141 ER 99. For more details on this development see Swain, 'Consideration', 59–61.
74 Duxbury, *Frederick Pollock*, pp 202–8.

and judges had wanted to abolish consideration, they were handicapped by the absence of an alternative. A separate doctrine of intention to enter legal relations began to appear in the textbooks in the mid-nineteenth century,[75] but was only explicitly recognized by the judges in the 1890s[76] – by which time it was too late; the future of consideration was secure.

The continued presence of the doctrine of consideration left judges and writers searching for a compromise. But it was not always possible for the common law to embrace all of Pothier's views even in a modified form. Pothier, like the natural lawyers,[77] was willing to set aside unequal bargains on the grounds of imperfect consent.[78] Ballow[79] and Powell[80] were also sympathetic to this view, as was Henry Colebrooke, who drew comparisons with the doctrine of *laesio enormis* in Roman law.[81] Many years earlier in *Nott v. Hill*, Lord Nottingham had contrasted equity with the civil law and complained that, 'by the civil law a bargain of double the value shall be avoided, and wish'd it were so in England'.[82] But the majority of English lawyers remained deeply uncomfortable about interfering with contracts on the grounds of inequality. In equity, which is sometimes seen as more paternalistic,[83] inequality alone was not enough to merit equity's protection even if it could, along with other factors, be received as evidence of fraud in order to justify refusing specific performance[84] or rescission.[85] Despite some lukewarm support for a principle of inequality, Pothier's theory ran into the

---

75 W. Fox, *A treatise on simple contracts* (London, 1842), pp 62–3; Leake, *Contract*, pp 9–10.
76 *Carlill v. Carbolic Smoke Ball Co.* [1893] 1 QB 256; A.W.B. Simpson, *Leading cases in the common law* (Oxford, 1995), pp 259–91.
77 H. Grotius, *The rights of war and peace*, trans. F. Kelsey (Oxford, 1925), 2.12–13; S. Pufendorf, *Of the law of nature and nations*, trans. C.H. & W.A. Oldfather (Oxford, 1934), 5.1.6.
78 Pothier, *Obligations*, 1.2.4 §33.
79 Ballow, *Equity*, c 2 § 9–12.
80 Powell, *Contracts*, i, pp 9–151.
81 H. Colebrooke, *Treatise on obligations and contracts* (London, 1818), p. 39. Given that *laesio enormis* was confined to land the comparison was not wholly accurate see P. Stein (ed.), W.W. Buckland *A textbook of Roman law from Augustus to Justinian* (3rd edn, Cambridge, 1963), p. 486.
82 (1682) 2 Ch Ca 120, 121, 22 ER 875.
83 The paternalism of equity in the eighteenth century is almost certainly a myth see A.W.B. Simpson, 'The Horwitz thesis and the history of contracts', *Univ Chicago Law Rev*, 46 (1979), 533; J. Barton, 'The enforcement of hard bargains' *LQR*, 103 (1987), 118. On the relatively narrow scope of fraud see M. Lobban, 'Contractual fraud in law and equity', *OJLS*, 17 (1997), 441. For the argument that eighteenth century equity was paternalistic see Atiyah, *Rise and Fall*, pp 169–77.
84 *Emery v. Wase* (1803) 8 Ves Jun 505, 517, 32 ER 451; *Coles v. Trecothick* (1804) 9 Ves Jun 234, 246, 32 ER 592.
85 *Low v. Bachard* (1803) 8 Ves Jun 133, 137, 32 ER 303; *Burrowes v. Lock* (1805) 10 Ves Jun 470, 475, 32 ER 927; *Lowther v. Lowther* (1806) 13 Ves Jun 95, 103, 33 ER 230.

buffers. In the common law there was a long standing maxim that the court should not inquire into the adequacy of the consideration so long as some consideration had been given.[86] Even those nineteenth century writers who were most enthusiastic about the will theory followed the traditional line.[87] Pothier's translator was forced to concede that, 'The Law of England has not in general admitted inequality as a primary and substantive objection.'[88]

THE WILL THEORY AND JUDICIAL INNOVATION

One of the reasons that the will theory was so successful in nineteenth century England was the way in which it could be blended with existing common law rules. Another attraction was the way that it proved useful when it came to solving practical problems. The adoption of offer and acceptance was not just about fidelity to the theory. Indeed it was still possible to provide a coherent account of the law of contract in the early nineteenth century without offer and acceptance. The doctrine was ignored by Samuel Comyn as late as 1824.[89] Rather more surprisingly, given his interest in the will theory, it was also missing from the first edition of Chitty's textbook.[90] Robert Belt, in the fifth edition of Brown's Reports published in 1820, on the other hand, used offer and acceptance in order to explain an exchange of letters.[91] Judges were quick to see the practical applications of offer and acceptance. It provided a solution to the difficulties of contracting by post in *Adams v. Lindsell*.[92] Lord Eldon had adopted a similar solution the year before in Chancery in *Kennedy v. Lee*.[93] Offer and acceptance also proved useful when it came to rationalizing the practice of auction sales.[94]

---

86 Ibbetson, *A historical introduction*, pp 72–4.
87 Chitty, *Contracts*, p. 7; Addison, *Contracts*, p. 39. S. Comyn, *A treatise on the law relating to contracts and agreements not under seal* (2nd edn., London, 1824), p. 7 wrote that that a contract for valuable consideration could not be impeached but does not link it to the adequacy rule. Pollock, *Contract*, p. 154 made the same point with a quotation from Hobbes. The passage is taken from *Leviathan*. Sir W. Molesworth (ed.), *The English works of Thomas Hobbes* (London, 1839), part 1; chapter 15 states, 'The value of things contracted for, is measured by the appetite of the contractors: and therefore just value, is that which they be contented to give.'
88 Pothier, *Obligations*, i, p. 23.
89 Comyn, *Contracts*.
90 Chitty, *Contracts*.
91 *Ford v. Compton* (1785) 2 Bro CC 32 note 2.
92 (1818) 1 B & Ald 681.
93 (1817) 3 Mer 441, 36 ER 441.
94 R. Babington, *A treatise on the law of auctions* (London, 1826), p. 30; Anon *A practical treatise on the law of auctions* (London, 1838), p. 23. Although offer and acceptance was not explicit in earlier times the practice of candle auctions seems to have been based on a similar idea see B. McConnell, 'Candle auctions', *NLJ* 143 (1993), 598.

The will theory of contract

For legal writers, offer and acceptance quickly became an integral part of a theory of contract premised on the meeting of wills. Much of the time judges were less concerned with determining the precise moment of a meeting of wills than they were to develop workable solutions. It made no difference, so far as a meeting of wills was concerned, whether a contract was accepted when posted or when it reached the offeror. One solution was simply more commercially convenient than the other.[95] Judges were even prepared to deploy offer and acceptance when a meeting of wills was never a possibility.[96] From the early nineteenth century it became more common for counsel and judges to deploy Pothier and other Civilian sources as a way of adding weight to a particular line of argument.[97] *Hadley v. Baxendale*[98] may have sprung from a desire to protect entrepreneurial activity and to insulate common carriers from unlimited liability, but during the course of argument the preferred solution was explicitly likened to the Code Civile by Parke B.[99]

Pothier's views were useful in developing legal doctrine in less specific ways which, although real enough, are harder to trace. One of the features of the will theory was the way in which intention was thrust into the spotlight. Once again this dove-tailed neatly with existing approaches.[1] In *Kingston v. Preston*,[2] Lord Mansfield held that conditions should be interpreted according to the intentions of the parties.[3] Ashhurst and Aston JJ agreed[4] and this quickly became the standard view.[5] Writing in the 1790s, Powell stressed

---

95 *Dunlop v. Higgins* (1848) 1 HLC 381, 400: see Gardner, 'Trashing with Trollope', 173.
96 For example in *Williams v. Carwardine* (1833) 4 B & Ad 621, 110 ER 570 which held that a plaintiff was entitled to a reward when giving information about a murder purely to assuage her own conscience. On this case see P. Mitchell & J. Phillips, 'The contractual nexus: is reliance essential?', *OJLS*, 22 (2002), 115 at 117–18.
97 This phenomenon is carefully explored by C. MacMillan, 'Mistaken agreements: the role of argument in the development of a doctrine of contractual mistake in nineteenth century England' in Lewis & Lobban (eds), *Law and history*, p. 284.
98 (1854) 9 Ex 341; 2 CLR 517; 23 LJ Ex 179; 18 Jur 358; 2 WR 302; 23 LT 69. For a detailed discussion of this case see Ibbetson, *A historical introduction*, pp 229–32; Simpson, 'Innovation', 273–7; R. Danzig, 'Hadley v. Baxendale: a study in the industrialization of the law', *Jour Leg Stud*, 4 (1975), 249; D. Pugsley, 'The facts of Hadley v. Baxendale', *NLJ* (1976), 420; F. Faust, 'Hadley v. Baxendale: an understandable miscarriage of justice', *Jour Leg Hist*, 15 (1994), 41; J. Barton, 'Contractual damages and the rise of industry', *OJLS*, 7 (1987), 40.
99 (1854) 9 Ex 341, 346.
1 Pothier, *Obligations*, ii, 35–6.
2 (1773) Lofft 194, 198 was also cited in argument in *Jones v. Barkley* (1781) 2 Doug 684, 689–691, 99 ER 434.
3 He was probably not the first judge to think in this way about conditions. There are earlier hints in *Thorpe v. Thorpe* (1701) 12 Mod 455, 460; *Russen v. Coleby* (1733) 7 Mod 236, 87 ER 1213.
4 (1773) Lofft 194, 198.
5 *Porter v. Shepherd* (1796) 6 TR 665, 668, 101 ER 761. For similar statements see: *Glazebrook v. Woodrow* (1799) 8 TR 366, 101 ER 366; *Campbell v. Jones* (1796) 6 TR 570, 101 ER 708;

the importance of intention when interpreting the meaning of agreements.[6] This approach was carried over into the nineteenth century. Henry Colebrooke insisted that: 'The leading principle is, that the intentions of the parties, as expressed or implied, shall be the rule of construction. Particular maxims of interpretation are illustrations of that principle, rather than substantive and authoritative rules of law.'[7]

Pothier's influence went beyond support for an intention orientated approach towards contractual interpretation. His *Traité des obligations* set down twelve rules of construction,[8] described by Samuel Comyn as, 'quite consonant to the principles of the English law, and to the practice of our courts'.[9] But in the hands of English writers Pothier's overarching emphasis on intention became twisted. It was buried under layers of rules of interpretation.[10] Like Lord Mansfield before him, he was not wholly successful in liberating English lawyers from rigid rules of interpretation.[11] In the 1820s Serjeant Williams complained that, 'almost all of the old cases, and many of the modern ones on this subject, are decided upon distinctions so nice and technical, that it is very difficult, if not impractical, to deduce from them any certain rule or principle'.[12] Rather than withering away in the face of intention, the rules of construction grew in importance. By the 1871 edition of Williams Saunders Reports the rules of construction were spread across five pages.[13] They were heavily relied upon in judgment[14] and in argument[15] and were repeated in the influential *Smith's leading cases*.[16]

Intention was often little more than a justification for mechanical application of the rules of construction. As with offer and acceptance there

Havelock v. Geddes (1809) 10 East 555, 103 ER 886; *Storer v. Gordon* (1814) 3 M & S 308, 105 ER 627.

6 Powell, *Contracts*, i, 243–4.
7 Colebrooke, *Contracts*, p. 73. Leake, *Contract*, p. 349 expressed similar sentiments.
8 Pothier, *Obligations*, 1.1.7.
9 Comyn, *Contracts*, p. 24.
10 Colebrooke, *Contracts*, pp 65–6; Chitty, *Contracts*, pp 19–22; Leake, *Contract*, p. 349; Pollock, *Contract*, p. 409.
11 For the position pre-Lord Mansfield see *Thorpe v. Thorpe* (1702) 1 Ld Raym 662, 12 Mod 455, 91 ER 1341, 88 ER 1448; *Blackwell v. Nash* (1722) 1 Stra 535, 8 Mod 105, 93 ER 684, 88 ER 83; *Dawson v. Myer* (1726) 1 Stra 712, 93 ER 801.
12 (1824) 1 Wms Saund 320 n 4. On his rules of construction see S. Stoljar, *A history of contract at common law* (Canberra, 1975), pp 161–3.
13 Edited by Sir Edward Vaughan Williams.
14 *Glazebrook v. Woodrow* (1799) 8 TR 366; *Carpenter v. Cresswell* (1827) 4 Bing 409, 130 ER 825; *Mattock v. Kinglake* (1839) 10 Ad & E 50, 113 ER 19; *Dicker v. Jackson* (1848) 6 CB 103, 136 ER 1190; *Thames Haven Dock & Railway Co. v. Byrmer* (1850) 5 Exch 696, 155 ER 305.
15 For example: *Ferry v. Williams* (1817) 8 Taunt 62, 129 ER 305; *Lloyd v. Lloyd* (1837) 2 Myl & Craig 192, 40 ER 613; *Lord Howden v. Simpson* (1839) 10 Ad & E 793, 113 ER 300; *Giles v. Giles* (1846) 9 QB 164, 115 ER 1237.
16 J.W. Smith *Leading cases on various aspects of the law*, 2 vols (London, 1837), ii, 9. This section increased in length see the fifth edition of 1856 see ii, 11–14.

was not always a genuine inquiry into the minds of the parties. English law had come full circle. Colin Blackburn, writing in the 1840s, was one of the few writers prepared to admit the deceit: 'the intention must be collected from the whole agreement, and the Courts have within the last fifty years adopted for this purpose some rules of construction which are, perhaps some of them a little artificial'.[17]

The same process was also played out in attempts to distinguish liquidated damages clauses which were perfectly valid from penalty clauses which were not. Looking back on the nineteenth century common law in his commentary on the Indian Contract Act Pollock admitted that: 'The truth is that here, as in some other branches of the law, what was a rule of policy overriding the intention of the parties has been turned into an artificial and more or less arbitrary rule of construction.'[18]

In *Astley v. Weldon* Lord Eldon laid down some guidelines for determining whether a clause was a genuine pre-estimate of loss and thereby escaped branding as a penalty clause.[19] The established position was clearly seen to be unsatisfactory:

> A principle has been said to have been stated in several cases, the adoption of which one cannot but lament, namely that if the sum would be very enormous and excessive considered as liquidated damages, it shall be taken to be a penalty though agreed to be paid in the form of a contract.[20]

Where the agreement contained a condition that money was to be paid and the sum in the clause was higher or there were several different conditions in the agreement and the sum in the clause was payable on breach of any of them, then it was branded a penalty clause. Rooke J was explicit about the role of intention, 'the determination of the court in construing this instrument must be guided by the intention of the parties'.[21] Initially some judges were prepared to overlook Lord Eldon's guidelines. Carrying the label 'liquidated damages' was enough to determine the character of a clause because the description reflected what the parties intended.[22]

---

17 *A treatise on the effect of the contract of sale; on legal rights of property and possession in goods, wares, and merchandize* (London, 1845), p. 151. Ibbetson, *A historical introduction*, p. 225 makes the same point.
18 F. Pollock with D. Mulla, *The Indian Contract Act with a commentary, critical and explanatory* (1st edn., London, 1905), p. 268.
19 (1801) 2 B & P 346, 350, 126 ER 1318.
20 (1801) 2 B & P 346, 351.
21 (1801) 2 B & P 346, 353 Chambre J. used similar language at 354.
22 *Barton v. Glover* (1815) Holt NP 43, 171 ER 154; *Reilly v. Jones* (1823) 1 Bing 302, 130 ER 172.

By the 1820s the courts began to adopt Lord Eldon's guidelines. Any inconsistent authorities were treated as wrongly decided.[23] In *Kemble v. Farren*[24] an agreement worded 'to be liquidated and ascertained damages, and not a penalty or penal sum'[25] was treated as a penalty because the clause applied to various breaches of differing severity. Lord Eldon's guidelines continued to be bound up with intention.[26] But, as elsewhere, rules of interpretation had less to do with intention than applying set rules, in this instance whether or not there was a genuine pre-estimate of loss. The search for intention came second to commercial convenience.

THE INTERACTION BETWEEN JUDGES AND TEXTBOOK WRITERS

The will theory made the impact that it did because judges and writers were engaged in a joint enterprise. Nowhere is this seen more clearly than in the development of a unified doctrine of mistake. In Pothier's mind 'error is the greatest defect that can occur in a contract'.[27] His analysis based on an absence of consent was slow to gain acceptance in England.[28] One reason was that, to begin with, there was no specific doctrine of mistake. Given that the parties were not competent witnesses in civil actions until 1851, it would have been difficult for mistake to be raised at all.[29] Where evidence was forthcoming, mistake was simply a matter that could be raised in evidence under the general issue and the jury were then entitled to find that no agreement had been reached.[30] It could also be raised indirectly through an allegation of breach of warranty or condition,[31] but the effectiveness of this method

---

23 Chitty, *Contracts* (2nd ed., 1834) p. 678 described *Barton v. Glover* and *Reilly v. Jones* as 'irreconcilable' with *Astley v. Weldon*. Addison, *Contracts*, failed to mention *Reilly v. Jones*.
24 (1829) 6 Bing 141, 130 ER 1234.
25 Such a clause looks like a standard form of drafting and may have been common practice. Evans recommended just such a clause see Pothier, *Obligations*, ii, p. 98.
26 *Davis v. Penton* (1827) 6 B & C 216, 222, 108 ER 433; *Kemble v. Farren* (1829) 6 Bing 141,148–49. Chitty, *Contracts*, p. 678; Leake, *Contract*, p. 578; Anson, *Contract*, p. 243.
27 Pothier, *Obligations*, 1.1.3.1§17.
28 For the development of a doctrine of mistake in England see Ibbetson, *A historical introduction*, pp 225–29; Simpson, 'Innovation', 265–69; MacMillan, 'Mistaken agreements', p. 284. For the influence of Pothier see J.C. Smith and J.A.C. Thomas 'Pothier and the Three Dots', *MLR*, 20 (1957), 38; C. Malecki 'L'Erreur sur la personne en anglais et en droit français déterminante de Pothier sur la Common Law?', *Revue de Droit International et Droit Comparé*, 72 (1995), 347.
29 (1851) 14 & 15 Vic c. 99 s 2.
30 For example: *Lindsay v. Limbert* (1826) 2 C & P 526, 172 ER 239; *Raffles v. Wichelhaus* (1864) 2 H & C 906, 33 LJNS 160, 159 ER 375.
31 J.L. Barton, 'Redhibition, error and implied warranty in English law', *Tijdschrift voor Rechsgeschiedenis*, 62 (1994), 317.

depended on a court's willingness to imply a warranty.[32] With the exception of Colebrooke's more theoretical work,[33] English writers largely ignored mistake.[34] Pothier's position was not totally ignored by lawyers, but as MacMillan has observed this was less because there was a deliberate end in mind than the fact that counsel resorted to arguments with a civilian flavour when the common law was against them.[35] In *Kennedy v. Panama New Zealand and Australian Royal Mail Company*,[36] Blackburn J. referred to a text from the *Digest* on mistake[37] but his reasoning stands out because it was so unusual.[38] Procedural developments including the availability of equitable defences in the common law and the decline of the jury all ensured that English law became more receptive to a doctrine of mistake.[39] It still needed the intervention of legal writers before civilian ideas really took hold. The catalyst may have been the Indian Law Commission report on contract, which gave Pothier's treatment of mistake pride of place.[40] In a book on Indian contract law a few years previously, the secretary to the commission, William MacPherson, had already praised Pothier's analysis.[41] Stephen Leake's *The elements of the law of contracts*,[42] which provided the first extended treatment of mistake, was published around the same time as the commission's report. Leake was also the first writer to draw parallels with equity.[43] In the hands of Pollock[44] and Anson,[45] Pothier's unified analysis of mistake became more deeply embedded. English authority was still scarce and these writers simply reinterpreted cases like *Couturier v. Hastie*,[46] *Boulton*

32 P. Mitchell, 'The development of quality obligations in sale of goods', *LQR*, 117 (2001), 645.
33 Colebrooke, *Contracts*, p. 46.
34 Comyn, Chitty and Addison were all silent on the subject.
35 MacMillan, 'Mistaken agreements', pp 292–93.
36 (1867) LR 2 QB 580.
37 (1867) LR 2 QB 580, 588. The texts were taken from Paul and Ulpian: A. Watson (ed.), *The digest of Justinian* (Philadelphia, 1985) D.18.1.9,10,11. Colebrooke, *Contracts*, p. 46 relied on a different text of Ulpian to illustrate the same point: D. 50.17.166.2.
38 MacMillan, 'Mistaken agreements', pp 301–2. Equitable defences were introduced into the common law by the Common Law Procedure Act (1854) 17 & 18 Vict c.125 ss 83–86. For a comment on equity's jurisdiction over mistake see *Murray v. Parker* (1854) 19 Beav 305, 308, 52 ER 367 and MacMillan, 'Mistaken agreements', pp 308–12.
39 MacMillan, 'Mistaken agreements', pp 289–90.
40 *The Report of the Indian law commissioners on the subject of contracts* (1867–68) PP HC vol xlix.
41 *Outlines of the law of contracts as administered in the courts of British India* (London, 1860), pp 2–5. MacPherson was a self-confessed admirer of Pothier: p. xi. On the influence of Pothier see Ibbetson, *A historical introduction*, p. 227.
42 Leake, *Contract*, pp 168–81.
43 Ibid., pp 179–81.
44 Pollock, *Contract*, pp 355–429.
45 Anson, *Contract*, pp 116–128.
46 (1852) 8 Exch 40 (Court of the Exchequer); (1853) 9 Exch 102 (Exchequer Chamber);

v. Jones[47] and *Raffles v. Wichelhaus*,[48] in order to make them fit with the new theory.

The influence of the will theory may not be confined to the common law. By the mid-eighteenth century, equity was no longer the loose coalition of former times. Precedent had a more important role.[49] In *The Earl of Chesterfield v. Jansen*,[50] Lord Hardwicke had brought together five grounds of equitable relief under the banner of fraud. A unified structure was still lacking.[51] In his, *A treatise on contract within the jurisdiction of courts of equity* of 1806, John Newland took his definition of contract from Blackstone's *Commentaries*: 'A contract is an agreement, upon a sufficient consideration to do or not to do a particular thing'.[52] The type of analytical approach which began to characterize the common law also began to appear in equity from around 1830. Newland's definition of contract began to look dated.

Attempts to introduce consensual ideas into equity had to compete with the existing order constructed around fraud. The new generation of writers were very receptive to principles gleaned from natural law and will theory. Writing in the 1830s, Joseph Story put forward a general principle, that 'in regard to acts done or contracts made by parties, affecting their rights and interests ... there must be a free and full consent'.[53] Edward Snell followed his example.[54] Some of this analysis reached a high level of sophistication, particularly in the work of George Jeremy.[55] Equity lawyers were also familiar with Pothier's work. In *Huguenin v. Baseley*,[56] Sir Samuel Romilly, who was one of counsel, put forward an influential argument, which would

---

(1856) 5 HLC 673 (House of Lords). MacPherson, *Contracts*, p. 3, Leake, *Contract*, p. 176; J.P. Benjamin *Treatise on the law of sale of personal property* (London, 1868), pp 57–58; Pollock, *Contract*, p. 398; Anson, *Contract*, p. 121.

47 (1857) 2 H & N 564, 27 LJ Ex 117, 157 ER 232. Leake, *Contract*, p. 16; Pollock, *Contract*, p. 381; Anson, *Contract*, p. 118 cf Benjamin, *Sale*, pp 303–306 who treats *Boulton v. Jones* as a case on set-off.

48 (1864) 2 H & C 906, 33 LJNS 160, 159 ER 375. Leake, *Contract*, p. 178; Pollock, *Contract*, p. 389; Anson, *Contract*, p. 122. For a discussion of the background of the case see Simpson, *Leading cases*, pp 134–62.

49 C. Croft, 'Lord Hardwick's use of precedent in equity' in T.G. Watkin (ed.), *Legal record and historical reality* (London, 1989), p. 121; D. Lieberman, *The province of legislation determined: legal theory in eighteenth century Britain* (Cambridge, 1989), pp 81–83.

50 (1750) 2 Ves Sen 125, 155–57, 28 ER 82.

51 Lobban, 'Contractual fraud', p. 448.

52 The passage is taken from W. Blackstone, *Commentaries on the laws of England*, 4 vols (Oxford, 1766), ii, 442.

53 *Commentaries on equity jurisprudence as administered in England and America* (2nd edn., London, 1839), p. 186.

54 *The principles of equity intended for the use of students and the profession* (London, 1868)

55 *A treatise on the equitable jurisdiction of the High Court of Chancery* (London, 1828).

56 (1807) 14 Ves Jun 273, 33 ER 526.

overshadow Lord Eldon's judgment,[57] that equity recognized a general principle of undue influence. Romilly based his argument on Pothier's treatise on gifts[58] but the principle can be traced in English authority.[59] In general, legal writers probably made less of an impact in equity than in the common law at this time. Their main contribution had more to do with looking at existing doctrines in new ways than the wholesale development of new legal principles.

THE LEGACY OF THE WILL THEORY AND THE LAW OF CONTRACT

The law of contract in England would almost certainly have gone in new directions in the nineteenth century even without the intervention of the will theory. All the ingredients were present. Economic growth combined with a restructuring of legal procedure and a more analytical mind set exerted strong pressures.[60] Alternative explanations for contractual liability based on the parties' expectations were favoured by some writers.[61] But it is unlikely that a structure as coherent as the one which was borrowed from the will theory would have emerged. Doctrinal development may even have followed a more conservative route. This is precisely what happened in the law of tort[62] and restitution[63] where such structures were lacking.

The way in which the will theory gave focus to doctrinal change provides some important lessons about legal change. It is a warning against drawing sharp lines between different periods. Legal change is both slow and messy. Even within the law of contract, there were times when doctrinal development was hampered by the continued presence of older rules. Some

---

57 *Dent v. Bennett* (1839) 4 My & Cr 269, 277, 41 ER 105; O.D. Tudor, *A selection of leading cases in equity*, 2 vols (1850), ii, p. 430; Pollock, *Contract*, p. 576.
58 *Traité des donations entre-vifs* (Paris, 1777) 1.2§8.
59 *Bates v. Graves* (1793) 2 Ves Jun 287, 288–89, 30 ER 637.
60 On the influence of commerce on nineteenth century contract law see S. Hedley, 'The needs of commercial litigants in nineteenth century contract law', *Jour Leg Hist*, 18 (1997), 85.
61 For example by Adam Smith, *Lectures on jurisprudence*,(ed.), R.L. Meek, D.D. Raphael & P. Stein (Oxford, 1978), esp. pp 87, 472. William Paley, *The principles of moral and political philosophy* (1785) 105, 121–22 made a similar suggestion. The idea was later taken up by Pollock see Duxbury, *Frederick Pollock*, 195–96.
62 On the slow development of a tort of negligence in the nineteenth century see D. Ibbetson 'The tort of negligence in the common law in the nineteenth and twentieth centuries' in Schrage (ed.), *Negligence*, p. 229.
63 There was a gradual retreat from Lord Mansfield's attempt to liberalise money had and received: W. Swain, 'Moses v. MacFerlan' in C. Mitchell & P. Mitchell (eds), *Landmark cases in the law of restitution* (Oxford, 2006), p. 19.

of these tensions have still to be resolved. One of the most powerful arguments for reforming privity of contract was the way in which the restriction was capable of frustrating the will of the parties.[64] The doctrine of consideration is still capable of preventing the will of the parties from being satisfied.[65]

---

[64] H. Gutteridge, 'Contract and Commercial Law' (1935) 51 LQR 91, 98; *Smith & Snipes Hall v. River Douglas Catchment Board* [1949] 2 KB 500, 514; *Scruttons Ltd. v. Midland Silicones Ltd.* [1962] AC 446, 489; Contracts (Rights of Third Parties) Act 1999 ss 1 (1) (a)–(b).

[65] This was one of the reasons behind Denning J's attempt to circumvent consideration using promissory estoppel in *Central London Property Trust v. High Trees House Ltd.* [1947] KB 130.

The 'creation' of the default judgment in nineteenth-century English procedural reforms

CARLA CRIFÒ

THIS PAPER CHARTS A SINGLE CHANGE in the procedural law in the maelstrom of the nineteenth-century reforms. This change can be considered either a small technical adjustment or a fundamental modification to underlying principles of procedure, of the role of courts and their sovereignty in the international arena. It is part of the socio-cultural landscape of its time, and it may have gone unnoticed amid some more evident changes to civil procedure and the law of evidence during the century.

The possibilities of obtaining a judgment in the continued absence of the counterpart (the defendant) in a 'personal' action were extremely limited up to the 1720s. The terms of the question can be easily summarized by reference to Maitland's lecture on the forms of action:[1]

> A court chosen, one must make one's adversary appear; [...] Suppose him contumacious, what can one do? Can one have his body seized? If he cannot be found, can one have him outlawed? [...] Again, can one have the thing in dispute seized? Can one obtain a judgment by default, obtain what one wants though the adversary continues in his contumacy?

Of course, there is a chasm between taking action when the defendant is contumacious and granting default judgment in the absence of a reply by the defendant. The former implies a value judgment on 'disobeying' the summons. Judgments based upon contumacy in this sense were well established in civil law systems in Maitland's time. Such judgments would be

---

This paper originates in a chapter of my DPhil thesis on 'default and *contumacia*.' A first version was presented at the Annual Meeting of the Law and Society Association, Las Vegas in June 2005, and a longer, amended version at the British Legal History Conference, London, in July 2005. Grateful thanks are owed to the Society of Legal Scholars and the Department of Law, University of Leicester for financial support, to the organizers of the conferences and to the participants for their insightful and helpful comments.

1 F.W. Maitland, *Equity; also the forms of action at common law: two courses of lectures* (Cambridge, 1920), pp 296–7.

for the most part on the merits (based more or less on evidence led by the plaintiff). Additionally, they would be perfectly 'regular' unless the defendant applied to have them set aside or appealed, often within a fixed time limit.[2]

Up to the eighteenth century default judgments could be obtained in English courts only in real actions, where the absence of the defendant did not prevent the issue of a judgment without consideration of the merits. The defendant who had lost possession in this way might then seek to recover possession, but could only do so by suing out a writ of right. On the other hand, there was entrenched reluctance in English law to award a judgment in an action *in personam* where no jurisdiction could be asserted over the defendant, either through submission (appearance), or institutional 'belonging',[3] with the exception of a few strictly limited statutory cases.[4]

It was not until 1832 that the modern 'default judgment' became the norm. Before its appearance on the statute books, generally the plaintiff at common law had to compel the appearance of the defendant by recourse to one of several means, of which the most important were:

1. process by (judicial writ of) *distringas* or distress infinite, which consisted in seizing the defendant's chattels until he put in an appearance; this was the only means available if the defendant had privilege against arrest and was in England.
2. Process by bill, closely followed by the writ of *latitat* leading to imprisonment and based on a fictitious violent act; the first bill did not disclose the true action (the debt) and the debtor could remain in prison until the creditor served a further bill disclosing the true cause of action.
3. The ultimate threat of outlawry, an expensive process by original writ to be used if the defendant remained absent from the start or could not be served with writ of summons or bill and was suspected of having absconded abroad.

Judgment in default of appearance is today one of the most common outcomes of a civil claim (statistics for 2004 show for example that out of 1,051 claims for debt issued in the Queen's Bench division, 657 default judgments were granted)[5] and the procedure has not undergone many changes of note since its introduction in the nineteenth century. A default judgment is not strictly a judgment on the merits (although it creates direct

---

2 See for example the *Code Louis*, Tit. V.
3 Prisoners and court officers were in the jurisdiction of a court. J.H. Baker, *An introduction to English legal history* (4th ed. London, 2002), p. 41.
4 12 Geo. I c. 29 s. 1 (Frivolous Arrests Act 1725); extended by 45 Geo. III c. 124 § 3 (Privilege of Parliament Act 1805); and 7&8 Geo. IV c .71 § 5 (Imprisonment for Debt Act 1827); W.S. Holdsworth, *A history of English law* (London, 1903–72), ix, 253.
5 DCA, *Judicial statistics 2004* (Cm 6565) p.39. In the county courts, out of 1,335,775 default actions entered only 14,670 were set down for trial.

res judicata, in the form of cause of action estoppel).[6] It certainly is not conceived nor understood as a punishment for failure to answer the summons.[7] The theoretical justification of the necessity of court intervention in the case of defendant's apathy is now to be found in the principle of access to justice.[8] A judgment may be entered either as soon as the time limits for serving an acknowledgment of service or a defence have elapsed, or after an application to the court and a hearing, depending on the subject matter of the claim.[9] The judgment may be set aside at any time, as of right if it was obtained in violation of any rules, or upon the discretion of the court.[10]

THE (NON-)EVOLUTION OF THE LAW AS TO DEFAULT IN PERSONAL ACTIONS AT COMMON LAW

Practice and procedure in the English courts has always varied widely between courts; under the writ system, they varied depending on the writ used. The entrenched common-law development of procedure in the courts requires at this point an historical excursus into the roots of the denial of default judgment in personal actions.

In the early twelfth century, the *Leges Henrici Primi*[11] described the different procedural rules pertaining to the different courts. Rules applying to seigneurial courts[12] or particular proceedings in the county courts[13] did in fact allow for default judgments. Moreover, the rule that civil cases could normally only be heard and determined in the presence of both parties or their duly authorized representatives under the English medieval common law was limited to personal actions, while in other types of action (such as the petty assizes of novel disseisin, mort d'ancestor and darrein presentment)[14] judgment would be given, even in default of appearance. There were sus-

---

6 *Kok Hoong v. Leong Cheong Kweng Mines Ltd* [1964] AC 993 (PC), 1010 *per* Viscount Radcliffe.
7 Although in a recent case decided on the Civil Procedure Rules, *Shiblaq v. Sadikoglu* [2004] EWHC 1890 (Comm), it was suggested that valid service creates a 'duty' to return an Acknowledgment of Service.
8 A.A.S. Zuckerman *Civil procedure* (London, 2003), p. 239.
9 Civil Procedure Rules (CPR) Part 12.
10 CPR Part 13.
11 L.J. Downer (ed.), *Leges Henrici Primi* (Oxford, 1972).
12 Downer, *Leges*, pp 164–5. Ch. 50 *De supersessionibus placiti*.
13 Ibid., pp 168–71. Ch. 53 *De supersessione comitatus*.
14 P. Brand, 'Delay in the English common law courts (twelfth to fourteenth centuries)' in C.H. van Rhee (ed.), *The law's delay: essays on undue delay in civil litigation* (Antwerp, 2004), p. 31. I am grateful to Dr Brand for his comments on the paper and for providing me with a copy of his article.

tained attempts to develop an efficient system of mesne process,[15] applicable to all or most actions, well into the following centuries,[16] that would allow the court to grant relief in the absence of a party in personal actions. However such attempts failed and the distinction between real and personal actions with regard to the possibility of default judgment was established.

The distinction appears in *Bracton*, which seems to set the most often cited golden standard in this matter.[17] The possibility of obtaining a default judgment depends on the type of property, the subject matter of the claim, or the type of writ. In personal actions, if the defendant does not appear after renewed summons and increasingly invasive mesne process (that is, mostly, distraint on the defendant's property), the plaintiff only has the nuclear option of petitioning for a declaration of outlawry. However, a declaration of outlawry does not satisfy the debt, but merely increases the pressure on the defendant to appear. In fact, declarations of outlawry lost at a very early stage their most serious consequences, while still maintaining the extensive and expensive formalities connected to the ancient procedure. Ironically, and as pointed out polemically in Pollock and Maitland's *History*,[18] the rule preventing the issue of a default judgment in personal actions is criticized by *Bracton's* author,[19] and the

---

15 Baker, *Introduction*, p. 64.
16 D.W. Sutherland, '*Mesne* process upon personal actions in the early common law', *LQR*, 82 (1966), 482; M. Blatcher 'Distress infinite and the contumacious sheriff', *Bull. Inst. Hist. Res.*, 13 (1935–36), 140 at 146ff.
17 E. Coke (*Institutes*, 128 and 259b) and C. Viner (*A general abridgment of law and equity*, vii, 'Default', pp 429ff) refer to Bracton as authority for the rules on default.
18 F. Pollock and F.W. Maitland, *History of English law* (2nd ed. Cambridge, 1968), p. 591: 'He has to suggest that there can be a minor outlawry just as there can be a minor excommunication: in other words, that a form of outlawry can be employed which will not involve a sentence of death {Bracton, fo. 441}. At a little later time a distinction is here drawn. In some of the forms of action, for example Trespass *vi et armis*, there can be arrest (*Capias ad respondendum*) and, failing this, there may be outlawry; in other forms "distress infinite" is the last process. At a yet later stage, partly by statute, partly under the cover of fictions, *Capias* and Outlawry became common to many forms, and "imprisonment upon mesne process" was the weapon on which our law chiefly relied in its struggle with the contumacious.' Bracton's arguing for a solution reinforces the view (P. Brand, 'Legal education in England before the Inns of Court' in A.A. Wijffels (ed.), *Learning the law*, London, 1999) of opposing views in the Treatise, and that *Bracton* is not necessarily to be taken as a description of the law of the time, but rather as a normative treatise.
19 'It would, so it seems, be well to distinguish between pecuniary actions arising from contract and actions arising from delict. In the former case it would be well to adjudge the plaintiff seisin of enough chattels to satisfy the debt and damages, and also to summon the defendant; and then, if he appeared, his chattels would be restored to him and he would answer to the action, and if he did not appear the plaintiff would become their owner. And in the case of delict it would be well that the damages should be taxed by the justices and paid out of the defendant's rents and chattels': S.E. Thorne (ed.), *Bracton on the laws and customs of England* (Cambridge, MA, 1968) fos. 440b, 368. Bracton's argument for outlawry

criticism is repeated in *Fleta*.[20] Nonetheless, the distinction is not challenged from then on. Coke does not debate the question, but merely refers back to *Bracton*.

Cases cited in Viner's abridgment provide a useful overview of the state of the law between the fifteenth and the eighteenth centuries. In personal actions, there are cases of judgments being given 'in default', but this possibility is limited to cases where the defendant has made at least one appearance,[21] since after appearance[22] default is always peremptory, the only possibilities being a judgment, if the thing is certain, or a writ *ad Audiendum Judicium*.[23]

True non-appearance, however, was still an insurmountable obstacle to the issue of a judgment. Therefore additional and new forms of 'process' were devised to compel the appearance of a determined absentee defendant.[24] The full process which eventually led to outlawry being used in actions *in personam* in the Court of King's Bench became extremely cumbersome. The *distringas* itself had lost most of its force by the fifteenth century.[25] As a consequence, compelling process was obtained by the parallel adoption and adaptation of the procedure by bill, which had been in use since the middle of the fourteenth century.[26] A fictitious bill of trespass in Middlesex would be issued, and immediately extended to other counties (*latitat*). Upon the presentation of the bill the defendant could be arrested (or forced to give bail for his appearance). This system therefore allowed the plaintiff to sue in debt without an original writ.[27] The procedure found favour in practice, at first for

   is that 'there is no greater crime than contempt and disobedience. For everyone in the realm is or ought to be obedient to the lord king and his peace.' Fo. 441, 368.
20 Bk. II, ch. 65: G.O. Sayles and H.G. Richardson (ed.), *Fleta (prologue and books I and II)* (Selden Society vol. 42: London, 1953), p 217: 'And immediately upon default made after attachment there follows the grand distress, which entails the forfeiture of goods to the king, but nothing for the party. This is an evil.'
21 *The Earl of Oxford's case* (1615) Ch Rep 1, 21 ER 485, citing [YB] 5 E[dw] 4, 38; *Porter v. Harris* (1662) 1 Levinz 63, 83 ER 298 on covenant; *Hodsden v. Harridge* (1670) 2 Wms Saunders 61, 85 ER 672 on debt. In both these cases judgment by default is equated with a confession, which suggests that they do deal with the jurisdictional problem of the presence of the defendant (they refer to default after appearance); also *Betton v. Ann* (1664–1665) Nelson 95, 21 ER 798 (judgment by default in an action of debt, but for arrears for rent in a lease of crown land).
22 'A man shall *not* be condemned by his default, *but after plea pleaded or imparlance*; for the dies datus is always before the count, and the imparlance is after the count. Note the difference, for it is good. Br. Default, pl. 1 cites [YB] 19 H.8, 6.' Viner, *Abridgment*, [476].
23 Viner, *Abridgment*, [472] 10, citing [YB] 2 H. 4, 23 (1401); and [474] 21, 22, citing [YB] 38 H 6. 33 and 39 H. 6 16 (1460).
24 W. Blackstone, *Commentaries on the laws of England* (19th ed. London, 1836) chapter xix.
25 Blatcher, 'Distress', pp 66–71.
26 Baker, *Introduction*, pp 41ff.
27 Ibid., p. 42. This allowed the King's Bench to expand its jurisdiction to the detriment of the Court of Common Pleas.

its low cost and simplicity,[28] but even after these benefits had palled, for the possibility of not stating, in the initial bill, the true cause of action.[29] Such was the success of the procedure that both the Court of Common Pleas and the Court of Exchequer[30] eventually adopted similarly fictitious procedures, the former by expanding its own bill jurisdiction against personnel and prisoners,[31] and the latter through the use of a fictitious *quo minus*,[32] and later the Exchequer *subpoena*.[33]

'By the end of the eighteenth century, the Bill of Middlesex or *latitat* [was] in general considered merely as process to bring the defendant into court.'[34] If the defendant to a suit by bill defaulted after his first appearance, the court could proceed to a verdict and judgment.[35] Procedure by original writ was still necessary, if the defendant had privilege of Parliament, or absconded, 'as a foundation of process in his goods, or in order to proceed to outlawry'.[36] Proceeding to outlawry was in fact the only way to obtain some sort of satisfaction if the defendant remained persistently absent and could not be served with any writ. The procedure required the return of a special writ of *capias utlagatum* (directing the sheriff not only to arrest the defaulter but also to inquire as to any previously undiscovered goods, available after outlawry), the inquisition by a jury into the estate of the defendant and finally the issue, by the Court of Exchequer, of writs to sell the goods, to recover the debts and to levy the issues and profits.[37] The moneys so raised belonged to the crown, but the plaintiff could petition to the Lords of the Treasury (unless the debt was for less than £50, in which case a simple motion to the Exchequer would suffice).[38] This procedure was the focus of much criticism during the earlier phases of nineteenth-century reform.

The procedure ought to have been reserved for cases where 'the defendant was neither within the jurisdiction nor had any fixed abode there, nor any property which could be distrained.'[39] However, in actual fact it would lead

28 Blatcher, 'Distress', pp 133, 120.
29 Ibid., pp 142–8, 154–62. Legislative attempts were made to curb the widespread use of the bill procedure between 1532 and 1661. The most important was the Act 13 C 2 S. 2 c.2 ss. 1–4, which required the true cause of action to be stated; practitioners circumvented this Act through the insertion of the clause *ac etiam* in the bill of Middlesex.
30 Baker, *Introduction*, p. 47 (Common Pleas) p. 49 (Exchequer); W.H. Bryson, *The equity side of the Exchequer: its jurisdiction, administration, procedures and records* (Cambridge, 1975), p. 25.
31 Baker, *Introduction*, p. 48.
32 H. Wurzel, 'The development of quo minus', *Yale LJ*, 49 (1939), 39.
33 Baker, *Introduction*, p. 49; Wurzel, 'Development', pp 55–61.
34 W. Tidd, *The practice of the Court of King's Bench in personal actions: with references to rules, and cases of practice, in the Court of Common Pleas* (4th ed. London, 1808), pp 78, 79.
35 Blatcher, 'Distress', pp 113, 134.
36 Tidd, *Practice*, p. 98.
37 Ibid., p. 137.
38 Ibid., p. 138.
39 Holdsworth, *History*, ix, 254ff.

(after a very long process) to the result of obtaining satisfaction without the defendant's participating in, or indeed, having any notice of the proceedings at all.[40] Moreover, the procedure was long and costly, and could be nullified at any point by the defendant's appearance, although not without paying full costs.

From 1725 onwards a series of statutes[41] attempted to introduce an important change to simplify the procedure for obtaining judgment in the absence of the defendant: in some cases, personal service of the summons or the original writ (later, even service at the defendant's abode, when it was attested by affidavit that the defendant could not be personally served), allowed the plaintiff to enter an appearance for the defendant. In these cases, as when the defendant had himself put in bail below (for appearance, to the sheriff who had made the arrest) or above (to the court, as undertaking of the satisfaction of judgment), the plaintiff might sign judgment in default even if the defendant did not put in an answer. This judgment by default was considered to be technically after appearance, 'an implied confession to the action,' and could be either by *nil dicit* (defendant appears but says nothing in bar or preclusion of the action),[42] or by *non sum informatus*, 'where [the defendant's] attorney says, he is not informed of any answer to be given thereto'.[43] Despite (or maybe because of) this potentially revolutionary innovation, the courts introduced so many fetters[44] on the exercise of the statutory power that it remained mostly unused. As Jacob put it, '[t]here was no machinery for the court to give judgment in default of appearance.'[45]

---

40 Holdsworth quotes from the *First report of commissioners on the courts of common law*, Parliamentary Papers 1829 vol. IX pp 93–4, reprinted in *The Irish University Press series of the British parliamentary papers. Legal administration. General* (Shannon 1969–1974) vol. 1: 'In its original design [outlawry] was intended to give the most ample and reiterated notice of the suit, and its penal operation attached only on the contumacious or fraudulent... But in its modern form it can scarcely be said to have any tendency even to apprize the defendant of the action, much less to warn him by distinct and repeated summons ... The original writ, *capias*, *alias*, and *pluries* ... are returned as a mere matter of form ... Nor does any greater effect in general attend to the proclamations ... A defendant against whom judgment of outlawry passes has therefore in general had no previous notice that the suit has been commenced, and may probably have had no opportunity of becoming acquainted with that fact, and it is quite possible that even his property may be seized and sold, and the proceeds paid over to the plaintiff, before he is aware that any action is pending against him.'

41 Above, n. 4.

42 In *Elmer v. Thacker* (1591) Cro Eliz 263, 78 ER 518 (action of waste), the difference between recovery by default and *nihil dicit* is described: the first is intended before appearance, while the '*nihil dicit*, ... is no default, but as a departure in contempt of Court, or rather a confession to the action, and a not denying the waste.'

43 Tidd, *Practice*, p. 496.

44 *First report of commissioners on courts of common law*, p. 87: the courts insisted that the summoner make affidavit also as to his belief that the defendant's absence was intentional and contumacious, and required at least three different applications.

45 J.I.H. Jacob, 'Civil procedure since 1800' in J.I.H. Jacob (ed.), *The reform of civil procedural law and other essays in civil procedure* (London, 1982), p. 198.

Nor did Chancery provide any relief to a creditor. One would expect that, since the Chancellor's court was free from the constraints of the strict rules of procedure which had been developed in the courts of Common Law, and 'defendants could not easily evade this new and powerful justice',[46] a solution to the non-appearance conundrum could be found. Indeed, in the early procedure, 'for contumacy', defendants 'could be imprisoned, or their property sequestered'.[47]

Chancery process started with a *subpoena ad respondendum*, 'the only original process of the Court of Chancery and the means whereby defendants were summoned to appear and make their answers'.[48] In default defendants were threatened with a monetary penalty; however, 'in practice the penalty was not enforced, but a disobedient defendant was subject to proceedings for contempt'.[49] Service of the *subpoena* could be effected in several ways: personally, either by giving it to the defendant or showing it to him and giving a note of the date of appearance; at the place of abode; or by giving or showing the writ to the defendant's wife, brother or servants.[50] While personal appearance of the defendant was theoretically necessary, the explosion of written pleadings and the possibility of appearance through attorneys transformed it into a 'procedure of formal convenience',[51] with the rule being enforced strictly only with regard to recalcitrant parties, after the answer had been put in. Neglect to appear or answer to a *subpoena* led (by an 'automatic presumption') to process for contempt,[52] by means of attachment, attachment with proclamation, and commission of rebellion.

Jones charted the progressive adding on of compelling process, 'from 1578 or thereabouts', as attachment became a formality. The main steps, return of a commission for rebellion, the involvement of the sergeant-at-arms and finally imprisonment, were established by the middle of the seventeenth century.[53] At all times 'imprisonment was regarded not so much as a punishment but as a means of retaining the defendant until he had made his apologies and put in satisfactory bonds for continued and permanent appearance'.[54] Eventually a decree of sequestration would be issued, and if

---

46 Baker, *Introduction*, p. 104.
47 Ibid.
48 W.J. Jones *The Elizabethan Court of Chancery* (Oxford, 1967) p. 177.
49 Baker, *Introduction*, p. 103.
50 Jones, *Elizabethan*, p. 179. Equity 'modified the *in personam* maxim to allow constructive service:' D.E.C. Yale, 'Introduction' in D.E.C. Yale (ed.), *Lord Nottingham's 'Manual'* (Cambridge, 1965), pp 45ff.
51 Jones, *Elizabethan*, pp 182–3; also Holdsworth, *History*, ix, 348–52.
52 Jones, *Elizabethan*, pp 229ff.
53 Ibid.; Holdsworth, *History*, ix, 350.
54 Jones, *Elizabethan*, p. 229. As Jacob, 'Civil procedure', p. 198, says, the right of arrest of the defendant, as in the common law procedure, was tolerated as 'one of the methods of exercising jurisdiction over the defendant'.

the defendant did not give himself up within a year, an injunction for possession could be granted to the plaintiff.[55] In its Tudor form, sequestration had been used when required by 'social and legal necessity', such as when a 'defendant had not been apprehended after the full range of process of contempt, and an injunction for possession awarded to the plaintiff had been thwarted'.[56] Sequestration did not pass title, nor did the eventual injunction for possession. Indeed, its use for enforcing decrees created concern, especially as it was applied to property which was not the subject matter of the dispute, and thus came to be frozen under the control of the Court.[57]

> [I]n Equity, if the defendant did not appear, the suit could not proceed nor could the bill be taken *pro confesso*[58] ... in original bills, or bills of revivor, if the defendant hath not appeared but stands out all process of contempt, the bill shall not be taken pro confesso; but this only where the defendant hath appeared, and stands out all process for want of an answer. ... [In] *Nodes v Batle*[59] ... the defendant refused to appear and 'sits out all process for contempt.' The Court could not decree the bill *pro confesso* but ordered a sequestration against all his property till the contempt was cleared. ... It was not until 1731 (5 Geo. II c. 25 s.1)[60] that the Court was enabled to enter an appearance on the defendant's behalf. After an appearance the bill could be taken *pro confesso* on no answer or an insufficient answer. In order to be liable to a decree in default of appearance the defendant must have been lodged in the Fleet and not in the custody of any other court. *Thomas v Jones* (1653), Nelson 50.[61]

Gilbert, writing in the 1720s on the procedure of Chancery,[62] referred by comparison to the canon law on contumacy, with its two decrees, the second of which did transfer the disputed property. In Chancery, on the other hand, there was upon the *subpoena* an '*apprehensio realis* (that is on the person of the

---

55 Yale, 'Introduction', p. 25.
56 Jones, *Elizabethan*, pp 302–3.
57 Ibid., citing Yale, 'Introduction', pp 30–1.
58 *Anonymous* (1667) 2 Freem 127.
59 *Nodes v. Batle* (1683/4) 2 Ch Rep 285.
60 Equity Procedure Act 1731: 'if the defendant was suspected of leaving the realm, or otherwise absconding to evade service of process, the plaintiff could, after certain formalities specified in the Act, apply to have his bill taken *pro confesso*, and the court could make such a decree as appeared to it to be just; and if a defendant was produced in court and refused to enter an appearance, the court could have an appearance entered for him': Holdsworth, *History*, ix, 350.
61 Yale, 'Introduction', p. 22.
62 G. Gilbert, *The history and practice of the High Court of Chancery (Forum Romanum)* (London, 1758), pp 32ff.

defendant), not a *missio in possessionem* by reason of the prejudice among the lawyers at the erection of the Court'.[63]

There could be cases of 'deemed or implied confession.' In one of these, the defendant appeared by attorney in court, and afterwards lay in prison. He was brought up three times by Habeas Corpus, had the bill read to him and he refused to answer: 'such public refusal in court does amount to the confession of the whole bill'.[64] In the second case, the defendant

> appears, and departs without answering, and the whole process of the court has been awarded against him after his appearance and departure to the sequestration. There also the bill is taken *pro confesso* [to be confessed], because it is presumed to be true when he has appeared, and departs in despite of the court and withstands all its process without answering; ... and it is so with us, that if the whole process of the law be spent, and the defendant never appears, you can never have a decree, for you can never make any proofs against an absent person, who is never brought into contest and there is no foundation for a decree without confession or proofs; however the plaintiff has the benefit of the sequestration, which answers to the *primum decretum*.

Of the other central courts, the Admiralty Court used a summary procedure of Continental origin much appreciated by those litigants (merchants and mariners) who could avail themselves of it.[65]

THE STEPS OF THE REFORM

At the beginning of the nineteenth century, England had two well-developed systems of law, each with its own procedure. In the courts of common law, immediate default judgment could be obtained only in the remaining real actions. In personal actions, the courts did not have jurisdiction over absent defendants. When an action was started by bill, the defendant could be

---

63 Ibid., p. 34: this is because the canonists viewed the first decree to be '*quasi litiscontestatio*, & that therefore the plaintiff may proceed to proof,' while the Chancery has 'no *quasi litiscontestatio* ... because, unless the defendant comes in and contests, there is no jurisdiction to a court of conscience; for unless the party confesses ... or it be proved upon him, there is no sufficient ground for a decree, which cannot be without *contestatio litis* (contesting the suit).'

64 Ibid., p. 36, citing Ch Rep 50 (*sic*: rectius *Thomas v. Jones* (1653) Nelson 50, 21 ER 787[?]) and *Anonymous* (1677) 2 Ch Cases 237, 22 ER 925.

65 Holdsworth, *History*, i, 300–37; B.P. Levack, *The civil lawyers in England, 1603–1641: a political study* (Oxford, 1973), p.155; T.L. Mears, 'The history of the admiralty jurisdiction' in J.H. Wigmore (ed.), *Select essays in Anglo-American legal history* (Cambridge, 1908), ii, 312.

arrested and held in prison and eventually forced to attend, leading to a judgment 'by confession' for failure to defend. However if he never appeared or was never 'in the jurisdiction of the court', the most common outcome would be a judgment of outlawry, which followed a complex and expensive procedure destined to apply in cases where no service of the writ had been possible. The judgment of outlawry could be the basis for some modicum of recovery of a debt, but that was not its primary function nor was it very effective. The *First report* by a commission into the procedure of the courts of law duly noted that the fundamental reason for proceeding to outlawry (that is, to provide notice of pending proceedings and compel appearance) was foiled by its very nature,[66] the essence of which was to lead to a judgment which would not be known to an honest defendant until execution, where possible, but which a dishonest defendant could apply to have set aside, or indeed reversed, almost as of course. Meanwhile, in the courts of equity, decrees would never be granted upon a complete failure to find the defendant, but if the defendant was present and merely refused to participate in the proceedings, it was possible to resort to the process of contempt to bring him in and eventually issue a decree *pro confesso* against him.

After more than a century since the first legislative attempts were made to loosen the rules regarding appearance, and decided resistance by the courts,[67] the adoption of the modern rules of default happened surprisingly quickly and without much apparent opposition. Brougham in his 1828 speech in the House of Commons had criticized outlawry for being absurd and suggested that no harm could come of its abolition.[68] The Commission, composed of eminent practitioners (Bosanquet, Parke, Alderson and Serjeant Stephen), devoted its entire first report published in 1830 to the question of the different modes of service and outlawry.[69] In 1832 an Act was passed taking up in part its recommendations. The Process in Courts of Law at Westminster Act (2 Will IV c. 39) allowed proceedings to be taken in default of appearance (s. 16). This procedure led to a judgment by default, although in form, it would be a judgment by confession or consent on the part of the defendant, who had been served in person but whose appearance had been entered by the plaintiff. When no personal service was possible, however, either because the defendant intentionally kept out of the way or because he was out of the jurisdiction, process by *distringas* on his property was necessary, either to compel appearance, again, or to proceed to outlawry.

Emboldened by the absence of a negative reaction and riding the momentum for reform, which included the abolition of imprisonment for

---

66 *First report of commissioners on the courts of common law*, Parliamentary Papers 1829, vol. ix.
67 Above, text at n.41.
68 *Lord Brougham's speeches* (Edinburgh, 1837), ii, 319, 409ff, 411.
69 *First report*.

debts in 1838[70] and the creation of county courts, with their own simplified procedure, in 1846,[71] the 1851 Common Law Commissioners returned to the problem of outlawry. The earlier commission, in its criticisms of this outdated procedure, had focused on the injustice to the (honest) defendant, who might not even be aware that proceedings had been commenced against him. The 1851 Commission on the other hand focused on the uncertainty and hardship to the plaintiff. The Commissioners noted how easily a judgment of outlawry could be displaced, set aside by entering an appearance and applying to a judge in chambers and paying the costs, or reversed 'upon a writ of error', for failing to comply with any of the formal requirements in the issue of mesne process (in which case the defendant would not even have to pay the costs of the previous action nor enter an appearance to that action). In fact, they wrote, 'the plaintiff is left in a worse position than he was before the proceedings to outlawry were instituted, by the delay which has intervened, and the costs that have been thrown away.'[72] Since the proceedings to outlawry could 'practically only be instituted in cases where the result is sure to be erroneous', for they were the

> result of the conflict between the rule of law that no man shall be outlawed who is not within the kingdom at the time of the exigent awarded, and the rule of practice adopted by the Courts, not to allow a *distringas* to issue for the purpose of proceeding to outlawry unless it be established that the defendant is out of the kingdom at the time,[73]

it was again recommended, after failure to implement the 1829 Report on the subject, that outlawry be abolished.

The result of these reports was incorporated in the Common Law Procedure Act 1852, best known for other important innovations to the jurisdiction and the procedure of the central courts.[74] By sections 24 and 26 the plaintiff was now allowed to sign judgment upon affidavit of personal service or best endeavours to effect it upon the defendant. On implementation, it was held that in order to have a regularly signed judgment set

---

70 Judgments Act 1838.
71 County Courts Act 1846.
72 *First report of the commissioners on the process, practice and system of pleading in the superior courts of common law*, Parlt. Papers 1851, vol.xxii, p. 6 (repr. in *British Parliamentary Papers. Legal Adminstration. General* (Irish University Press, Shannon, 1969–72) 9, p. 18), citing *Matthews v. Erbo* (1698) Carthew 459, 90 ER 865, where the court refused to set aside on motion a judgment of outlawry against a person not within the jurisdiction, but stated that on the same grounds (the defendant never having been in the jurisdiction) a writ of error would have succeeded.
73 Ibid.
74 Baker, *Introduction*, pp 68, 90, 303.

aside, the defendant must make an affidavit of a good defence on the merits, such as a plea of infancy, bankruptcy, or the Statute of Limitations.[75] Outlawry became unnecessary due to the possibility, granted in sections 18 and 19, to serve the summons on the defendant even if he was abroad.

In Chancery, the Improvement of the Jurisdiction of Chancery Act, also passed in 1852, made similar inroads. The time limits for the taking of procedural steps were bolstered by more effective sanctions, and section 15 of that Act provided that

> [t]he plaintiff in any suit commenced by bill shall be at liberty, at any time after the time allowed to the defendant for answering the same shall have expired (but before replication), to move the court ... for such decree or decretal order as he may think himself entitled to ...

The court would have a discretion whether to grant or refuse the motion, 'or to make an order giving such directions for or with respect to the further prosecution of the suit as the circumstances of the case may require, and to make such order as to costs as it may think right'.[76]

Roughly twenty years later, another round of reforms was inaugurated with the appointment of a commission on the judicature. Its recommendations, aimed at the fusion of the two systems into a single Supreme Court of Judicature, were implemented in the Supreme Court of Judicature Act 1873 and its amendments. The question of which procedure to adopt in the resultant new court was answered in the commission's first report which reflected that

> [i]n a considerable number of suits there is no substantial question as to the right of the plaintiff to, at least, some relief. ... In all cases in which the plaintiff seeks to recover a money demand, whether founded upon a legal or equitable right, the practice established by the Common Law Procedure Act, 1852, should we think be adopted ... Further, in all cases in which a special endorsement has been made on a writ, and the defendant has appeared, the plaintiff should be entitled, on affidavit verifying the cause of action, and swearing that in his belief there is no defence, to take out a summons to show cause why he should not be at liberty to sign judgment; upon which summons such order may be made as the justice of the case may require.[77]

---

75 *Delafield v. Tanner* (1814) 5 Taunton 856, 128 ER 930; *Evans v. Gill* (1797) 1 B & P 52, 126 ER 773, *Maddocks v. Holmes* (1798) 1 B & P 228, 126 ER 875.
76 S. 16.
77 *First report of the judicature commission*, Parlt. Papers 1868–69, vol. xxv , p. 10 (repr. in *British Parliamentary Papers. Legal Adminstration. General* (Irish University Press, Shannon, 1969–72) 13, p. 9). The last part, with the special endorsement, reflects the procedure of

The report further recommended that a more extensive power of obtaining judgment by default be available in the county courts, with special provision made as to the nature of the notice to be served, in order to draw the attention of defendants (who, in smaller cases, were presumed to be less adept with the law) to their liability to such judgments.[78]

The courts, reluctant until just fifty years previously to award judgment by default in any case, had taken to the new procedure with a vengeance, once it had been clearly introduced by the legislature, first in 1852 and again in 1873.[79] A pressing need was felt for streamlining the court system and allowing undefended and indefensible claims to reach a speedy and satisfactory conclusion. However, the very contrast between the courts' positions before and after the reform rounds must indicate that in their view, the political choice indicated a momentous change in the law, which they had not felt able to make on their own motion. The next two sections will examine some of the elements that made such changes possible and their consequences.

ENABLING FACTORS

The change to the procedure itself was momentous, yet there is very little contemporary systematic analysis as to the rationale of the rule and justifications for its abandonment. Even Brougham's speech[80] does not deal with the central tenet of a rule whose first appearance is in the *Leges Henrici Primi*: the (mostly common-law) courts' lack of jurisdiction over a defendant who has not accepted, in a way or another, their authority. The reformists' arguments are for the most part deliberately non-technical and in effect a series of non-legal factors seem to enable the change to the rules of procedure but do not overtly address the jurisdictional point at all. Such factors can be gleaned from some generalist literature, in fiction, reviews and pamphleteering and even Brougham's speech.

Firstly, there is a general push for modernization of the system of procedure, by removing antiquated procedures whose *raison d'être* had been lost in the mists of time. In this context, reform of procedure is a philosophical, political and social preoccupation, dealing mostly with the consequences of the rule against judgment by default, that is, the possibility of imprisonment and the absurdity of outlawry. On this point, the heated criticism of the *status quo* goes unchallenged from a legal community under assault on too many fronts. Secondly, there is the emergence of a strong

summary judgment, introduced for merchants by Keating's Act in 1855: J.A. Bauman, 'The evolution of the summary judgment procedure', *Ind. L. J.*, 31 (1955–6), 329.
78 *First report of the judicature commission*, above n. 77, p. 16.
79 Supreme Court of Judicature Act 1873 s. 7.
80 Above n. 68.

merchant and industrial class, which requires clear and certain procedures for the satisfaction of debts. The introduction of the procedure of summary judgment facilitates the abandonment of long-held traditions and the emergence of new legal perspectives. The commingling of the requirements for a summary judgment and those relating to a default judgment persists to this day,[81] despite the wide ranging differences in nature, rationale and procedure. However, openly or not, the Common Law Procedure Act 1852 changes the jurisdictional position. A different vision of the state and its sovereignty colours the very technical field of domestic civil procedure. This latter aspect will be addressed in detail in the next section.

It is well established that the early- to mid-nineteenth century was awash with reformist movements. Sunderland described the powerful and well-organized movement of public opinion relating specifically to the law and the reform of the law.[82] Its origins may be found in the all-pervasive Benthamist influence;[83] it is characterized by a commonsense approach to the civil justice system, and its evils of complexity and delay. However, Bentham himself did not address the issue of service of process and outlawry specifically: a direct influence on the drafting of the statutes may be discounted. His influence may be found in the general attack on the use of fictions (both process by bill of Middlesex and process to outlawry were riddled with fictional steps and characters). In a sense, it is possible to identify this line of influence in a series of arguments for change made on the basis of a rational and systematic approach to the law. These arguments appear in various forms in articles in the *Edinburgh Review*,[84] the *Quarterly Review*[85] and the *Westminster Review*[86] in support and following the publication of the First Report of 1829. The clearest expression is to be found in that Report, with the definition of appearance as 'some act by which the defendant first admits that he has had sufficient intimation of the suit';[87] and that the antiquity of a procedure is not enough to justify it.[88] When Brougham addressed in his speech the

---

81 The most striking similarities between the two procedures lies in the grounds for setting them aside; see *Alpine Bulk Transport Co. Inc. v. Saudi Eagle Shipping Co. Inc. (The Saudi Eagle)* [1986] 2 Lloyd's Rep 221 (CA).
82 E.R. Sunderland, 'The English struggle for procedural reform', *Harv. L. Rev*, 39 (1925–26), 725.
83 J.F. Dillon, 'Bentham's influence in the reforms of the nineteenth century' in Wigmore (ed.), *Select essays in Anglo-American legal history*, i, 492. Also, G.J. Postema, 'The principle of utility and the law of procedure: Bentham's theory of adjudication', *Ga. L. Rev.*, 11 (1976–7) 1393.
84 H. Brougham, 'Law reform', *Edinburgh Review*, 51 (July 1830), 478.
85 Anon, 'Common law reforms', *Quarterly Review*, 42 (Jan. 1830), 181.
86 W. Gordon, 'Imprisonment for debt', *Westminster Review*, 9 (Jan. 1828), 41; J. Bentham and G. Bentham, 'Bentham, Brougham and law reform', *Westminster Review*, 11 (Oct. 1829), 447; Anon., 'Law of arrest', *Westminster Review*, 12 (April 1833), 359.
87 1830 Report (n. 40) p. 71.
88 Ibid., p. 79, following a citation from Bracton.

question of outlawry and the necessity of appearance, he did it with simple rhetoric:[89]

> My next objection to the present system under this head is, that no proceeding can take place in our courts unless there be an actual appearance. We outlaw a man to compel an appearance. Why do so? Why can we not proceed as in the case of ejectment, where a notice is left at the dwelling-house? Why can we not leave a writ at a man's house, stating what we sue him for; and only when we think him about to fly call upon him to give surety? I repeat, why not send a writ to the known domicile or house of business of the debtor? A writ, too, which shall plainly describe the cause of action, instead of serving him with a writ that only tells him he is a prisoner for some reason or other, which in due time he will be informed of; and, if he cannot be found, outlawing him after nine months' delay? This is done in Holland, a mercantile country, and in Scotland, a wary country, where too great charity is not generally shown to the debtor; at least the Scotch have not the reputation of being unnecessarily merciful on such occasions; yet a writ to take the debtor's person is only obtainable there if he be *in meditatione fugae*. Our process of outlawry is, in its nature, extremely foolish; its object being to compel an appearance, which, after all, is not necessary, provided the party wilfully absents himself after due notice. If a man chooses to keep away, why not proceed without him after such a delay, and so many services at his place of residence, as shall ensure him having knowledge of the action? As for any scruple about proceeding against an absent man, without making perfectly sure of his having notice, the present law has no right to say a word on the subject; for the process of outlawry is neither more nor less than a mean by which you harass an absent man, without even pretending to give him notice. He may be in the Greek Islands, on the coast of Africa, or in the backwoods of America, and his creditor can outlaw him, and proceed to have his goods forfeited without his being aware of the transaction, and without the proceeds of the forfeiture necessarily benefiting any one but the Crown. In Exchequer cases, it is true, the debt and costs, not exceeding 50l., are paid out of the fund which arises from selling the goods; in all other cases a party must apply to the Lords of the Treasury. Why should this be? What have the Lords of the Treasury to do with the legal remedy of plaintiffs in suits? Why send any one to the executive power for the redress which the judicial authority alone ought to administer?

---

89 *Speeches*, ii, 412–13.

This extract shows that the positively technical question of service and appearance, and the slightly more 'popular' issue of outlawry, are to be seen in the wider context of a growing commercial empire and the corresponding influence of the mercantile class.[90] The problem is not so much to be found in the law of procedure: the central complaint is that imprisonment for debt, which was a necessary corollary of the uncertainty in the law of debtor and creditor, was an inefficient practice, and thus a sufficiently familiar target for zealous reformers. Dickens and Thackeray had publicized the horrors of debtor's prison. While Bentham is said to have approved of it,[91] imprisonment for debt or upon outlawry was variously criticized in the pamphlet literature[92] and even charged of unconstitutionality, for it imposed the criminal sanction of imprisonment without a jury in violation of Magna Charta.

In 1838, preventive imprisonment for debt was abolished.[93] However, the momentum for the reform of the rules of service, default and outlawry did not stop, but indeed grew to encompass a wider scope. As hinted in Brougham's speech, in the passage quoted above, other countries had systems of procedure which favoured the expedited collection of monetary claims. The countries mentioned by Brougham are Holland and Scotland, the first a mercantile country, the second boasting a hybrid common law–civil law system. At this stage of the debate, the focus was firmly on the necessities of plaintiffs to recover swiftly what was owed to them. Continental jurisdictions had efficient special procedures[94] which indeed were not unknown to English merchants who had traded there or made use of the summary procedures of the Admiralty Court or the earlier piepowder courts in town fairs.[95] The introduction of the procedure leading to summary judgment, precisely in order to assist collection of indefensible claims for money, has been mentioned:[96] Brougham had suggested a transplant from Scotland, but Keating's proposed all-English procedure was instead adopted.

Echoes of the summary judgment debate appear in the 1851 Report. Until 1850, appearance, even if fictitiously entered by the plaintiff, was a formal necessity. The 1851 commissioners dispensed with it, recommended the abolition of the 'special' forms of action, and suggested a new and improved system of summoning persons who were not already within the jurisdiction

---

90 For Brougham's political relationship with this class, see M. Lobban, 'Henry Brougham and Law Reform' in *EHR*, 115 (2000), 1184.
91 Bentham and Bentham, 'Bentham, Brougham'.
92 Anonymous, *On the law of debtor and creditor* (London, 1833), appended to W. Glover, *Lord Brougham's law reforms* (London, 1834); see also the articles cited above at n. 86.
93 Judgments Act 1838.
94 See generally A. Engelmann and R.W. Millar, *A history of continental civil procedure* (London, 1928).
95 Holdsworth, *History*, v, 103–20.
96 Above n. 77.

of the courts. Against British subjects resident abroad a writ of summons should be issued regardless of their whereabouts, while if it was necessary to summon 'foreigners resident abroad', there should be simplified proceedings (serving a notice that a writ had been issued, not the writ itself) 'enabling persons within the jurisdiction to prosecute actions against [them]'.[97] On the international stage, this extension of the jurisdiction – or rather, this disregard for previously held strong notions of jurisdiction – was justified by the simultaneous existence of extensive powers to sue foreigners in other legal systems (France in particular).[98]

On the domestic side, however, the spotlight had definitely moved from general concerns of injustice to the defendant, to concerns about the costs and delay to which the plaintiff (the creditor) would be exposed in order to recover his debts. Moving from the premise that in actual fact the presence of the defendant was not needed, the commissioners recommended abolishing the entry of appearance by the plaintiff for the defendant, but 'retain the substance by permitting the plaintiff, on making … an affidavit [of personal service having been effected], to proceed as though the defendant had been served'.[99] Their second premise was that a plaintiff should not be subjected to additional procedural costs and delay in recovering what was owed to him. This required some statistical evidence, which was duly brought, that only a very limited number of cases were actually defended.[1] The commissioners deduced then

> the fact, as ascertained from the returns referred to, that in the vast majority of actions commenced there is no disputed question between the parties, either of law or fact. The defendant perfectly well knows what the claim is, and requires no information on the subject, and the writ merely operates to compel immediate payment from a necessitous or backward debtor of a known and admitted debt.[2]

Thus it was suggested that

> when the defendant does not appear, and has neither the power nor the intention to defend the action (which is the case, as we have shown, in a great majority of instances) … in all actions for liquidated demands, if there be indorsed on the back of the writ a substantial particular of the plaintiff's claim, the declaration may be safely dispensed with altogether.[3]

---

97 Common Law Procedure Act 1852 ss. 18–19; First Report 1851 (n. 72) p. 8.
98 Ibid., p. 8.
99 Ibid.
1 Ibid. The statistics as to writs issued and actual declarations are at pp 35–6.
2 Ibid., p. 37.
3 Ibid.

The default judgment

A liquidated demand was exemplified as that arising on a bill of exchange, promissory note, or cheque, or other simple contract debt or on a bond or covenant under seal or on a statute where the sum sought was a fixed sum of money, or on a guarantee where the claim against the principal was one of the previous types of liquidated demand.[4] It must be noted that these instances were to be the basis upon which a summary judgment could be granted.[5] At this point it was merely suggested that non-appearance after the time specified in the writ would entitle the plaintiff to sign judgment, as was already the case when the defendant had failed to plead.[6] The defendant could appear at any time before judgment, save the need to give notice of appearance to the plaintiff if his appearance was after the time specified in the writ.

Finally, new commercial realities also required, from a completely different perspective, the abolition of imprisonment: Joint-Stock Companies could enter into contracts for money or services,[7] but it would be impossible to obtain satisfaction through imprisonment, and distress would not have served much in the event of insolvency. Surprisingly, there does not seem to be any mention of this very practical problem in the run-up to the 1852 Act.

THE CONSEQUENCES OF THE REFORM AND THE QUESTION OF JURISDICTION

It appears that the legal system and the procedure of the courts, exposed to the glare of public opinion, could not withstand a concerted effort to dismantle old-fashioned institutions and procedures whose justification was not offered up for the public debate. History was not used as an example of the evils that the current procedures were meant to avoid – nowhere in the rather limited eighteenth and nineteenth century literature on procedure is there any analysis of the early procedures or the procedures of the local courts which did allow default judgment in the claims under their jurisdiction (with the exception of Pollock and Maitand's polemic in historical terms).[8]

---

4   Ibid., Appendix A p. 70.
5   By reference to the existing continental forms which A. Engelmann and R.W. Millar, *A history of continental civil procedure* (London, 1928) calls in German law the 'mandate procedure, both for documents and negotiable instruments' (pp 584–5) and the 'order for payment' or *Mahnverfahren* (p. 612), and 'mandate procedure' for Italy (p. 831). See above, n. 77, for the express juxtaposition of default judgment and summary judgment – with the necessary distinctions – in the Report on the Courts of Judicature.
6   First Report 1851 (n. 72) 40.
7   Created in 1844. The point was made to me by a participant at the 2005 British Legal History Conference, whose name I unfortunately did not catch and whom I am thus forced to thank anonymously.
8   Above text at n.18. See also Gordon, 'Imprisonment for debt' (n. 86).

The prohibition of court activity in the absence of a party, abroad or within the country, had to go, not because its inherent rationale was challenged, but because of the detrimental consequences on commerce, certainty of debt enforcement, and, if one is to believe that Brougham had all the influence he claimed for himself, its capacity for tarnishing the reputation of English law when confronted with the laws of Holland, Scotland, Denmark[9] and France.[10] One of the first consequences of the reform is that, like many other parts of the statute book, English procedural law shifted from a debtor-friendly to a creditor-friendly perspective.[11] In technical terms, it suffices to consider the 1829 and the 1851 Reports on the point of outlawry to be struck by the change in tone. While the earlier Commission, though critical of the system, had noted the injustice to a (honest) defendant, the 1851 Commission focused on the ease of challenge, which made the institution of proceedings to outlawry at best a gamble, at worst a costly and useless waste of time for the plaintiff. The definition of injustice had changed: from the defendant's right not to be arrested and kept in jail in order to compel his appearance and his right not have a judgment of outlawry pronounced against him unawares, in the Report of 1829, to the relevance of the plaintiff's 'costs and delay' (Report of 1851).

Another change occurred in the twenty years separating the institution of the Commissions, relative to the jurisdictional powers of the court(s). In 1829 there was little mention of[12] and no debate as to the need for some sort of defendant action (or knowledge, or even notice) in order to found the jurisdiction of the court. In other words, the common law rationale of 'submission', though unexpressed, was also unchallenged. In 1851 the main proposal of the Commission, and the main innovation in the Common Law Procedure Act, was a single summons that could be served in England or abroad, on British and non-British citizens (if the court was satisfied that there was a cause of action which arose within the jurisdiction).[13] Technically it could be said that there is an apparent inversion of the relationship between substance and procedure: in the modern system, it is the summons

---

9 Mentioned in Brougham's speech, together with France and Holland, in defence of arbitration as a mode of settling disputes in preference to adjudication.
10 France is mentioned several times in the documents here cited: Brougham appeals to the House of Commons to outstrip Napoleon of the mantle of modern lawgiver; and the 1851 Commissioners refer in particular to France as having a long-arm jurisdiction over citizens and non-citizens alike, within or without the borders.
11 This characterization I owe to a comment made at the 2005 British Legal History Conference.
12 Above, n.87.
13 Cases construing 'cause of action which arose within the jurisdiction' can be found in W.D. Griffith, *The Supreme Court of Judicature Acts 1873 & 1875: with the rules, orders and costs ...* (London, 1875), p. 130.

of the court that founds jurisdiction, not the existence of a jurisdictional ground that enables the court to summon a party.

It is quite instructive to consider the English courts' response to the separate, but kindred problem of the recognition and enforcement of foreign judgments. In the conflict of laws there are three main questions, two of which have a procedural slant. The first is whether, and under which conditions, the national court will assume jurisdiction in a case involving one or more elements pertaining to a foreign legal system (jurisdiction); the second seeks to find criteria by which the law applicable to the action or one of the parties may be found among all those relevant (choice of law); finally, the third question concerns the recognition and enforcement of a judgment issued by a foreign court in the domestic system.[14] Most of the case-law up to the nineteenth century developed in the Admiralty Court, and, if principles were mentioned, more often than not they were of Roman origin and akin to continental solutions. In the case of recognition of foreign judgments, especially of colonial provenance, however, other central courts might be seised (the Queen's Bench in particular), since the basis for recognition and enforcement of a judgment in a commercial context was that the judgment itself created an obligation to perform, similar to a contract.[15]

The effects of the Common Law Procedure Act 1852 on the conflict of laws were noticeable. On jurisdiction, the question became inextricably linked with the (new) possibility of effecting service abroad. The debate at first raged around the interpretation of the clause granting discretionary jurisdiction to the court (permission to serve abroad if satisfied that 'there is a cause of action, which arose within the jurisdiction').[16]

The first edition of Dicey's *Conflict of Laws*[17] explains the situation with regard to the jurisdiction of the English court in respect to any cause of action, when the defendant is in England:

> Every action in the High Court now commences with the issue of a writ of summons, which is in effect a written command from the Crown to the defendant to enter an appearance in the action: and the service of the writ, or something equivalent thereto, is absolutely essential as the foundation of the Court's jurisdiction. Where a writ cannot legally be served upon a defendant, the Court claims no jurisdiction over him. In an action *in personam* the converse of this statement holds good, and wherever a defendant can be legally served with a writ, there the Court, on service being effected, has jurisdiction

---

14 C.M.V. Clarkson and J. Hill, *Jaffey on the conflict of laws* (2nd ed. London, 2002), p. 1.
15 Ibid., p. 153; *Russell v. Smyth* (1842) 9 M & W 810, 152 ER 343.
16 ss.18 and 19. *Allhusen v. Malgarejo* (1868) 3 QB 340, *Jackson v. Spittall* (1870) LR 5 CP 542; *Western National Bank of the City of New York v. Perez, Triana & Co.* [1891] 1 QB 304 (CA).
17 London, 1896.

to entertain an action against him. Hence, in an action *in personam*, the rules as to the legal service of a writ define the limits of the Court's jurisdiction.[18]

The law is stated in the following terms: at common law a writ could never be served on a defendant when out of England. However, RSC Order 11, r 1[19] gave the court discretion to allow service abroad, in particular when the cause of action had arisen in England, therefore granting jurisdiction. It may be the case that here the exceptional and discretionary power of the court is a better indication of the underlying policy and the consequences of the new, commercially oriented common law writ of summons. The original prohibition is tempered to the point of losing most of its force.

On recognition and enforcement of foreign judgments, on the other hand, the question is slightly more complicated. The first criterion for recognition is that the foreign court must be 'a court of competent jurisdiction'. Although this criterion is not necessarily connected to the rules for *assuming* jurisdiction in an 'international' case, it appears from the early reported cases that the courts were (wrongly) influenced by notions of reciprocity when considering it; that is, they believed that if the English court would have had jurisdiction in the same circumstances, the criterion would be met with regard to the foreign court. There was a wavering of opinions,[20] and arguments made in the cases suggest that the *new* English procedure (domestic and international) allowed the *English courts* to understand a primarily foreign concept of sovereignty, exemplified in the relationship between a country's courts and its citizens.

Dicey in 1896 tentatively admitted allegiance as a criterion for competent jurisdiction:

> The Courts of this country consider the defendant bound when he is a *subject* of the foreign country in which the judgment [against him] has been obtained.' [*Rousillon v. Rousillon* (1880) 14 Ch D 351, 371, judgment of Fry J. See *Douglas v. Forrest* 1828, 4 Bing 683[21]] Allegiance, that is to say, is, independent of residence, a ground of jurisdiction. The reason of this is that a subject is bound to obey the commands of his sovereign, and therefore, the judgments of his sovereign's Courts. ... The doctrine, however, that allegiance is sufficient to give jurisdiction, though supported by judicial dicta, cannot be established by

---

18 At p. 234.
19 Implementing the 1873 equivalent of ss. 18 and 19 Common Law Procedure Act 1852.
20 Blackburn J refers to his own, later corrected, acceptance of such an argument in *Schisby v. Westenholz* [1861–1873] All ER Rep 988 (QB).
21 130 ER 933.

any reported decision. In *Douglas v. Forrest*, which goes near to a decision on this point, the Court dwell on the fact of the defendant having at the time of the judgment possessed property in Scotland.[22]

In continental systems, it was often the case that a national court would assume jurisdiction over its own citizens, regardless of their presence, submission or other criteria. One of the leading treatises on private international law, which sank its roots firmly into the practice of the Admiralty courts and openly discussed the applicability of Roman law to their practice, had this to say in a rare historical excursus, once the dust had settled on the 1873 procedure:[23]

> ... the *forum rei* is admitted in England as a sufficient ground of competence for a foreign judgment which it is sought to enforce, whether that forum be grounded on political nationality; on domicile in the sense admitting but one domicile .... as the criterion of personal law; or on domicile in the looser sense in which it may be taken in those countries which are familiar with it as the ground of jurisdiction. ... *Schisby v. Westenholz* 1870 LR 6 QB 161.
>
> This doctrine long remained obscure, as might be expected from the fact that the competence of the English courts themselves with regard to personal obligations had not been based either on allegiance or on domicile. In the older cases, where the foreign judgment had been pronounced against an absent defendant, the endeavour was to determine in each instance whether it was agreeable to natural justice that the defendant should be held to be bound.[24]

In the long run, allegiance by itself ceased to be considered a valid criterion. Although it was listed as one of five criteria in *Emanuel v. Symon*,[25] later dilution took advantage of the earlier limitation of the allegiance precedent to cases where any duty of allegiance was made 'correlative to the

---

22 At 375.
23 J. Westlake, *A treatise on private international law* (5th ed. London, 1912) p. 401.
24 Citing *Buchanan v. Rucker* (1807) 1 Camp 63, 170 ER 877 and 921 and, further, (1808) 9 East 192, 103 ER 546, a case on the recognition of a money judgment from Tobago. Lord Ellenborough is cited at 878: 'it is contrary to the first principles of reason and justice that either in civil or criminal proceedings a man should be condemned before he is heard'. However, Westlake and Dicey have been characterized as belonging to a tradition of the 'positivist theory of international law for private international law' by A. Mills, 'The private history of international law', *ICLQ*, 55 (2006) 1, 30–1, with Westlake primarily concerned with 'determining which sovereign has the power to command the duty which is correlative to the disputed right', and Dicey presenting the purely English cases he cited 'almost as if they were a set of sovereign commands.'
25 [1908] 1 KB 302 (CA) (*per* Buckley LJ).

protection given by State' which could 'only' happen when it coincided with 'presence'.[26] In *Schisby v. Westenholz* the equation citizenship-duty of allegiance was made in the context of a French rule of law which bound French subjects to French courts' judgments, an argument of choice of law rather than recognition. Today, the nationality of the parties is not sufficient to found jurisdiction by itself for the purpose of recognition or enforcement of a judgment.[27] The courts have succeeded in cutting short any parallelism between the criteria by which the English court *assumes* jurisdiction in an 'international' dispute (the first question), and the criteria by which it admits that a foreign court was a court of competent jurisdiction for the purpose of recognizing or enforcing a foreign judgment (the third question).

For an all too brief moment, however, amid the uncertainty of practice and the giddiness of reform, we catch a glimpse of a different facet of the new procedure. Allegiance, as the duty to obey the sovereign and the judgments of its Courts, would not have looked out of place in the medieval seigneurial and local courts. In the Royal courts at Westminster, on the other hand, the lines were firmly drawn between the sovereign and his courts, who issued different kinds of summons (original and judicial writs) with varied effects when it came to obtaining a binding judgment in the absence of the defendant. Gilbert talked of the 'prejudice of lawyers at the erection of the Court [of Chancery]'.[28] Intentionally or not (but as we have seen, this is not apparent in the declarations of intent), the possibility in principle of affirming jurisdiction over defendants and issue binding judgments, regardless of their participation, changes the relationship between an Englishman and the English courts. The only cases where such a change is acknowledged seem to be in the field of private international law, where notions of 'sovereign' and 'sovereignty' were not unknown nor could be avoided, both in the literature and in the practice.[29] It is conceivable that some judges, unfamiliar with the Admiralty tradition and law, show an awareness in the recognition cases of the new role thrust upon them by the Common Law Procedure Act 1852.

CONCLUSION

The reformist intent broadened and intensified considerably with each new Commission. The law concerning default changed drastically. First to undergo drastic surgery was the common law procedure, perhaps by reason

---

26 *Carrick v. Hancock* (1895) 12 TLR 59, 60 (Lord Russell of Killowen).
27 *Adams v. Cape* [1990] Ch 433 (CA); L. Collins et al. (eds), *Dicey and Morris on the conflict of laws* (13th ed. London, 2000), i, 291ff.
28 Above n. 63.
29 Mills, 'Private history'.

of its being more in need of reform than the procedure of the court of Chancery. Thus, the early tentative statutory attempts to overcome the jurisdictional hurdle of the presence of the defendant, dating back at least to Norman times, were first extended to all cases (1832). Then the procedure was even more aggressively simplified by systematically granting the common law courts the power to assert jurisdiction over all persons within England and Wales, and Britons and foreigners resident abroad, while the court of Chancery expanded its jurisdiction to pronounce decrees upon plaintiff's motion. Eventually, the 1852 Common Law Procedure Act default procedure became the most favoured of innovations, was extended (in a better guaranteed form) to county courts, and became the only procedure applicable to the unified Supreme Court of Judicature (although some resistance remained, for instance in the Admiralty division, to its sweeping application).

The ease with which the change was accomplished has probably less to do with procedure and rationality than with the unenviable consequences of the old system, on the certainty and diffusion of credit – imprisonment and outlawry were easy targets for social reformers and politicians seeking to curry favour with the commercial classes. The law's perspective became creditor-oriented, and age-old obstacles in the path of a pragmatic enforcement of liquidated debt were bulldozed with but little thought for their rationale. Certainly the legal professions felt it as a revolution, which perhaps went further than anticipated by the practitioners involved in the reforms – heralding, or perhaps only crystallizing, a modern construction of the State and its citizens.

Poor law in the city: a comparative analysis of the successful legal resistance to the implementation of the Poor Law Amendment Act 1834 in the cities of Chester and Liverpool

LORIE CHARLESWORTH

IT HAS BEEN A TENET of many poor law histories that the implementation of the Poor Law Amendment Act 1834 was eventually effected without much real difficulty across England and Wales. That is, apart from initial localised resistance, sometimes with riots, and an ongoing political debate, largely in the contemporary press.[1] This statement should not be taken at face value, as in fact, a number of localities were able to resist the implementation of the Act by using unreformed legal 'rules' concerning Local Act Incorporations. In order to explore this matter, this chapter reflects upon a series of legal questions and local issues raised by a comparison of two geographically proximate, but in some ways rather different examples of such resistance. To be precise, those events that took place in the city ports of Liverpool and Chester when the central poor law authorities attempted to impose the terms of the Act upon both cities.[2] In order to achieve this purpose, I have drawn upon archival research amongst poor law and other local and national records, based around a study of poor law in the North West of England; in other words, the chapter will contextualize that legal history. To be precise, the work has adopted an interdisciplinary approach, drawing upon the methodologies of doctrinal black letter law and social history.

The chapter opens with a short legal history of poor law and of the implementation of the 1834 Act. It includes a brief discussion of some of the local protests that accompanied it. The terms of the Act authorised a 'compulsory' national system of workhouses arranged on a regional basis as poor law unions throughout England and Wales.[3] These poor law unions

1 M.E. Rose, 'The anti poor law movement in the North of England', *Northern History*, 1 (1966), 70–91; Nicholas C. Edsall, *The anti-poor law movement* (Manchester, 1971); John Knott, *Popular opposition to the new poor law* (London, 1986).
2 4 & 5 Will. IV c. 76. The Poor Law Amendment Act 1834.
3 'It shall be lawful for the said commissioners, by order under their hands and seal, to declare

were composed of groups of parishes and townships amalgamated together and administered by poor law guardians elected from each parish, under delegated regulations issued by the Poor Law Commission in London. In retrospect, it can be concluded that the Act marked the first centralized system of delegated bureaucratic law making. A new national system of inspectors was introduced, to advise and ensure that all the unions complied with the legislation.[4] Prior to the Act, poor relief operated through a 'system' of local parish autonomy (see below) within a legal framework. However, the new system was implemented in order to achieve a uniform, standardised system to relieve poverty throughout England and Wales. By the end of the nineteenth century this was indeed the case. Even so, the Act was not immediately adopted everywhere in spite of the intention of Parliament that it should be so. Some towns, such as Huddersfield, actively and forcefully resisted its implementation. In other areas there were anti-poor law riots, but in the end they succumbed.

There were, nevertheless, some rare exceptions. Those places that had set up their own workhouses, either managed by Select Vestries,[5] or under the authority of private acts,[6] continued to operate outside the terms of the Act after 1834. Although they were still subject to inspection from the central bureaucracy, some of those places remained free of the minutiae of financial

so many parishes as they think fit to be united for the administration of the laws for the relief of the poor, and such parishes shall thereupon be deemed a union for such purpose, and thereupon the workhouse or workhouses of such parishes shall be for their common use'; ibid., s. 26.

4 Mark Blaug, 'The myth of the old poor law and themaking of the new', *Journal of Economic History*, 23:2 (June 1963), pp 151–84; 'The Poor Law Report re-examined', *Journal of Economic History*, 24 (1968), 229–45; George R. Boyer, *An economic history of the English poor law 1750–1850* (Cambridge, 1990); A. Brundage, *The making of the new poor law* (London, 1978); Maurice Caplan, 'The new poor law and the struggle for union chargeability', *International Review of Social History*, 22 (1978), 267–300; Anne Digby, *Pauper palaces* (London, 1978); *The poor law in nineteenth century England and Wales* (London, 1982); Derek Fraser (ed.), *The new poor law in the nineteenth century* (London, 1976); Norman Longmate, *The workhouse* (London, 1974); Peter Mandler, 'The making of the new poor law redivivus', *Past and Present*, 117 (1984), 131–57; D. Roberts, *Victorian origins of the British welfare state* (London, 1960); 'How cruel was the Victorian poor law?', *Historical Journal*, 6 (1963), 97–106; M.E. Rose, *The relief of poverty, 1834–1914* (London, 1972); M.E. Rose (ed.), *The poor and the city: the English poor law in its urban context, 1834–1914* (Leicester, 1985); K.D.M. Snell, *Annals of the labouring poor: social change in agrarian England, 1660–1900* (Cambridge, 1985); Pat Thane, *Foundations of the welfare state* (2nd ed. London 1996); R.N. Thompson, 'The working of the Poor Law Amendment Act in Cumbria, 1836–71', *Northern History*, 15 (1979), 117–37; S. and B. Webb, *English poor law history: Part II, the last hundred years* (1929).

5 58 Geo. III. c. 69 and 59 Geo III. c. 12. The Sturges Bourne Acts 1818 and 1819. Even after implementation three quarters (15,635) of all parishes remained unreformed; S. and B. Webb, *English local government, vol. I, The parish and the county* (1906) p. 164.

6 Gilbert's Act 1782.

and other controls that were eventually to standardise poor relief in England and Wales. One such example was Liverpool, whose Select Vestry was responsible for the largest workhouse in Britain; another was the Chester Incorporation, relieving its poor under the legal authority of a private Act.

This chapter will examine and compare these two exceptions and consider why they were able to continue with their own anomalous poor relief systems, and could not be forced to comply with the terms of the 1834 Act.[7] In order to understand the legal framework that allowed this resistance, the next section will briefly consider the legal history of poor relief and the reforms implemented under the 1834 Act. This brief reconstruction will serve as a framework for the individual case studies of the two cities that follow.

THE LEGAL FRAMEWORK OF THE POOR LAW

The relief of poverty in England and Wales was established under statute by the Act for the Better Relief of the Poor 1601.[8] This Act formalised and codified a quasi-customary system of poor relief where a duty to relieve the poor was combined with a funding system which was eventually raised by a locally set poor rate.[9] In summary, the history of the relief of poverty both prior to, and after, this date indicates that such entitlement to relief was the right only of those who were settled in a place. This was finally enshrined in the Poor Relief Act 1662,[10] whose terms state that only the settled poor were entitled to a share of the poor rate.[11] Hence, poor law, consisting of all that law relative to the relief of poverty, was in reality the law of settlement and removals. The preamble to the 1662 Act set out its purpose in describing the mischief that it proposed to cure:

> poor people are not restrained from going from one parish to another and therefore, do settle themselves in those parishes where there is the best stock, the largest commons or wastes to build commons and the

---

[7] This chapter will not consider the nineteenth-century political tensions between Tory localism and Whig centralization; Lorie Charlesworth, 'Salutary and humane law: a legal history of the Law of Settlement and Removals, *c.*1795–1865' (PhD, University of Manchester, 1998), pp 234–7.

[8] 43 Eliz.I c. 4 (1601).

[9] Lorie Charlesworth, 'The law of settlement and removals viewed as a model of property rights for the poor', in Robert Holmes (ed.), *Squatters and settlers* (London, forthcoming).

[10] 13 & 14 Car. II c. 12. Poor Relief Act 1662.

[11] The term 'settlement' meant ' a permanent right to take the benefit of the poor laws in a particular parish or place which maintains its own poor. A settlement is not forfeitable, and may be communicated from person to person. It ceases and is destroyed in the parish or place where it once existed upon the acquisition of a settlement in any other parish or place'; Herbert Davey, *Poor law settlement* (London, 1908), p. 1.

most woods for them to burn and destroy and when they have consumed it then to another parish and at last become rogues and vagabonds to the great discouragement of parishes to provide stocks where it is liable to be devoured by strangers.

The chief provision under s.1 was that, any person coming to settle in a tenement valued at less than £10 per annum could be removed to their last settlement, that is, until 1795: 'any person or persons that are likely to be chargeable to the parish'.[12] This removal was to be achieved by the order of any two justices of the peace upon a complaint made by the overseers of the poor or churchwardens of any parish, within 40 days of the pauper arriving. There was a right of appeal to Quarter Sessions by: 'all such persons who think themselves aggrieved by any such judgement' (s.3). In legal terms, this meant the other named parish. Under the authority and terms of the 1662 Act, a formal legal process evolved for asking and answering the settlement questions. This was based upon a fundamental legal presumption, that every person born in England and Wales possessed a settlement.[13]

In its earliest form, settlement was acquired simply through birth or residence. However, gaining and proving a legal settlement became an increasingly technical matter. This law continued to evolve from those terms introduced into the 1662 Act, via further amending statutes and case law, to become extremely complex and a major source of contemporary lawyers' incomes.[14] The rules of settlement were only a problem for those who could not automatically qualify for a settlement by renting property at £10 per annum. This meant that the poor were less fortunate and moreover, often could not qualify as settled by the other, increasingly complex, methods of gaining a settlement. As a result of not acquiring a settlement, the destitute poor were vulnerable to the legal processes of removal; thus they could be returned by the operation of law to their settlement parish. Nevertheless,

---

12 35 Geo. III c. 101, (1795). The terms of this Act ended an area of great legal difficulty. As a result, from this date only paupers, that is those actually in receipt of relief, were vulnerable to removal. Rogues, vagabonds and disorderly persons were not protected.

13 'Prima facie every English-born subject has a settlement, and that settlement is the place of birth ... [unless] displaced by any other settlement'; *R v. All Saints, Derby* (1849), 14 QB 207.

14 The proportion and volume of income generated by settlement issues was equivalent to that earned from criminal law practice today. In 1888, Montague wrote, of the volume of legal material settlement law had produced: 'the statutes relating to the subject are more than thirty in number and their number gives no measure of their difficulty ... new law is frequently grafted on the old without repealing the old, so that it becomes difficult even for a lawyer ... to know what the law really is. But the statutes are a trifle to the case law. The cases indexed under the heads of settlement and removal in the latest index of Fisher's *Digest* occupy one hundred columns. More than five hundred pages of Burn's *Justices* are filled with them': F.C. Montague, 'The Law of Settlement and Removal', *Law Quarterly Review*, 13 (1888), 40–51 at 41.

those who became destitute away from their settlement parish were entitled to aid until the legal issue was decided. The 1601 Act remained the legal basis for all poor relief and welfare payments until 1948.[15]

More significantly for a legal history, before 1834 poor law was local law operating within a common legal framework throughout England and Wales.[16] To be precise, each person resident in a parish or township had a legal obligation to contribute to the poor rate; in amounts set relative to the value of property they occupied, against sums required to relieve the poor the previous year, minus any amount in surplus. As with English Council Tax today, failure to pay led to the distress of goods, and possible imprisonment. However, this 'structure', administered by local vestries composed of ratepayers under the web of statutory authority, permitted great flexibility by vestries in the manner and amount that they relieved their poor. At the same time, the justices at the Quarter Sessions oversaw all their accounts, the appointment of unpaid officials and many other activities. In fact, from a purely 'legal' perspective, the obligation to carry out poor law duties remained the legal and financial responsibility of local vestries until the Local Government Act 1894.[17] In order to perform this specific obligation, the ratepayers of each local vestry in England and Wales had to meet annually to set a poor rate, and appoint, from among its number, an unpaid overseer of the poor. S/he served for one year, and was responsible for collecting the poor rate and giving relief payments to the poor.[18] The overseer had a legal obligation to account to the vestry, and the justices, for all activity and expenditure.

By the nineteenth century, parochial autonomy was a well-established legal fact. To be precise, it was intrinsic to the legislation, fully evidenced in practitioners' texts and found expression within the settlement and removal case law.[19] Contemporaries and later commentators, believed that this had led

---

15 11 & 12 Geo.VI c. 29. The National Assistance Act 1948.
16 Lorie Charlesworth, 'The poor law: a modern legal analysis', *Journal of Social Security Law* 6 (1999), 79–92.
17 55 & 57 Vict. c. 71. Local Government Act 1894.
18 Overseers were generally men. However, women appear occasionally in that role. Thus the Tranmere (now part of Birkenhead, Merseyside) vestry, appointed two women as overseers in the late eighteenth century, but none in the nineteenth; Wirral Museum (WM) 1783–1827, BC VI 387 (Archives) CR/C 7745, Tranmere Vestry Records; Toulmin, Smith *The parish: its powers and obligations at law* (2nd ed. London, 1857).
19 Richard Burn, *The history of the poor laws with observations* (London, 1764); *The Justice of the Peace and the Parish Officer* (London, 1757); Michael Dalton, *The Countrey Justice* (1618); London, 1630 ed.; London, 1635 ed.; London, 1727 ed.; London, 1742; H.J. Hodgson, *Steer's Parish Law, being a digest of the law Relating to the civil and ecclesiastical government of the parishes, friendly societies etc. and the relief, settlement and Removal of the poor* (3rd ed London, 1857); Michael Nolan, *A treatise of the laws for the relief and settlement of the poor*, 2 vols (2nd ed.1805) ; The Honourable Roger North, *Discourse on the pernicious*

to a situation the Webbs described as a 'state of constitutional anarchy'.[20] This contemporary perception, combined with the increased cost of parish rates rising between c.1770 and 1819,[21] are deemed to have been influential in both the House of Commons and the House of Lords setting up two *Select Committee on the Workings of the Poor Laws* in 1817. These Committees were established with the specific purpose of reducing the poor rate.[22] The Commons' Committee was presided over by the Rt. Hon. William Sturges Bourne, who was influential in introducing two Acts to regulate the procedure of some vestry meetings.[23] These Acts introduced a scale of plural voting in proportion to the amount of rates paid by individuals. In short, their terms authorised the setting up of a system of Select Vestries, whose members were elected every year by the open vestry. The overseer had a duty to act as the Select Vestry instructed, and was a salaried employee.

THE POOR LAW AMENDMENT ACT 1834

It is probable that the most persuasive impetus for reform of the old poor law was the escalating poor law costs. These were due to many factors, including the considerable social and economic changes in the lives of the labouring classes during the first part of the nineteenth century. Such changes occurred at a time when new theories of political science were influencing the centralising tendencies of the Whig reformers. The old poor law epitomized the Tory traditions of localism and paternalism that, many believed, stood in the way of reform. The reforming impetus of the Whigs, combined with the influence of the development of legal positivism which suggested new ways of looking at law, can be seen as expressed most fully in the Poor Law Amendment Act 1834, particularly in its innovative approach to the organization of poor relief on a national scale. Moreover, Bentham's influence pervaded the new poor law, not only through his privately circulated writings, but also via his former secretary, William Chadwick. Chadwick was

---

Tendency of the laws for the maintenance and settlement of the poor 1689 (London, 1753); J. Shaw, *The parochial officer; or Churchwardens' and overseers' guides and assistance* (4th ed. London, 1833); W. Toone, *A practical guide to the duty and authority of overseers* (2nd ed. London, 1815); *The magistrate's manual* (2nd ed.) (London, 1817).

20 Webb, *The parish*, p. 152.
21 Total rates levied in England and Wales in 1758 were a little over £2m; in 1802 £5.3m; by the desperate years of 1818–19 the total was more than £10m; ibid., pp 152–3.
22 *Report of the House of Lords Committee on the Poor Laws*, 10 July 1817; *First Report from the House of Commons Committee on the Poor Laws*, 10 March 1818; *Second Report from the House of Commons Committee on the Poor Laws*, 28 April 1818; *Third Report from the House of Commons Committee on the Poor Laws*, 26 May 1818, p. 153.
23 The Ats did not apply to the operation and powers of vestries governed by Local Acts or established custom, nor to the closed vestries.

the author of the 1834 *Poor Law Report*.[24] In summary, the Report was based upon the findings of the earlier *Royal Commission on the Poor Laws*, set up in 1832 to examine the operation and costs of the old poor law. Chadwick helped to draft the 1834 Act and was appointed Secretary to the three Poor Law Commissioners who headed the bureaucratic centre of the new poor law in London. The new system outlined in the Act was slowly introduced throughout England and Wales, By the 1860s it had largely transformed the formerly local and autonomous poor law administration to a consistently run national, bureaucratic, administrative system.

Nonetheless, after 1834 each parish still remained financially responsible for its settled poor. Moreover, each retained their poor law responsibilities to those poor and much of their former discretion in poor law activities. For example, overseers continued to be appointed after 1834. The overseer remained the person or authority responsible for the making, collection and recovery of the poor rate. His, or occasionally her, official duties for the payment of out-relief were, in theory, transferred to the boards of guardians after 1834 as out-relief became prohibited under the terms of the 1834 Act. However local records indicate that overseers still made payments to casual and other poor.[25] The Poor Law Commission and its successors, the Poor Law Board (1846) and the Local Government Board (1871), recognised and deplored this situation. Article V of the Out Door Relief Prohibitory Order of 1844, issued by the Commission on 21 December 1844, in force into the twentieth century and binding all the unions listed in its schedule to the Order,[26] stated for example, that overseers were forbidden to pay rent: 'except in an emergency'. All relief given contrary to such an order was declared to be unlawful.[27] However, the Poor Law Board in their circular dated 9 December 1868 impressed upon local guardians the importance of strict compliance with the Order, as did a letter from the President of the Local Government Board on the 21 March 1894. Clearly unions were still not complying with its terms. Vestries and overseers also retained legal authority in one very important matter. That is, the right to initiate and enforce pauper removals. This was not transferred to the relieving officers and poor law guardians of the unions until 1865.[28]

24 S.G. and E.O.A. Checkland (eds), *The Poor Law Report of 1834* (London, 1974).
25 Lorie Charlesworth, 'Tranmere township in the nineteenth century: an introduction to the operation of the Tranmere Vestry', *Cheshire History*, 40 (2000–1), 40–56.
26 These were mostly in the South of England.
27 W.C. Maude, *The poor law handbook* (London, 1903), p. 87.
28 The office of overseer of the poor was finally abolished in the Rating and Valuation Act 1925 when rating powers and duties were transferred to public authorities. These comprised the councils of county boroughs, non-county boroughs, urban districts and rural districts: John C. Clarke, *Social administration including the poor law* (2nd ed.) (London, 1935), p. 65.

Far more significantly for the lived experience of the poor, after 1834 the new system imposed severe controls upon them. This was because the terms of the Act stated that the able-bodied poor (and their families) could only be relieved in a workhouse, under conditions of 'less eligibility'.[29] There families were split up, husbands from wives, parents from children, girls from boys, and all were subject to discipline and control in a quasi-prison environment. A family entered together, and technically could only leave together. Nevertheless, in spite of the primary requirement that the able-bodied poor could only be relieved in the workhouse, payments continued to be made to paupers outside the workhouse, both by individual parish overseers and by order of the guardians. In addition, the Poor Law Commissioners themselves could, by order or regulation under s.52 of the 1834 Act, declare to what extent and under what conditions out-relief might be administered to able-bodied persons or their families. This was an acknowledgement that the union workhouses could not hold all those made destitute in times of great dearth.

Thus, it is apparent that such *ad hoc* arrangements, although not within the spirit of the 1834 Act, continued after 1834 and, in fact, well into the twentieth century. This was perhaps, a legacy of parochial and local autonomy. There are detailed records in some areas for the payments of nonresident relief after 1834; for example as practised in Kirby Lonsdale, and recorded in the records of Garnett the overseer.[30] Evidence in letters and correspondence indicated that money was often paid as a supplement to wages or for rent, particularly to large families. Quite often, a settlement parish paid small sums of money to those families possessing a settlement but resident elsewhere. The financial benefit to the settlement parish was that the relieved family was still largely self-funding, and that comparatively small payments kept them financially independent elsewhere. Thus for example, in Manchester a considerable number of the non-settled poor were relieved in Manchester by their settlement parishes.[31] Such payments were largely

---

29 'Less eligibility' has been understood to mean that the able-bodied pauper in the workhouse should not experience a better standard of living than that available to the labourer outside the house. The *Royal Commission on the Poor Laws* defined 'less eligibility' with reference to discipline, '... although the workhouse food be more ample in quantity and better in quality than that of which the labourer's family partakes, and the house in other respects superior to the cottage, yet the strict discipline in well-regulated workhouses, and in respect the restrictions to which the inmates are subject ... are intolerable to the indolent and disorderly ...', Checkland, *Poor law report*, p. 338.

30 Cumbria Record Office, 1809–36 WPR/19, 'Kirby Lonsdale. Township Letters', cited in J.S. Taylor, 'A different kind of Speenhamland: nonresident relief in the Industrial Revolution', *Journal of British Studies*, 30 (1991), 183–208 and 195.

31 In the 1840s numbers equalled that of payments to the settled poor. The costs quintupled between 1847 and 1848, probably as an effect of the 1846 Act; Liverpool Central Library (LCL), M3/3/4/6, 'Churchwardens' Accounts. 1809–48'.

minimal and, in the case of utter destitution, pauper families were faced with no alternative but to return to their settlement parish.

However, this was in the future and, at the time the Act was passed, many were very concerned about the form that future would take. In consequence, there were protests against the imposition of poor law unions. These became enmeshed within the movement for factory reform and Chartism, but also represented the independent spirit of localism, as many from all walks of life viewed the new poor law as an attack on local autonomy. As a consequence, poor law protest, in spite of some massed demonstrations in the north of England, remained essentially local protest.[32] The national battle was waged mainly in print; a section of the press virulently opposed the Act. This included local papers, journals and national publications, for example William Cobbett's *Political Register,* the *Quarterly Review* and *The Times*.[33] The initial protests in the south and west of England took the form of riot.[34] There was no leadership or formal organisation. On the contrary, responses consisted of spontaneous panic initiated by a mixture of local inefficiency in introducing the new system, some mischief making by opportunists and, perhaps, a sense of lost rights by the poorest section of society.[35]

Tory radicals supported both the protests and the resistance to the Commissioners' orders in the North of England, again on the basis that the orders threatened established institutions and local autonomy. This view dominated rural areas and some new industrial areas. For example, Huddersfield resisted the imposition of the new poor law for a year due to the timely interventions of a well-led mob.[36] The *Northern Star*, founded by the radical O'Connor (in November 1837) was, perhaps, most influential in the debate. The journal covered the minutiae of local protests and poor law developments fully and was a truly popular newspaper.[37] Localism was such a fundamental feature of protest, as it had been of the operation of the old poor law itself that no successful national opposition emerged. As a result, much of what opposition there was focused upon responding to the actions of the Poor Law Commission as they attempted to impose the new administrative order upon each individual newly-established union.[38] Local vestries and their inhabitants continued to resent central interference in matters which remained locally funded. It is therefore not surprising that central government, at least for a while, tolerated pre-existing schemes where

---

32 Knott, *Popular opposition*, p. 270.
33 Edsall, *Anti-poor law*, p. 25.
34 Ibid., p.31.
35 Lorie Charlesworth, 'The poet and the poor law. Reflections upon John Clare's *The Parish*', *Liverpool Law Review*, 23 (2002), 167–78.
36 Edsall, *Anti-poor law*, p. 100.
37 Ibid., p. 121.
38 Ibid., p. 178.

the local establishment also resisted the new system, but where the pre-existing poor relief systems resembled the new poor law unions. Chester and Liverpool fell into this category.

POOR RELIEF UNDER THE CHESTER INCORPORATION

Chester is an ancient city situated on the River Dee in Cheshire; it was founded by the Romans and, unusually, much of Roman Chester survives today. In the Victorian era it lay close to industrialising areas but was not part of them. Moreover, it did not benefit from the canal and turnpike revolutions although it possessed some minor industrialization.[39] It had once been a busy port, but as the River Dee gradually silted up, so the wharves and docks were moved downriver to Parkgate and by 1830 the port was completely eclipsed by Liverpool, seventeen miles away. Thus, Chester had suffered stagnation, however, after the arrival of the railway in 1840 it became prosperous. In spite of its current charm, in the nineteenth century Chester also contained some appalling slum housing in its courts.[40]

The Chester Incorporation was formed in 1761 when Chester obtained a Local Act of Parliament.[41] The impetus for this costly and complex procedure came from Chester's particular parish make-up. Although Chester is a small city, it contains 9 separate parishes, including the extra-parochial cathedral chapter. Each of these had a separate vestry to administer the poor law for their settled poor, raise a poor rate, appoint officials and so on. Before the Local Act, the Chester parishes had built their own individual workhouses under the authority of the Parish Workhouse Act of 1723. After Incorporation, Chester used a workhouse built by Chester Town Council, completed by sometime between 1759 and 1762.[42] It is significant that the members of all the vestries together formed a small tightly knit community. These men (always men) were also often both members of the town council and the closely knit Chester Guilds. As a result, the Town Council and local vestry members were connected by their local duties. This enabled the group to be both in a position to see the need for a Local Act, and to have the means to carry out the necessary expensive and complex processes to obtain the required legislation. That is to say, they shared mutual interests and met

39 J. Herson, 'Victorian Chester: a city of change and ambiguity', in R. Swift (ed.), *Victorian Chester* (Liverpool, 1996), p. 14.
40 Courts are small blind alleys off streets. Often entered though narrow entrances with housing on at least two sides, usually back to back. Such housing was multiple-occupancy, squalid, unsanitary and caused public health disasters. Liverpool had huge numbers of these, but only a few have survived.
41 2 Geo. III (1761).
42 Chris Lewis, 'Building Chester's first workhouse', *Cheshire History*, 38 (1998–9), 50–4, p. 52.

regularly in different settings. Moreover, they possessed the legal authority to raise a rate to fund the procedure.

Those who obtained the new Act ensured that guardians elected from each parish managed the Incorporation, and its workhouse.[43] This resulted in the Chester Incorporation actually having seventy-four guardians elected annually. This was an extraordinary number for a single institution in a small city, but it reflected the inclusive nature of its membership and the large number of parishes the City contained. In addition, Chester town council, the mayor, recorder and aldermen were *ex officio* members. The Incorporation had the sole power of raising the rate, to be in proportion to the number of paupers from each parish who were maintained within the workhouse. This innovation was far from the poor law norm, as it took rating, the fundamental basis of local autonomy, away from the vestries. This deliberate change reflected the unity of purpose and trust of the membership of the new Chester Incorporation board of guardians, and the mutuality of those who ran the City administration. As a result, it was clearly of great interest to all the ratepayers of the City to have representation on the board of guardians.

The poor rate continued to be collected by the overseers of each parish, and the guardians had the right of appointing and removing officials and fixing their salaries. Paupers were only to be relieved in the Incorporation's workhouse. They could be provided with employment there or hired to harvest or to perform other work.[44] In addition, the guardians had the power to search for the poor in the city and compel them to enter the workhouse; a power never envisaged nor contained in the later 1834 Act. Unlike other Local Acts, Chester guardians could contract for the maintenance of the poor of any of the parishes in the neighbourhood, a process known as 'farming' the poor.

The Chester guardians not only had a workhouse, rented at £99 per annum for a term of 99 years, they also ran an industrial farm, situated in Saltney, 2 miles from the city.[45] This had been leased from the Chester Town Council for 40 years at a rent of £21 per annum. The guardians let small portions of the land to industrial labourers who cultivated them after their day's work.[46] This practice was not allowed under the 1834 Act, although

---

43 M.A. Handley, 'Local administration of the poor law in the Great Boughton and Wirral Unions and the Chester Local Act Incorporation, 1834–71' (MA, University of Bangor, 1969–70).

44 Mothers of bastard children, even if not chargeable, could be punished, not only by hard labour and the wearing of a badge, but also by public whipping. In reality they were paid 2s. a week and not punished as the Local Act stipulated; *Royal Commission on the Administration of the Poor Laws*, PP, 1834, xxxv, Appendix B, Part I.

45 Ibid., Appendix A, Part I, at 205a.

46 Ibid. The labourers paid a small rent to the guardians and yet managed a small profit to supplement their wages. D.C. Maylan reported that the farm 'had been the means of preventing numerous applications for assistance that would otherwise have been granted'.

local vestries could hold land to fund poor relief purposes. In spite of the draconian provisions of the Local Act, it is clear from evidence given to the *Royal Commission on the Administration of the Poor Laws* (1834) that the Incorporation were also giving out-relief payments to the poor.[47] The Chester Incorporation was governed under the term of that Act from 1762 until 1869, for, as we shall see below, until then the guardians refused to surrender their Act to the Commission.

The social composition of the guardians in Chester was mixed, but the majority were merchants and craftsmen, with retail shopkeepers and innkeepers in the majority. Unlike the surrounding areas, particularly the Wirral Peninsular, the clergy did not take a significant role in the administration of poor relief.[48] Perhaps the fact that Chester is a cathedral city, with the bishop in residence sitting in the centre of a spider's web of many parishes, ensured that the clergy had more interest in ecclesiastical politics than secular matters.[49]

In order to administer the Chester Incorporation, the guardians held a weekly 'court' to hear applications for relief and a monthly 'court' that made policy decisions. Handley notes that, in common with the practice in many later poor law unions, the guardians appeared most preoccupied with finishing meetings quickly and keeping down relief costs.[50] It is arguable that this attitude demonstrated little sympathy for the occupants of the workhouse, or the rest of Chester's poor. As a result, in 1858 when Dr Bedford a new reforming guardian accused the master of the workhouse of 'having provided meat for the inmates that was unfit for human food', he received little support.[51] The *Chester Chronicle* reported that: '[The] governor of the board told the doctor that he was decidedly disorderly'. Bedford's attempts at reform subjected him to much ridicule and abuse from the other

---

47 Ibid. John Babb, overseer of the parish of St Martin, stated that such relief was only given 'after a home visit and upon the advice of a magistrate'; ibid., Appendix B, Part 1.
48 For example; Revd Joshua King, rector of Woodchurch on the Wirral from 1821, was a Tory and ardent anti-poor law activist; *Chester Courant*, 14 June 1836; Revd R.M. Fielden, magistrate and rector of Bebbington on the Wirral, was chairman of the Wirral Poor Law Guardians from 1838. Fielden also chaired the vestry meetings of Tranmere Township on the Wirral regularly and supported the new poor law; Chester Record Office (CRO), LGW 1/1, *The Minutes of the Board of Guardians*, Wirral Poor Law Union, vol. 1, 17 March 1836–23 March 1838; WM, BC VI 837, 'Tranmere Township Overseers Poor Rate Accounts 1827–38 and Minutes of Township and Vestry Meetings, 1831–38'.
49 For a contemporary account of ecclesiastical preoccupations, published between 1855–1867 see; Anthony Trollop, *Barchester Chronicles*.
50 Handley, 'Local administration', p. 69. The neighbouring Wirral Poor Law Union records reveal the same tendency, plus appalling attendance during cold weather and full meetings when Sir Charles Stanley of Ness or Sir Thomas Stanley of Great Sutton were present as chair; CRO, LGW/1/ series, 'Wirral Poor Law Union, 1836–1931'.
51 *Chester Chronicle*, 29 May 1858.

guardians, eventually leading to him being forcibly ejected from meetings and thereafter excluded. He complained of this to the Poor Law Board in London but, significantly for this writer's purpose, again they were unable to actively interfere in the operation of a Private Act Incorporation.[52]

In general, it appears that the guardians shared the unsympathetic view of the upper and middle classes towards paupers. In the Chester Incorporation, their aims were to prevent the working class from starving and rioting whilst preventing the poor rate from becoming too great a burden upon themselves and other ratepayers.[53] At the time of the Royal Commission *Report* of 1834, the greatest number of paupers admitted into the Chester workhouse was 317.[54] Excluding the cost of clothing, fuel and medicine, which were charged to each pauper's settlement parish, it cost 4s. per week to maintain a pauper in the workhouse.[55] The paupers worked at various tasks including street sweeping, or within the workhouse and all received the same diet.[56] The Incorporation farmed the poor of Cheshire, Flintshire and Denbighshire parishes under contract, a profitable practice strictly at variance with the terms of the 1834 Act. However, this practice and its profits stopped once those other parishes were formed into poor law unions and had built their union workhouses.

The Chester guardians had shown an interest in the 1834 Act from its introduction as a bill; mainly to oppose it's passing.[57] The 1834 Act set out precisely the manner in which a private act Incorporation was to be brought under its new administration. S. 32 stated that an Incorporation had to be dissolved by agreement: '... a Majority of not less than Two Thirds of the Guardians of such Union shall so concur therein'. This was something the first Assistant Poor Law Commissioner for the area, Richard Digby Neave, was never able to achieve. Moreover, by 1837 it was established case law that the Commissioners could not force Local Act Incorporations to comply with the new Act.[58] In fact, no changes were made in the administration of the poor law in Chester as a result of the 1834 Act.[59]

---

52 National Archives (NA), MH 12/904, 30 June 1858; 15 July 1858; 30 October 1858; 8 March 1859; 24 March 1859; 'Dr. Bedford to the Poor Law Board'.
53 Handley, 'Local Administration', p. 41.
54 21 January 1830. The average number was 250; *Royal Commission*, PP, 1834, xxviii, Appendix A, Part I, at 265a.
55 NA, MH 12/900. 1/10/1834, 'Incorporation Clerk to Poor Law Commission'.
56 Ibid. Inmates above the age of 50 could receive allowances of tobacco, snuff or gin.
57 George Harrison, a plumber and the mayor, was reported as stating: 'I shall use my best exertions to prevent aged people from going to the workhouse. I must have the certificate of a surgeon first, before that I allow that an old man's wife be taken from him'; *Chester Courant*, 28 October 1834.
58 *R v. Poor Law Commissioners (ex parte St Pancras)* (1837). This case stated that the Poor Law Commissioners could not force the guardians of a parish where a Local Act was in force to elect a board of guardians under the 1834 Act.
59 The Poor Law Commissioners were not allowed to alter the boundaries of local

At his first meeting with the Chester guardians, in an attempt to bring the Incorporation under the control of the Commission, Neave suggested that if Chester agreed to adopt the new Act he would ensure that the new union comprised all the townships within seven miles. If not, he threatened to detach all those parishes that had contracted (lucratively for Chester) to put their poor in the Incorporation's workhouse.[60] In fact, this happened anyway. Two thirds of the guardians did agree at a vote put at this first meeting, but later after reflection they decided not to comply. They wrote to the Commission to enquire if the new union would run under the Local Act.[61] Their concern was that they held the workhouse under a beneficial lease and did not wish the considerable expense of buying it from the town council, as required under the terms of the 1834 Act. In spite of their initial support for Neave's plan this issue proved a stumbling block. As a result, the necessary formal agreement required to impose the terms of the Act was never given; the guardian's opposition to change continued. They rejected an amended plan suggested by Neave, and resisted his persistent attempts which continued until 1841, to bully and cajole them into surrendering the Act.

Although retaining legal autonomy, the Chester Incorporation was still subject to inspections from the Commission, but these only occurred regularly from 1848. Data was collected and reports written with suggested improvements. Most significantly these comments had the effect of advice rather than instruction upon the Incorporation as the Poor Law Commission had no means of enforcement. A case in point occurred in 1841, when William Day, a later Assistant Poor Law Commissioner, was seriously unimpressed with the workhouse: 'as badly regulated as any in the kingdom'.[62] A year later, conditions were still inadequate.[63] The classes of pauper were not separated;[64] the school and children's dormitories were detached from the main building; as was the House of Separation (for lunatics), then being converted into sick wards; the women's apartments were ill-ventilated; forty boys occupied eleven beds; and in a recent smallpox epidemic mortality had been high. However, by June Day was reporting improvements but was still unhappy about the general lack of classification.[65]

administrations without their consent, in those parishes where a Local Act was in force; M.A. Crowther, *The workhouse system, 1834–1929* (London, 1981), p. 45.
60 *Chester Courant*, 19 April 1836.
61 NA, MH 12/900, 21 May 1836, 'Chairman of the Incorporation and other Guardians to the Poor Law Commission'.
62 Ibid., 1 December 1841, 'William Day to the Poor Law Commission'.
63 Ibid., 6 January 1842, 'William Day to the Poor Law Commission'.
64 The Commission devised a sevenfold classification; aged and infirm men; able-bodied men and youths over 13 (increased to 15 in 1842); boys aged from seven to 13; aged or infirm women; able-bodied women and girls over 13 (increased to 16 from 1842); girls from seven to 13; children under seven; Crowther, *Workhouse system*, p. 42.
65 'There is only one general yard of the main quadrangle into which all the staircases open';

In addition, in 1843 Day commented that in Chester the Local Act itself was not being followed with respect to rating; that apportioning pauper costs to parishes was in breach of the 1834 Act and that the keeping of accounts and the collection of rates were unsatisfactory. He noted that the master held considerable funds over time and also acted as clerk; a practice utterly disallowed under the 1834 Act. Furthermore, it was one that depended entirely upon the reliability of the master.[66] In 1848, the next Assistant Commissioner, Aneurin Owen, reported that Day's advice had been taken to divide the paupers' exercise yard.[67] Continued inspections revealed a pattern of inadequacy, but much to the inspector of the day's chagrin, when the workhouse lease expired in 1861 it was renewed and the Incorporation continued.[68]

One characteristic that Chester shared with Liverpool was the disproportionate numbers of Irish in the poor law costs. This section will consider what role, if any, this may have played in Chester's ability to resist the implementation of the Act of 1834. By the late eighteenth century, the Irish visited England in seasonal migrations for harvesting. Although the Welsh and Scots also followed a seasonal labour migration pattern, by the nineteenth century the Irish were the largest number. They did work the English disliked because it was dirty, disreputable or otherwise undesirable.[69] Numbers travelling to England increased in the nineteenth century and by 1816 Parliament's attention was drawn to the increased problem of Irish paupers in Manchester and the seaports and surrounding districts.[70] An Act of 1819 facilitated the passing of the Irish and the Scottish vagrants back to their places of origin. This was successful and rather popular with these 'vagrants' who obtained free travel home thereby. Their numbers increased, as did the pressure on the ports whose vestries were responsible for returning these non-settled poor home. The settlement rules allowed settled migrant workers to travel by means of certification. However, the Irish could not produce such certificates, as the poor law did not run in Ireland until 1838 and then in a truncated form.[71] Even so, they found a demand for their services which kept them arriving.

NA, MH 12/900, 29 November 1842, 'William Day to the Poor Law Commission'.
66 *9th Annual Report of the Poor Law Commission*, PP, 1843, xxi, p. 306.
67 NA, MH 12/901, 28 March 1848, 'Aneurin Owen to the Poor Law Board'.
68 *Chester Courant*, 15 February 1861.
69 In Birkenhead across the River Mersey, the Irish specialized in collecting and selling cockles and mussels, or sold sand and rubbing stones; Arthur Redford, *Labour migration in England, 1800–1850* (2nd ed. Manchester, 1964).
70 *The First Report on Mendicity in the Metropolis 1815*, pp 5–9 and 138.
71 Poor relief was a different matter in Ireland where the Act of 1601 did not run. As a result, in 1838, Parliament was able to pass an Act establishing the Irish poor law system without any right to relief. For a full discussion of the Irish poor law and its implications for the deaths of famine victims in the 1840s; Christine Kinealy, *This great calamity: the Irish famine, 1845–52* (Dublin, 1994).

In the 1740s, the Irish harvesters had arrived through Parkgate (technically the Port of Chester) on the Dee estuary. They continued to arrive at the port until 1815 when that coastal stretch of the River Dee had silted up and the traffic moved to the Port of Liverpool.[72] The names of 25,325 individuals are recorded in the accounts of the Neston House of Correction, (in Parkgate) between 1750–1800. These records reveal that it was in fact rarely used for Rogues (vagrants), but for the destitute in need of shelter.[73] This practice ended with the silting of the port.[74]

Meanwhile, a considerable number of Irish lived in Chester, largely as the City's position lay on the well-defined migrant route in England that lay through the Wirral Peninsular to and from Ireland.[75] This large number of mainly poor Irish living in the city was of some concern. Travelling harvesters also passed through the City, these traditionally included many Irish workers and there were also Irish vagrants.[76] In 1841, 4.4% of the population of Chester were Irish born, and by 1851 the proportion was 7.3%. [77] Contemporary reports in the *Chester Chronicle* reveal that there was a great deal of suffering among the Chester Irish during the famine period of the 1840s. In 1847 the *Chester Chronicle*, at the height of the famine influx, expressed concern that: 'a great deal of distress prevailed' with: 'more suffering among the lower orders than is generally imagined'.[78] On 14 February 1847 the *Chronicle* reported over 300 destitute Irish had been relieved with soup, coal and money from Father Carberry and his Charity. The newspaper noted that these: 'unfortunate and starving creatures were huddled up in large numbers in very confined and filthy dwellings'.

The problem of relieving large numbers of poor in Chester continued. Finally, by the 1860s the Chester workhouse was seriously overcrowded; the problem exacerbated by agricultural labourers in Cheshire who were thrown out of work by the cattle plague. Driven by destitution, they flooded into the city to seek employment and by April 1869 there were 400 inmates in the workhouse.[79] At long last, the Incorporation Management Committee recommended building a new workhouse as the old building was so

---

72 Geoffrey Place, *The rise and fall of Parkgate, passenger port for Ireland, 1686–1815* (Manchester, 1994), p. 174.
73 Ibid., pp 183–7.
74 'Irish vagrants. The Magistrates of this county have given notice by circulars, which the Dublin packets did not now sail from Parkgate but from Liverpool. Magistrates … are requested to direct passes in future to Liverpool'; *Chester Chronicle*, 28 July 1815.
75 K. Jeffes, ' The Irish in early Victorian Chester: an outcast community?', in Swift, *Victorian Chester*, p. 85.
76 Ibid. A local magistrates' report on vagrancy in 1785 showed that 4,686 Irish vagrants had been conveyed through the county of Chester during the previous three years.
77 CRO, census abstracts, 1841 and 1851.
78 *Chester Chronicle*, 15 January 1847.
79 NA, MH 12/906, 7 April 1869, 'Reverend George Salt to the Poor Law Board'.

overcrowded. The financial difficulties this presented to the City drove the guardians to surrender the Incorporation to the Poor Law Board. They formally dissolved the Chester Incorporation, relinquishing their control to the central authority. A subsequent rearrangement of the neighbouring Great Boughton Poor Law Union was achieved to incorporate some of its townships into the new Chester Poor Law Union. This action finally brought Chester into compliance with the terms of the 1834 Poor Law Amendment Act.

LIVERPOOL AND THE SELECT VESTRY

Liverpool presented a very different picture to Chester in the nineteenth century as today, and yet it resembled Chester after 1834 in its retention of some legal autonomy in poor relief administration.[80] It too was (and still is) a port, albeit on the River Mersey. However, Liverpool became a port on a massive and very successful commercial scale. The City of Liverpool was composed of one parish unlike Chester's nine, and therefore a single vestry was responsible for the administration of poor relief.[81] The city is and was much larger, had and has a much bigger population and its social and public health problems dwarfed those of Chester. As a consequence, Liverpool, in poor law terms, was a pathological case. Its workhouse was the biggest in Britain, with over 5,000 pauper inmates by the end of the nineteenth century, compared to Chester's overcrowded workhouse when 400 paupers were in residence. Both cities attracted poor Irish immigrants, but as we shall see below, Liverpool did so during the Irish famine on an almost unimaginable scale. Yet these two ports, very different in size with problems on a vastly differing scale, both successfully legally resisted the imposition of the terms of the 1834 Poor Law Amendment Act.

Liverpool does not share Chester's ancient origins. King John established the city by charter in 1207; this specifically invited settlers to the new town.[82] Chandler points out that it was a feature both of Liverpool's status as a port and of its geographical position that the city attracted great numbers of poor, not only from the immediate locality, but also from Ireland and Wales.[83]

80 A minor poor law connection between the two cities is that the Liverpool Vestry minutes of 1724 record that a small rent was received for two houses in Forrest Street, Chester, which had been devised for the benefit of the Liverpool poor by Mr Bird; W. L. Blease, 'The poor law in Liverpool 1681–1838', *Transactions of the Historic Society of Lancashire and Cheshire*, 61 (1909) 97–182, p. 101.

81 Liverpool was originally a part of the parish of Walton-on-the-Hill, it became a separate parish in 1699; G. Chandler, *Liverpool* (London, 1957), p. 97.

82 Ibid., pp 13–20.

83 Ibid., p. 371. Bye laws in 1540 and 1541 provided that no person within the town shall receive: 'eny maner of beggars or vacabound … upon payne of every defaulte 6s. 8d.'; ibid., p. 372.

During the seventeenth century many poor were transported from Liverpool to America. From 1682, Liverpool's Vestry Books reveal extensive out-relief payments by overseers to the poor. In 1685 the Council ordered that all persons whose names were in the Poor Book were to wear a pewter badge with the Town's Arms engraved on it, all who refused were to be denied relief.[84] After the opening of the first dock in Liverpool in 1715, the poor rate began to rise as the numbers of destitute in-migrants increased. In response to this problem, in 1723 the vestry discontinued out-relief in favour of parish work.[85] By 1732 the vestry had decided to build a workhouse to reduce poor law costs, end out-relief and impose a test of labour and residence in the workhouse.[86] The growth of poverty outpaced this early workhouse accommodation and in 1772 a new workhouse was built on Brownlow Hill, where it remained and grew until the empty building was demolished to build the Metropolitan Cathedral.[87]

In 1733, the vestry had set up a parish committee that became over time a standing committee dealing with all poor law matters on behalf of the ratepayers of Liverpool. In consequence, when Liverpool elected its first Select Vestry in 1821 under the authority of the Sturges Bourne Acts of 1818 and 1819, some elements of the old parish committee remained, with new title and statutory powers, but pursuing largely the same objects as before.[88] However, the vestry minutes do reveal that the Select Vestry made strenuous efforts to reduce relief payments, investigate abuses and stop some of the rather corrupt practices that had previously become institutionalized within the operation of the system.[89]

Every matter concerning the relief of poverty in Liverpool was on a vast scale. Even the composition of the Select Vestry was different from that of the Chester guardians. Unlike Chester, with its Incorporation run largely by tradesmen of the 'middling' sort, the Select Vestry was composed of extremely wealthy merchants and professional men.[90] The ratepayers elected

---

84 Ibid., p. 383.
85 S. Kelly, 'The Select Vestry of Liverpool and the administration of the poor law, 1821–1871' (MA, University of Liverpool, 1971), pp 8 and 10.
86 Blease, 'The poor law', pp 109–110.
87 The scale of the problem of poverty in Liverpool was enormous. Vestry minutes of 1813 reveal that there were 1,300 paupers in the workhouse, 8,000 receiving relief on the streets and one inhabitant in ten received relief in one form or another. By the 1830s the workhouse housed more than 1,500 people and was the largest in Britain; ibid., pp 128 and 146–7.
88 Ibid., p. 114.
89 Extravagance on the part of the churchwardens included inflated payment of salaries, expenditure on wine and spirits, the non collection of rates and so on; Blease 'The poor law', pp 160–1.
90 Much of the mercantile wealth of Liverpool at this time came from the slave trade; the 'professional men' were largely lawyers whose financial interests also included taking shares in slaving ventures.

these members in a system where votes were proportional to the amount of poor rate paid. The Vestry was divided into five boards; one sat every weekday except Tuesday, a secretary attended each. All applicants for relief were interviewed, with the Irish treated particularly severely. The Select Vestry built up a large staff and paid a high salary for professional managers for its institutions including the workhouse.[91] Thus, in 1869 Liverpool paid the master of the workhouse, then with 3,500 inmates, a salary of £350. By comparison, the Wirral Poor Law Union fifteen miles away with an average of 200 inmates, paid the master £50 per annum. In 1849 the Select Vestry employed 187 officers, 64 full-time, including 94 teachers in the Industrial Schools. The workhouse was run on strictly regulated lines, a formal uniform was issued.[92] In 1814 it cost about a pound a week to keep a family in the workhouse, a similar cost to Chester. However the scale of the workhouse operation in Liverpool meant that the annual costs for the Liverpool workhouse were much higher.[93] As a result, the records of the Select Vestry of Liverpool reveal similar pre-occupations with parish economy. The Chester Incorporation failed to divide paupers into classes and apply a labour test to those receiving out-relief payments.[94] The Select Vestry, on the other hand, applied a rigorous labour test to paupers, requiring those in receipt of relief to work both in the workhouse and elsewhere.

As with Chester, the Select Vestry were particularly concerned with the numbers of Irish poor entering Liverpool. These were either arriving in some destitute state as migrant labour, or were awaiting their return to Ireland under the vagrancy pass system. All too frequently, vestry records reveal that two thirds of the poor who received casual relief were Irish.[95] The first failure of the Irish potato crop in 1821 was followed by famine in 1822 and from this period the numbers of Irish entering England increased dramatically.[96] Lancashire contained a greater number of Irish settlers than any other county. The great famine of the 1840s brought in huge numbers of destitute Irish.[97] In 1846, over 280,000 immigrants arrived in Liverpool from

---

91 In recognition of the scale of the problems of poor relief in the city, Liverpool had a tradition of paid officials. The first was Edward Crane, overseer who, in 1724, was allowed £15 'for his trouble'; Blease, 'The poor law', p. 108. This practice was later authorized by the terms of the Sturges Bourne Acts.

92 Blease noted that from the time the Select Vestry was established, the records were better kept, minutes more formal and always signed by the chairman; 'The poor law', p. 159.

93 The annual cost of the workhouse in 1834 was £15,638, 25 March 1834; H. Peet (ed.), *Liverpool Vestry Books, 1681–1834* (Liverpool, 1915), ii, 339; 1857–8 it was £120,121; PP 1857–8, xlix, Part I, p. 309.

94 LRO, 355 Par 1/4/3/, Liverpool Parish Records, 'Annual Report of the Select Vestry for 1834'.

95 1 October 1824; Blease, 'The poor law', p. 165.

96 Redford, *Labour migration*, p. 140.

97 Cecil Woodham-Smith, *The great hunger: Ireland 1845–1849* (London, 1962).

Ireland and less than half sailed on to other countries; in 1847, over 300,000 arrived in Liverpool and again over half remained behind. Of the total, 50,000 travellers were passengers on business; the remainder were paupers suffering dire effects from the famine. Their local vestries had 'paid' them to emigrate.[98]

Under the terms of the 1834 Act Liverpool, along with Bristol, Manchester and much of London (all with Select Vestries), were able to retain their own administrative system. However, unlike Chester, they were expected to run their poor relief administrations in conformity with the regulations of the central authority. The first mention of this control appears in Liverpool Vestry minutes in 1836. It records an order read out in a Vestry meeting, for a revaluation of the county rate and to appoint a constable to deal with illegitimacy.[99] The order is explicit that these matters were to be taken out of the Vestry's hands. In response, the Vestry minutes note that the Poor Law Commissioners had asked for, and received, full information regarding the management of the parish.[1] As a consequence, and perhaps as a sign of their growing resistance, the Vestry record that they will make no changes until they know if the Commission 'have any plans of their own to suggest or enforce'.[2] Interestingly, the minutes conclude by noting that the Parish is in good financial shape, all debt has been paid off and more than five thousand pounds is held in their bankers' hands. The act of specifically recording such an extraordinarily large sum outside the annual accounts may be understood today as the Vestry's attempt to demonstrate the efficiency of their poor law administration to the Commission.

It is noticeable, that the Vestry minutes are carefully nuanced and anodyne, for as later developments reveal, the Vestry followed a 'wait and see' tactic with the central authority. The Vestry's resistance to the imposition of the 1834 Act finally reveals itself in the minutes taken at a meeting held 5 April 1836, although as we shall see, that resistance had begun earlier. At this meeting a Vestry member, Cholmley Woodward, introduced a perverse motion, utterly out of sympathy with the attitude of the majority.[3] He

---

98 The terms of an Act of 1846 authorized the purchase of labourers' interests in their small plots of land in order to allow them to emigrate. However, it was subsequently used by local vestries to force those who sought relief to give up their land in return for passage out of Ireland. The peak arrival in Liverpool was the first four months of 1847 when 144,000 destitute Irish arrived in Liverpool.

99 21 April 1835; Peet, *Liverpool Vestry*, p. 346.

1 Ibid., p. 347.

2 Ibid.

3 Woodward proved himself an equally unpopular and contentious vestry member and chair of the Tranmere Vestry in 1857, when he moved to live across the Mersey; WM, BC VI 385, 'Tranmere Township Minute Book of Vestry Meetings, October 1850–May 1897'; Charlesworth, 'Tranmere Township'.

suggested a petition to Parliament for the repeal of the Sturges Bourne Acts so that Liverpool would come under the authority of the 1834 Act. This was roundly defeated on the grounds that: '... the affairs of this Parish have been well and economically administered under the Act'.[4]

In fact, the Sturges Bourne Acts did not prove to be a legal barrier, but the sheer scale of Liverpool's poor relief responsibilities, combined with its nature as a single parish, may have encouraged the Poor Law Commission to delay implementing the terms of the Act. Liverpool presented a very different administrative problem to that posed by Chester where the Commission simply wished to graft on some of the townships surrounding the city to create a single poor law union. In 1837, perhaps in an effort to placate the Commission, the Select Vestry adopted a new system of rates collection: 'In conformity with the spirit of the New Poor Law Act [sic]'.[5] This conciliatory measure did not work and in 1841 the Vestry were faced with notice from Mr. Mott, Assistant Commissioner, that the Poor Law would be introduced into Liverpool 'immediately after Easter'.[6]

However, whilst the events discussed above were taking place, some of the ratepayers were pursuing an alternative course of action. Whatever the Commission ordered, they still constituted an elected portion of a parish vestry with all the legal powers, authority and autonomy of any other local vestry. In that capacity, they petitioned the overseers and churchwardens of the parish to call a: 'Special Vestry to take into consideration the propriety of adopting such measures as may prevent the introduction of this Act into the Parish'.[7] That meeting duly called, in the correct, legally authorized manner, discussed the attending ratepayers' objections to the imposition of the terms of the 1834 Act. In short, the likely increase in cost, the satisfaction with the status quo and the great dissatisfaction the introduction of the terms of the Act would cause in Liverpool.[8] The Commission continued on its course regardless. At the Easter Select Vestry Meeting, the minutes record: 'That, the administration of the affairs of the Parish and the government of the poor are transferred ... to the Guardians of the Poor, elected under the Poor Law Amendment Act'.[9] The minutes also record that the ratepayers had some hope that a bill then in Parliament would restore the: 'management of its own parochial affairs' to the Parish of Liverpool.[10]

Meanwhile, although this is not in the minutes, the Liverpool vestry members had taken serious action in opposition to the implementation of the

4 Peet, *Liverpool Vestry*, p. 350.
5 Ibid., 28 March 1837, p. 352.
6 Ibid., 11 March 1841.
7 Ibid., 6 March 1841.
8 Ibid., pp 360–1.
9 Ibid., 13 April 1841, p. 363.
10 Ibid.

1834 Act in the city. They had again used their legal authority and autonomy, this time to authorize and initiate an application for a private Act from parliament. What they were trying to do was place themselves into the legal position occupied by Chester, and operate the poor law under a Local Act Incorporation, taking the Select Vestry and poor relief in Liverpool away from the control of the Commission. In November 1841, the ratepayers requested and held a Special General Vestry to seek further support for that private act to restore Liverpool's autonomy in poor law matters.[11] This action was successful, aided by the continuing Tory parliamentary opposition to the new poor law. As a result, in July 1842, an: 'Act for the administration of the laws relating to the poor in the Parish of Liverpool, in the county of Lancaster' was passed and elections were held to appoint twenty-one Select Vestrymen.[12]

This marked the end of the new poor law's sway in Liverpool. The Select Vestry, even when replaced by poor law guardians, had retained its residual legal powers as a part of a parish vestry. These included the power to set and collect a rate, which they had used to fund the expenditure of a considerable sum of money in the pursuit of a private act.[13] What the vestry members also possessed was an almost unanimous agreement to restore local autonomy within a wealthy city where men of influence took an active role in local administration. Thus, Liverpool successfully challenged and overcame central bureaucracy. The Poor Law Commission made no serious attempt to reverse this position. The fact that the Select Vestry's administration was close enough to that set up under the authority of the 1834 Act, coupled with the scale of poverty in Liverpool, including the Irish dimension even before the famine, may have discouraged the Commission from serious opposition to a private bill. Once the famine devastated the labouring classes in Ireland, sending them to and through England, the Poor Law Board (the Commission's successors) appeared to lose all interest in assimilating Liverpool back into the national system.

CONCLUSION

As we have seen above, the Poor Law Amendment Act 1834 was passed by Parliament with a number of aims. In summary, these were; ending the practice of out-relief for the able-bodied poor across England and Wales; reducing the cost of poor relief by putting to an end what was perceived as

11 Ibid., 4 November 1841, p. 365.
12 Ibid., 28 July 1842, p. 367; 5 & 6 Vict. c. 88 (30 June 1842).
13 Peet, *Liverpool Vestry*, 29 March 1842, p. 366, 'Summary of the Church Accounts ... Expenses incurred in applying for Local Act, £350 0s. 10d.'

local profligacy in relief payments; and finally, limiting local autonomy in poor law administration. To that end, a uniform system of workhouses was to be introduced and there the poor were to be housed, and receive aid. A central bureaucracy, the Poor Law Commission, was appointed to oversee the introduction of this system and a system of inspectors ensured compliance. In spite of this, Chester and Liverpool (the latter apart from a brief hiatus) retained autonomy in the relief of poverty in their cities. A comparison of their circumstances reveals, that in spite of some shared characteristics (geographical proximity; both sea ports; numbers of Irish immigrants and so on) the vast differences of scale in the numbers of poor in the two cities made them very different cases. However, they both either retained or recovered their previous position through the operation of law.

Chester retained its autonomy through the Local Act Incorporation that made it exempt from the terms of the 1834 Act. It remained outside the national poor relief system in some particulars, whilst still reporting to, and remaining in contact with the Poor Law Commission and the later Poor Law Board respectively. Its autonomy was a feature of a lacuna within the 1834 Poor Law Amendment Act that barred the Commission from interfering with pre-existing private act Incorporations, unless a majority of their guardians concurred. The refusal by Chester's guardians stopped the Commission from imposing the terms of the Act. Necessity (the disrepair and lack of space in the workhouse) and economic pressure (the financial cost of replacement) eventually forced the guardians of the Chester Incorporation to succumb to the centralized bureaucratic system that operated for the relief of poverty in England and Wales. Chester remained a small city with a small problem, yet it successfully, albeit passively, was able to resist the implementation of the 1834 Act for 35 years.

Liverpool, as a Select Vestry, was already running a system similar in many ways to that set up under the Act. As a very wealthy city, it had the good fortune to consist of a single parish. Moreover, even when operating in compliance with the terms of the 1834 Act, Liverpool retained sufficient autonomy in rating matters to arrange parish vestry meetings to agree the funding for a private act. Liverpool actively resisted and was able, using the law itself as weapon, to circumvent any further attempts by the Poor Law Commission to enforce the Act. Once it had obtained its Local Act, Liverpool was in the same legal position as Chester and could resume its autonomy in poor relief. Thus any characterization of the Poor Law Amendment Act 1834 as setting up a national system can be seen as an over simplification. The explanation for these two anomalies within the system can be found within the pre-existing framework of legal authority under which the cities of Liverpool and Chester, although experiencing very differing poor law responsibilities, were both able to continue their stubborn maintenance of local customs in the face of central government authority and pressure.

This writer has not examined the other localities that also enjoyed the benefits of the legal autonomy granted by administering poor relief under the terms of their Local Act Incorporations. This brief reconstruction demonstrates however, that the Poor Law Amendment Act 1834 was successfully resisted in at least two places, using the legal mechanisms left unaltered by the terms of the Act. The explanation for that resistance has been revealed by an interdisciplinary approach, moving beyond the territorial integrity of the sub discipline of doctrinal legal history. In other words it has been revealed by an historical reconstruction of the lived experience of those who administered the poor law and were able to succeed using legal means. In this context, it is the more historical aspects of this research that have revealed, in part at least, some of the motivation of the participants. Furthermore, it is possible that future research, combining a doctrinal legal study with local archival research could reveal other examples of successful legal resistance. In turn this may modify our current understanding of the 'successful' national implementation of the 1834 Act. A purely legal approach, which bracketed out and excluded the local histories of these two examples, would be limited to a narrative doctrinal black letter description of law. This writer would argue that this study demonstrates that certain types of scholarship should no longer be excluded or marginalized in researching legal history; that the study of history in its own right is not merely auxiliary to the main task of legal analysis. On the contrary, the archival skills of the professional historian are a vital component if we are to truly understand the operation of law as experienced in the past.

The lord chancellor, the poets and the courtesan: public morality and copyright law in the early nineteenth century

ISABELLA ALEXANDER

Distortion of Nature's the Taste of the age. –
Make a story obscene, – 'twill be read every page.[1]

THE EARLY NINETEENTH CENTURY saw the arrival of a new doctrine in the common law of copyright. This was the principle that copyright protection would not be accorded to works with indecent, immoral, irreligious or libellous tendencies. The doctrine entered the law through the court of chancery and Lord Eldon has long borne the brunt of accusations that the doctrine sprang fully-formed from his reactionary, Tory forehead. The *Edinburgh Review* reported in 1823 that it could not 'sufficiently regret [that] ... Lord Eldon should, upon a new principle, be the first to deny to authors a temporary refuge against common robbers ...'.[2] Lord Campbell, writing a generation later, wrote that 'the decisions of Lord Eldon which I most object to, are those by which he erected himself into a Censor of the Press, and gave himself power to protect or to extinguish all literary property at his pleasure'.[3] Sir William Holdsworth concurred, noting in his history of English law that Lord Eldon's decisions in certain copyright cases 'aroused the fiercest and, from the point of view both of technical correctness and public policy, the most justifiable criticism'.[4]

I would like to thank Professor W.R. Cornish, Dr M. Conaglen, Dr J Schramm and Ms E. Turnbull for reading and commenting upon earlier drafts of this paper. Any errors are, of course, my own.

1 H.J. Luke Jnr, 'The publishing of Byron's "Don Juan"', *PMLA*, 80:2 (1965) 199–209 at 203. The poem was published in the *Dorchester Guide*, and attacked Lord Byron as well as the well-known radicals Henry Hart, Major Cartwright, William Hone and Francis Burdett.
2 'Late judgments of the Lord Chancellor', *Edinburgh Review*, 38:76 (1823) 281–314 at 283. (Authorship of this article has been attributed to William Empson or Henry Brougham.)
3 Lord Campbell, *Lives of the Lord Chancellors*, 10 vols (5th ed. London, 1868), x, 254.
4 W. Holdsworth, *History of English law*, xiii (London, 1952), p. 637.

The doctrine may have been new, but it re-connected copyright law with its roots in the censorship regimes of the Tudors. In the sixteenth and seventeenth centuries, regulation of the book trade had been carried out through the Stationers' Company, fortified by decrees of the Star Chamber and a series of Printing Acts.[5] For the crown, books presented a threat to public order, as they provided a means for spreading dissent and heresy. The system of regulation that grew up around the Stationers' Company held that nobody could publish a book which had not first been inspected by an official of the company, and entered on the company register. Later, inspection of the books was carried out by a licensor appointed by the crown.

The advantage of the system to the Stationers' Company was that it concentrated power in the book trade among its members and allowed it to regulate the trade through use of the register. Registration signified ownership of a manuscript and the sole right to print, publish and sell copies of it. This right was enforced by internal company sanctions and, on rare occasions, by litigation. The advantage to the crown was that it could control what was being printed. The Statute of Anne (as the first copyright act has come to be known) was passed in 1710 and severed the link between censorship and trade regulation by giving the right to print a book for a limited number of years to any person, not just members of the Stationers' Company, unless that book was a reprint of a book that had already been printed by someone else.[6] The added requirement of licensing was removed, thereby laying the foundations for the modern law of copyright.

However, the Statute of Anne could not erase the longstanding perception of the power of books to undermine public order and influence social change. The statute's title proclaimed that it was an Act for the Encouragement of Learning. Its practical effect was to create a property right in the printing of books, albeit one that was limited in time.[7] The doctrine that no copyright would subsist in a books of 'non-innocent tendencies' brought these two elements of the statute into conflict. It revealed that in Regency England the encouragement of learning was a double-edged sword and that the state's perception of where the public interest lay might still trump the private property rights of authors.

---

5 For a history of regulation of the book trade in Britain see C. Blagden, *The Stationers' Company: a history, 1403–1959* (London, 1960), J. Feather, *A history of British publishing* (London & New York, 1988).
6 8 Anne c. 19.
7 8 Anne c. 19, ss 1, 11. The act provided that the right to print a book would last for fourteen years, and that after the expiration of that period, the right would return to the author for a further fourteen years, if he or she were still alive.

THE READING PUBLIC IN THE REGENCY PERIOD

The end of the eighteenth century saw a growing concern among the middle and upper classes for the education of the poor.[8] Until this period, learning had largely been the province of the higher echelons of society. However, after 1780, the Sunday School movement began to provide religious-based education for the children of the poor, and was soon joined by the schools of Lancaster and Bell. Moves towards adult education were also made, first by the Society for the Promotion of Christian Knowledge, then through the Sunday Schools, and finally by the Mechanics' Institutes. The latter originated in Glasgow, when George Birkbeck, professor of natural philosophy and chemistry, began holding lectures for working men. Birkbeck left Glasgow for London where he founded the London Mechanics' Institute, and other Mechanics' Institutes were soon set up in other towns.[9]

Another leading supporter of the Mechanics' Institutes was Henry, later Lord, Brougham. Brougham believed that it was:

> highly useful to the community that the true principles of the constitution, ecclesiastical and civil, should be well understood by every man who lives under it. The peace of the country, and the stability of the government could not be more effectually secured than by the universal diffusion of this kind of knowledge.[10]

Brougham also sought to encourage education for the masses by means of cheap publications. In 1826, he established the Society for the Diffusion of Useful Knowledge, and began to issue monthly publications with the publisher Charles Knight. The first volume of the *Penny Magazine*, as it was called, included short articles on Van Dieman's Land, the Zoological Gardens and the history of beer, as well as an extract of the poetry of the recently deceased Revd George Crabbe. It also contained several homilies, of varying length, no doubt intended to edify, improve and instruct in the value of scientific knowledge.[11] Brougham and Knight then started the Society for the Diffusion of Useful Political Knowledge. Around the same time, the

---

8 For the history of education of the lower classes see M. Sturt, *The education of the people: a history of primary education in England and Wales in the nineteenth century* (London, 1967), S.J. Curtis, *History of education in Great Britain* (7th ed. London, 1967).
9 L. Woodward, *The age of reform* (Oxford, 1962), pp 494–5.
10 H. Brougham, *Practical observations on the education of the people addressed to the working classes and their employers* (London, 1825), p. 5.
11 An example of such a homily is as follows: 'When the air-balloon was first discovered, someone flippantly asked Dr Franklin what was the use of it? The doctor answered this question with another: "What is the use of the new-born infant? It may become a man,"': *Penny Magazine*, 1:1 (1823), 8.

radicals Hume, Grote, Warburton, Place and Roebuck founded the Society for the Diffusion of Political and Moral Knowledge. Although these two latter bodies had short life-spans, their establishment demonstrates that working class education had moved firmly onto the radical agenda.

The objectives of most schools aimed at working class children were limited. As the evangelist Hannah More noted, 'My object has not been to teach dogmas and opinions, but to form the lower classes in habits of industry and virtue.'[12] However, even with such limited aims, education remained an object of concern and fearfulness to more conservative members of society. When the French Revolution broke out, fear of the power of the masses reached new heights. In 1792, a Royal Proclamation against seditious writings was passed, and led to a number of state trials. Blame for the unsettled state of society was laid on the Sunday Schools, which had been the most prominent advocates of working class education.[13]

In 1797, the *Gentleman's Magazine* worried that 'A little learning makes a man ambitious to rise, if he can't by fair means then he uses foul ... A man of no literature will seldom attempt to form insurrections, or form idle schemes for the reformation of the state.'[14] The destabilizing potential of print appeared, to the upper classes, to be realized in the unprecedented sales and dissemination of Tom Paine's response to Edmund Burke, *The Rights of Man*. Although first published at 3*s*., a price that the Tories considered high enough to keep the book out of the reach of the lower classes, copies spread like wildfire.[15] When Paine dropped the price to 6*d*., and arranged for the distribution of copies among workers in manufacturing cities, the government panicked. Having refused a thousand guineas for the purchase of the intellectual property rights, Paine was convicted *in absentia* of seditious libel, and several booksellers who had been selling the pamphlet were prosecuted.[16]

Reading matter was subject to the same duality of attitudes as education and most attacks focussed on the novel. This was not entirely a nineteenth century development. In 1750, Samuel Johnson wrote of novels,

---

12 Sturt, *The education of the people*, p. 13.
13 R.D. Altick, *The English common reader* (Chicago, 1957), pp 72, 73.
14 Sturt, *The education of the people*, p. 4.
15 Altick, *The English common reader*, p. 69. Altick states that within weeks the first volume had sold 50,000 copies and by 1793 an estimated 200,000 copies were in circulation. By 1802, Paine estimated that 400,000 to 500,000 copies were being circulated, and seven years later there were thought to be 1,500,000 copies of Part 2 alone (pp 69–72). St Clair considers that such claims were greatly exaggerated: W. St Clair, *The reading nation in the Romantic period* (Cambridge, 2004), p. 256. However, even allowing for hyperbole, the circulation of the pamphlet was unprecedented, especially judging by the government's reaction.
16 St Clair, *The reading nation*, p. 256.

> These books are written chiefly to the young, the ignorant, and the idle, to whom they serve as lectures of conduct, and introductions into life. They are the entertainment of minds unfurnished with ideas, and therefore easily susceptible of impressions ... not informed by experience, and consequently open to every false suggestion.[17]

Women were seen as particularly vulnerable to corruption by novels. Hannah More believed that, for women, novel reading 'prepares for the surrender of virtue'.[18] She attempted to counteract the effects of novel reading, as well as the bawdy chapbooks carried around by hawkers, by producing the Cheap Repository Tracts series. These little books were priced at the same low prices as chapbooks and were peddled by the same hawkers, but their content combined Bible teaching and moral lessons.[19] This view of books as both poison and antidote encapsulates the ambiguity of the attitudes of the middle and upper classes towards the education of the lower classes.[20]

Similar contradictions are apparent in relation to the circulating libraries. The libraries serviced and supported the rapidly expanding novel-reading market, particularly for those who could not afford to purchase new books, and were in consequence considered by many as the wellspring of decadence. However, Mudie, the proprietor of the largest and most powerful of these libraries, exercised a firm hand of censorship over the novels he stocked. His influence and market power were such that if he refused to stock a book, it would remain unsold and unknown.[21]

In 1816, Samuel Coleridge characterized the reading public as 'the misgrowth of our luxuriant activity'.[22] Learning and reading, he implied, should be limited to the upper classes, and the creation of a mass reading public merely debased them. However, the relationship between class and morality was more nuanced than the simple dichotomy between a virtuous middle and upper class and the depraved masses which was so often asserted. This was demonstrated by the moral crusading movement that emerged at the end of the eighteenth century. Associations such as Wilberforce's Proclamation Society, the Society for the Suppression of Vice, and Wellington's Constitutional Association, sought to improve public morals

---

17 *The Rambler*, 31 Mar. 1750, quoted in P. Brantlinger, *The reading lesson: the threat of mass literacy in nineteenth-century British fiction* (Bloomington, 1998), p. 27.
18 St Clair, *The reading nation*, p.283.
19 Feather, *A history of British publishing*, p. 162; Altick, *The English common reader*, pp 73–5.
20 Brantlinger notes that the contradiction inherent in trying to address the poisonous effects of reading with books of curative power is reminiscent of Derrida's analysis of the *pharmakon* in Plato's *Phaedrus*: Brantlinger, *The reading lesson*, p. 7.
21 On Mudie, see G.L. Griest, *Mudie's Circulating Library and the Victorian novel* (Newton Abbot, 1970) and J.L. Sutherland, *Victorian novelists and publishers* (London, 1976).
22 *Lay Sermons*, p. 36, quoted in Brantlinger, *The reading lesson*, p. 3.

generally by focussing on the middle and upper classes as an example. The most influential of these was the Society for the Suppression of Vice, or Vice Society as it was called, which passed information to magistrates and brought actions itself against works of pornography (obscene libel), as well as blasphemous libel, such as *Paine's Age of Reason*.[23] Fear of immoral books reached such heights that even Shakespeare was not immune. Thomas Bowdler bequeathed his surname to the English language when he produced his 'Family Shakespeare' in 1818 with the aim of producing an edition of Shakespeare that a father could read to his daughters 'without incurring the danger of falling unawares among words and expressions which are of such a nature as to raise a blush on the cheek of modesty.'[24]

These were also years of considerable political unrest among the working classes, characterized by renewed interest in Major Cartwright's Hampden Club and outbreaks of machine breaking and rioting. In the wake of the French Revolution the State sought to bring reading matter under control by increasing the amount of the newspaper stamp. The first Stamp Act to apply to newspapers had been introduced in 1712,[25] although stamp duty had applied to paper and other documents for over a decade prior to that.[26] The Stamp Act of 1712 raised tax on newspapers, pamplets and advertisements as well as paper and was calculated according to size.[27] Its main aim was to raise money to pay for Marlborough's foreign wars.[28] Contemporary writers, such as Swift, identified a secondary objective of discouraging the periodical press and the opposing political views it expressed.[29] Certainly, numerous publications were forced to shut down by the Act, but many survived and found ways to circumvent its operation. Following the French Revolution, numerous radical publications were surreptitiously printed and circulated among the working class, leading to what became known as the war of the unstamped press.

In 1819, the 'massacre of Peterloo' and the subsequent political unrest led the government to pass the Six Acts. Two of these were directly aimed at press control by further increasing the price of the newspaper stamp, as well as the publications to which it applied, and by giving magistrates greater

23 D. Thomas, *A long time burning: the history of literary censorship in England* (New York, 1969), pp 200–1.
24 Ibid. p. 186.
25 10 Anne c.18.
26 D. Foxon, 'The Stamp Act of 1712: Sandars Lectures 1978' (unpublished, copy in Cambridge University Library), p. 3.
27 Over the course of the eighteenth century further stamp acts were introduced to close loopholes, assist with enforcement and increase the level of the tax, before finally being repealed in the middle of the nineteenth century: F.S. Siebert, *Freedom of the press in England* (Urbana, IL., 1952), pp 318–22.
28 Foxon, 'The Stamp Act of 1712', p. 2.
29 Ibid.; Siebert, *Freedom of the press*, p. 304.

search and seizure powers in relation to blasphemous and seditious literature. In the same year, the Attorney-General brought thirty-three prosecutions against radical publishers, and local magistrates continued to apprehend and punish hawkers of radical pamphlets.[30] In 1820, the prince regent succeeded his father as George IV, and soon had his wife tried for adultery before the house of lords. The radical press rallied to the queen's support, and further prosecutions for seditious libel ensued.[31] In the minds of the ruling classes during this period immorality, profanity and civil disorder were all intrinsically linked, not only with each other, but also with books as the conduit by which they were spread.

LITIGATING 'DUBIOUS' BOOKS

It was against this background of political unrest and contradictory attitudes towards education, reading matter and public order that Lord Eldon formulated the principle that no copyright would subsist in immoral, libellous or blasphemous books. Lord Eldon's key role came about partly as a result of the central function of the court of chancery in eighteenth and nineteenth century copyright litigation. The Statute of Anne[32] had provided for penalties recoverable at common law,[33] but what copyright owners really wanted was to prevent their books being copied, multiplied and distributed. The best remedy was, therefore, the injunction. Consequently, the usual course of action for a copyright owner who considered his work was being pirated was to bring a bill before the court of chancery, praying an account of profits and an injunction.[34] If the copyright owner could establish title to the work, an interim injunction was usually granted,[35] and the defendant was issued with a subpoena to appear and make answer. If the answer was considered sufficient, the injunction would be dissolved; if not, it would continue.

Over the course of the eighteenth century, it became increasingly common for lord chancellors granting injunctions to order also that the plaintiff proceed to establish his legal title at law.[36] Sometimes, an injunction was

---

30 Thomas, *A long time burning*, p. 163.
31 Ibid., pp 164–5.
32 And its successor, 41 Geo. III c.107, s.1.
33 8 Anne c. 19, s.1. These penalties could be sued for by a common informer, who would receive half the amount awarded, with the other half going to the crown.
34 As Eden wrote in 1821, 'The jurisdiction of the courts of equity in interposing by injunction to restrain the violation of copyright has been assumed merely for the purpose of making effectual the legal right': R. Eden, *A treatise on the law of injunctions* (London, 1821), p. 264.
35 Although the expression interim injunction was rarely used.
36 At common law a claim could be made for the recovery of damages, which was preferable

suspended until after the plaintiff established such title.[37] In practice, however, it was unusual for parties to continue to law and so the lord chancellor's decision generally ended the litigation. Permanent injunctions were, however, also rare. In 1817, Sir William Grant MR expressed considerable annoyance towards a plaintiff seeking a perpetual injunction at hearing in a case where the defendants had not challenged the interim injunction. The master of the rolls claimed that he could recall no instance where such a request had been granted, and he dismissed the bill.[38]

The first case involving a work of dubious political tendency to come before Lord Eldon was *Walcot v. Walker*.[39] In 1802, John Walcot, a former physician and clergyman, better known by his pseudonym Peter Pindar under which he published satirical works that frequently targeted George III, was granted an interim injunction against two booksellers for publishing two editions of his works without consent. Walcot applied to make the remedy permanent, but Lord Eldon entertained suspicions that the works were libellous. He suggested that if they were libellous then an action would not lie and the court of equity would give no account of profits, stating that 'the Court ought not to give an account of the unhallowed profits of libellous publications'. Nor, it seemed, would it give an injunction, for he dissolved the injunction already awarded unless the books were brought into court so that he could inspect them.[40]

The authority that Lord Eldon relied on for his view that no action would lie in respect of libellous works was a case involving Dr Priestley, the well-known scientist, dissenter and republican sympathizer, who had brought an action against the hundred for damage sustained as the result of the Birmingham riots of 1791.[41] Among the property he had claimed was destroyed were certain unpublished manuscripts, and he offered to lead evidence of what booksellers would have paid for them. Counsel for the hundred alleged that the works were seditious. Lord Eyre CJ held that if

---

to the penalties provided for by the Statute of Anne which were low and half of which had to go to the crown.

37 For an outline of this practice, in the context of a patent case, see *Bacon v. Jones* (1839) 4 My & Cr 433, 436; 41 ER 167, 169, per Lord Cottenham LC.
38 *Whittingham v. Wooler* (1817) 2 Swan 428; 36 ER 679.
39 *Walcot v. Walker* (1802) 7 Ves 1; 32 ER 1.
40 Ibid., 2; 1.
41 The ability of citizens to bring actions for damages against the hundred dated back to the ancient principle that the individual inhabitants of the hundred were liable for damages to any person who had sustained harm from a robbery or other felony unless they raised the hue and cry and captured the criminal within forty days: Holdsworth, *History of English law*, iv, 521. This was extended to cover damages caused by rioting by an act of George I (1 Geo. I c. 5). See also 19 Geo. I c. 22, 41 Geo. III c. 24, 52 Geo. III c. 130, 56 Geo. III c. 125, 57 Geo. III c. 19 and 3 Geo. IV c. 33 (consolidation and reform).

counsel for the hundred had produced evidence of the claim, then he would have allowed it to be received 'as against' the plaintiff's claim.[42]

There was, however, an earlier case to which Lord Eldon could have looked for authority for a different approach. In 1720, a work of dubious morality had come before the court of chancery.[43] The work was by the late Dr Thomas Burnett, the well-known natural philosopher. It was written in Latin and claimed that the Bible's stories were allegorical, thereby threatening the divine authority of the scriptures. Dr Burnett had taken steps to suppress the book during his lifetime and, after his death, his son sought an injunction to prevent the book's publication in English. The view taken by Lord Macclesfield LC distinguished between knowledge in the hands of the upper and lower classes. Having read the book, he concluded that it 'contained strange notions, intended by the author to be concealed from the vulgar in the Latin language, in which language it could not do much hurt, the learned being better able to judge of it.' He granted the injunction, on the basis that the court of chancery had 'superintendency over all books, and might in a summary way restrain the printing or publishing any that contained reflections on religion or morality'.[44] This case therefore provided authority for the granting of an injunction to prevent publication of immoral works, where such injunction would prevent publication altogether. Such a situation would come before Lord Eldon fifteen years later, but, in the interim several cases involving immoral works were brought before the common law courts.

In 1803, the case of *Hime v. Dale* came before Lord Ellenborough in the king's bench.[45] The case involved the alleged piracy of the words of a song and counsel for the defendant argued that the song was libellous against the government. Lord Ellenborough was clearly influenced by Lord Eldon's decision in *Walcot* because, although he found that the song was not libellous, he stated by way of *obiter dictum* that if it were a libel 'so gross as to affect public morals' the court of chancery would grant no injunction and he would advise a jury to grant no damages.[46]

Several months before Lord Eldon's decision in *Walcot v. Walker*, the case of *Fores v. Johnes* had been heard by the court of king's bench.[47] In that case the plaintiff brought an action of assumpsit to recover the value of several caricature prints he had sold to the defendant but which the defendant had refused to receive on the grounds that some of them were libellous and

---

42 Noted by counsel in *Southey v. Sherwood* (1817) 2 Mer 435; 173 ER 1006. It is not clear whether 'as against' means as a bar to or as a defence to the plaintiff's claim.
43 *Burnett v. Chetwood* (1720) 2 Mer 441; 173 ER 1008.
44 Ibid., 441; 1009.
45 *Hime v. Dale* (1803) 2 Camp 27n; 170 ER 1070.
46 Ibid., 27n; 1071.
47 (1802) 4 Esp 97; 170 ER 654.

obscene. Lawrence J held that the plaintiff could not recover for those prints which were obscene, libellous or immoral or for which a criminal action could be brought. Lord Ellenborough also heard two actions involving claims for damages in respect of works of dubious content. In 1810, Du Bost brought an action for damages against Beresford, who had destroyed Du Bost's painting of Beresford's sister and her husband.[48] The defendant claimed that the picture was libellous and Lord Ellenborough accepted that evidence, instructing the jury that damages could be awarded only for the cost of the canvas and paint, and not in respect of any anticipated profits from its exhibition. In the 1817 case of *Gale v. Leckie* Lord Ellenborough suggested he would have allowed evidence of the libellous nature of the books to be brought as a defence against an action of assumpsit to recover damages against a printer who had refused to print a book.[49] It is not clear from these three cases whether the principle emerging is that no property could subsist in an immoral or libellous work, or whether works of such a nature could not claim the protection of the law for other, possibly public policy-based, reasons.

Nor was clarity reached in the next case to come before Lord Eldon, *Southey v. Sherwood*.[50] Twenty-three years earlier, Southey had left a poem entitled *Wat Tyler*, expressing the radical views of his youth, in the hands of a publisher. In 1817, the publisher Sherwood began to print and sell the poem to embarrass him, as Southey was by now a Tory and poet laureate. Southey sought an injunction to restrain publication. Lord Eldon read the poem and refused the injunction until Southey had established his right to the property at law. As Southey wanted to suppress publication entirely, this case could have fallen within Lord Macclesfield's judgment in *Burnett v. Chetwood*.[51] However, Lord Eldon made no mention of it. Once again, he referred to Lord Eyre CJ as having 'expressly laid it down that a person cannot recover damages for a work which is, in its nature, calculated to do injury to the public'.[52] At the same time, however, Lord Eldon seems also to have based his decision on the fact that Southey had left his work in the hands of the publisher for so long that it could amount to abandonment.[53]

The next work to come before Lord Eldon was by a much more controversial poet: Lord Byron. Lord Eldon and Lord Byron represented the two extremes of Regency England. One, cautious, conservative and highly

---

48 *Du Bost v. Beresford* (1810) 2 Camp 411; 170 ER 1235.
49 (1817) 2 Stark 107; 171 ER 588.
50 (1817) 2 Mer 435; 173 ER 1006.
51 See above. *Burnett v. Chetwood* was at that time unreported but was later appended to the report of *Southey v. Sherwood* by the reporter Merivale.
52 (1817) 2 Mer 435, 439; 173 ER 1006, 1008.
53 Ibid., 440; 1008

moral, the son of a coal factor who ended up as the highest legal officer in the land; the other, a hereditary peer and flamboyant flouter of almost every moral, and sexual, code. Both Byron and his publisher Murray had been reluctant to seek the protection of chancery, despite the fact that Byron's poems were extremely popular targets for the pirates. Murray feared prosecution for publishing an immoral work, and went to the lengths of publishing it anonymously. Byron's anxiety stemmed from fear of the effect that refusal to protect his poem, based on its immorality or blasphemy, might have on his right to custody of his daughter, Ada.[54] This concern was not unreasonable. In 1817, Lord Eldon had refused Byron's friend Shelley custody of his children due to his 'highly immoral conduct', established in part by reference to his poem *Queen Mab*.[55]

Although Murray had considered taking action against the numerous piracies of *Don Juan*, in the end he brought an action in respect of *Cain* against the radical political publisher William Benbow.[56] Advice was sought from Lancelot Shadwell, king's counsel and later Vice-Chancellor, and Shadwell consented to lead the case, considering the poem no worse than *Paradise Lost*.[57] However, Shadwell's view was not shared by Lord Eldon. The Lord Chancellor considered that Milton's poem promoted Christianity, rather than bringing it into disrepute, and he doubted that Byron's work had the same innocent intent. Implying that no action would lie in respect of a work which undermined Christianity, he refused the injunction.[58]

Lord Eldon expanded upon this view a month later, in respect of Lawrence's *Lectures on Physiology, Zoology and the Natural History of Man*, which contained some metaphysical and theological argument.[59] Lord Eldon held

---

54 See L. Marchand (ed.), *Byron's letters and journals*, 12 vols (London, 1976) vii, 238.
55 *Shelley v. Westbrooke* (1817) Jac 266n, 37 ER 850.
56 *Murray v. Benbow* (1822) Jac 474n; 37 ER 929n and 6 Petersdorff Abr. 558n. Murray's biographer, Smiles, states that an injunction was sought in respect of *Don Juan* in 1819 and granted, as do Robinson Blann and Hugh J. Luke Jnr. However, I have been unable to locate a reported or unreported case concerning *Don Juan* at this time. In 1823, when Byron did bring an action against Hodgson for publishing cantos 6, 7 and 8 of *Don Juan*, his counsel assured the court that no injunction had ever been sought in respect of the whole work. The Vice-Chancellor was particularly insistent upon the point, stating he had been under the impression that an injunction had been sought in the past, but Wakefield firmly denied it. Moreover, the piracy of *Don Juan* continued at the same high levels in the period after 1819, and Byron's concerns about his daughter were not assuaged. See S. Smiles, *A publisher and his friends: memoir and correspondence of the late John Murray*, 2 vols (London, 1997), i, 408; R. Blann, *Throwing the scabbard away: Byron's battle against the censors of 'Don Juan'* (New York, 1991), p. 72; Luke, *Publishing of Byron's Don Juan*, p. 202, Marchand, *Byron's letters and journals*, vii, 238. Also *The Times*, 19 July 1823, 2 July 1823.
57 Smiles, *A publisher and his friends*, i, 428.
58 6 Petersdorff Abr. 558n.
59 *Lawrence v. Smith* (1822) Jac 471; 37 ER 928.

that the law gave no protection to those who contradicted the Scriptures. Since he had a 'rational doubt' as to whether the book violated the law, he was unable to say definitively that the plaintiff had a right of property in the book and, consequently, was unable to continue the injunction. In this case, as in *Murray v. Benbow*, he suggested that the plaintiff could seek to establish his right at law, and apply for an injunction again if the action were upheld.[60]

An action to halt the piracy of Byron's *Don Juan* was eventually brought before the court of chancery by Wakefield, acting for Lord Byron, in 1823. Sir John Leach, the Vice-Chancellor, granted an injunction against the publisher Hodgson, which Hodgson did not contest.[61] Several days later, Shadwell sought an injunction on behalf of Murray against another publisher, Dugdale, for publishing *Beppo*. This time, Shadwell was able to persuade a rather reluctant Lord Eldon that there was nothing objectionable about the poem and the injunction was granted.[62]

A month later, Wakefield, acting for Byron, sought an injunction against Dugdale for publishing cantos six, seven and eight of *Don Juan*.[63] Sir John Leach V-C granted the application, but Dugdale moved for its dissolution, arguing that the work was 'immoral in the highest sense of the word, most calculated to taint the minds of the public, licentious, in every way dangerous, and most destructive of the morals of the community at large.'[64] Pleading inexperience, Sir John Leach consulted with Lord Eldon before delivering his decision, which was to refuse the requested injunction. Leach stated that the rule was:

> Wherever, therefore, a court of law would grant a reparation by damages for the piracy of a work, there, as a general principle, the court of equity would grant a more perfect remedy to prevent further injury of the property. Where, on the contrary, a court of law would refuse a reparation by damages, it necessarily followed that a court of equity must withhold its injunction.[65]

The rule established in this series of cases was clear: where it was doubtful whether a work was of an 'innocent' character, the court of chancery would grant no injunction. The basis for the rule was, however, less clear. Sometimes Lord Eldon had suggested that no action at common law would lie because there could be no property in such a book, while at other times he had suggested that no damages would be granted at common law, which was

---

60 Ibid., 474; 929.
61 *The Times*, 19 July 1823, 22 July 1823.
62 *The Times*, 23 July 1823.
63 *Byron v Dugdale*, *The Times*, 2 August 1823.
64 *The Times*, 9 August 1823.
65 *The Times*, 11 August 1823.

the aspect emphasized by Leach V-C. If the former were the case, no equitable remedy would be available as they lay only to protect property rights; if the latter view was adopted, then Lord Eldon's refusal to grant an injunction rested either on the principle that no right exists without a remedy, or on the principle that if no damages would be awarded then the injunction would not be protecting against anything, or on a combination of the two. The significance of the distinction was probably lost on the plaintiff who was denied his injunction. However, it was raised when the issue was squarely considered by a common law court for the first time in 1826.

This case involved the memoirs of the well-known Regency courtesan, Harriette Wilson.[66] Harriette is famous today for having been told by the duke of Wellington to 'publish and be damned' but, in the event, it was her publisher who suffered when the memoirs were pirated.[67] Harriette persuaded Henry, later Lord, Brougham, her friend and former lover, to act for her in exchange for keeping his name out of her book. At the hearing, Lord Abbott CJ held that: 'The law cannot recognize as property the history of the low amours of a notorious courtezan.'[68]

Brougham moved for a new trial, this time founding his argument on the distinction between refusing an injunction on the basis that damages would not be granted, and holding that no action would be maintainable.[69] He claimed that the principle that no property existed in such a work was sustained only by a *dictum* of Lord Eyre CJ.[70] In addition, Brougham argued that the decisions of the lord chancellor were no authority for the court and that the question was still open and worthy of further consideration.[71] The significance of Brougham's argument was that, if the court accepted that the correct principle was that property subsisted *prima facie* in all publications, then the burden of proof fell upon the person denying or defending the infringement.

The reports of the case differ slightly. However, it is clear in all of them that even in the absence of clear authority, Lord Abbott CJ was in no doubt as to what the law should be. Although he agreed with Brougham that the cases in equity provided no authority for the courts of law, he considered that

---

66 *Stockdale v. Onwhyn* (1826) 5 B & C 173; 108 ER 65 and 2 Car & P 163; 172 ER 75.
67 However, it is hard to feel too sorry for Stockdale, who had used the argument that the book was obscene in order to avoid paying the printer, Poplett. When Poplett brought an action in common pleas to recover the amount Stockdale owed him, Best CJ refused the assistance of the court to 'the person who lends himself to the violation of the public morals and laws of the country', adding that he would not 'take an account between two robbers on Hounslow Heath': *Poplett v. Stockdale* (1825) Ry & Mood 337, 338, 339; 171 ER 1041, 1041.
68 *The Times*, 12 January 1826.
69 2 Car & P 163, 168; 172 ER 75, 77.
70 Ibid., 167; 76.
71 *The Times*, 28 January 1826.

'upon the plainest principles of common law, founded as it is, where there are no authorities, upon common sense and justice, this action cannot be maintained. It would be a disgrace to the common law could a doubt be entertained upon the subject; but I think no doubt can be entertained, and I want no authority for pronouncing such a judicial opinion.'[72] The other three judges of the court of king's bench concurred.

A KNOT TWISTED BY A SINGLE HAND?

Unsurprisingly, in light of the strong feeling surrounding the moral content of books and the widespread discontent with chancery practice and procedure in this period, Lord Eldon's judgments were attacked in the periodical press. These attacks mixed proprietarian concerns that the decisions undermined private property rights, utilitarian fears regarding the practical effects of the decisions, and more general stabs at the court of chancery and the role of the Lord Chancellor. The *Quarterly Review*, which was, incidentally, owned by John Murray, claimed that 'no sooner was it whispered that there was no property in "Don Juan" than ten presses were at work, some publishing it with obscene engravings, others in weekly numbers and all in a shape that brought it within the reach of purchasers on whom its poison would operate without mitigation.'[73] Pirated copies of *Don Juan* and *Cain*, it warned, would be exposed to 'thousands totally unfitted by knowledge and habits of thinking to grapple with its difficulties',[74] thereby echoing the judgment of Lord Macclesfield one hundred years before.[75] The reviewer also worried that the rule would have a chilling effect on freedom of the press, as learned men such as Malthus and Locke might be discouraged from writing books for fear of suffering the stigma of the disapprobation of chancery.[76]

The *Edinburgh Review*, which numbered Brougham among its founders, argued that the rule would result in the whole property of modern literature turning 'on the pendulous oscillations in the mind of the person who, for the time being, may hold the Great Seal'.[77] The reviewer also considered that 'the single hand that twisted [the knot] is of itself competent to untie it ... we believe that Lord Eldon, should he have occasion to review his own

---

72 5 B & C 173, 176; 108 ER 65, 66.
73 'Cases of *Walcot v Walker, Southey v Sherwood, Murray v Benbow* and *Lawrence v Smith*', *Quarterly Review* 27:53 (1822) 123 at 128 (The authorship of this article has been attributed to either Southey or Nassau Senior)
74 Ibid., p. 128.
75 In *Burnett v Chetwood*, see above, p. 239 n. 51.
76 'Cases of *Walcot v. Walker*', *Quarterly Review*, 27:53 (1822) 123 at 136.
77 'Late judgments of the Lord Chancellor', *Edinburgh Review*, 38:76 (1823), 300.

decisions, will find no authority but that of Lord Eldon which it will be necessary to overrule.'[78] The lawyer Joseph Parkes also condemned Lord Eldon's rule, stating,

> Two extraordinary and recent stretches of the prerogative of a Lord Chancellor cannot pass unnoticed, viz: the assumption of the offices of *Licensor of the Press*; and of *Censor*, an office of the Roman Emperors who in the height of their power styled themselves *morum praefecti*.
>
> In the former jurisdiction nothing can be more anomalous than the effect of Lord Eldon's interference under the powers given him as the arbiter of copyright. His Lordship would not *protect* a bad book, but assisted to bring (what he deemed) licentiousness and irreligion into notice by cheap pirated publications, thus stimulating and disseminating that which otherwise would be smothered in its own obscurity and insignificance. The liability to error in the selection of the judge, and the possibility of error in his judgment, unite to make this a dangerous power in the hands of any individual.[79]

These accusations of judicial overreach and capriciousness would have been particularly galling to Lord Eldon, who had explicitly sought to endow equity with principles as settled as those of the common law. In 1818, in *Gee v. Pritchard*, he famously noted 'I cannot agree that the doctrines of this court are to be changed by every succeeding judge. Nothing would inflict on me greater pain in quitting this place, than the recollection that I had done anything to justify the reproach that the equity of this court varies like the Chancellor's foot.'[80]

Set against the argument that refusal of injunctions would lead to greater and cheaper numbers of such books being printed was the claim that denying publishers the profits from their works would discourage such works from being printed at all. *Blackwood's Magazine* claimed that in this way, Lord Eldon's rule had 'kept a flood of improper books from the market, without recurring to the unpopular method of prosecution, and has neutralized the power of those which have already crept in.'[81]

In fact, it seemed that those who attacked the rule were correct. Lord Eldon's refusal to protect books against piracy had indeed operated to multiply such books and to drive down prices. Southey's *Wat Tyler*, which would normally have sold for 10s. 5d., was sold in Sherwood's pirated edition

---

[78] Ibid., 314.
[79] J. Parkes, *A history of the Court of Chancery* (London, 1828), p. 438.
[80] 2 Swan 402, 414; 37 ER 670.
[81] 'Letters of Timothy Tickler to eminent literary characters', *Blackwood's Edinburgh Magazine*, 14:79 (1823), 217.

for 2s. in 1817, but within the year had dropped to 3d.[82] Southey's son estimated the total sale of the book to be 60,000 copies, making it twice or three times as popular as the rest of Southey's poems put together. *Don Juan* had a similar fate, with copies appearing in the year of its first publication for 4s., an eighth of Murray's original asking price.[83]

Lord Eldon was undoubtedly aware that his decisions would result in increased circulation of these works, as this was argued by plaintiffs in almost every case that came before him. In *Walcot v. Walker*, he appeared to endorse the opposing argument (that refusal to protect books would mean that publishers could no longer afford to print them) when he noted that he would not protect 'the unhallowed profits of libellous publications.'[84] However, in later cases Lord Eldon emphasized that instrumentalist approaches were not the role of his court. In *Southey's case*, he noted 'It is very true that, in some cases, it may operate so as to multiply copies of mischievous publications', but held that he had nothing to do with such a question.[85] In *Murray v. Benbow*, he pointed out that 'the duty of stopping the work does not belong to the court of equity, which has no criminal jurisdiction, and cannot punish or check the offence.'[86]

For Lord Eldon, the public interest was recognized in making the law an instrument of a well-ordered constitutional monarchy and Christian society. It could not, therefore, be used to protect elements that undermined it. In *Stockdale v. Onwhyn*, Bayley J suggested that a practical solution to the dissemination problem would be for the court of chancery to grant an injunction, requiring at the same time an undertaking by the owner not to publish the work himself.[87] Such an approach would not have accorded with Lord Eldon's ideas about the role of the court of chancery: if property existed in the work, it was the role of the court to protect it; if there was no property, there would be no protection.

An important corollary of Lord Eldon's position was that criminal prosecutions were undertaken against publishers, whether piratical or not. This did occur in some cases. William Clark was prosecuted by the Vice Society for piratically publishing Shelley's *Queen Mab*, and John Hunt was prosecuted for legitimately publishing Byron's *Vision of Judgment*. A second supplementary element of Lord Eldon's view was that he was not denying all relief to the plaintiff, who was always free to bring an action at common law to establish his right and then return to chancery for his injunction. However, the fear of criminal prosecutions, combined with financial considerations,

---

82 St Clair, *The reading nation*, p. 318.
83 Ibid., pp 317, 324.
84 7 Ves 1, 2; 32 ER 1, 1.
85 2 Mer 435, 439–40; 173 ER 1006, 1008.
86 Petersdorff Abr. 558n, 559n.
87 *The Times*, 28 Jan. 1826.

meant that, with the exception of *Stockdale v. Onwhyn*, no plaintiffs took their cases to the common law courts, and the court of chancery decision was the final settlement of the matter.

It was for this reason that the American academic, George Ticknor Curtis, argued in his mid-nineteenth century treatise on copyright law that it would be a far sounder rule to hold that every work was entitled to protection *prima facie*, unless malicious or mischievous intention appeared on its face, and if no such intent appeared then it rested on those who relied on the intent to establish it.[88] He particularly objected to Lord Eldon's decision in *Southey v. Sherwood*, arguing that the right to publish or withhold from publication a manuscript was a common law right of possession and control, and the question of the work's innocence or otherwise did not arise, because that question related only to the right to publish and make a profit.[89]

Joseph Story, Dane Professor of Law at Harvard University, was also critical of Lord Eldon's decisions. In his *Commentaries on Equity Jurisprudence*, published in the United Kingdom in 1839, Story stated that Lord Eldon's view that equity would not protect immoral, irreligious or blasphemous books was correct, and he agreed that the effect of such a finding on the book's circulation should be no concern of the court of equity.[90] However, Story noted that the rule was difficult to apply in practice and expressed concern that conferring an absolute power on a court of equity over the subject of literary property might 'sap the very foundations' of the law of literary property and 'retard, if not entirely suppress the means of arriving at physical as well as metaphysical truths.'[91]

CONCLUSION

After the decision in *Stockdale v. Onwhyn*, the principle of non-protection of immoral and blasphemous works moved sideways, and was applied to refuse

---

88 G.T. Curtis, *A treatise on the law of copyright* (London & Boston, 1847), pp 165–6.
89 Ibid., pp 157–61.
90 J. Story, *Commentaries on Equity Jurisprudence*, 2 vols (London, 1839), pp 192–3.
91 Ibid., p. 193. Between the mid-nineteenth and mid-twentieth centuries, some United States courts took that view that copyright protection would be denied to obscene works: see Z. Chafee, 'Coming into equity with clean hands', *Mich LR*, 47:8 (1947) 1065, 1065–7 and B. Wilkinson, 'Recent developments', *Fordham LR*, 46:5 (1978) 1037. Interestingly, an alternative justification sometimes offered for refusing protection in the US was that it arose from the limitations in the Constitution, which provided that copyright must 'promote the Progress of Science and the Useful Arts'. E.g. *Martinetti v. Maguire* 16 F Cas 920 (C.C.D. Cal. 1867) (No 9,173). However, the principle of non-protection was decisively abandoned in the 1979 case of *Mitchell Brothers Film Group v. Cinema Adult Theater* 604 F 2d 852. See also M.B. Nimmer and D. Nimmer, *Nimmer on Copyright* (New York, 1996), §2.17.

protection to deceptive and fraudulent books.[92] In 1848, an injunction was refused in respect of a libellous book,[93] and Kekewich J dismissed an action without costs relating to two indecent pictures in 1899, with very little discussion of the principle.[94] The last time that the principle was directly considered and applied was in the 1915 case of *Glyn v. Western Feature Film Company*.[95] In that case, Younger J noted: 'It may well be that the Court in this matter is now less strict than it was in the days of Lord Eldon, but the present is not a case in which in the public interest it ought, as it seems to me, to be at all anxious to relax its principles.'[96]

Although the case has never been explicitly overruled in the United Kingdom since this time, it has long since ceased to be applied in relation to immoral, blasphemous and even pornographic works. The rule of non-protection of immoral works, in fact, might have completely slipped off the judicial radar if it had not been referred to approvingly in 2001 by Aldous LJ in *Hyde Park v. Yelland* as belonging to the inherent jurisdiction of the court.[97] Although this was *obiter dictum*, it was implicitly adopted by Lord Phillips MR in *Ashdown v. Telegraph Group* when he concluded that Aldous LJ's approach to the public interest defence was too restrictive.[98] The rule was also recently discussed in Australia in the federal magistrates court but the magistrate declined to make any finding on the point.[99]

This unwillingness to overrule the principle directly, but concomitant reluctance to apply it, attests to its historical specificity. The hand that tied the knot may have been Lord Eldon's but the rope with which he was supplied was woven from the particular ideals, fears, and political pressures of Regency England. Although books continued to be viewed as morally corrosive and a threat to social order into the Victorian era, the copyright cases challenging the moral and religious content of individual books ceased after 1826. This may be due to a change of political atmosphere. The threat of immoral and irreligious works had been closely linked to the cause of radical reform because it was largely the radical publishers, such as Dugdale and Benbow, who were involved in the piracies. These publishers were not averse to publishing the works of living writers who might forward the

---

92 *Wright v. Tallis* (1845) 1 CB 893; 135 ER 794; *Slingsby v. Bradford Patent Truck and Trolley Company* (1906) WN 51.
93 *Clark v. Freeman* (1848) Beav 112; 50 ER 759.
94 *Baschet v. London Illustrated* [1900] 1 Ch 73.
95 [1916] 1 Ch 261.
96 Ibid., 269.
97 [2001] Ch 143, 161. Note that in *Attorney-General v. Guardian*, Lords Griffiths and Jauncey also considered that *Glyn v. Western Feature Film* was good law: [2002] Ch 149, 275–6, 294.
98 [2002] Ch 149, 171.
99 *Fraserside Holdings & Anor v. Venus Adult Shops & Ors* [2005] FMCA 997.

radical agenda.[1] Nor were they averse to linking piracy and reform. In 1822, following his success against Murray, Benbow wrote:

> The enormous high price of books has long prevented the humble in place and purse from acquiring information, and we are not sorry to see the 'gates of knowledge' opened, so that all ranks may enter therein for a mere trifle; and, we trust, that cheap editions of dear and valuable works will rapidly proceed from the press, in spite of threats and animadversions.[2]

After Dugdale's victory over Lord Byron, a pseudonymous writer, probably either Dugdale or Benbow, wrote a letter directed at Byron's publisher John Hunt for publication in Benbow's *Rambler Magazine*: 'I trust that the next excellent thing you bring out will spread in similar manner to Don Juan and disappoint the avarice of such fellows as you, who think, that knowledge should be given only to them who can afford to buy it at high price.'[3]

Following Castlereagh's replacement by Canning in 1822, the Tory administration took on a new tone, gradually becoming more open to reform.[4] Perhaps more significantly, Michael Lobban has also demonstrated that the law of seditious libel had become increasingly unworkable from the late eighteenth century and, after the 1820s, the authorities looked increasingly to the law of unlawful assembly to control threats to public order. Physical force, not radical ideas, thus became the main focus of conservative fear.[5]

The relationship between copyright law and immoral or blasphemous works in the early nineteenth century reveals that the public interest in the encouragement of learning proclaimed by those involved in debates over copyright law was a deeply complex and ambivalent issue. In the words of Brantlinger, the threat posed by reading matter in this period was 'of mass literacy producing the opposite of enlightenment.'[6] The principle of non-protection subordinated private property rights to a concept of public interest. However, it was not the public interest championed by the radical publishers of making cheap books available to the masses that triumphed, but rather Lord Eldon's notion that the law should serve the public interest in an altogether stricter and more principled sense by refusing to grant property rights over books that undermined public order, morality and religion.

1 Luke, 'The publishing of Byron's "Don Juan"', 199.
2 Ibid., 205–6.
3 Ibid., 207–8. The comment was unfair, as Hunt had attempted to avert the threat of piracy by issuing the new cantos in a 1s. for an 18mo edition, advertising the cheap edition as a substitute for the Lord Chancellor's protection; ibid.
4 Thomas, *A long time burning*, p. 173; Woodward, *The age of reform*, p. 69.
5 M. Lobban, 'From seditious libel to unlawful assembly: Peterloo and the changing face of political crime, c.1770–1820', *Oxford Journal of Legal Studies*, 10 (1990).
6 Brantlinger, *The reading lesson*, p. 3.

Legal education in England and the German historical school of law in the nineteenth century

MARCEL SENN

THE PROBLEM AND THE GOAL

THE HISTORICAL SCHOOL OF LAW dominated legal education in Germany during the nineteenth century. This school also exerted influence on the development of American law and American law schools in the late nineteenth and the early twentieth century. We have further evidence of a certain influence of the German historical school of law on legal education in other countries such as France, Austria and Switzerland. We know, however, less about a parallel in England during the nineteenth century,[1] although a certain general influence of German on English culture existed during the classic and romantic period.[2] There had also been an evident

---

Many thanks for helpful assistance to Prof. Andreas Buja, University of Pennsylvania, and Prof. Wolfgang Ernst, University of Zürich.

[1] Knut Wolfgang Nörr, 'The European side of the English law: a few comments from a continental historian' in Helmut Coing and Knut Wolfgang Nörr (eds), *Englische und kontinentale Rechtsgeschichte: Ein Forschungsprojekt* (Berlin, 1985), pp 15–30. The developments described by Nörr concentrate on some aspects from the twelfth to the seventeenth century and some influences of English Law on the continent in the nineteenth century. He mentions constitutional ideas, judiciary (the jury), the practice of using standardized contractual terms, the concept of trust, labour law and especially factory laws; *see also,* Marcel Senn, *Rechtsgeschichte – ein kulturhistorischer Grundriss* (3rd ed. Zürich/Basel/Genf, 2003), pp 334–8.

[2] Andreas B(ertelan) Schwarz, 'John Austin and the German jurisprudence of his time', *Politica,* 8 (1934), 178–99, 179f. Schwarz cites the following literature: Leslie Stephen, 'The importance of German', in *Studies of a biographer,* ii (1898), 38; John L. Haney, 'The German influence on S.T. Coleridge' (thesis, Philadelphia 1902); W. Streuli, *Th. Carlyle als Vermittler deutscher Literatur und deutschem Geiste* (Zürich, 1895); C.E. Vaughan, *Carlyle and his German masters* (Oxford, 1910); René Wellek, *Immanuel Kant in England, 1793–1838* (Princeton, 1931); J.H. Muirhead, 'How Hegel came to England', *Mind,* 36 (1927), 423ff. Further: Janet Ross (ed.), *Three generations of English women: memoirs and correspondence of Sunnah Taylor, Sarah Austin and Lady Duff Gordon* (2nd ed. London, 1893), Chap VII–XVII, XV; Jack Beatson, 'Aliens, enemy, and friendly enemy aliens: Britain as a home for emigré and refugee lawyers', in Jack Beatson and Reinhard Zimmermann (eds), *Jurists*

influence by German authors of natural law in England and Scotland during the eighteenth century.[3] It seems, however, that there was no connection in legal education between England and Germany in the nineteenth century.

In this essay I would like to establish whether this impression, that the historical school of law had little influence on English law, is correct as well as where this impression comes from, and I wish to conclude with a critical discussion of the merits of the German historical school of law.

In the following I translate the traditional German term *Historische Rechtsschule* as 'historical school of law', and I use the abbreviation 'HSL' henceforth.[4] Further I shall use the notion of 'reception' in the meaning that a methodological paradigm – not only a concrete method – is accepted and adapted to local cultural conditions.[5] My own method does not follow a theoretical mainstream. I just try to reconstruct the facts as lawyers do in court, and I wish to be methodically correct and fair in my descriptions, aware that there always exists more than one way to present the facts.

The present investigation shall address the following topics: an introduction to the intentions of the HSL and legal education in Germany against the background of its political, social and economic conditions in the nineteenth century, the influence of the methodological programme in Germany in the nineteenth and twentieth century, the reception of the programme of the HSL in Switzerland, Austria, France and USA, the approaches of the English legal education to US-legal science and thereby indirectly to the HSL, and the merits of the HSL-concept for legal education.

THE INTENTIONS OF THE HISTORICAL SCHOOL OF LAW (HSL) AGAINST THE BACKGROUND OF ITS POLITICAL, SOCIAL AND ECONOMIC CONDITIONS

The HSL was a German phenomenon of its time. It was the answer of mostly conservative intellectuals to the overwhelming political events that had occurred in France and to the economic developments in England.[6]

---

uprooted: German-speaking emigré lawyers in twentieth-century Britain (Oxford, 2004), pp 73–104, pp 75, 80 (for the nineteenth and early twentieth century).

3 Klaus Luig, 'Institutionenlehrbücher des nationalen Rechts im 17. und 18. Jahrhundert', in H. Coing (ed.), *Ius Commune*, iii (Frankfurt/Main, 1970), 64–97, 91–94; Klaus Luig, 'Zur Verbreitung des Naturrechts in Europa', *Tijdschrift voor Rechtsgeschiedenis*, 40 (1972), 539–57, 546; Michael H. Hoeflich, 'Law & geometry: legal science from Leibniz to Langdell', *American Journal of Legal History*, 30 (1986), 95–121, 108–12.

4 Schwarz, 'John Austin', p. 184.

5 As developed by Thomas S. Kuhn, *The structure of scientific revolution* (Chicago, 1962).

6 Senn, *Rechtsgeschichte*, pp 294–301, 327–35.

The French revolution as well as the English industrialisation meant the breakdown of an old social order and legal system that had endured on the continent since the late Middle Ages. The political revolution brought a collapse of the old social order in Europe as well as a time of occupation and war for almost twenty years. After the Vienna Congress of 1815 there was, however, no rebuilding of the former structures for the common people but a political and social alliance among the upper classes. The industrialisation was led by the middle classes, one of the former three estates, but without concern for public welfare. The experience of the collapse of the social and political structures after 1806 was therefore an enormous collective trauma for Germany. Everything seemed to be lost: political autonomy, social safety nets and economic prosperity. In those days, the main concern of the wider public was not freedom. Freedom was the political demand of only a minority, the middle classes, those who later wrote the books about liberty as the historical issue of the nineteenth century and who therefore passed their interpretations on to subsequent generations. But the majority of the population was (as we face this issue again today) looking for social guarantees. Freedom was a welcome but lesser gift.

The collapse of the political and social system gave people a deep-seated feeling that the changes in the social environment were driven by incomprehensible circumstances and influences of the time. A shared tragic sense of life was fundamental for most of the subsequent social developments. This tragic sense was reflected in German philosophy and in the emerging 'Geisteswissenschaften (*humanities*)' where it was translated into the terms of scientific historicism. On the political level, after the decline of the Holy Roman Empire, one was compelled to ask: was Germany at all a nation like France, England or other countries? And, in general, what were the significant elements that constituted a nation?

At the time the debate over these questions was led by an elite of German conservative and liberal law professors. The liberals held that the German nation could be given an identity by a national code of law. Bavaria, Prussia, France and Austria had already such codes but Germany as a whole had none.[7] This is why one of the celebrated professors of civil law, Anton Friedrich Thibaut in Heidelberg, demanded such a national code of private law for Germany in 1814. He was countered by the young conservative professor Friedrich Carl von Savigny who had just started teaching at the newly founded Humboldt University in Berlin.[8] Savigny held that there was no necessity for a national code and that, on the contrary, a national code

---

7 Ibid., pp 263, 266–9.
8 The two treatises by Thibaut and Savigny have been reprinted with a comment by Hans Hattenhauer (ed.), *Thibaut und Savigny. Ihre programmatischen Schriften* (2nd ed., München, 2002).

would only petrify the law and inhibit further development. In his eyes the advancement of law rested not on a nationwide code but on serious legal education in the national spirit.

The problem with this view was that at the time legal education was largely oriented on the principles and methods of Roman law. For this reason Roman law would be the framework in which the principles and specific rules of law would be discussed and developed by the intellectual elite for the foreseeable future. But how could ancient Roman law – in its various manifestations of byzantine, scholastic, humanistic and forensic practice – fit Germany's needs for a modern law? And how could such a law advance the reunification of a country that was split into forty political entities? A link had to be found between the dogmatic and technical aspects of the law on the one hand, and political questions of nation building on the other hand. This link was found in the idea that law had its own organic history, that it naturally developed and adapted over time as part of a larger culture and spirit. Law was to be understood as part of tradition and social evolution, as opposed to law imposed by political revolutions. Roman law should therefore not be understood as a substantive law, but as an analytic method embodied in the corpus of Roman law. Consequently, substantive law was to be derived by lawyers from the people's historical spirit ('Volksgeist') which in turn was to be recreated from old home-grown sources with the methods of 'historicism'. Lawyers would then use the analytic method derived from Roman law to intelligently and fruitfully apply the law in society.

THE RECEPTION OF THE HSL IN OTHER COUNTRIES

The reception or non-reception of the HSL programme with its orientation on the principles of Roman law is not be reduced to differences between legal systems, as one might expect at first sight. Switzerland and Austria belong both to the German type of legal system and had a moderate reception. France belongs to the Roman type of legal system but the reception was blocked by the Code Civil. The United States belong to the Anglo-American legal system and had a reception.

Austria

Within the Holy Roman Empire Austria played the dominating political part until 1803. When, however, Franz II had taken the imperial crown of the Austrian monarchy in 1804 and made himself Emperor Franz I of Austria (imitating Napoleon, who had taken the imperial crown of France a few months earlier), it became obvious that Austria would separate itself from the Holy Roman Empire. The kingdom of Prussia assumed the new political leadership in the nationalised Germany. Since the Seven Years War in the 1750s, there had been permanent conflict between Austria and Prussia. Both were sovereign states and both had therefore their own legal codes: Prussia the ALR (the Common Law of Prussia) of 1794 and Austria the ABGB (the Code of Private Law) of 1811. As different as both codes were – the Prussian Code was still responding to the society of the ancient régime – they belonged both to the era of the enlightenment and the natural law. Against this background it is to be understood that the Code was defended as imperial decree and the Emperor's prerogative. In the first half of the nineteenth century Austria was dominated by a school of lawyers who defended the Code's exegetically correct interpretation as the "legal gospel" against the HSL. But thereafter a reception of the HSL took hold in Austria. The initial rejection of the HSL gave way after a polemic attack by the responsible minister for education, Leo Graf Thun-Hohenstein in 1852. The result was a discussion between both parties in Austria and from there on one finds a reception of the methodological programme of HSL, too, which led to a more serious and academic debate of the legal system in Austria.[9]

France

In France, the situation was similar to that in Austria. However, 'la Grande Nation' had the unimpeachable Code Napoléon where any exegetical interpretation was prohibited. Therefore, legal education meant simple indoctrination as if there were no historical development of law and social problems that would drive such developments.

This situation changed after 1850 under the influence of authors such as Pellegrino Rossi, Jean-Jacques Gaspard Foelix and, after 1900, by François Gény, Marcel Planiol and Henri Capitant. This meant that in the second part of the nineteenth century there emerged historical and comparative studies in the manner of the HSL inspired by men who had become acquainted with the HSL-programme.[10]

Switzerland

In Switzerland – a nation of twenty-two states[11] and four different languages and cultures – one finds influences of the codes of Austria, France as well as

9 Hans Schlosser, *Grundzüge der neueren Privatrechtsgeschichte. Rechtsentwicklungen im europäischen Kontext* (9th ed. Heidelberg, 2001), p. 139.
10 Helmut Coing, *Europäisches Privatrecht 1800 bis 1914. 19. Jahrhundert* (München, 1989), ii, 35ff; Olivier J. Motte, Articles on 'Capitant', 'Foelix', 'Gény', 'Planiol', in Michael Stolleis (ed.), *Juristen – Ein biographisches Lexikon von der Antike bis zum 20. Jahrhundert* (2nd ed. München, 2001), pp 117, 215, 236, 502, 540ff; Ernst Holthöfer, Article on Rossi, in Stolleis, *Juristen*, pp 555ff; Max Gutzwiller, *Der Einfluss Savignys auf die Entwicklung des Internationalprivatrechts* (Freiburg, 1923), pp 141ff.
11 Bundesverfassung der Schweizerischen Eidgenossenschaft vom 12. September 1848, Art.

of the HSL in the mid nineteenth century. There existed a direct link between Zürich and the HSL bolstered by personal friendships with Savigny. Professors Keller and Bluntschli, who both had studied in Berlin with Savigny, introduced the methodological programme at the University of Zürich, just founded in 1833. Keller published parts of Savigny's programme as early as 1828.[12] Based on the ideas of the HSL the two professors created a new private law code for Zürich, thereby responding to the actual needs of the time. The Code of Zürich from 1855 was the basic reference for the national Swiss Code of Private Law in 1907 (ZGB). This is a good example of a fruitful development of the programme of the HSL. Even Turkey became connected with this development when it adopted the Swiss Code in 1926.

The United States

The US also had a longstanding connection with Germany, a tradition that dated back to earlier than the mid-nineteenth century: more than 10,000 Americans studied at German universities prior to 1900. Johns Hopkins University, the Universities of Chicago and of Michigan all had a special relationship with Germany.[13] Mathias Reimann – now at the University of Michigan – showed that there had been an extensive reception of the HSL in the US between 1860 and 1920 – the so-called 'classical era' – until the sociological method became dominant in the 1920s.

What were the reasons for this reception? First, Savigny's theory provided a foundation to a new generation of lawyers searching for a historical understanding of the common law in the dispute with the ahistorical analytical jurisprudence of John Austin. Savigny's theory made it possible to explain why Austin's command theory was wrong: law always had a historical basis; its core did not consist of everlasting ideas, a will of God or natural

---

1, in Alfred Kölz (ed.), *Quellenbuch zur Neueren Schweizerischen Verfassungsgeschichte. Vom Ende der Alten Eidgenossenschaft bis 1848*, (Bern, 1992) p. 447.

12 F.L.K. [=Friedrich Ludwig Keller], *Die neuen Theorien in der Zürcherischen Rechtspflege* (Zürich, 1828), 42 pages; reprint by Organisationskommittee des „Schweizerischer Juristentag", 8./9. September 1940, pp 6ff, 18ff, 32ff.

13 John Roberts & Edward Shills, 'Nordamerika', in Walter Rüegg (ed.), *Geschichte der Universität in Europa. Vom 19. Jahrhundert zum Zweiten Weltkrieg (1800–1945)*, (München, 2004), iii, 146–56, especially 148–54; Marcus Lutter, Ernst C. Stiefel and Michael H. Hoeflich (eds), *Der Einfluss deutscher Emigranten auf die Rechtsentwicklung in den USA und in Deutschland. Vorträge und Referate des Bonner Symposions September 1991* (Tübingen, 1993); Michael H. Hoeflich, 'Transatlantic friendships and the German influence on American law in the first half of the nineteenth century', *American Journal of Comparative Law*, 35 (1987), 599–611: Hoeflich opens with the remark that there was a tendency in recent decades to pass over the importance of German influences on American law; Hoeflich, *Roman and civil law and the development of Anglo-American jurisprudence in the nineteenth century* (Athens, GA, and London, 1997), esp. pp 52–7.

causality; its essence was its history. Second, Savigny's theory convinced through its consistency of thought demonstrated in his *System des heutigen römischen Rechts* (The legal system of contemporary Roman law). Earlier authors such as Montesquieu, Gibbon or Hugo presented their ideas unsystematically whereas Savigny formed an intellectual system that could serve as a framework of law. Third, because it was methodological rather than substantive, Savigny's theory also lent itself to new developments such as psychological and sociological analysis. The organic theory based on the idea of 'Volksgeist' could be transformed into social Darwinism as occurred at the end of the nineteenth century, certainly an avenue Savigny would not have pursued, but the price of the absence of substantial law in my opinion. Fourth, Savigny's thinking had also certain limited practical implications which were significant for American audiences.[14] Here they found a lucid theory that combined the ideas of Montesquieu with the practical efforts of Blackstone. Fifth, one found in Savigny also a brilliant style of calm and simple clarity, although much of it may have been lost in the translation by Hayward.

APPROACHES OF ENGLISH LEGAL EDUCATION TO US LEGAL SCIENCE AND THE HSL

From the extensive academic and organisational exchanges between the US and Germany in the nineteenth century it is evident that the HSL programme could develop an influence in the United States of America, as it was demonstrated by Michael H. Hoeflich in 'The Americanization of British legal education in the nineteenth century', and that therefore the changes in England in the nineteenth century were inspired by American academic influence. Hoeflich observed that English legal education was excellent during the early modern period, but that it broke down at the universities as well as at the Inns during the eighteenth century.[15] The only major achievement during that time was Blackstone's *Commentaries* on the laws of England (1765–70). Until the mid-nineteenth century there was a period of decline so that, in the words of William Holdsworth, legal education became a melancholic topic.[16]

---

14 Mathias Reimann, *Historische Schule und Common Law. Die deutsche Rechtswissenschaft des 19. Jahrhunderts im amerikanischen Rechtsdenken*, (Berlin, 1993), pp 89f; further Reimann (ed.), *The reception of continental ideas in the common law world, 1820–1920*, Berlin, 1993, *see* Introduction, esp. pp 13ff; further Reimann, 'The historical school against codification: Savigny, Carter, and the defeat of the New York Civil Code', *American Journal of Comparative Law*, 37 (1989), 95–119, especially 107ff; Gutzwiller, *Der Einfluss Savignys*, pp 112ff, 121.

15 Michael H. Hoeflich, 'The Americanization of British legal education in the nineteenth century', *Journal of Legal History*, 8 (1987), pp 244–59, esp. 246.

16 William Holdsworth, *A history of English law* (London, 1903–72), xii, 77f.

Legal education in England was lacking, for example, comprehensive treatises; worse, it was generally devoid of a comprehensive method. Students had to search for the principles of law on their own from a large mass of details.[17] In this relatively disorganized condition lectures were often held without much enthusiasm. If we had to single out one major contributing factor to this decline, it would be the fact that professorial salaries at universities were so extraordinarily low.[18] An impulse to revive legal education came only from University College, London, with its three new chairs in law including Roman law, jurisprudence and English law. John Austin was the first incumbent in the chair of jurisprudence, but he was a failure as a lecturer. Soon he had no students and resigned. The active role to improve legal education was still with the Inns of Court.

In response to the perceived problems in English legal education, the English parliament appointed in 1846 a select committee on legal education in England and Ireland. The task of the committee was to investigate English legal education and propose improvements. It published its report in August 1846.[19]

The drive to improve legal education was powered by a simple but mighty imperative: England was a global empire whose lawyers, diplomats and administrators were inadequately equipped to resolve legal conflicts. Thus arose an awareness of the need for comparative legal studies and studies in the differing developments of legal systems. The reforms promoted by the select committee were intended to establish law as a principled discipline, amenable to systematic study and able to transcend the limitations of a case-by-case approach. Legal education should strive for high quality by international standards and establish itself as a serious discipline in the university community.[20]

---

17 Anonymous (referring to Lord Brougham), 'Legal education', *Law Magazine or Quarterly Review of Jurisprudence*, 37 (1847), pp 175–200, esp. 175f, 189f.

18 Hoeflich, 'The Americanization of British legal education', pp 246, 248.

19 *Report from the select committee on legal education, together with the minutes of evidence, appendix and index* [351 pages]. Ordered by the house of commons, to be printed, 25 August 1846.

20 Peter Stein, 'Continental influences on English legal thought 1600–1900', in *La Formazione Storica del Diritto moderno in Europa. Atti del terzo Congresso internazionale della Società italiana di Storia del Diritto*, (Firenze, 1977), pp 1105–25, esp. 1121; the contemporary example was delivered by Justice Joseph Story (*see* below note 21) in his *Commentary on the conflict of laws* (1832–45), see the contemporary review on this commentary by Carl Joseph Anton Mittermaier, 'Collision der Gesetze verschiedener Staaten', in *Kritische Zeitschrift für Rechtswissenschaft und Gesetzgebung des Auslandes* 7 (1835), 228–49. However, I learnt from a handout entitled 'Empire's Law' by William Cornish from Magdalene College, University of Cambridge, to the [Deutscher] Rechtshistorikertag at the University of Bonn, 2004, that Britain handled the problem in a far different way: the necessity of a serious legal education was replaced by a system of fraternity beyond the judges and lawyers (in Britain) and the lawyers of the colonies were sent to London for the bar to become successful barristers and solicitors in their countries in the nineteenth century (p. 12).

A greater part of the committee's testimony focussed on the means and methods of international legal education, especially in the USA and in particular at the Harvard Law School. The experts on the committee favourably received works of American legal educators such as Kent and Story. Like Blackstone the American legal educators were not just academics but practising lawyers and judges who integrated legal theory and practice in their lectures and treatises. The American law schools became a shining example, and to many English educators they seemed as important for their times as the law school of Bologna for the Middle Ages.[21]

If there had been an influence of the HSL in England, it was mediated by the American reception. There are very few indications of a direct influence, and we find only isolated reactions to the educational programme of the HSL in England but no coherent commentary. While there existed a general influence of German legal thinking in England as well as a reception of concrete dogmatic figures, e.g., into contract law, neither should be confused with a concrete influence of the HSL and specifically Savigny.[22] We are therefore unable to follow Peter Stein who holds that there had indeed been a real and full reception.[23] By comparison Enid Campbell's study of 1959 was

21 Hoeflich, 'The Americanization of British legal education', 249f, 253. Hoeflich shows the positive paradigm of the American educational model. In general the experts accepted either James Kent's *Commentaries on American law* (1826–30) or Wheaton's *Treatise on international law*, another American textbook, to be the best elementary work in the English language. The most important American legal educator in the mid-nineteenth century, however, was – as above mentioned (note 20) – Mr Justice Joseph Story from Harvard University with his *Commentary on the conflict of laws* (1832–45).

22 The English system of law had need of concrete dogmatic elements: there were received the 'will-theory' in the law of contract by Pollock and the notion 'consensus' by Anson, further the notion and construction of 'possession' or 'legal person' (*see* Stein, 'Continental influences', pp 1120–3). The plausible reason for these concrete dogmatic receptions was: German Roman law supplied the abstract elements which were lacking in English law. Roman law was considered at this time as a part of jurisprudence: see Peter Stein, 'Legal theory and the reform of legal education in mid nineteenth century England', in *L'Educazione Giuridica, Profili Storici* (Perugia, 1977), ii, 185–206, p. 195f; further: Basil S. Markesinis, 'Homage an das deutsche Recht', in *European Review of Private Law*, 4 (1999), 429–44.

23 Stein, 'Legal theory', p. 205 n. 10. Stein just mentions two influences. Firstly it was the Prussian school system which was on a high level and admired; but one knew as well that the English system had no chance to reach this level, as the committee itself very well realized. And admiration as there was in some heads does not mean reception as I do understand. Further, the school system in general has nothing to do with the University itself. The other influence was by admired persons as John Austin who studied in Heidelberg and Bonn; he lived afterwards in Berlin and Dresden, too, but was influenced by Thibaut, the before mentioned antipode of Savigny. Stein however does not let us know clearly what the essence of the influence could have been; but no matter, because Austin was certainly not the man to improve the method in legal education at his time. Two other translations are to be mentioned: Ferdinand Mackeldey's *Lehrbuch des heutigen römischen*

more differentiating when she stated that the 'question of influence is a delicate one [...] and in the present context does not necessarily mean that German ideas may have been accepted by English lawyers', or to quote from her conclusion: 'Although legal scholars of the nineteenth century gave more to German legal scholarship than to the work of any European lawyers, there is little evidence that German ideas penetrated very deeply into the fabric of English legal thought except in one limited field, i.e., legal historiography. One cannot say even that the inspiration for the reform of English legal education was German in origin.'[24]

Nevertheless, there existed a few enthusiastic followers of Savigny, such as Markby and Maitland. Savigny's 'Pandektensystem' was first adopted in William Markby's book *Elements of Law* in 1871. Savigny's own writings, however, were not very intensively adopted, and they had yet to be translated. Volume one of his *System des heutigen römischen Rechts* appeared in translation by George Long not before 1867, a quarter of a century after its initial publication. A reviewer uttered with barely concealed disdain: 'Mr. Long must take especial care not to be led by Savigny (to whose valuable work he expresses his obligations) into too abstract and Germanized a system of lecturing.'[25] This is concrete evidence for Campbell's thesis of non-acceptance and non-penetration in general. It seems that there was just one case of genuine reception: Frederic William Maitland, the founder of Selden Society (1887) and editor of many documents and historical analyses of English legal history.[26] He was the only scholar who truly represented the ideas of the HSL in England in the nineteenth century. By comparison, Henry James Sumner Maine's notion of development has more to do with evolutionary thought and geological science than with the model of the HSL in the sense of Savigny. Maine's work on *Ancient Law*, based on the early history of society and its relation to modern ideas, was edited not before 1861, and it was a complementary work to that of Austin.[27]

Rechts (1841) – a completely forgotten author within Germany and even at his time of no special importance – and Lord Lindley's translation of Thibaut's *Pandektenrecht* as it was the typical system to present Roman law.

24 Enid Campbell, 'German influence in English legal education [and] jurisprudence in the 19th century', in *University of Western Australia Annual Law Review*, 4 (1959), 357–90, 358, 388.

25 *Law Magazine*, 37 (1847), p. 238 after Stein, 'Legal theory', 194f and esp. p. 205 n. 21.

26 Kent Lerch, [Article on] 'Maitland', in Stolleis, *Juristen*, pp 412f.; T.F.T. Plunkett, *Early English legal literature* (Cambridge, 1958), pp 2–18; Michele Graziadei, 'Changing images of the law in XIX century English legal thought (the continental impulse)', in Mathias Reimann (ed.), *The reception of continental ideas in the common law world, 1820–1920* (Berlin 1993), pp 115–63, especially pp 158ff; Stein, 'Continental influences' 20, p. 1123 saying that Maitland established also that Savigny's thoughts were criticized and rejected in England.

27 Frederick Pollock, 'The history of comparative jurisprudence', in Frederick Pollock, *Essays in the law* (London, 1922), pp 10f; Peter Stein, 'Legal theory', pp 198f, Kent Lerch, in Stolleis, *Juristen*, pp 410ff. There could be perhaps a parallel to Georg Friedrich Puchta (see

THE HISTORIOGRAPHICAL CONTROVERSY SURROUNDING THE ABOVE ISSUES

Now we have to ask why England was resistant to a direct influence by Germany in legal education. Such resistance is particularly puzzling because German culture was influential among the English upper classes who were attracted to the music of the Austria-German composers and to the liberal and individualistic conception of society in German classical literature and philosophy.[28] Although some English professors had studied in Germany[29] they generally did not speak German fluently, with the exceptions of Bryce, Long and Hayward. Jurists in general read only translations.[30] Those, however, who studied in Germany did so in Bonn, Heidelberg or Göttingen, but not in Berlin with Savigny.[31] They therefore learnt the methods of the schools of Göttingen or those of Thibaut, Savigny's antipode, in Heidelberg.

Turning to the conditions in England, it seems that the English legal environment was not sufficiently prepared for a reception of the HSL. The reasons can be traced to the differences between the English and German legal systems: the German system had been based for a greater part on codified law since the eighteenth century. By contrast, English legal authority was vested in the Royal Courts of Justice. Germany, unlike England, did not have this strong and specific tradition of practice of courts as ground for legal education. Another difference between the legal systems, established by Andreas Schwarz (1934), stems from the fact that English jurisprudence in general lacked a home-grown quality, and therefore the German traditional elements were inappropriate for English law[32], as several contemporary commentators also recognized.[33] Furthermore, on the continent legal

---

Hans-Peter Haferkamp, *Georg Friedrich Puchta und die „Begriffsjurisprudenz"* (Frankfurt/Main, 2004)), but I did not find any hint of a connection with Puchta. Maine's work did not seriously challenge the dominant position of Bentham or Austin. As Stein says, until after the Second World War, jurisprudence as a subject of study meant analysis of legal concepts in the way of Austin and Bentham. Historical thoughts as postulated by the HSL were very far different from that.

28 See works listed in n. 2 and Campbell, 'German influence', pp 372ff.
29 See the list in Reimann, *Historische Schule*, pp 289–307: Austin (Bonn, Heidelberg, living later on in Dresden and Berlin), Bryce (Heidelberg), Hayward (the famous translator never studied there but spoke German), Lindley (Bonn), and Reddie (Göttingen). George Long also studied in Göttingen. James Bryce published in 1864 the book about the Holy Roman Empire (with 18 editions or reprints), and John Reddie in 1826 his *Historical notes of the Roman law and the recent progress of its study in Germany*.
30 Michael H. Hoeflich, 'Savigny and his Anglo-American disciples', *American Journal of Comparative Law*, 37 (1989), 17–37, 18ff.
31 See however the opposite examples of Keller and Bluntschli in Switzerland mentioned under heading 3.
32 Schwarz, 'John Austin', p. 188.
33 *e.g.* Henry James Sumner Maine, *The nature of positive law* (London, 1883), pp 253–69.

education took place at the universities. In the Holy Roman Empire it was of importance to hold a higher degree from a qualified university.

In addition to institutional differences between English and German law that inhibited communication, there also exist indications of a chasm between English and German legal thinking. A good example is the contemporary reviewer of the translation of Savigny's first volume of the *System* mentioned earlier. It seems that there was not only no enthusiasm for, but outright scepticism toward German legal thinking which was seen as 'abstract' in a derogatory sense.[34] If this chasm existed in the nineteenth century, it was not helped in the twentieth century by the two World Wars caused by Germany.[35] The deep seated scepticism expressed by the above nineteenth century reviewer may have persisted throughout the twentieth century.[36]

THE MERITS OF A RECEPTION OF THE HSL

Bologna was the birthplace of the European university in the Middle Ages. The spirit of Bologna, the belief in seeking deeper truth through education of, and inquiry by free individuals, was present again in the HSL's methodological programme against the background of the reform of the universities in the spirit of Humboldt.

In spite of its roots in the German romantic tradition, the HSL encompasses an element of the Enlightenment when it seeks the solution to national problems in legal education. One believed that education would achieve desirable goals in time and in 'organic' ways, namely, compatible with

---

34 The chasm was stressed at the end of the nineteenth century by the more racial thoughts which began to increase in England and on the Continent and got public the more this argument won its strategical value in discussions, see Senn, *Rechtsgeschichte*, pp 350ff, 357ff; Marcel Senn/ Lukas Gschwend, *Rechtsgeschichte II – Juristische Zeitgeschichte* (Zürich/Basel/Genf, 2004), pp 73–111; Sven Oliver Müller, 'Recht und Rasse. Die Ethnisierung von Staatsangehörigkeit und Nationalvorstellungen in Grossbritannien im Ersten Weltkrieg', *Geschichte und Gesellschaft. Zeitschrift für Historische Sozialwissenschaft* 30 (2004), pp 379–403, pp 389f, 394f.; Robert von Friedeburg, *Konservativismus und Reichskolonialrecht. Konservatives Weltbild und kolonialer Gedanke in England vom späten 19. Jahrhundert bis zum Ersten Weltkrieg*, pp 345–93, 345f, 358, 366.

35 One argument was that the two World Wars – caused by Germany – should have been a reason (e.g. see Michael H. Hoeflich, 'Savigny', p. 18). But on the other hand, if so, why is there still a positive connection between USA and Germany, but not between England and Germany?

36 e.g. the statement by the former Director of the Institute of European and Comparative Law in Oxford Basil S. Markesinis, 'Homage an das deutsche Recht', 435, 441 saying that there has always been a tendency to demonstrate an insular isolation of the home-grown English law and there was no encouragement to the students to deal with other cultures.

the people's historically developed spirit, against the brutality of the French revolution. Thus, the emphasis on, and trust in legal education of the HSL incorporates an enlightened element worth our consideration. Even if some of the terminology used by the HSL has fallen into disrepute after the Third Reich ('Volksgeist', for example), this fact would be a shallow pretext for ignoring an intellectual tradition with considerable progressive ideals.

If we could agree that legal education should have these goals: that it should produce a liberal and autonomous intellect capable of understanding the contexts of, and differences among legal systems, furthermore that this intellect should be able to distinguish the fundamental questions and principles of law and of justice from more practical skills, then we should accept that the HSL deserves our attention not only today but even with regard to the English legal education of the nineteenth century that had missed the opportunity of its reception while struggling for higher academic quality.

Law and India at King's College London

PAUL MITCHELL

ON 20 SEPTEMBER 1862 a terse advertisement appeared in the Athenaeum magazine:

> KING'S COLLEGE, London – The PROFESSORSHIPS of HINDUSTANI and of INDIAN JURISPRUDENCE are NOW VACANT. For particulars apply to J. W. CUNNINGHAM, Secretary

This was the first public appearance of the Professorship of Indian Jurisprudence at King's. Over the course of the next forty years it was to be held by a succession of diversely talented scholars – including a judge-poet, a barrister-mathematician and a mainstay of the *Oxford English Dictionary*. The teaching of Indian law subjects was to have a profound influence on the nature of legal education offered by the College. Indeed, at the height of its success (between about 1865 and 1875) the Indian theme was integrated into more mainstream material to such an extent that students were instructed, at the outset, to focus on the similarities and differences between English, Roman, Hindu and Islamic laws. It was a remarkably ambitious and distinctive approach to law teaching.

ESTABLISHING THE PROFESSORSHIP

King's College London in the early 1860s was not a likely location for innovative legal education. Indeed, it was not a likely location for any legal education at all. The College had been fortunate to appoint the distinguished scholar J.J. Park as its first Professor of English Law.[1] But Park's successors contributed little by way of scholarship and less as teachers.[2] In 1849, when

---

First published in *King's College Law Journal*, 17:27 (2006). Republished by permission of Hart Publishing.
1   Park's most famous work is *The dogmas of the constitution* (London, 1832).
2   See generally, C. Morse, 'Dower, dogma and grand designs: law at King's, nineteenth century style' in C. Kenyon Jones, *King's College London: in the service of society* (London, 2004), p. 60.

the 'almost sinecure and honorary position of professor of law'[3] was vacated by its latest undistinguished holder, the Council commissioned a report on what form, if any, legal education at King's should take. A committee including Coleridge and Patteson JJ advised that it was hopeless to attempt to teach law as a professional subject, but that it should not be abandoned altogether:

> What should be aimed at is to give *all*, whether intended to be practical lawyers or not, such sound elementary information as may make the former more fitted to enter readily and usefully on a strictly professional course of study; and to give to the latter that acquaintance with the constitution of the country and the spirit and outline of its legal system without which no gentleman or member of any profession can be considered completely educated.[4]

The Council decided to persevere with law, and appointed G.K. Rickards. He resigned within months, and was replaced by James Stephen in 1851. There was still no progress. In the academic year 1861–2 no legal subjects were being offered.[5]

But during the 1850s, whilst legal education at the College was non-existent, developments elsewhere were creating a more favourable environment for certain types of legal study. In particular, the method of recruitment to the Indian Civil Service was changing: the Government of India Act 1853 introduced open competitive examination, and abolished the previous practice of nominations by Directors of the East India Company.[6]

The change in recruitment method had been a long time coming: it had first been introduced in the Charter Act of 1833, but the Directors of the Company had succeeded in having the provision deferred.[7] It proved to be neither a successful nor universally popular reform. Those who favoured it had anticipated that large numbers of the best university students would be attracted to Indian posts. This expectation was disappointed,[8] and it was even questioned whether the aim was worth achieving at all. As one anonymous pamphleteer asked, rhetorically, would the mundane duties of an Indian civil servant really be performed better 'if every servant had begun by being a senior wrangler or a double first-class man?'[9]

3   F. Hearnshaw, *The centenary history of King's College London, 1828–1928* (London, 1929), p. 180.
4   Ibid.
5   *The calendar of King's College London for 1861–1862* (London, 1862).
6   E. Blunt, *The ICS: the Indian civil service* (London, 1937), pp 45–6; N. Ferguson, *Empire: how Britain made the modern world* (London, 2003), p. 186.
7   Blunt, *ICS*, 46.
8   B. Spangenberg, 'The problem of recruitment for the Indian civil service during the late nineteenth century,' *Journal of Asian Studies*, 30:2 (1971), 341.
9   *An examination of the competitory mode of admission into the civil service of the East India Company. By a close observer* (London, 1855), p. 8.

The change in recruitment was not limited to the initial selection process – it also applied to the preparatory training given to successful candidates before they were sent to India. This preparatory training included instruction in Indian languages, geography and history, as well as English and Indian law.

The importance of legal knowledge for Indian civil servants could be seen as early as 1623, when the East India Company's charter authorized senior officers of the Company to try offences committed by the Company's servants.[10] As the Company took on a more political, governing role, the need for legal expertise increased. Thus, for instance, from 1672 onwards there was a 'regular judicial system'[11] in place in Bombay; from 1728 onwards there were courts of record, under the auspices of the Company, in Bombay, Madras and Bengal. The expertise required of the Company's servants was not limited to English law: as early as 1654 the Company took over the 'choultry' court in Madras, which dealt with disputes between Indians.[12]

Despite the obvious importance of legal expertise, little was done to ensure that the Company's servants acquired it. Perhaps the assumption was that one learned about legal practice through practice. A notable exception was Warren Hastings (the Governor-General of the East India Company), who founded the Calcutta Madrassa, an Islamic law school, in the 1770s – but that seems to have been more a reflection of personal enthusiasm than systematic reform.[13] By 1800 the only educational requirement for Indian civil servants was still, merely, the rudiments of commercial knowledge.[14]

In the early years of the nineteenth century, however, this *laissez-faire* approach was replaced by its complete opposite. Now nominated candidates were to receive systematic instruction in languages and law at the Company's College at Haileybury. As the College's first prospectus made clear, it was not in the business of education for its own sake:

> The object of this establishment is to provide a supply of persons duly qualified to discharge the various and important duties required from the civil servants of the Company in administering the government in India.[15]

So the 1853 Act, by introducing examinations in Indian languages and in law (both English and Indian) for selected candidates, was a direct challenge

---

10 Blunt, *ICS*, p. 22.
11 Ibid., p. 23.
12 Ibid., p. 24.
13 Hastings apparently told Lord Mansfield that 'Muslim law is as comprehensive, and as well defined, as that of most states in Europe'. Ferguson, *Empire*, pp 38–9.
14 Blunt, *ICS*, p. 34.
15 Ibid., p. 35.

to the monopoly Haileybury had enjoyed for the previous fifty years or so. Such a challenge might have been withstood, but when a committee was appointed to advise on how the 1853 Act should be implemented, it recommended the abolition of Haileybury College altogether.[16] Its recommendation was accepted; and the College closed permanently in 1857. There was now a gap in the market.

King's in the late 1850s was a college desperately seeking such gaps. Its financial state was dismal, it was undermanned, and what staff it had were underpaid.[17] As the College's historian puts it,

> The urgent need to secure new sources of supply made the principal, the secretary, the staff, and the council quick and eager to discern new educational demands, and to start new activities in order to satisfy them.[18]

The changes in civil service recruitment were exactly the kind of opportunities that the College craved. Indeed, it had already attempted to capitalize on the introduction of the open competitive examination by setting up a Civil Service Department in 1854. That department lasted only a year.[19] But the principal, undaunted, was clearly determined to exploit the situation. On 9 May 1862 he put before the College Council

> the details of a scheme for an Oriental Section of the Department of General Literature and Science, prepared chiefly with the view of preparing Candidates selected for the Indian Civil Service for their further examination.[20]

The scheme was distributed among the oriental professors for consideration, and on 16 June 1862 the Council approved the prospectus for the new section.[21]

The original scheme cannot have included lectures in Indian law, for at its meeting on 11 July 1862 the Council agreed the following modification:

> On the recommendation of Mr Leitner [Professor of Arabic and Mohammedan Law at King's] and Mr Maitland the Secretary of the Civil Service Commission, it was resolved, subject to the approval of the Principal, to add to the Lectures proposed for the Oriental Section of the Department of General Literature and Science a course on the

---

16 Ibid., p. 198. The Principal of Haileybury, the Revd H. Melvill, was a member of the Committee.
17 Hearnshaw, *Centenary*, p. 206.
18 Ibid., p. 207.
19 Ibid., pp 251–2.
20 *King's College London; minutes of the Council*, volume I, item 120.
21 Ibid., item 133.

"Jurisdiction and Procedure of Courts of Law in India", and the Principal was requested to make enquiries for some one competent to undertake this subject.[22]

But before a penny in fees was received, the oriental section was plunged into crisis by the resignation, in late August 1862, of the professor of Hindustani, who had obtained an appointment in India from the bishop of Calcutta.[23] Hence, just over a week before the academic year began, the College was advertising to fill two key vacancies in its new oriental section.

APPOINTING THE FIRST PROFESSOR

The standard of applicants responding to the College's advertisement was not universally high. For instance, one candidate drew to the college secretary's attention: 'that I resigned the Service in 1856, and have since been two years in madhouses upon a false Certificate of Insanity'.[24] He enclosed a handwritten pamphlet on madhouses 'to be circulated to the Professors'. There were several applications from retired Indian army officers.[25] But the outstanding candidate was Fitz-Edward Hall.

Hall had several advantages. The first was his impeccable Indian academic background. He had been, amongst other things, a tutor, then professor of English and Sanskrit at the government college at Benares and an inspector of public instruction[26]. As he pointed out in his application letter, he had taken 'much pains to acquaint [him]self with various Indian languages' as shown 'by some twenty volumes which I have published and edited, chiefly in the Bibliotheca India of the Asiatic Society of Bengal'.[27] He was also fortunate in his choice of referees. One was the Revd S. Slater, the recently departed holder of the chair of Hindustani. The second, James Ballantyne, was the professor of Sanskrit at King's, and had been the principal of Benares government college during Hall's tenure. His reference, preserved in the college secretary's correspondence, was enthusiastic, to say the least:

---

22 Ibid., item 139.
23 Ibid., item 147, 1 October 1862 (recording receipt of resignation letter on 28 August).
24 King's college secretary's incoming correspondence, KA/IC/H46, 26 September 1862 (King's College archives).
25 See the bundle of correspondence received by the college secretary KA/IC/H46. Generally some of this correspondence is organised by correspondent, some by subject-matter. The H46 bundle contains letters from Fitz-Edward Hall (filed under Hall) and several from other applicants on the basis that they related to the professorship of Hindustani.
26 *Oxford dictionary of national biography* (Oxford, 2004).
27 KA/IC/H46, 22 September 1862 (King's College archives).

His knowledge of Hindustani is unusually accurate and extensive; and in the Hindi dialect I am not aware of any scholar equal to him.

One of Dr Hall's favourite studies while at Benares was Hindu Law. When questioned as to his remarkable fondness for this very dry line of Sanskrit reading, he justified himself by the remark that he came of a legal family & inherited the fancy. As regards conversancy with the Sanskrit original treatises, I am not aware of any one else with Dr Hall's pretensions to be regarded as an authority on Hindu Law.

I need scarcely add that I would rejoice to find myself associated in any collegiate institution with Dr Hall.[28]

Ballantyne's reference was as modest – he himself was a great scholar of Sanskrit and Hindi[29] – as it was effective. Hall's appointment to both Professorships was recommended by an informal committee (of which Ballantyne was a member), and the Council approved it.[30] The Council minutes indicated the extreme time pressure under which the appointment was made, by recording that the Council

> departed from their usual custom of referring the applications and testimonials to a Special Committee, solely because from the fact that the College Academical Year was just beginning, and that it was necessary that the new Professors should be at their posts at the end of the present week, there was not time for the usual reference.[31]

The oriental section was now, finally, complete.

On the face of it, the College had been extremely fortunate to secure the services of such an eminent scholar at such short notice. But appearances may be deceptive. It was, perhaps, odd that the council had resolved to appoint a professor of Indian jurisprudence in July, but that there had been no advertisement until late September. The delay is all the more surprising given that the oriental section was the principal's personal project. It may be that the college secretary was (uncharacteristically)[32] disorganized; or that the College's optimism about finding a suitable candidate bordered on complacency.

There is, however, a third possibility. In 1865, when Hall's relationship with the College had soured following a dispute about the use of substitute teachers, Hall wrote to the principal in the following terms: 'Dr Ballantyne,

---

28 Ibid., (with Hall's application letter).
29 See his entry in the *Oxford dictionary of national biography* (Oxford, 2004).
30 *King's College London; minutes of the council*, volume I, 1 October 1862, item 147.
31 Ibid., item 148.
32 Hearnshaw, *Centenary*, p. 202, describes Cunningham's appointment as college secretary as 'a singularly prudent and fortunate one'.

I would remind you, was allowed to act by a proxy, myself, from the day of his appointment to the Sanskrit chair, until the day of his death, nearly two whole collegiate years'.[33] The principal's reply did not dispute Hall's claim about either Ballantyne's absence or Hall's performance as a proxy.[34] The fact that Hall was effectively carrying out the duties of the professor of Sanskrit before October 1862 puts his appointment in a rather different light. Ballantyne's effusive reference and recommendation to council begin to look as if he was returning a favour. The appointment itself starts to look less like an excellent piece of good fortune, and more like the formalisation of an existing position. In other words, the professorship of Indian jurisprudence may well have been earmarked for Hall from the moment it was created; and the advertisement of the post may have been a mere irrelevant formality.

LEGAL EDUCATION IN THE ORIENTAL SECTION

The law courses offered by the oriental section, and the professors in charge of them during the first year of operation[35] were an impressive array. In addition to Hall's course on the jurisdiction and procedure of the courts of India, there was Hindu law taught by Ballantyne (or his substitute), Mahommedan law by Leitner and English law and jurisprudence by James Stephen. Ballantyne and Leitner deserve particular attention. The former was at the end of a highly distinguished academic career[36], in the course of which he had published grammars of Hindi, Sanskrit, Maratha and Persian and translations of Hindu philosophy and linguistics, some of which were recently still in print.[37] Leitner was at the very start of his career. He had been appointed professor of Arabic with Mahommedan law in 1861, aged twenty-one. Three years later he became principal of the government college at Lahore and, during the next fifteen years, founded several journals, including the *Civil and Military Gazette*, where Kipling published many early stories and verses.[38]

It was, perhaps, too much to hope that the distinction of the professoriate would be enough in itself to attract students. The College, therefore, offered discounts for bulk purchases: Hindu and Mahommedan Law cost £8 8s. for

---

33 KA/IC/H52, 31 January 1865.
34 Copy of principal's letter to Hall, filed in KA/IC/H52, 1 February 1865. The Principal pointed out that Ballantyne's leave of absence had been sanctioned by the college council.
35 *The calendar of King's College London 1862–1863* (London, 1862), p. 93.
36 See his entry in the *Oxford dictionary of national biography*.
37 E.g. S. Acharya, J. Ballantyne and J. Murdoch, *Selections from the Upanishads, Bhagavad Gita, Vedanta Sara and Laws of Manu* (Delhi, 1988).
38 For more details see his entry in the *Oxford dictionary of national biography*.

the year if taken alone; £5 5s. if taken with a language.[39] We do not know how many students availed themselves of this special offer.

However, we can begin to piece together what was taught. As the college calendar announced, 'The object of this Section is to meet the wants of candidates for the Indian Civil Service, particularly those selected for the "further examination"'[40]. The language classes in Sanskrit and Arabic might have helped candidates for the initial examination – where there were translation and grammar papers in those subjects[41] – but the law classes were clearly targeted only at selected candidates (i.e., those who had succeeded in the first examination). The further examination papers for 1863 show that, if King's was giving its students value for money, an impressive level of legal analysis was being taught. Thus, for example, in Hindu law candidates were required to demonstrate detailed knowledge of different schools of analysis:

> State whether a daughter's son has, in any and what case, a right to inherit the property of his maternal grandfather, according to the several schools of Bengal, Benares and Mithila.[42]

They also needed some comparative understanding, with another question asking about 'the principal points of resemblance and difference between the Hindoo system of *Adoption* and that of ancient Greece'.[43] Mahommedan law made similar demands.[44] The questions on procedure were, perhaps understandably, more factual.[45] But the really striking paper was general jurisprudence. Here the range of questions demanded both insight and analytical ability. Thus, for instance, question 3 asked candidates to:

> State Bentham's objections to the principle of giving judges the power of interpreting the Laws; how has this danger been foreseen by and provided for by the framers of the Indian Penal Code? Were Bentham's objections intended to apply at all to English Jurisprudence?[46]

A more philosophical approach was needed for Question 10:

---

39 *The calendar of King's College London 1862–1863* p. 94.
40 Ibid., p. 93.
41 See e.g. *East India Company's civil service examination papers*, July 1857.
42 *Ninth report of her majesty's civil service commissioners, together with appendices* (London, 1864), 263 (Question 7).
43 Ibid., (Question 9).
44 Ibid., 263–4.
45 Ibid., 264–6.
46 Ibid., 261.

> Does Savigny's dictum 'that all property is founded on adverse possession ripened by prescription,' agree with Bentham's views as to what is the proper foundation of property? What light is thrown upon speculations regarding the origin of property from the Hindoo village community?[47]

And Question 16, which started out as an orthodox problem question, took a surprising turn:

> A. in London sells a horse to B. in York; the price is paid, and the animal is sent by railway to York; on the journey it is injured, and a serious loss ensues. On which of the parties, according to Bentham, ought the loss to fall? On which would it fall by the Roman and English Law respectively?[48]

More detailed information exists about the Oriental Section's second year[49]. Hall was now listed as the Professor for two courses: Hindu law as well as jurisdiction and procedure of Indian courts.[50] Perhaps as the result of a successful first year, the discount for taking Hindu or Mahommedan law with a language had been dropped[51]. Most importantly, for our purposes, the professors told the students which books they needed[52]. For Mahommedan law and Indian jurisprudence one needed Macnaghten's *Principles and Precedents* and *Hindu Law* respectively. For procedure in Indian law courts it was Macpherson's *New civil procedure for* British India, the Indian criminal code and the Code of criminal procedure. The most eclectic selection, however, was needed for English law and general jurisprudence: Blackstone's *Commentaries*, *Institutes of Justinian* (Sandars' edition), *Traités de legislation de Bentham par Et Dumont*, Maine's *Ancient Law* and Mackenzie's *Studies of Roman Law*.

This was a daunting array of material for students to master. But the professors could not be criticized for imposing an excessive workload, since all but one of these books – Maine's *Ancient Law* – was prescribed by the civil service commissioners themselves.[53] Nonetheless, students struggled, as one former King's student was later to recall vividly. Arthur Frederick Cox

---

47 Ibid., 262.
48 Ibid.
49 *The calendar of King's College London 1863–1864* (London, 1864), pp 99–103.
50 Ibid., 99.
51 Ibid., 100.
52 Ibid., 102–3.
53 *Ninth report of her majesty's civil service commissioners, together with appendices* (London, 1864), 198–200. The Commissioners were optimistic that a translation of Bentham would be published 'shortly' (see footnote on 198).

started at King's College school in 1862, progressed to the College in 1866 and passed the first Indian civil service examination.[54] He then went to a crammer 'and discovered for the first time what real hard work meant',[55] passing the second competitive examination in 1869.

> Then followed two years study of special Indian subjects, and I found that I had to read as hard as for the competitive exam. The task required of us was then excessive, and of my year three men lost their reason soon after reaching India, while two failed in their final medical examination. Questions were, in consequence asked in Parliament, and the result was that the amount of reading was much reduced.[56]

Cox's memoir also makes clear that the selected candidates were under enormous examination pressure. During their two years' training there were examinations every six months, with prizes for the best paper. Failing to obtain more than half marks, on the other hand, resulted in a deduction of £10 per subject from the candidate's half-yearly civil service allowance of £50. And any failure in the final exam meant being turned out altogether.[57] This combination of excessive workload and severe penalties for shortcomings made a mockery of the commissioners' claim that there was no necessity to obtain 'the assistance of qualified instructors'.[58]

'THE PERSONNEL OF THE SECTION ... CAUSED AN UNUSUAL AMOUNT OF TROUBLE'[59]

In 1864 there would have been some cause for optimism about the future of the oriental section, and of its law courses: there was a constant supply of students, who needed all the help they could get, and a prestigious professoriate to teach them. But despite the initial success of the section, its professors were not financially secure, and held other posts.[60] Ballantyne, for example, was the librarian of the India Office. When he died in early 1864, Hall became the new librarian, and resigned the professorship of Indian jurisprudence, although he still continued as professor of Sanskrit.[61] 'Careful

---

54 Hearnshaw, *Centenary*, p 274.
55 A. Cox, *Reminiscences of seventy years* (1995, written 1922–3), p. 10.
56 Ibid., p. 12.
57 Ibid., pp 12–13.
58 *Ninth report*, 200.
59 Hearnshaw, *Centenary*, p. 250.
60 Ibid. The problem was not confined to King's: for the difficulties over financial security at University College see J. Baker, 'University College and legal education, 1826–1976' *Current Legal Problems*, 30 (1977), 1 at 5.
61 *King's College London: minutes of the council*, volume I, 22 April 1864, item 327.

inquiries'[62] were made for a replacement, and resulted in the appointment of John David Bell,[63] a barrister, who had previously been an advocate in the High Court at Calcutta. But five months later Bell resigned, explaining that 'circumstances had occurred which compelled him immediately to return to Calcutta'.[64] The College appointed Thomas John Mazzinghi as a temporary substitute.[65] The Chair of English Law also became vacant in late 1864, when James Stephen accepted what he described as 'a valuable appointment in the Court of Bankruptcy at Leeds'.[66]

Hall's continuing association with the College was not a happy one. Illness, later attributed by him 'solely ... to over-zeal in the performance of my professional work in connexion with King's College',[67] prevented him from teaching, and a substitute was found for the October term 1864. The day before the start of the following term, the substitute resigned. The principal wrote to Hall, proposing that he should give up his professorship at once if unable to perform his duties, and adding that Hall's class was waiting. Hall explained that a further substitute had been found by his efforts.[68] But the principal was in no mood to compromise. 'I have been & still am in considerable difficulties with the Oriental Section',[69] he explained.

> These difficulties may be partly traced to the sudden departure of some of the principal Professors, &, to the temporary expedient of *substitutes* which the emergencies so caused rendered necessary & justifiable *for a time*.
>
> Things have now come to such a pass, that I must either advise the abandonment of the Oriental Section, or adopt at once decisive measures for the real organization of an effective staff.[70]

He outlined some of the difficulties with the Sanskrit class – the new substitute was, for instance, insisting that students attend classes '*at his own house*' – and stated, ominously, 'The past cannot be helped; but I must guard myself for the future as far as I can against the possibility of such serious irregularities recurring.' He again presented Hall with the choice of

---

62 Ibid., 1 July 1864, item 346.
63 Ibid.
64 Ibid., 18 November 1864, item 368.
65 Ibid., item 369.
66 Ibid., 14 October 1864, item 358. Oddly, the council minutes recorded Stephen as having been professor since 1862; he had in fact been appointed in 1851, but seems to have been inactive for eleven years.
67 Hall to Jelf (principal), KA/IC/H52, 31 January 1865.
68 Ibid.
69 Jelf to Hall, KA/IC/H52, 1 February 1865 (marked 'Copy').
70 Ibid.

resuming teaching, or resigning, and added a third option: referral to council. Hall chose the latter,[71] but the council's letter to him, though evidently less confrontational, was similar in substance.[72] He resigned on 21 February 1865.[73]

Although Hall was notoriously difficult to work with,[74] it is difficult not to feel some sympathy for him. For two years he had performed Ballantyne's professorial duties, but when he tried to take the benefit of a similar arrangement himself, he incurred the displeasure of the principal. The real reason for the principal's annoyance was that Hall's substitute was less reliable than Hall had been when acting in the same way for Ballantyne. In any case, the College had no better luck with Hall's successor – who was lost for months, finally discovered in Munich and brought back to the Strand, only to vanish again shortly afterwards.[75] Hall spent four more years at the India Office, and then devoted himself to work on the *Oxford English Dictionary* – where his help supplying quotations and reading proofs was crucial, and greatly appreciated.

So in 1864, as in 1862, there were two professorships to be filled in the oriental section. The professorship of English law was to be dealt with by Sir John Coleridge and a Mr Cheese, the principal having power to appoint a temporary replacement.[76] No similar provision seems to have been made for the professorship of Indian law, it being left to the Principal to bring the matter before the council.[77]

The temporary replacement for the professor of English law was John Cutler, a junior barrister. Cutler quickly set about making a good impression. And the way to do that at King's in the 1860s was to bring in money. Cutler did this by setting up an evening class in law for articled clerks,[78] which was a great success. He also kept the principal up to date with reviews of his work in the press.[79] In fact, Cutler's ability was so conspicuous that it started to cause anxiety among candidates for the permanent post. One of them, George Wells, wrote to Sir John Coleridge in March 1865 to complain about the delay in making the permanent appointment, and pointed out that:

71 Hall to Jelf, KA/IC/H52, 9 February 1865.
72 See the terms of the Council's resolution in *King's College London: minutes of the council*, volume I, 10 February 1865, item 411.
73 Hall to Cunningham (College Secretary), KA/IC/H52, 21 February 1865.
74 S. Winchester, *The meaning of everything: the story of the Oxford English dictionary* (Oxford, 2003), 190–4. See also Hall's entry in the *Oxford dictionary of national biography*: 'In 1869 he retired, or was forced to retire, from the India Office ...'
75 Hearnshaw, *Centenary*, p. 250.
76 *King's College London; minutes of the council*, volume I, 14 October 1864, item 358.
77 Ibid., 18 November 1864, item 369.
78 Cutler to Jelf, KA/IC/C57, 28 December 1864.
79 Ibid.

there seems every reason to suppose that Mr John Cutler's temporary engagement will end in his obtaining the permanent appointment simply from his having discharged the duties of acting Professor for so long a time.[80]

The reason for the delay was that Coleridge had not been told that he was jointly responsible for appointing the new professor: Wells' complaint was the first he knew of it.[81] He promptly wrote to the principal, asking that he be taken off the committee, and urging that the appointment be made quickly.[82] A week later the council elected Cutler to the professorship of English law, adding that he had 'discharged the duties of this office with great satisfaction to the Principal since October last'.[83] They also elected him to the vacant professorship of Indian jurisprudence. One can imagine Wells' reaction.

The principal was evidently delighted, writing to Cutler in person to give him the good news. The College bureaucracy was a little slow in catching up, and there is a slightly awkward letter from Cutler to the college secretary that refers to the principal's note, and asks, 'Will you kindly let me know if it is so. My excuse for troubling you must be that I wish to get a notice in the Papers.'[84]

CUTLER'S LECTURES

As it turned out, Cutler's was an appointment that merited a fanfare. He was to hold the professorship of English law for the next fifty years, and wrote books on subjects as diverse as naturalization[85] and passing off.[86] His tenure of the professorship of Indian jurisprudence, though shorter, was to be no less significant: the two Indian lectures that he chose to publish demonstrated excellent teaching skills combined with original thought.

Perhaps the most immediately striking aspect of his lectures was how skilfully he recognized and met his students' needs. His advice on studying English, Roman, Hindu and Mahommedan law was aimed primarily at preventing candidates being confused by the different systems.[87] When he

---

80 Wells to Coleridge, enclosed in letter from Coleridge to Jelf, KA/IC/C57, 23 March 1865.
81 Coleridge to Jelf, ibid.
82 Ibid.
83 *King's College London: minutes of the council*, volume I, 31 March 1865, item 425.
84 Cutler to Cunningham, KA/IC/C57, undated.
85 J. Cutler, *The law of naturalization, as amended by the Naturalization Acts, 1870* (London, 1871).
86 J. Cutler, *On passing off: or Illegal substitution of the goods of one trader for the goods of another trader* (London, 1904).
87 J. Cutler, *On the study of English, Roman, Hindu & Mahommedan legal systems, with especial*

felt that the set text was 'rather chaotic'[88] he recommended, instead, the use of a shorter introductory work, which noted how the law of evidence differed in India from its English counterpart.[89] The style was always clear and accessible.

Cutler's skills as a teacher were best shown by his lecture on reporting cases.[90] This task was given great weight by the civil service commissioners, who required candidates to report a total of forty-one cases during their two years' training; they allocated 500 out of the possible 1,250 marks for law to reports. A wide range of cases were required, ranging from county court decisions to Indian appeals to the privy council.[91]

As Cutler explained to his students, there was good reason for the commissioners to place such emphasis on reporting. First, it ensured that a candidate was familiar with procedure; second, it meant that any candidate would have a sense of how legal principles were applied in practice.[92] But Cutler also suggested a further reason, which the commissioners had not explicitly articulated. Much Indian judicial work required taking down evidence, drafting judgments or making reports,

> all of which may and often will come before Superior Courts, and which, if done correctly and in lawyer-like style, will create a favourable impression of your ability and capacity for legal business; but, if on the contrary such portion of your work is carelessly of clumsily done, your promotion may be seriously retarded.[93]

That would have ensured his audience's full attention.

He then explained the principle of reporting:

> There are two ways of reporting; you may report as a lawyer or as a short-hand writer. A short-hand writer may take down *verbatim* every word that falls from judge, counsel and witnesses, and yet know as little

---

regard to their salient points of agreement and difference: being a lecture delivered at King's College London (London, 1865), 5 at 22.

88 J. Cutler, *On reporting cases for their periodical examinations by selected candidates for the civil service of India: being a lecture delivered on Wednesday, June 12, 1867 at King's College London* (London, 1868), 14. He was referring to J. Taylor, *A treatise on the law of evidence as administered in England and Ireland; with illustrations from the American and other foreign laws* (4th ed. London, 1864).

89 E. Powell, *The new practice of evidence* (2nd ed. London, 1859). Cutler later edited five editions of this work, beginning with the third edition in 1869: *The principles and practice of the law of evidence*, third edition by John Cutler and Edmund Fuller Griffin (London, 1869).

90 Cutler, *Reporting*.

91 For details see Cutler, *Reporting*, 5.

92 Ibid.

93 Ibid., 6.

about the case which he has reported as a man who grinds a barrel-organ does about music. On the other hand, a lawyer in reporting takes down only those things which are material, omitting mere surplusage.[94]

The rest of the lecture contained invaluable advice about how to achieve a lawyer's report, and please the commissioners. Some of his points have a familiar ring – 'a careful observation of small *minutiae* creates a favourable impression on the mind of an examiner'[95] has probably been paraphrased every year since 1867 by a King's law teacher. But perhaps most useful to students were his comments about the short analysis, which the commissioners required at the conclusion of each report. Many candidates, he explained, found this 'a stumbling-block'.[96] A mere resumé was not enough; rather, what was required was an explanation of the legal context and importance of the decision. He made it clear that this was not mere guesswork on his part:

> in this supposition I am confirmed by the circumstance that the students in the Oriental Section at King's College, who have by my advice not confined themselves to a mere *resumé*, have almost invariably obtained the largest number of the marks allotted to notes of cases; in more than one instance, I am happy to say, obtaining the prize.

Cutler's other published lecture also aimed to help his students do well, but it was more intellectually ambitious. *On the study of English, Roman, Hindu & Mahommedan legal systems*[97] seems to have been his first lecture to new students. It was designed to give them a way of approaching the daunting task of studying four very different legal systems at the same time, without getting confused. Cramming, he asserted, was not the answer:

> What is really required is, that a Candidate should so thoroughly understand the leading principles of these four legal systems, as to be competent afterwards upon the foundation thus laid to raise a superstructure of legal knowledge, both by further study and by practical experience, which will enable him to discharge satisfactorily the duties of his future position. The question then is, How is this general knowledge to be best obtained in the time which the Candidate has at his disposal? The answer appears to be: By taking one of the

---

94 Ibid., 7.
95 Ibid., 8.
96 Ibid., 13.
97 *On the study of English, Roman, Hindu & Mahommedan legal systems, with especial regard to their salient points of agreement and difference: being a lecture delivered at King's College London* (London, 1865).

legal systems prescribed for your study as a standard, acquiring a general knowledge of its leading principles, and then observing where the three other systems agree, and where they differ from it.[98]

He then went on to develop this theme using illustrations. For instance, the principles governing the powers of parents over their children differed widely in the four systems.[99] In English law such power could only be exercised over legitimate children. In Roman and Hindu law, by contrast, the power of adoption meant that parental power could be exercised more widely. But, it was also important to remember that the Roman and Hindu methods of adoption were very different, with Hindu law being far more restrictive. A similar analysis of the law of succession revealed that 'English law gives the most unfettered power over property, but the interests of the heirs-at-law are protected under the three other systems'.[1]

He concluded the lecture with a significantly modified method for the students to follow:

> I should strongly advise you in your reading to take the English or Roman law as your standard, and to note up all the points on which the other systems differ from your standard. You will thus avert the otherwise imminent danger of getting confused between the different doctrines.[2]

Cutler's claims for his method were modest – it helped prevent confusion – but that should not distract us from its wider significance. In fact, he was advocating nothing less than an entirely comparative method of legal study in his very first lecture. Such a method went far beyond the requirements of the civil service papers, where no systematically comparative knowledge was expected. But it was not entirely unheard of, particularly to readers of Maine's *Ancient law*.[3]

Although Maine's jurisprudential ideas are notoriously difficult to summarise, one recurrent theme in his work was that no adequate understanding of law could be gained by examining only one system or historical period.[4] Bentham, for instance, had erred in claiming that law's

---

98 Ibid., pp 6–7.
99 Ibid., p. 13.
1 Ibid., p. 20.
2 Ibid., p. 22.
3 H. Maine, *Ancient law: its connection with the early history of society and its relation to modern ideas* (London, 1861). Subsequent page references are to the 1906 edition, with an introduction and notes by Pollock.
4 R. Cocks, *Sir Henry Maine: a study in Victorian jurisprudence* (Cambridge, 1988), pp 1–78 is an invaluable guide to the ideas in *Ancient law*.

definitive characteristic was the command of a sovereign: an examination of different societies and different historical periods showed this to be false. Furthermore, legal concepts could only be understood if one had a sense of their historical development. As Maine put it, in a famous passage:

> The mistake ... is ... analogous to the error of one who, in investigating the laws of the material universe, should commence by contemplating the existing physical world as a whole, instead of beginning with the particles which are its simplest ingredients.[5]

Maine also argued that valuable lessons could be learnt from observing the development of law in Asiatic societies and setting it against similar Western developments.[6]

That Cutler took inspiration from Maine's work is highly plausible. *Ancient Law* became a bestseller,[7] and it was the only book that Cutler's predecessor, James Stephen, had added to those works prescribed by the civil service commissioners. By 1867 Cutler was referring to it, in passing, as if it were a set book.[8]

There is also internal evidence, in the lecture text, that Maine's influence was at work. For instance, the discussion of paternal power and adoption mirrored Maine's extensive treatment of the subject.[9] And Cutler may deliberately have been engaging with Maine's claim that English judges were like the Roman jurists[10] when he stated that the jurists 'held a somewhat analogous position to the pundits in India, but to whom there is nothing similar in England'.[11]

As Cutler was meeting his students for the first time, if is hardly surprising that he did not elaborate in his lecture on the wider benefits of a quadruple comparative approach. He did not want to terrify. But students who followed his method, and read Maine (as they were advised to do) had the means to embark on an exciting intellectual journey. They may also have been influenced in their later work in a less positive way: taking English law as a 'standard' and noting how other systems differed might easily slip from being a mere method of classification into an assumption of superiority. As Pollock later observed, in his notes to *Maine's Ancient Law*, when British judicial officers in India applied rules about "justice" or "equity", the results

---

5 Maine, *Ancient law*, p. 128.
6 See further Cocks, *Maine*, pp 34–5 on Maine's comparative method.
7 Ibid., p. 1.
8 Cutler, *Reporting*, p. 7.
9 Maine, *Ancient law*, pp 140–53.
10 Ibid., pp 37ff.
11 Cutler, *Study*, p. 9.

bore the stamp of the common law.¹² This tendency could be attributed, indirectly, to an approach like Cutler's, although there was little support for it in Maine.¹³

Despite Cutler's efforts, by the mid-1870s the oriental section was in decline. In the academic year 1875–6 no Indian law classes were offered.¹⁴ The section was not abandoned, but by now Cutler's career at the bar was taking off, and in July 1879 he resigned the professorship of Indian jurisprudence, saying that he could no longer 'give the time necessary to do the entire Law work for the Oriental Section when revived'.¹⁵ He thoughtfully suggested a successor: Almaric Rumsey, whom he had sounded out about taking over. 'A more competent man', Cutler assured the college secretary, 'it wd be hard to find in this country & I need only point to his well known books on Hindu and Mohammedan Law as proofs of his ability'.¹⁶

MATHEMATICS AND POETRY: THE LAST TWO PROFESSORS

Rumsey was keen. Three days after Cutler's resignation he wrote to the college secretary to offer his services, volunteering to be 'Acting Professor' pending the decision of the council.¹⁷ He summarised his qualifications as a first in mathematics from Oxford, twenty-two years as a barrister, and the authorship of two books on Indian inheritance law that were recommended by the civil service commissioners. He cannot have received a satisfactory reply, because on 7 August 1879 he wrote again, with reference to the acting professorship, saying 'if I am the man, I should like to begin preparing my first term's lectures as soon as may be'.¹⁸ We can guess the tenor of the college secretary's reply from Rumsey's next letter: 'I am sorry that you think there is a little hope of getting a class'.¹⁹ But an absence of students did not inhibit Rumsey from pushing for the appointment to be confirmed,²¹ and in October 1879 the council elected him professor of Indian jurisprudence 'on [Cutler's] recommendation'.²¹

For the first five years of Rumsey's tenure, the oriental section offered no teaching. That was a shame, because the College had once more succeeded in

12 *Ancient law*, p. 78.
13 See particularly Maine's discussion of the role of lawyers in adapting the law to social conditions: ibid., pp 88–90; Cocks, *Maine*, pp 5, 67–8.
14 *The calendar of King's College London for 1875–76* (London, 1875).
15 Cutler to Cunningham, KA/IC/C90, 11 July 1879.
16 Ibid.
17 Rumsey to Cunningham, KA/IC/R57, 14 July 1879.
18 Ibid., 7 August 1879.
19 Ibid., 11 August 1879.
20 See his letters to Cunningham in ibid., 13 August 1879 and 24 September 1879.
21 *King's College London: minutes of the council*, volume M, 11 October 1879, item 587.

appointing a first-rate scholar. Rumsey's specialism was Islamic inheritance law, a subject to which he was particularly suited. As he explained in his first work in the area, *A Chart of Family Inheritance, according to orthodox Moohumudan law, with an explanatory treatise*,[22] very strict and complex rules governed the disposition of property on death. European attempts to master the subject had been hampered 'by want of method, and still more by the retention of ancient modes of calculation which have long been superseded in European countries by the march of science.'[23] Using his mathematical expertise, Rumsey aimed to set aside the 'complicated machinery' of Arabic calculation, which previous writers had copied slavishly, 'just as the Japanese are said to copy a watch or a steam-engine, without understanding it'.[24] In its place, he solved the problems of inheritance by harnessing 'the power of European arithmetic'.[25]

Rumsey's second work on Islamic inheritance must be one of the most intellectually rigorous and strange law books ever written. It was, apparently, an edition of *Al Sirajiyyah*, an early Arabic treatise, translated by Sir William Jones seventy years earlier, with notes and appendices by Rumsey.[26] But its formal description belied Rumsey's contribution. As his Preface made clear, he was dismayed by the fact that where his *Chart* differed from Macnaghten's *Principles*, the Courts were inclined to follow Macnaghten. This, he pointed out using several examples, was a mistake.[27] It was, in fact, 'impossible to feel a reasonable hope of being able, by [Macnaghten's] aid, to work out any given problem'.[28] The full extent of Rumsey's bitterness came through in the next paragraph:

> If Mr (afterwards Sir W.H.) Macnaghten had lived to this day, he would, no doubt, have rewritten his book long ago. Unfortunately he died early; and his book, in the temporary absence of other treatises, acquired, soon after its publication, that exaggerated fame which an unintelligible disquisition on an obscure subject can sometimes command.[29]

The book was, in essence, Rumsey's proof that he was right. This was partly accomplished by footnotes, but its main expression was thirty pages of

22 (London, 1866).
23 A. Rumsey, *A chart of family inheritance, according to orthodox Moohumudan law, with an explanatory treatise* (London, 1866), p. 2.
24 Ibid., p. 3 in footnote.
25 Ibid., 3.
26 *Al Sirajiyyah: or the Mohammedan law of inheritance*. With notes and appendix by Almaric Rumsey (London, 1869).
27 Ibid., pp ix–xii.
28 Ibid., pp xii–xiii.
29 Ibid., p. xiii. Cf. Rumsey, *Chart*, 3–4: 'we have derived much assistance from the valuable labours of Mr Macnaghten.'

mathematical appendices, where a reader could find demonstrated, beyond any mathematical doubt, how an estate would be divided in a bewildering number of hypothetical situations.

From 1884 onwards Rumsey may have been able to share some of his erudition with his classes, for the oriental section was offering courses once more.[30] Its new Dean[31] was Leitner, previously professor of Arabic and Mohammedan law at King's, who had returned to England after fifteen years in India in order to found an oriental institute.

For the next five years the oriental section continued to offer its courses (including Indian law), but in 1889 the college calendar announced the foundation of a school for modern oriental studies, established by 'the Imperial Institute of the United Kingdom, the Colonies and India, In Union with University College and King's College, London'.[32] The school's promotional literature mentioned languages, history, literature, etc, but there was no law.[33] Furthermore, all of the Indian subjects were to be taught at University College.[34] The oriental section at King's, and its associated legal education, were gone. Rumsey never taught again.

The disappearance of the oriental section marked the end of an era; but it was not the end of legal education at King's. Cutler's evening class had proved a great success, and had led to daytime classes too. There was, therefore, still scope for a contribution by a professor of Indian jurisprudence, and in 1899 the Council elected Alec McMillan as Rumsey's successor.

McMillan had little in common with his predecessor. Whilst Rumsey had devoted himself to working through the recondite problems of Islamic inheritance, McMillan's Indian connection was a career as a judge in the Bengal civil service. And where Rumsey favoured mathematics, McMillan preferred verse. This is how he described judicial business:

> All day I swelter in my chair,
> Administ'ring the law's redress,
> Bewildered, dazed, provoked to swear
> By perjured 'clouds of witnesses'.
> Lord! how they lie, unmoved by fear
> Of all their million ugly gods;
> I make out scarcely half I hear
> But then it's lies, so what's the odds?[35]

---

30 *The calendar of King's College London for 1884–1885* (London, 1884), p. 179.
31 Ibid.
32 *The calendar of King's College London for 1889–1890* (London, 1889), p. 143.
33 Ibid., p. 145.
34 Ibid., p. 147.
35 A. McMillan, 'Address to the wallahs of 1869' in *Divers ditties* (London, 1895), p. 18.

To judge by his book of poetry, he was obsessed by perjury in Indian courts.[36] He even suggested that it would be more appropriate to decide Indian cases by rolling dice, since 'as is well known to all persons who have had any experience of Courts, the decision of cases by a laborious consideration of evidence is an empty and delusive mockery'.[37] He also seems to have had a jaded view of new recruits to the Indian civil service, describing them, mockingly, as being 'Of schools, of cramming dens the choice'.[38] In another poem there is a wistful reference to 'Haileybury's hall of fame'.[39] We can only imagine how he felt about teaching the finer points of Indian civil procedure to students who had proved themselves in the competitive exam.

CONCLUSION

McMillan was the last professor of Indian jurisprudence at King's, offering the final classes in Indian law in 1901–2.[40] He brought to an end a succession of very different, but highly distinguished scholars. Individually their publications illustrated a remarkable sweep of interest in, and responses to, law and India in the second half of the nineteenth century. But perhaps their greatest significance was collective: they represented an important, successful, yet overlooked facet of nineteenth century legal education, in which theory and comparative insights were paramount. Of course, theoretical aspirations in London were nothing new – Austin's lectures at University College thirty years earlier had epitomised the theoretical approach[41] – but the practical requirements of the Indian civil service examination created the conditions in which such teaching could flourish as never before. In an era when legal education elsewhere was still struggling to find its feet, the oriental section at King's was offering an ambitious and challenging curriculum that was well ahead of its time.

---

36 See, for instances, 'Anundorum borooah' (p. 4 at 5), 'Address to the Wallahs of 1869' (p. 15 at 18), 'The Model Alibi' (p. 25), 'The *Alibi* of the East' (p. 128), 'Justice à la Bridoye for India' (p. 131).
37 Ibid., p. 132.
38 Ibid., p. 15 (the opening line of 'Address to the Wallahs of 1869').
39 Ibid., p. 4 ('Anundorum Borooah').
40 *Calendar of King's College London for 1901–1902* (London, 1901), p. 113. There is no mention of Indian law in the *Calendar* for 1902–3.
41 H. Hale Bellott, *University College London 1826–1926* (London, 1929), pp 96–102.

Dragging the law into disrepute[1]

RUTH PALEY

THE ARREST OF ERNEST BOULTON AND FREDERICK PARK

LATE ON THE EVENING OF 28 APRIL 1870 police arrested 22-year-old Ernest Boulton and 23-year-old Frederick Park as they were leaving the Strand Theatre with their companion, a recent acquaintance named Hugh Alexander Mundell. Boulton and Park appeared in the dock of Bow Street magistrates' court the next morning, still dressed for the theatre. Ernest Boulton was wearing a cherry coloured silk evening dress, trimmed with lace. There were bracelets on his arms and he wore a wig and a plaited chignon. Frederick Park's dress was low-necked, made of dark green satin and trimmed with black lace. His accessories included a lace shawl and white kid gloves.

Boulton and Park's alleged crimes and the publicity generated by attempts to prosecute them reveal a great deal about Victorian attitudes to and assumptions about manliness and male sexuality. For the modern gay community Boulton and Park's brief moment of fame represents a strand of historical continuity that is vital to the construction of a social identity. To one gender historian the ultimate failure of the prosecution and the self-censorship of press reports of their trial represents the state's inability to cope with 'a fundamental challenge to the hegemonic power of middle- and upper-class men'.[2] That the trial revealed deep concerns about what was perceived to be the increasing decadence of Victorian society is undeniable. Newspaper reports depicted homosexual behaviour as alien to contemporary mores. Homosexual behaviour was almost to be expected from foreigners and members of the inferior races and it was just possible that such people might be joined by a few Englishmen drawn from the dregs of the labouring classes: 'the lowest, the most ignorant, and the most degraded' but it was most emphatically not to be associated with the upright, manly English middle classes and their imperial mission. Commentators came perilously close to declaring that the British Empire was not won by men in frocks.[3]

---

1   I am indebted to Paul Mitchell and Elaine Reynolds for comments on an earlier version of this paper.
2   Charles Upchurch, 'Forgetting the unthinkable: cross-dressers and British society in the case of the queen vs Boulton and others' in *Gender and History*, 12:1 (April 2000), 130.
3   *The Times*, 31 May 1870.

Boulton and Park's 'guilt' stemmed as much from a perception of their middle class social origins as from the contents of their wardrobes. Park's family were well known in upper middle-class circles. His grandfather was the judge, Sir James Alan Park, whilst his father, Alexander Atherton Park, was senior master in the court of common pleas.[4] Census records confirm a comfortable upper middle class lifestyle serviced by large numbers of servants.[5] The Park family represented what to contemporary commentators was both the best and the worst of their society. Frederick Park's eldest brother, Lieutenant Atherton Allen Park, had been killed in 1858 defending the empire during the Indian Mutiny.[6] Another brother, Edward Henry Park, had fled London in 1862 rather than face a charge of indecently assaulting a police officer.[7] Newspaper reports implied that Ernest Boulton came from a similar upper middle-class background but in reality his social origins were rather more humble than he cared to admit. His claim that his father was a stockbroker does not stand up to scrutiny. Thomas Boulton was certainly listed on the 1871 census as a gentleman, but his household was a very modest one, lacking even a single live in servant.[8] A decade earlier he had been trading as a wine merchant in Greenwich but even then the household had been a relatively humble one, consisting of himself, his wife, two sons and a teenage female servant.[9] Ernest Boulton's own employment history included a spell as a bank clerk: a respectable but relatively lowly occupation.

The story of Boulton and Park, veering as it does so quickly from tragedy to farce and back again, is a fascinating tale in its own right. Yet for legal historians its real significance lies not in the social context of the case but in the immense detail with which it was reported. Here, somewhat unusually, we can trace the workings of the Victorian criminal justice system from arrest to acquittal, through a combination of newspaper accounts and court records. Unusually those court records also include a complete transcript of the trial. Through the lens of *R. v Boulton and others* we can study the role of committing magistrates, discover the extensive rather than nominal control that the Home Secretary exercised over the newly appointed Commissioner of the Metropolitan Police (Sir Edmund Henderson) and, perhaps most important of all, uncover public concerns about the process of criminal investigation that had resulted in what *The Times* called 'popular impatience with the increasing impotence of our means of detecting crime.'[10]

4 Law List, 1865; Boase, *Modern English biography*.
5 The 1861 census listed five members of the family and nine servants, TNA, RG 9/72/66/3. By 1871 the household consisted of three members of the family and six servants, RG 10/1312/58/5.
6 *The Times*, 6 May 1858.
7 *The Times*, 2 Apr. 1862, 26 July 1870.
8 TNA, RG 10/18/43/77.
9 TNA, RG 9/399/50/6.
10 *The Times*, 17 Jan. 1873.

BUILDING THE CASE FOR THE PROSECUTION

Boulton and Park had been observed attending restaurants, theatres, and other public places of entertainment dressed as women on several occasions over a period of some four years. They were so successful as female impersonators – or as they termed it (in a word that was apparently new to mainstream English) going about in drag – that many people believed them to be women. Their determination to transcend standard gender stereotypes meant that even when dressed as men they wore make up and behaved so effeminately that onlookers were convinced that they were women dressed as men. Whether dressed as men or as women, they revelled in outraging convention. Boulton and Park dressed like fine ladies: the police superintendent who was responsible for their arrest told the committing magistrate that on the night of his detention Boulton had been pointed out to him as the duchess of Manchester. But their behaviour mimicked that of London streetwalkers looking for clients: on their visits to London they walked the streets by day as well as by night, smiling invitingly at men and making lascivious noises at them, they frequented public houses and when in the theatre they rather than the actors on stage became the centre of attention. Their behaviour was so outrageous that they had been 'marched out' of the Alhambra Theatre on several occasions and had been the subject of several complaints to the police.

Although some people seem to have been genuinely confused about their gender, there is little doubt that Boulton and Park were arrested as men rather than as women. The arresting officer, Detective Sergeant Kerley, reported that he had told them that he had reason to believe them to be men dressed as women and, in the course of their journey to Bow Street police station, Boulton and Park both admitted that they were men.[11] In the absence of the relevant police correspondence it is not clear what prompted the arrests. In dealing with prostitution at this time it was common police practice to ignore the activities of streetwalkers unless they constituted a threat to public order. Just six months before Boulton and Park's arrest public dismay at a brief campaign against prostitutes in the West End involving the use of indiscriminate arrests and orders to move on had resulted in a police order emphasizing that prostitutes could not be arrested simply because they were prostitutes.[12] Rather bizarrely therefore, Boulton and Park's behaviour was, if not exactly acceptable, at least within the bounds of toleration – but only so long as they were thought to be women.

---

11 TNA, KB 6/3, Frederick Kerley, 30 Apr. 1870.
12 Stefan Petrow, *Policing morals: the Metropolitan Police and the Home Office, 1870–1914* (Oxford, 1994), p. 130.

Prosecution papers in the Boulton and Park case reveal that in the weeks immediately before their arrest the police had invested a considerable amount of time and effort in collecting information about the two men and their circle. On the night of the arrest, Detective Officer Chamberlain had followed them to the theatre and observed their behaviour there. He had been aware of them dressing as women and 'talking to gentlemen' for over a year 'and suspecting them I have watched them'. He had started to watch the lodging house that they used when in London some nine months earlier, though not it would seem in a concerted or targeted manner.[13] Constable Walker had been watching their activities for a fortnight prior to their arrest during which he had seen them repeatedly dressed as women as late as 3 a.m. and 'at all hours of the night'.[14] Last and not least the divisional superintendent, James Thompson, was in attendance at the Strand theatre to watch Boulton and Park arrive and to see that his men were in place.[15] Boulton and Park had attended the theatre with two male companions; one of them ran off when the police moved in, the other (Hugh Alexander Mundell) decided to accompany them to the police station, apparently in hopes that he might be able to secure them bail.[16]

It is possible that even at this stage the police thought they were dealing with something rather more serious than mere nuisance or an offence against public decency but it is on the whole unlikely. Certainly at the moment of arrest there was no indication of an intention to charge them with felony – that is of actual anal intercourse. The police may already have suspected that Boulton and Park were behaving in a manner designed to entice other men into homosexual acts but at the time of their arrest Boulton and Park were told only that the charge was one of going about in women's clothes.[17] A later statement by defence counsel indicates that the original intention had been to charge them with a 'common' offence under the Vagrancy Act.[18] Defence counsel protested early in May that 'he had sought in vain' to discover details of the offences alleged.[19] The precise nature of the charges to be brought against them was not settled until their eighth and final appearance in the dock at Bow Street magistrates' court on 30 May.[20]

The morning after the arrest Detective Officer Chamberlain together with Inspector Shenton visited Boulton and Park's lodgings in Wakefield Street.

13 TNA, KB 6/3, William Chamberlain, 30 Apr. 1870; further statement of William Chamberlain, 30 Apr. 1870.
14 TNA, KB 6/3, Charles Walker, 30 Apr. 1870.
15 TNA, KB 6/3, James Jacob Thompson, 30 Apr. 1870.
16 He was to be disappointed: Boulton and Park were remanded to gaol where they remained until bailed by the Lord Chief Justice in July. *The Times*, 7 July 1870.
17 *The Times*, 11 May 1871.
18 *The Times*, 21 May 1870.
19 *The Times*, 7 May 1870.
20 *The Times*, 31 May 1870.

These, it transpired, were not lodgings where they lived but rooms that they took from time to time on visits to London in order to store their drag outfits. The police had no warrant and Martha Stacey (who managed the lodging house on behalf of her mother) was too confused to demand that they produce one. When her mother remonstrated with them, Chamberlain insisted that he had a right to search the premises and continued to do so. In the course of his search he discovered and removed a number of items that appeared to substantiate suspicions of homosexual activity. Boulton and Park possessed an extensive (and expensive) female wardrobe, they had photographs of themselves dressed in female clothing, and they also had a collection of letters. Some of these letters were dull and prosaic: Messrs Kennington and Jenner of Edinburgh for example demanded payment of their bill and feigned surprise that no remittance had yet been received. Others were personal and extremely affectionate. Many of them were written by men: John Fiske for example addressed Boulton as 'My darling Ernie' and wrote, 'Believe me darling a word of remembrance from you can never come amiss'. Some of the letters referred to Boulton and Park as Stella and Fanny. If the police had not been suspicious before they certainly were now. They concluded that Boulton and Park's behaviour was designed to entice other men into homosexual acts. On 30 April, *The Times* in its first report of the case indicated that they were going to be charged with frequenting the Strand Theatre with intent to commit felony.[21] The two men were remanded to gaol.

Boulton and Park's letters brought more men under suspicion of homosexual acts. All but one were members of otherwise respectable middle class families. The one exception was the former naval officer and MP for Newark, Lord Arthur Pelham Clinton, whose father the 5th duke of Newcastle had been Colonial Secretary under Palmerston. Boulton, it seems, frequently referred to himself as Lady Stella Clinton and as Lord Arthur's wife. If the Home Office had not been involved before, the realization that Boulton and Park were part of an extensive cross dressing community and that Boulton might be involved sexually with an aristocrat whose social connections included senior members of the royal family was more than enough to prompt the intervention of the Home Secretary. Within days the Home Office had directed the Treasury Solicitor to take charge of the prosecution. The Home Office note authorizing this betrays more than a little urgency: 'Do this at once I forgot it yesterday.'[22] Taking charge of the prosecution involved interviewing witnesses before their appearance in the magistrate's court in a way that we would now expect to be the responsibility of the police. The letters at Boulton and Park's lodgings led to the discovery

21 *The Times*, 30 Apr. 1870.
22 TNA, HO 12/192/91575, 5 May 1870.

of further letters and photographs through an equally unauthorized search of premises in Edinburgh. Others were handed to the police by Clinton's former landlady. Whether she had any right to do so is unclear but both her actions and her testimony were motivated by a grudge against Clinton whose recent bankruptcy had left her with no redress for his unpaid rent.

The publicity afforded to the case brought further witnesses to the fore. They included the superintendent of the Alhambra music hall and the former beadle of Burlington Arcade, both of whom were able to contribute new stories of Boulton and Park's exploits on the streets and in the theatres of London. Tales of Burlington Arcade were perhaps a little double edged for although the beadle insisted that Boulton and Park behaved like female prostitutes eyeing up potential clients, he also revealed one essential difference between them. The real prostitutes were working class women who knew their place. They treated the beadle with respect and paid him to turn a blind eye to their activities; Boulton and Park not only treated him contemptuously as a social inferior, they also refused to offer the customary bribe.

Perhaps more usefully from the prosecution point of view, Francis Kegan Cox also came forward to describe his meeting with Ernest Boulton. He had been introduced to Boulton (whom he regarded as 'a fascinating woman') by Clinton. He and Boulton flirted together, they made Clinton jealous and Cox 'kissed him, she or it'. When Cox realized his error he was furious and made a public scene. Another equally useful witness was Richard Barwell, senior surgeon at Charing Cross Hospital. On 14 May he attended Bow Street and identified Park as a former outpatient – a patient who had been treated for an anal sore, which Barwell had diagnosed as a symptom of primary syphilis. Here for the first time was positive evidence of an illegal sexual act. On 19 May the police divisional surgeon, James Paul, dramatically confirmed Barwell's opinion. Paul had been summoned by the police to examine Boulton and Park after their arrest. Beyond confirming their sex he had not disclosed his conclusions to anyone. He had not even made notes about the examination. Now however he told the Treasury Solicitor that he had (of his own volition) conducted an intimate examination of their anuses. According to Paul it had taken no more than a brief examination of their genitalia to convince him that he was dealing with a pair of homosexuals. Boulton's penis was of 'an inordinate length' as was Park's and this was clear evidence, at least as far as Paul was concerned, of a propensity for anal intercourse. The anal examination simply confirmed his diagnosis. He concluded that Boulton's anus was abnormally dilated 'the muscles surrounding the Anus easily opened and I could see right into the Rectum and the appearance I saw could be accounted for by the insertion of a foreign body … numerous times'. He came to a similar conclusion about Park and declared that 'The insertion of a man's person would cause the appearances I have described.'

PREPARING FOR TRIAL

By the end of May 1870 almost all the evidence that could be mustered against Boulton and Park was in place, as was the case for the defence. Let us review the state of the case. The evidence consisted of:

1. A statement by Barwell that he had treated a man whom he believed to be Park for syphilis caused by anal intercourse. Barwell, who treated between 150 and 240 outpatients a week, had no medical records to support his claim and relied on his memory to identify Park as the patient concerned. Barwell's clinic treated the labouring poor; he had noticed nothing about the patient he identified as Park to suggest that the man was of higher social status than the usual run of patients. Barwell had no relevant training or expertise in identifying symptoms of anal intercourse.

2. A statement by Dr Paul, whose examination took no more than 3 minutes and was carried out in a poorly lighted room and whose conclusions were not reported to anyone for nearly three weeks. Like Barwell Paul had no relevant training or expertise in the diagnosis of anal intercourse; he did however read a book on the subject the day *after* he reported his findings to the Treasury Solicitor. At a time when even searching an accused person without 'strong necessity' was held by the courts to be illegal it is clear that Dr Paul's examination of Boulton and Park was unlawful.[23]

3. A collection of dresses and jewellery which Boulton and Park claimed was for use in their appearances in private theatricals.

4. Letters in which men used extravagantly affectionate language to other men. It should be noted that the language of the letters was emotional rather than erotic. Extravagantly affectionate language may not fit our stereotypical picture of the emotionally constipated Victorian middle classes, but it clearly was part of the common coin of life for some Victorians, perhaps particularly for those whose interests focussed on the theatre. Same gender intimacies have clearly varied over time and probably also between different sub-groups within the same larger community. This makes it particularly difficult to interpret the social or sexual significance of flowery or emotional prose written by men to men without a far wider knowledge of the social conventions of the day.[24] Boulton was certainly no stranger to the everyday

---

[23] Samuel Stone, *The justices' manual, or guide to the ordinary duties of a justice of the peace* (11th edn, 1865), p. 120.

[24] One might usefully compare the difficulties of interpreting the correspondence in this case to the controversial 'outing' by C.A. Tripp of Abraham Lincoln. Tripp's arguments are based partly on evidence of bed sharing and partly on the affectionate content of his letters to other men. C.A. Tripp, *The intimate world of Abraham Lincoln* (New York, 2005); Doris Kearns Goodwin, *Team of rivals: the political genus of Abraham Lincoln* (New York, 2005).

use of extravagant language. One of the letters opened with the words 'My darling, I am so longing to see you dearest'. This was a letter written to Ernest Boulton by his mother. The police acquired some 2,000 letters in the course of their investigation. Only a few were produced in court. Among those *not* produced in court were several which showed that Clinton was contemplating marriage; understandably these were not used to prove that he was heterosexual.

5. A number of photographs in which Boulton and Park appeared dressed as women. Copies do not survive amongst the prosecution papers but such information as we have (including photographs that survive elsewhere) indicates that although these were described as indecent they were simply standard studio portraits that were produced and sold as souvenirs of Boulton and Park's theatrical performances.

6. Evidence that Boulton expected to get money from Clinton who, although unmarried, had purchased visiting cards for Lady Arthur Clinton, that Boulton and others had referred to Clinton as Boulton's husband and contradictory evidence that the two men had on occasion shared a bed.

7. Evidence that Boulton and Park had, on occasion, shared a bed.

8. Testimony from Cox that he had kissed Boulton in the belief that he was a woman.

9. Testimony from Mundell that he had met Boulton and Park whilst they were dressed as women, that they told him they were men but that he did not believe them. Convinced that Park was a woman, he tried to put his arm round 'her' and had his advances rebuffed.

10. And finally, of course, evidence that Boulton and Park had appeared in public on a number of occasions dressed as women, that they 'chirruped' and glanced at men after the fashion of prostitutes, and that on other occasions when dressed as men they had assumed 'an air of studied effeminacy'.

From a twenty-first century vantage point we might certainly suspect that Boulton and Park were members of a homosexual circle but we would also recognize that cross dressing is a heterosexual as well as a homosexual activity and that our limited information about Boulton and Park means that we cannot know whether these men were transvestites, transsexuals or actors showing off their skills. To the Victorian authorities – that is, to the Metropolitan Police, the Home Office and the Treasury Solicitor – matters were very much simpler. To them it was patently obvious that the only possible explanation for Boulton and Park's conduct was that they were homosexuals who deliberately set out to entrap other young men into homosexual activities in order to blackmail them. The problem was that both the official mind and the law suffered from a very limited sexual imagination.

Sodomy and buggery had been removed from the list of capital offences just nine years earlier but were still serious crimes punishable by imprisonment for between ten years and life. To prove such offences to the satisfaction of a court of law required proof of actual penetration – evidence that by definition was unlikely to be available in cases of consensual sex.[25] As in all criminal indictments it would also be necessary to make a specific charge as to time and place. A lesser offence of indecent assault had evolved under common law but until the passage of the Criminal Law Amendment Act in 1885 – fifteen years in the future – it would be difficult to argue that consensual sex falling short of penetration was illegal, especially if practiced in private.

Given this kind of legal background, it comes as no surprise to learn the opinion of learned counsel. On 28 May 1870 prosecution counsel (Harry Bodkin Poland QC) told the Home Office that 'there are *many* difficulties in the way of this prosecution, and that it is doubtful whether a conviction against either Boulton or Park will be obtained ...'. The correspondence suggests that by now the role of the Metropolitan Police was a peripheral one and that the investigation was being controlled by the Treasury Solicitor under the direction of the Home Office. Further enquiries were instigated. The various letters that had been seized did suggest that Boulton and Park's activities extended to Edinburgh. The case against them would be strengthened if were possible to use a conviction in Scotland to corroborate the prosecution case in London but the Lord Advocate clearly thought the evidence to be as shaky under Scots law as it was under English law and declined to intervene.[26]

The difficulties anticipated by Poland were rehearsed by defence counsel during the final examination of their clients at Bow Street magistrates' court on 30 May. They insisted that there was no evidence to sustain any charge beyond a misdemeanour, if indeed there was enough evidence even on that accusation. Any more serious charge, they argued, was based 'upon the merest conjecture' and no more than 'vague and irregular surmises'. Despite all this at the end of May the presiding Bow Street magistrate charged Boulton and Park with buggery, conspiracy to commit buggery, outraging public decency and corrupting public morals. The two men, who had already been in custody for a month, were again refused bail even though the statutory framework declared that accused persons could be remanded in custody for examination for a maximum of only eight days.[27] By the time they faced the grand jury on 6 June the charges had been extended to include Clinton and other members of the cross-dressing community. The charges

25 John Jervis, *Archbold's Pleading and Evidence* (17th edn, 1871), 716–17.
26 TNA, HO 12/192/91575, 23 May 1870.
27 TNA, KB 6/3, 30 May 1870; *The Times*, 31 May 1870; 11&12 Vict. c. 42.

at this stage still included felony. The remaining charges were now framed into two indictments for misdemeanour. The first and more serious set of charges alleged that since 1 January 1868 Boulton, Park, Clinton and five other named individuals had conspired to commit buggery, to solicit others unknown to commit buggery, to commit buggery together, to have a venereal affair together and carnally to know each other and commit buggery. The second indictment alleged that since 1 January 1867 they had either together or separately conspired and confederated with others unknown 'to disguise themselves as women and being so disguised to frequent and be present at divers places of public resort to wit streets, highways, theatres, music halls, licensed public houses etc. thereby to inveigle induce and incite divers of the male subjects of her majesty improperly lewdly and indecently to fondle and toy with them as women and openly and scandalously to outrage public decency and offend public morals'.[28]

Before the case came to trial Clinton had died. His doctor certified that the cause of death was scarlet fever but his solicitor made it clear that 'the awful nature' of the charges 'in no slight degree accelerated his end'. Further public sympathy was elicited by what was in effect a deathbed letter in which Clinton insisted that he was guilty of no more than 'a foolish continuance of the impersonation of theatrical characters, which arose from a simple frolic in which I allowed myself to become an actor'.[29] In describing Boulton and Park's behaviour as a mere frolic, Clinton was following the line already set by the defence in the magistrates' court. It was a line that was to remain central to the defence case. Clinton himself already had a well established reputation for imprudence. Just over a year before Boulton and Park were arrested, he had declared himself bankrupt. He attributed his debts to 'insufficiency of income' rather than extravagance but evidence about his lifestyle, including his habit of giving lavish presents to his friends, fellow officers and even to his solicitor, together with his resort to money lending 'rogues' suggested otherwise.[30]

The indictments were scheduled for trial at the Central Criminal Court (Old Bailey) but Boulton successfully applied for a writ of *certiorari* to remove them to the Queen's Bench. In so doing he ensured that evidence would be heard by a special jury – that is, one in which the jurymen were likely to be of substantially higher social status than was commonly the case. Removing an indictment by *certiorari* was, by 1870, an unusual proceeding and suggested that there was a vigorous legal battle to be fought. On 6 July 1870 the prosecution, recognizing that they were unlikely to be able to prove actual buggery in sufficiently specific detail to sustain a conviction, agreed to

---

28 TNA, KB 12/99, Trin. 33 Vict., 4, 5.
29 *The Times*, 20 June 1870.
30 *The Times*, 10 Nov. and 31 Dec. 1869.

drop the charge of felony and to allow Boulton and Park, who had been in custody since their arrest on 28 April to be released from Newgate on bail. The amount of bail was very high (£1,000 plus two sureties of £250 for Boulton and £1,000 plus two sureties of £500 for Park) and, unusually, had been set by the Attorney General rather than by the judges.[31]

THE TRIAL OF BOULTON AND PARK

The trial on the first and more serious conspiracy charge opened in May 1871. Despite the delay the prosecution was in no better shape than when the charges were originally brought. It soon became clear that the prosecution strategy was to compensate for the lack of evidence by confusing the jury. The indictment had been carefully drawn to include charges that covered both private and public behaviour. Although the counts were quite distinct the jury were effectively being invited to use a combination of medical evidence and details of public conduct in order to draw conclusions about the private relationships of the defendants. The central plank of the prosecution case was the medical evidence to the effect that Boulton and Park had taken part in acts of anal intercourse. Unable to prove any specific act of buggery the prosecution hoped that proving a general history of acts of buggery would persuade the jury to draw inferences about Boulton and Park's sexual activities that could not otherwise be substantiated. Unfortunately as indicated above the medical evidence was all too easily impugned, especially when Dr Paul had to admit that during his supposedly careful (if speedy) anal examination of Boulton he had failed to notice a scar from a previous operation for fistula. The jury's attitude to Paul's evidence can scarcely have been helped when Cockburn CJ lambasted him for conducting an unauthorized intimate examination: 'You should be more careful in future or you may find yourself involved in very unpleasant consequences, because I am not aware that the mere fact of your being surgeon to the police force entitles you to send a man behind a screen and examine him for any purpose you may think necessary.'[32] The prosecution had additional medical witnesses at its service – but so had the defence. In the course of the trial it was readily admitted that not one of the medical witnesses had any real expertise in the subject and the defence undoubtedly came off best, partly because it was able to show that throughout the period of conspiracy specified in the indictment, Boulton had been suffering from a painful fistula, thus making his participation in anal intercourse decidedly unlikely. Even the attorney general was forced to admit that allegations that Boulton and Park had a long history of illegal sexual intercourse could not be sustained.

31 *The Times*, 6 and 11 July 1870.
32 TNA, DPP 4/6.

In the course of the trial the defence easily established Boulton and Park's interest and participation in private theatricals. They established that their female costumes were originally bought as theatrical costumes and that Boulton in particular was regarded as a talented performer. Boulton had given up his job as a bank clerk to become an actor: his subsequent career (see below) confirms that for him acting was not a pastime but a vocation.[33] Had Clinton still been alive there would have been still more evidence about the theatrical ambitions of this little group. Amateur dramatics had brought Boulton and Clinton together. Clinton had organized a number of successful music hall evenings in West End theatres for charity and after his bankruptcy had thoughts of repairing his finances by becoming an impresario.[34]

The defence rested on the claim that Boulton and Park wandered the streets in female clothes for 'a lark' and that the use of female names and references to a male 'husband' were simply a private joke stemming from the fact that Boulton had played opposite Clinton as his wife in one of their productions. 'What was there' demanded defence counsel 'beyond these dresses and photographs? Nothing but a few ambiguous passages in boyish and foolish letters.' The prosecution rested on the claim that Boulton and Park behaved in a way calculated to 'excite each others passions and to make themselves objects of desire to persons of their own class' and that cross dressing was more than a frolic: it was 'in a great degree the occupation and business of their lives'.[35] Even the choice of words suggests that Boulton and Park's guilt was as much to do with their social standing as with their actual sexuality. The prosecution was however unable to produce any evidence that either had ever been guilty of inciting a sexual act. Francis Kegan Cox had died before the trial, but even his pre-trial statement amounted to no more than that he had made advances to and had kissed Boulton rather than that Boulton had attempted to kiss him. Alexander Mundell the only prosecution witness who could have testified to having been incited to an 'immoral' act testified unambiguously to the propriety of Boulton and Park's behaviour towards him. The attorney general tried to rescue his case by suggesting that their arrest had protected Mundell from Boulton and Park's advances but a case that so clearly rested on what might have been was scarcely impressive. Cockburn CJ had no doubt that the public behaviour of Boulton and Park amounted to an outrage on public decency and that such behaviour 'is not to be tolerated even when done for a mere frolic and amusement' but he warned the jury against allowing natural indignation to 'warp your judgments' because the question at issue was not whether they had outraged public decency – which was covered by a separate indictment – but whether the

---

33 *The Times*, 12 May 1871.
34 *The Times*, 10 Nov. 1869.
35 *The Times*, 15 May 1871; TNA, DPP 4/6.

defendants had acted with 'the intention and design imputed to them.' Cockburn left the jury in little doubt that the prosecution had struggled to prove its case.

As to the private relationship between the parties, the evidence was suggestive but scarcely conclusive. One defendant, Clinton, was already dead and could not defend himself. Testimony as to whether any of these men had shared a bed was contradictory – and, at a time when bed sharing was not uncommon, did not elucidate what if anything they had done in bed together other than sleep. Of the other five additional individuals named in the indictment, three could not be found and two, John Fiske and Louis Hurt, were resident in Scotland. There was hardly any evidence against any of the five and it rapidly became apparent that the only reason that they had been named as defendants was to allow the introduction of additional evidence to corroborate the extent of cross dressing activities. Cockburn was particularly scathing about the inclusion of Fiske and Hurt in the indictment. It was he said 'a part of the case that I approach with considerable pain'. Cockburn was in no doubt that they had been included as part of a prosecution attempt to conflate evidence that would otherwise have been outside the jurisdiction of the court. 'Mr Fiske and Mr Hurt ought never to have been put on their trial in this country at all ... gross injustice is done to them, as they are mixed up with things with which they had nothing at all to do, but which are calculated to excite great prejudice ... If there was a conspiracy in Scotland, if there was immorality in Scotland, it is in Scotland that they should have been tried.' The only evidence against them came from the letters and as Cockburn pointed out the indictment was not for incitement to immorality but for conspiracy to incite immorality 'and to make out conspiracy there must be a concurrence of both minds ...'. Even if the jury believed the contents of the letters represented more than 'personal admiration and affection' the charge of conspiracy required evidence that they were received and responded to.

Given the very clear direction given by Cockburn in his summing up, it is perhaps surprising that it took the jury an hour to reach a verdict. Counsel for both sides had certainly appealed to popular prejudices, the one silently benefiting from Boulton and Park's effeminacy and evidence that Boulton possessed a fine soprano (or as we would now say counter-tenor) singing voice, the other by ensuring that their clients countered allegations of effeminacy by appearing in court sporting that most masculine of accoutrements – facial hair. On 15 May 1871 Boulton and Park were acquitted to a burst of applause.[36] In the wake of the verdict the police were uncertain as to how to deal with the unexecuted warrants against the remaining defendants. What, asked Metropolitan Police Commissioner Henderson, should they do?

36 *The Times*, 16 May 1871.

Home Office officials, dissatisfied with the verdict, decided that there should be no official response to his query but declared that Henderson should be told confidentially not to execute them. This they hoped would ensure that the defendants remained '*in terrorem* & keep out of the way for a bit.'[37]

Quite what happened in respect of the second indictment (outraging public decency) is unclear. According to *The Times* it was scheduled for trial at the next sitting.[38] The Home Office file indicates that Cockburn CJ and the attorney general settled an order of court between them requiring Boulton and Park to enter a plea of guilty and to enter into recognizances of £500 each to be of good behaviour for two years and to appear in the Queen's Bench on the first day of Michaelmas term to receive sentence, but no such order has yet been traced amongst the Queen's Bench records[39] and it seems likely that the indictment was quietly forgotten, in the hope that Boulton and Park would disappear back into obscurity. In reality, just like any modern pseudo celebrity Boulton exploited his notoriety by going on tour. Reviews of his performances were highly favourable and remarked on his 'genuine histrionic talent'. He then crossed the Atlantic and performed on the New York stage under the name of Ernest Byne, accompanied by his brother Gerard. Suspicions that Gerard Byne was an alias for Frederick Park are dispelled by the 1861 census entry for the Boulton family, which reveals that Ernest Boulton did indeed have a younger brother called Gerard.[40] Our last glimpse of Ernest Boulton/Byne is in the 1881 census when he was again living in London and gave his occupation as 'actor'.[41]

BOULTON AND PARK IN CONTEXT

Boulton and Park were by no means the only cross dressers in nineteenth century London. Newspaper reports make it clear that cross dressing, though not exactly commonplace, was by no means unusual. Reactions were often ambivalent. Cross dressing was not of itself illegal and the well known story of the early eighteenth century Londoner John Cooper and his *alter ego* the Princess Seraphina suggests that it was once tolerated with ease.[42] By the early nineteenth century many middle and upper class men clearly regarded

---

37 TNA, HO 12/192/91575, 17 May 1871.
38 *The Times*, 16 May 1871.
39 TNA, KB 21/77.
40 Laurence Senelick, 'Boys and girls together: subcultural origins of glamour drag and male impersonation' in Lesley Ferris (ed.), *Crossing the stage: controversies on cross dressing* (London, 1993), pp 87–8; John Charles Franceschina, *David Braham, the American Offenbach* (London, 2003), p. 84; TNA, RG 9/399/50/6.
41 TNA, RG 11/198/100/15.
42 *Old Bailey Proceedings*, 5 July 1732, trial of Thomas Gordon.

cross dressing with considerable anxiety. There are some grounds for suspecting that those anxieties increased as the century wore on[43] but up to and even immediately after the Boulton and Park case, the treatment cross dressers actually received varied according to the prejudices of individual magistrates. A young man who caused a disturbance when he paraded up and down outside the Coburg Theatre in female clothes in the summer of 1824 was simply discharged after a night in the cells and an apology.[44] A similar attitude was taken by the Marlborough Street magistrate in 1864.[45] Yet in 1849, long before the magistrate realized that the case before him also involved an allegation of indecent assault, a teenage cross dresser was told that 'the assumption of woman's attire by a man in the public streets was an offence from which great abominations might possibly arise'.[46] An incident in 1854 revealed that cross-dressers had been attending balls at London's Druids Hall and indulging in 'disgusting conduct' there for some two years. The presiding magistrate was appalled to learn that the local police sergeant had told his men not to interfere unless they witnessed 'such conduct take place in the public street.' When he discharged transvestite Edward Holmes, his homophobic comments made it clear that this was an exceptionally magnanimous decision. His fellow magistrate made it equally clear that Holmes should have been jailed as a rogue and a vagabond.'[47] In 1870, whilst the Boulton and Park case was still being heard, Walter Thurston was arrested for being in the street dressed as a woman. Although he produced a number of witnesses to testify that he was simply trying to win a bet he was remanded in custody for nearly a week before being released without charge. According to the committing magistrate his imprisonment was 'richly deserved'.[48] Whether the wider public agreed with such pronouncements remains a matter for speculation. Boulton and Park fared better at the hands of a judge and jury than in the magistrates' court. In 1879 two less well known transvestites, Harry Newman and Arthur Smith, had a similar experience. Once again the prosecution tried to use evidence of long term cross dressing to support otherwise unproveable allegations of homosexual activity. Once again a judge had to explain that 'the mere act of putting on female attire and wearing it in the public streets was no offence ... the act of

---

43 Cf. Cocks' findings about the marked increase in prosecutions of homosexual/indecent assault cases over the same period. H.G. Cocks, 'Trials of character: the use of character evidence in Victorian sodomy trials', in R.A. Melikan(ed.), *Domestic and international trials, 1700–2000: the trial in history* (Manchester, 2003), ii, 38.
44 *The Times*, 24 Aug. 1824.
45 *The Times*, 20 Sept. 1864.
46 *The Times*, 7, 18 and 25 Apr. 1849
47 *The Times*, 27 July, 1 and 2 Aug. 1854.
48 *The Times*, 29 June and 4 July 1870.

so dressing up only became unlawful when it was used as the means of carrying out other objects ...'. Once again the jury found them not guilty.[49]

THE CRIMINAL JUSTICE SYSTEM IN MID-VICTORIAN ENGLAND

The Boulton and Park case does not simply highlight the contrast between the types of justice meted out in summary and jury trial. It also shines a light into otherwise murky recesses of the Victorian criminal justice system. In 1870, despite the increasingly active role in prosecutions played by the Metropolitan Police, the criminal justice system was still very dependent on private prosecution. Nationally, nearly 7% of defendants were acquitted simply because the prosecutor failed to appear at the trial.[50] Boulton and Park's crimes – if crimes they were – were victimless. There was thus no readily identifiable person or agency to take the lead in either the investigation or the prosecution. Today we would take it for granted that the principal investigative agency in any crime would be the police, but this was not so in the England of the 1870s. Even in this high profile case where the authorities were particularly anxious to obtain a conviction responsibility was split between at least four agencies – the Metropolitan Police, the Treasury Solicitor, the Home Office and the Bow Street magistrate who conducted the examination of witnesses. Additional input came, from the earliest stages, from Harry Bodkin Poland, counsel to the Treasury and adviser to the Home Office on criminal matters. As indicated above Poland acted as an investigator and interviewed potential prosecution witnesses before they testified at Bow Street. These agencies had overlapping roles and it is not clear which of them had overall control of the case – if indeed anyone could be said to have been in charge.

To complicate matters still further, cases involving suspicious deaths were also investigated by a coroner.[51] In 1876 when the investigation into the death of Charles Bravo was bungled, blame fell on the coroner rather than the police. It was seen as his responsibility to conduct a search for any remaining poison on the premises and to question witnesses about the food and drink consumed before death.[52] His failure to do so led to a successful application to the courts for a rule to quash the inquest verdict; the second inquest amounted to a virtual trial of Bravo's young widow for murder.[53] In the

---

49 *The Times*, 23 Sept. 1879.
50 *The Times*, 7 May 1870.
51 *The Times*, 26 May 1871.
52 *The Times*, 20 June 1876.
53 *The Times*, 13 May, 19, 27 June 1876.

meantime the Home Office had also instructed the police and the Treasury Solicitor to make preliminary enquiries. Any decision about prolonging the investigation was to be taken, not by the police, but by the Home Office acting on the advice of the Treasury Solicitor.[54] Boulton and Park's case similarly suggests that the Metropolitan Police were junior partners in an enquiry directed by the Home Office and Treasury Solicitor.

In the course of Boulton and Park's trial an incidental exchange between Supt. Thompson and Cockburn CJ added another layer of complexity to the question of investigative responsibility, confirming not only that the police were not seen as independent investigators but that the separation of the executive and judicial roles of the magistracy was still far from complete. It reveals that the proceedings at Bow Street magistrates' court were not committal proceedings in the modern sense of the term but part and parcel of the investigation. The magistrate's investigative role was so great that on occasion it entirely superseded the need for a police investigation. When a group of police detectives arrested Daniel Mathieu for attempted pick pocketing in June 1870 they took him straight to Bow Street police court to be dealt with by the magistrates there. He was taken to a police station only when it became clear that pressure of business (the examination of witnesses in the Boulton and Park case) meant that his case would not be heard that day.[55] Legal manuals as well as reports of other cases show that verbal statements made to the police were formed into written depositions in order to be sworn and signed on a separate occasion in the magistrate's court and that witnesses in that court were examined in the presence of the accused who could question them. In London, the over zealous nature of such magisterial investigations and their admission of 'rambling statements and miscellaneous accusations' had led in the opinion of *The Times* to unwarranted delays and increasing expense.[56] Standard legal manuals assumed that the examination of defendants occurred in the context of a known accusation but when defence counsel in the Boulton and Park case asked the magistrate to clarify the charges faced by their clients, claiming not unreasonably that 'it was compulsory on the part of the prosecution to define exactly the offence alleged and the time and place of its commission' and pointing out that it was impossible to mount a defence without 'a definite statement of the actual charge' the presiding magistrate insisted that such a rule applied only to trials 'and not the preliminary examination of the accused before the magistrate.' Prosecution counsel then intervened saying that it was obvious that 'the police could not be expected to know how to shape a charge of this kind.'[57]

54 *The Times*, 20 May 1876.
55 *The Times*, 3 and 17 June 1870.
56 *The Times*, 7 May 1870, 10 Oct. 1877.
57 *The Times*, 21 May 1870.

The reports of the hearings at Bow Street, particularly the final one, show that the charges against the two men were being formulated by the magistrate rather than by the police. It was the magistrate's evaluation of a letter in which Park referred to Clinton's 'matrimonial squabbles' with Boulton that confirmed his belief that Boulton and Park should be charged with felony. It was not until the end of the hearings in the magistrates' court that Boulton and Park were charged and cautioned. Nearly a hundred years earlier in the mid 1770s the Attorney General had complained that newspaper reporting of the public examinations of suspected criminals at Bow Street was prejudicial to justice. On that occasion he had been worried about the rights of defendants and the erosion of due process; his concerns were shared by Lord Mansfield who described the reporting of public examinations as 'subversive of every principle of justice'.[58] Such concerns were markedly absent from the conduct of the case against Boulton and Park – so much so that it seems that publicity about their prolonged imprisonment, the death of Clinton, the unauthorized medical examination, the illegal searches and the reluctance of the prosecution to disclose evidence attracted public sympathy to their cause.

When the police first arrested Boulton and Park they probably did think that they were laying down some sort of warning about what was and what was not acceptable behaviour in London's public spaces. It is likely that all they wanted to do was to reinforce social norms about appropriate masculine behaviour. Instead they found themselves in a bizarre legal world in which structural flaws in the criminal justice system enabled matters to escalate out of all proportion to reality, partly because homophobic officials in the Home Office insisted on a prosecution in a case in which there was virtually no evidence and partly because Park's family were sufficiently wealthy and knowledgeable to make a fight of it. The impression that the police were out of their depth when called upon to deal with anything out of the usual was reinforced when the spectacular collapse of the case against Boulton and Park was matched by the almost contemporaneous and equally spectacular collapse of a high profile murder prosecution. Seventeen year old Jane Maria Clousens was two months pregnant, allegedly by her employer's son, Edmund Pook, when she was brutally murdered in April 1871. Pook was the only viable suspect but was nevertheless acquitted. Pook had been so obvious a suspect that the police had failed to follow up any other line of enquiry. They had allowed Pook's clothing to be contaminated before it was examined, they had not kept a full record of objects found at or near the scene of the crime, they had ignored evidence that did not fit their pre-conceptions of Pook's guilt and they had lied to Pook about the existence of

---

58 *British Mercury and Evening Advertiser*, 11 Dec. 1780. I am indebted for this reference to Prof. John Beattie.

evidence linking him to Clousens' pregnancy. Unfortunately for them, Pook, like Boulton and Park came from a prosperous middle class family and had a close relative who was a solicitor with an extensive criminal practice. The prosecution case was torn to shreds at trial. The police were roundly berated for their incompetence by the presiding judge (once again Cockburn CJ) and even by the leader of the prosecution team, the solicitor general (John Duke Coleridge).[59]

THE DEMAND FOR REFORM

The criticism levelled at the police during these cases was by no means unusual. Despite considerable complacency about the decline in street crime, there remained a vociferous demand for the reform of the criminal justice system, which was fuelled by the growing realization that the introduction of the 'new' police had not succeeded in delivering the full range of improvements that had been promised. In a plea that would have been familiar half a century earlier to proponents of police reform, critics demanded a system that delivered 'greater certainty in the detection and punishment of crime'.[60] They accepted that the new police had their uses but they also believed that a body of men drawn from the ranks of the working classes could not be expected to handle anything other than the most routine of cases. A small detective force had been formed in 1842 and further expanded in 1869.[61] These early detectives, just like Dickens' fictional Inspector Bucket in *Bleak House*, were determined, streetwise individuals who had acquired an extensive knowledge of London's underworld and of the men and women who inhabited it. Such qualities were admirable in their own way but were not suited to complex cases, especially those involving their social superiors. Critics feared that the police had become, virtually by default, investigators akin to the continental *juges d'instruction* in a way that 'would never be tolerated if it affected to any appreciable degree the higher or middle classes of society' and all the worse for the lack of an adequate supervisory framework.[62] As *The Times* put it in 1873 after another spectacular failure of justice (this time the arrest and detention of a respectable middle class and palpably innocent, though foreign, minister of religion on a charge of murder), 'It is too much to expect that half-educated men raised from the ranks of the police force can accurately weigh facts so as to see their precise bearing in evidence.'[63] Such defects could perhaps have been cured by careful

---

59 *The Times*, 5, 15 May, 14, 15 and 17 July 1871
60 *The Times*, 23 May 1873.
61 Clive Emsley, *The English police: a political and social history* (London, 1996), p. 72.
62 *The Times*, 18 July 1871.
63 *The Times*, 3 Feb. 1873.

oversight from the Treasury Solicitor but here too the system was perceived to have failed: 'the imbecility which has long directed Treasury prosecutions', concluded the *Pall Mall Gazette*, 'has reached a limit it will be difficult to surpass.'[64]

Although the criminal justice system was still essentially dependent on the willingness of victims to prosecute, the role of the central government had expanded because the Treasury had been authorized by statute, since 1840, to underwrite the costs of prosecution. Unfortunately the regulations surrounding these payments had led to something of a bureaucratic mess in which prosecution costs were examined at a number of different levels. Local officials authorized the initial expenditures, the actual costs incurred were then inspected by county taxing officers before being forwarded to the Treasury who then taxed them a second time. The Treasury (according to its critics) habitually disallowed perfectly reasonable items of expenditure, thus leaving the shortfall to be made up by local authorities. The Treasury's 'culpable parsimony' was regularly blamed for the inadequacy of prosecutions. Feeling against the Treasury's apparently petty and arbitrary interventions led in 1871 to an action by the county palatine of Lancaster for a writ of mandamus to compel payment of expenditure incurred.[65] The action had to be dropped when the judges declared that a mandamus could not lie against the crown, but the Treasury seems to have agreed to pay up anyway.[66] A year later Warwickshire attempted to form a coalition of counties to take similar action.[67] The subject continued to exercise letter writers to *The Times* over a period of several months.

The perceived defects of the criminal justice system – the inadequacy of investigative procedures, dissatisfaction with the performance of the Treasury Solicitor and concern that the effectiveness of prosecutions was further diminished by the niggardliness of the Treasury – all contributed to demands for a radical reform of the criminal justice system. The reform most commonly suggested was the creation of a public prosecution service. This idea had been part of the common coin of reform proposals from at least the eighteenth century. It was advocated by the Royal Commission on Criminal Law in 1845 and by a select committee of the House of Commons in 1855, by the Judicature Commission in 1874 and bore fruit in the 1850s and 1870s in the form of several abortive attempts at legislation. Until the 1870s the essence of such proposals was to draw a distinction between the detection and apprehension of criminals and the direction and management of preparations for trial. What was envisaged was a network of state prosecutors

---

64 Cited in *The Times*, 25 July 1871.
65 *The Times*, 24 Jan., 28 Apr. 1871, 25 Dec. 1872; LR 7QB 387–403.
66 *The Times*, 28 Apr. 1871, 25 Dec. 1872.
67 *The Times*, 3 Jan 1872.

rather similar to the U.S. system of district attorneys with powers to intervene at an early stage of prosecution. Cockburn CJ, in his minority report of 1874, vigorously supported the proposition that 'no prosecution should be left to the uncontrolled management of the police'. In practice such a reform seems never to have received serious ministerial attention. It would be expensive to implement and leave the government open to allegations of patronage creation. Some also feared that turning such a large number of lawyers into state employees posed a threat to their much prized professional status.[68]

In the event the prospects for, and the shape of, reform were decisively altered by two entirely unrelated events. The first was the election in 1874 of a Tory government and the appointment of the indefatigable Richard Assheton Cross as a reforming Home Secretary. The second was the 'turf fraud' scandal of 1877, which resulted in the conviction of three of the four chief inspectors in the Metropolitan Police detectives department on charges relating to corruption.[69] Whilst it is clear that some reform of the criminal investigation process had been under discussion for a long time, the scandal of 1877 provided the final impetus to action. In March 1878 – just four months after the conviction of the turf fraud detectives – the Metropolitan Police purged its existing detective force, reorganized its services and announced the creation of a centralized, specialist detective unit, the Criminal Investigation Department. One of the few detectives to survive the purge was Boulton and Park's old foe, Detective Sergeant Kerley, now promoted to the rank of Inspector.[70]

The new department was the brainchild of soldier turned barrister Howard Vincent and resulted from his study of the organization of the police of Paris. Appointed Director of the new CID, Howard ensured that his men were of higher calibre and better paid than ordinary uniformed constables. To Vincent the certainty of detection and conviction was an integral part of deterrence and hence of the Metropolitan Police's core function, the prevention of crime. Although his men were given no formal training for detective work, they were nevertheless subjected to a somewhat rapid process of professionalization, one that transformed the reputation of the police and boosted public confidence in the criminal justice system. This professionalization was accomplished by the dissemination of rules and procedures designed to ensure a more systematic approach to the detection of crime. Dissemination was in part through the established and recognized channel of

---

68 Parl. Papers (1845), xiv. 1, (1856), vii. 1; Judicature commission, 5th report (1874; C 1090); TNA, HO 45/9499/8002, 8002A, 8002C; Arthur D. Douglas, *Criminal procedure in England and Scotland* (London, 1878), pp 35, 38–45.
69 Emsley, *The English police*, p. 72.
70 *The Times*, 8 Apr. 1878.

police orders: it was for example Vincent's influence that led to the police order that ensured that the bodies of murder victims should not be moved prior to examination and that crime scenes be secured. Dissemination also occurred through conventional publication. Vincent's *A police code and manual of criminal law*, first published in 1881, became the standard textbook for police forces throughout the empire. Its practical usefulness can be gauged from the fact that it was regularly revised and republished over a period of some 60 years. Vincent also published a manual of procedures for dealing with extradition cases.

Cross lost office at the general election of 1880. One of his last achievements as Home Secretary was to push through the Prosecution of Offences Act of 1879, which finally authorised the appointment of a Director of Public Prosecutions.[71] This was scarcely the extensive reform that had been demanded. Yet hidden within its clauses were provisos that addressed the two remaining most often rehearsed criticisms of the existing system of criminal justice. Firstly the new Director of Public Prosecutions was authorized to take over prosecutions if the prosecutor refused or was unable to proceed. Secondly he could authorize specific costs such as extra fees to counsel, the preparation of scientific evidence or of plans or models needed to present an effective prosecution case thereby reducing the ability of the Treasury to refuse reimbursement of the full costs of a prosecution where it was deemed necessary to incur extra expenditure.

Less than ten years after Boulton and Park's ordeal therefore the criminal justice system had been overhauled in a way designed to boost public confidence in its ability to ensure that the guilty were apprehended, convicted and punished. Had the criminal justice system been organized in this way in 1870 it is just possible that Boulton and Park would have faced a far more effective prosecution case, one that would have made them as well known as martyrs for the cause of gay rights as Oscar Wilde. Yet on the whole one suspects not – for a truly effective criminal justice system would have abandoned this prosecution at an early date, recognizing that there is a world of difference between grounds for suspicion and evidence that proves guilt beyond reasonable doubt.

---

[71] 42&43 Vic. c.22.

What *were* the principles of nineteenth-century contract law?

STEPHEN WADDAMS

'IT IS SOMEWHAT CURIOUS,' Pollock told his readers in 1876, 'that no such thing as a satisfactory definition of Contract is to be found in any of our books.'[1] Similar statements have been made in the twentieth century, and in the twenty-first. James Gordley wrote (1991) that 'today we have no generally recognized theory of contract',[2] and Stephen Smith has said (2004) 'there is no single theory of contract that is universally accepted; rather there exists a variety of mutually exclusive theories, with few elements in common.'[3] Despite much writing on contract theory no consensus has emerged on a single explanation or justification for contractual liability, nor is there any agreed definition. A number of ideas have been in play, including those of will, autonomy, mutual consent, agreement, promise, bargain, reliance, expectation, entitlement, utility, efficiency, convenience, common sense, good faith, and public policy. Abstract debate conducted in terms of 'What is the true nature of contract law?' has often seemed to run into an impasse, with insistence on one side on rigorous exclusion of all considerations of utility, convenience, or policy, and assertion on the other side that such are the *only* relevant considerations. A historical enquiry tends to show that the truth has been both more complex and more interesting than what is suggested by this sharp dichotomy. A question about the past, unlike an abstract or theoretical question, may be demonstrably answered by historical evidence, and some evidence is available of what the nineteenth-century writers meant by 'principle' and how they attempted to grapple with the inter-relation of the various concepts just mentioned.

Blackstone's *Commentaries on the Laws of England* (1765–69) allowed no explicit place to contracts as a distinct part of English law.[4] The first treatise

---

1 F. Pollock, *Principles of contract at law and in equity, being a treatise on the general principles concerning the validity of agreements with a special view to the comparison of law and equity and with references to the Indian Contract Act and occasionally to Roman American and continental law* (London, 1876), p. 1 (opening words of text).
2 J. Gordley, *The philosophical origins of modern contract doctrine* (Oxford, 1991), p. 230.
3 S. Smith, *Contract theory* (Oxford, 2004), p. viii.
4 W. Blackstone, *Commentaries on the laws of England*, 4 vols (Oxford, 1765–9).

on English contract law (Powell, 1790) gave conceptual unity to the subject,[5] and this was extended by the appearance in English translation (1806) of Pothier's treatise on obligations,[6] and by at least twelve nineteenth-century English books.[7] The demarcation of contract law had far-reaching implications, including a division between property and obligations, and divisions among various classes of obligations. Some writers also implied that English contract law was a manifestation of a universal order. This attitude is well illustrated by Charles Addison, who wrote (1847) that English contract law was founded 'upon the broad and general principles of universal law' and that 'the law of contracts may justly indeed be said to be a universal law adapted to all times and races, and all places and circumstances, being founded upon those great and fundamental principles of right and wrong deduced from natural reason which are immutable and eternal.'[8]

By far the most influential of the nineteenth-century English contract books were those of Frederick Pollock (1876)[9] and William Anson (1879).[10] The titles of both books commenced with the word 'Principles'. Neither Pollock nor Anson spoke in such strong terms as Addison, but they nevertheless implied, both by the titles to their books and by remarks addressed to their readers, that there were certain propositions about English contract law, deserving of the name 'principles', that had some sort of special status as primary, fundamental, or indisputable, or that constituted a source from which rules used to determine particular cases were derived, and that those propositions could be identified and formulated.

But if we ask precisely what *were* these principles, the answer proves surprisingly elusive, even, as we shall see, in relation to the supposedly simple rules of offer and acceptance. Part of the reason for this is the indeterminacy of the word 'principle': the word has been used in many different senses, the meaning varying according to what is implicitly contrasted with it (principle and rule, principle and policy, principle and precedent, principle and authority, principle and pragmatism, principle and practice, principle and convenience, principle and utility, general principle and particular rule, general principle and particular case); on a controversial legal question two or more conflicting principles can usually – perhaps always – be identified;

5 J.J. Powell, *An essay upon the law of contracts and agreements*, (London, 1790).
6 R.J. Pothier, *A treatise on the law of obligations or contracts*, trans. W.D. Evans (London, 1806). The words 'treatise' and 'contracts' are in (contrasting) italics on the title page, showing that Evans regarded the work as primarily a treatise on the law of contracts.
7 See A.W.B. Simpson, 'Innovation in nineteenth century contract law', *Law Quarterly Review*, 91 (1975) 247, repr. in *Legal theory and legal history* (London, 1987), p. 171.
8 C. Addison, *A treatise on the law of contracts and rights and liabilities ex contractu* (London, 1847), preface, pp iv–v.
9 Note 1, above.
10 W. Anson, *Principles of the English law of contract* (Oxford, 1879).

principles may be stated and restated at an infinite number of levels of generality, and commonly the word has been used to mean no more than a reason or rule framed at a higher level of generality than another; sometimes a principle has meant more than a rule – a rule that is absolutely stringent, but at other times the word has signified something less than a rule – an objective desirable in general terms but liable to be outweighed by countervailing considerations, and here the meaning of the word merges with the idea of 'maxim;' very commonly also it has signified a legal rule, or a reason in support of a rule, that the writer considers persuasive, legitimate, or satisfactory.

Let us consider, as an illustrative example, the simple question of whether an offer could be effectively withdrawn without communication to the offeree. If there were a stringent principle that contractual obligation depended on intention, or on mutual consent, or concurrence of wills, it would follow that there ought to be no liability where the offeror had demonstrably intended to withdraw the offer. A much-discussed test case was that of an offer sent by mail, with a subsequent retraction also sent by mail; the legal issue was whether the offeror was bound if the offeree purported to accept the offer without notice of the offeror's change of mind. On this issue Pothier, the great French jurist, had expressly said that there could be no contractual liability because 'there is not that consent, or concurrence of ... wills, which is necessary to constitute the contract of sale.' This was a legal conclusion derived from a principle, and one at a very high level, namely mutual consent. But Pothier, aware of the inconvenient and potentially unjust consequences of this conclusion, added that, although there could be no contractual liability, an equivalent liability could be imposed on the offeror on a non-contractual basis: 'this obligation results from that rule of equity (*équité*) that no person should suffer for the act of another: *nemo ex alterius facto praegravari debet*.'[11] By this means Pothier preserved the principle (no *contractual* liability without consent), while suggesting a solution that protected the expectation of the promisee and answered to his and his readers' instinctive sense of fairness.

Whatever the merits of Pothier's approach as a matter of French law, it could not, despite Pothier's very high reputation in England, appeal to the nineteenth-century English mind. English equity could not have imposed such a liability as Pothier contemplated, and there was no tort known to the common law that fitted the facts. Moreover the Latin maxim relied on by Pothier (no one shall suffer by the act of another) would have struck an English lawyer of Pollock's time as far too wide, and the refusal to impose contractual liability, followed by the imposition of a non-contractual liability equivalent to – or even more extensive than – what the contractual liability

---

11 Pothier, *Treatise on sale* [1817] trans. L.S. Cushing (Boston, 1839), p. 18.

would have been had it existed, appeared to the English legal mind to be fictitious, convoluted, and potentially unjust.

Pothier's approach to this question was accepted by Chitty (1834) but Chitty omitted altogether any discussion of Pothier's suggestion of non-contractual liability.[12] Benjamin (1873) subjected Pothier's reasoning to very severe criticism.[13] Pollock (1876) also rejected Pothier's approach. Pollock commented on 'the manifestly unjust consequences' of permitting the offeror to retract after reliance by the offeree, and rejected Pothier's non-contractual solution, calling it 'cumbrous and inelegant.' Pollock then asserted that 'the declaration of an *animus contrahendi* [intention of contracting] ... when once made must be regarded as continuing so long as no revocation of it is communicated to the other party. A revocation not communicated is in point of law no revocation at all.' Pollock then added: 'These principles, it seems to us, are entirely right if tested by common sense and convenience, and are in accordance with the authorities of the common law when rightly understood.'[14]

This last sentence deserves a little attention. Pollock, having set out two rather specific propositions ('an offeror's declaration of intention must be regarded as continuing,' and 'a revocation not communicated is no revocation') evidently formulated to support the conclusion he favoured on the point in issue, then called these propositions principles ('these principles'), while Pothier's idea of concurrence of wills, which might more naturally be considered a general or fundamental principle, but the apparent consequences of which Pollock was in the process of rejecting, was not, in this particular passage, called a 'principle. Writers rarely designate lines of reasoning that they are in the course of rejecting as 'principles.' Pollock was conscious of expressing a personal opinion, and was somewhat embarrassed by this, as is shown by his awkward use of the editorial plural ('it seems to us'). His opinion, moreover, was plainly based primarily on general considerations of justice and policy ('common sense and convenience,' and avoidance of 'manifest injustice'). It is significant that principles were to be 'tested' by common sense and convenience: in case of conflict, it would seem, it was the principles (or apparent principles) that must give way. These considerations were then made to conform to the convention within which Pollock was writing, that of a barrister indirectly addressing an English judge on the actual state of English law ('in accordance with the authorities of the common law'). This last phrase sounds impressive but, since no authorities

---

12 J. Chitty, *A practical treatise on the law of contracts not under seal and upon the usual defences to actions thereon* (2nd ed. London, 1834), pp 12–13.
13 J. P. Benjamin, *A treatise on the law of sale of personal property with references to the American decisions and to the French code and civil law* (2nd ed. London, 1873), pp 58–9.
14 Note 1, above, at p. 11.

were mentioned, it can claim little independent substance. Moreover, it is evident from the next three words ('when rightly understood') that the search for authorities was neither a technical nor primarily a historical enquiry. 'Right understanding' impliedly imports the author's own opinion, primarily informed, as the context shows, by considerations of common sense, convenience, and avoidance of injustice.

It is tempting to suppose that a choice must be made between two views: either Pollock reached his conclusion on the basis of pure principle, or, on the other hand, he must have reached it on the basis of common sense, convenience, and justice, the appeal to principle being mere form. But this dichotomy tends to over-simplification. To call form in legal reasoning 'mere form' is to underestimate its historical significance, and is to overlook the possibility that Pollock was influenced *both* by the argument of principle *and* by the argument of convenience, common sense, and justice. That Pollock, like all other legal writers, including judges, found it necessary to cast his argument in the form of deduction of results from previously existing principles may not by any means be a trivial or accidental aspect of legal reasoning.

Pollock's approach to this question was rewarded with almost immediate success, for, in a decision of 1880, Mr Justice Lindley, to whom, incidentally, Pollock's book had been dedicated, expressly rejected Pothier's view and adopted Pollock's, calling his book the 'excellent work on *Principles of Contract*', and showing none of the later reluctance of English judges to cite modern authors (he referred also to Benjamin and Leake).[15] Lindley J went on 'to point out the extreme injustice and inconvenience which any other conclusion would produce,' adding that 'both legal principles and practical convenience require that a person who has accepted an offer not known to him to have been revoked shall be in a position safely to act upon the footing that the offer and acceptance constitute a contract binding on both parties.' Shortly afterwards, in *Stevenson v. McLean*,[16] Lindley J was expressly followed on this point by another judge.

'Principle' has often been contrasted with 'policy' and in some contexts the contrast is apt, but in this instance it is evident that principle and policy were not opposed, either in Pollock's mind or in Lindley's. Indeed, it was the flexibility of the concept of principle that enabled Pollock to give expression to his views on justice, protection of reliance, convenience, and common sense – considerations often summarized as 'policy' – while adhering to the conventional framework within which he was writing. Lindley J also perceived harmony, not opposition, in the concepts of legal principles, practical convenience, and protection of the promisee's reasonable expectation.

15 *Byrne v. Leon van Tienhoven* (1880) 5 CPD 344 (March 6).
16 (1880) 5 QBD 357 (Lush J, May 25).

In his third edition (1881), Pollock was able to cite the two judicial decisions of 1880 as authoritatively settling the question, omitting the awkward phrasing of his first edition, and substituting this much smoother formulation: 'In the earlier editions of this book the question was treated as practically settled, but only in 1880 was it actually decided ... [citing the two cases]'.[17] Thus the mutual interaction between writer and judge enabled each to disclaim an unmediated appeal to such very general considerations as common sense, convenience, and justice. Pollock, though influenced, as we have seen, by these considerations, relied also, in his first edition, on the assertion that his proposed principles were 'in accordance with the authorities of the common law when rightly understood.' Pollock's conclusion in turn enabled the judges to rest their decisions not simply on their own opinion of what was just and convenient, but on a previously recognized principle, and, from the third edition, Pollock, in turn again, was able to omit his own opinion with the supporting arguments and inform his readers that the law on the point had now been satisfactorily settled.

Another contrast often made is between contract law as giving effect to the will of the promisor and contract law as protecting the reliance, or the expectation of the promisee. It will be seen from this example that both ideas were present in Pollock's treatment of the question in issue, and that they were inter-related. Pollock spoke of the promisor's *animus contrahendi* (intention of contracting), suggesting the primary importance of intention, but he said that intention 'must be regarded as continuing' until notice of revocation had been given. This is a fictitious reason, because, on the assumed facts, it is known with certainty that the promisor's intention does *not* continue. Pollock evidently thought the fiction to be necessary, and his principal reason was the 'manifest injustice' that would otherwise ensue if the offeree had acted on the offer without notice of its retraction, that is to say, the need to protect the offeree's reasonable reliance, or expectation.

Meanwhile Anson, in his first edition (1879) had taken a different view of revocation of offers. Anson, while conceding that a rule protecting the offeree was needed in cases of correspondence between parties at a distance, asserted that 'when the parties are in immediate communication a proposal may be revoked without notice to the person to whom it is made', and added a footnote expressly critical of Pollock's view: 'Mr Pollock, in his work on Contract, p. 10, lays it down that "a proposal is revoked only when the intention to revoke it is communicated to the other party." We venture however to think that this rule must be received with the limitations suggested by the cases cited in the text [*Cooke v. Oxley*,[18] and *Dickinson v. Dodds*[19]].'

17 F. Pollock, *Principles of contract* (3rd ed. London, 1881), pp 25–6.
18 (1790) 3 TR 653.
19 (1876) 2 Ch Div 463.

Pollock's reply (third edition) pointed out that the headnote to *Dickinson v. Dodds* was misleading insofar is it implied that the court decided that an offer could be effectively withdrawn without communication to the offeree. Pollock gave similarly short shrift to Anson's treatment of *Cooke v. Oxley*, being enabled, by the decisions of 1880, summarily to foreclose further discussion: 'It is right to add that *Cooke v. Oxley* may be so read as to support the opinion that a tacit revocation need not be communicated at all. But the apparent inference to this effect is expressly rejected in *Stevenson v. McLean*, and therefore need not be discussed here.' He added a footnote (omitted in later editions), emphasizing, perhaps rather unkindly, Anson's evident reliance on the erroneous headnote: 'Sir W.R. Anson, writing in 1879, and troubled by this construction of *Cooke v. Oxley*, and apparently accepting the head-note in *Dickinson v. Dodds*, makes a distinction between cases "where the parties are in immediate communication" and where they "communicate by correspondence." In the light of the latest authorities no such expedient seems necessary.'[20] Anson was still arguing the point in his fifth edition (1888),[21] but substantially conceded to Pollock in the sixth (1891).[22]

Thus it came to be established as a matter of English law, and not subsequently doubted, that the 'true principle' applicable in these circumstances was that retraction of an offer requires communication to the offeree. But what kind of enquiry established this truth and this principle? It is evident in the particular instance that this was not a principle discoverable by logic, or by historical research, or by anything analogous to enquiries engaged in by natural scientists. It required argument based, in part, on personal judgment, guided by very general considerations of convenience, justice, and common sense, and accurate prediction by academic writers of what would be acceptable to English judges.

The resolution of this issue might naturally be summarized by saying that the principle (concurrent intention required for contractual obligation) was subject to an exception. But this way of putting the matter raises further questions. Is the exception to be framed narrowly (retraction of offers requires communication), or broadly (the reasonable expectation of the offeree is to be protected)? Is the exception itself based on a competing principle, and is the number of potential exceptions and competing principles indeterminate? Is the resolution of conflicts between competing principles itself based on any principle that can be articulated? These questions are partly conceptual, partly logical, and partly linguistic. They are not questions about the past, and they cannot be answered by historical evidence.

---

20 Pollock, *Principles of contract* (3rd ed., 1881) p. vi, p. 29.
21 Anson, *Principles of the English law of contract*, 5th ed., p. 33.
22 Ibid., 6th ed., p. 34.

Did English contract law in 1880 depend on concurrence of intention? This is a question about the past, and it can be answered by historical evidence. The answer is, no. The issue of retraction of offers is only one example of imposition of liability contrary to the intention of the promisor. It was also the law at this date that a promisor might be bound by a contractual term she never intended to agree to, if the promisee reasonably thought that she had agreed to it; that words in documents were to be construed according to the meaning reasonably ascribed to them by the promisee, not the meaning intended by the promisor; and contracts made by an agent acting within his apparent authority were binding on the principal even though the agent had acted in plain defiance of explicit instructions. All these rules tended to protect the reasonable expectation of the promisee where it conflicted with the actual intention of the alleged promisor.

The assertion that nineteenth-century contract law rested on a 'will theory' has been so often repeated as almost to attain the status of received wisdom. The historical evidence, however, does not support it: the will of the promisor was neither necessary nor sufficient. The rules mentioned in the last paragraph show that, in many important respects, the will of the promisor was not necessary for contractual obligation. The need for consideration shows that neither was the will of the promisor sufficient. A clear, simple, elegant, orderly, consistent, and logical explanation of contract law would, no doubt, be desirable, if attainable, but it cannot be a virtue to misdescribe the past, or to impose upon it an order that was not there.

Pollock's third edition (1881) introduced many important changes. The introduction to that edition included the following remarkable passage: 'The first chapter, which deals with the fundamental definitions, and the first conditions of the formation of a contract, has been *almost entirely re-written*, partly because some of the questions there discussed have been put on a new footing by recent decisions, partly because the treatment of first principles appeared on revision to be in sundry respects inadequate' (emphasis added).[23] An acknowledged change of opinion is usually to be counted to the credit of an author, but the re-writing, within five years, of the most fundamental part of a book entitled 'Principles', and on the grounds here stated (new judicial decisions, and appearance of inadequacy, on revision, of the author's treatment of *first principles*), must engender doubt about the eternal and immutable nature of the principles – those asserted in 1881 as well as those asserted in 1876.

In the third edition the Preface was replaced by a lengthy and discursive 'Introduction' which included, at its sixteenth page, the following passage:

---

23 Pollock, *Principles of contract* (3rd ed. London, 1881), p. vi.

The law of contract is in truth nothing else than the endeavour of the sovereign power, a more or less imperfect one by the nature of the case, to establish a positive sanction for the expectation of good faith which has grown up in the mutual dealings of men of average right-mindedness....The most popular description of a contract that can be given is also the most exact one, namely that it is a promise or set of promises which the law will enforce.... The primary questions ... of the law of contract are first, what is a promise? and next, what promises are enforceable? To examine these questions is the object of the present book. The importance and difficulty of the first of them depends on the fact that men can justly rely on one another's intentions, and courts of justice hold them bound to their fulfilment, only when they have been expressed in a manner that would convey to an indifferent person, reasonable and reasonably competent in the matter in hand, the sense in which the expression is relied on by the party claiming satisfaction.[24]

In the fourth edition this passage was sharpened, and made much more conspicuous by being promoted to the opening words of the Preface. The concept of reliance and expectation and their relation with intention was elaborated by this sentence: 'He who has given the promise is bound to him who accepts it, not merely because he had or expressed a certain intention, but because he so expressed himself as to entitle the other party to rely on his acting in a certain way.'[25] In the fifth edition (1889) these passages (slightly revised) were moved from the Preface, and promoted to still greater prominence as the opening words of the first chapter of the text itself.[26]

Connected with these changes was the development of the concept of 'promise.' The tentative opening note of the text of the first edition ('it is somewhat curious that no satisfactory definition of contract is to be found') is replaced by 'a series of statements in the form of definitions, [which] though necessarily imperfect may help clear the way.' The first of these was that 'every agreement and promise enforceable by law is a contract,' and a definition of 'promise' followed.[27] In the fifth edition the concept of promise was given further prominence, and the description of a contract as 'a promise or set of promises which the law will enforce' appeared in the second sentence of the main text.[28]

In a letter to Holmes in 1920, Pollock, commenting on recent American writings, said, 'It is rather amusing to see your new lights trumpeting

---

24 Ibid., (3rd ed. London, 1881), p. xx.
25 Ibid., (4th ed. London, 1885), Preface.
26 Ibid., (5th ed. London, 1889), p. 1.
27 Ibid., (4th ed. London, 1885), p. 1.
28 Ibid., (5th ed. London, 1889), p. 1.

reasonable expectation as the real fundamental conception in contract. I agree, of course, having put it in my 3d edition, ad init., nearly forty years ago, only without a trumpet obligato.'[29] This comment reveals that Pollock was conscious that his views of 'the real fundamental conception in contract' had altered in the five-year period between the dates of the first and third editions (1876 and 1881). It also shows that reasonable expectation was, in Pollock's mind, an aspect of reliance, and that protection of the one was the natural corollary of protection of the other.[30]

The fact that a concept seen five years later as 'the real fundamental conception' should have eluded the author during the years of work he put into the first edition of a treatise on general principles is revealing. Also revealing is Pollock's reference to the absence of 'trumpet obligato'. It certainly is true that the passages in question were introduced without fanfare. Buried as they were in the long introduction (not exactly, therefore, *ad init.* [at the beginning]), they could hardly have been less conspicuous in the third edition, and they were only gradually promoted, first to the beginning of the preface in the fourth edition, and then to real prominence in the fifth, and subsequent, editions. This suggests that Pollock was by no means sure of his ground in 1881, and was not ready to commit himself fully to a rejection of the idea that contractual obligation depended on intention. It is doubtful whether Pollock would have used the phrase 'real fundamental conception' in this context in 1881, but it is significant that, when he looked back forty years later, he then thought that his insight on this point dated from that time.

The idea of reasonable expectation gained further ground in successive editions. In the fifth edition (1889), under the headings 'Interpretation generally,' and 'Effect of promise,' Pollock wrote:

> The nature of a promise is to create an expectation in the person to whom it is made. And, if the promise be a legally binding one, he is entitled to have that expectation fulfilled by the promisor. It has, therefore, to be considered what the promisor did entitle the promisee to expect from him. Every question which can arise on the interpretation of a contract may be brought, in the last resort, under this general form.[31]

---

29 Underlining in original. A later letter (vol. ii, pp 53–4) shows that the reference was to the Wigmore Celebration Volume, *Celebration: legal essays to mark the 25th year of service of John H. Wigmore* (1919), and especially to Roscoe Pound.

30 See Fuller and Perdue, 'The reliance interest in contract damages', *Yale LJ*, 46 (1936) 52.

31 Pollock, *Principles of contract* (5th ed. London, 1889), p. 234. The passage was maintained in subsequent editions. See also article by Pollock, 'Contract' in *Encyclopaedia Britannica* (11th ed., London, 1910), vol. 7, p. 38: '... the guiding principle is, or ought to be, the consideration of what either party has given the other reasonable cause to expect of him.'

The idea of reasonable expectation is given prominence, indeed ultimate precedence here, and associated also with the idea of entitlement. As we have seen, Pollock was anxious in 1920 to claim credit with Holmes for anticipating American scholars on this point, and Pollock's next published edition (ninth edition, 1921) gave very prominent approval to 'the modern tendency to look to "the realization of reasonable expectations" as the ground of just claims rather than an artificial equation of wills or intentions,' with reference to Roscoe Pound, and the work mentioned in Pollock's letter to Holmes of 1920.[32] The express rejection here of 'an artificial equation of wills and intentions' indicates, as Neil Duxbury has pointed out, a marked departure from continental theorists, particularly Savigny,[33] and Pollock's open recognition that the concept of intention could not, on its own, supply a complete explanation of contractual obligation.

Pollock did not, however, reject the idea of intention as irrelevant. He did not see intention and expectation as exclusive alternatives, but as complementary. In his article on contract in the *Encyclopaedia Britannica* (1910) he wrote, 'The obligation of contract is an obligation created by the will of the parties. Herein is the characteristic difference of contract from all other branches of law,' – an endorsement, it would seem, of the 'will theory' – yet he added, a few lines later, that 'the guiding principle still is, or ought to be, the consideration of what either party has given the other reasonable cause to expect of him.' Intention, expectation, entitlement, and good faith were not, in Pollock's mind, alternatives, of which one only was to be chosen to the exclusion of the others, but complementary aspects, all of which were necessary for an understanding of contract law.

The demarcation of contractual liability from other sources of legal liability is, as Pollock's reference to 'the characteristic difference of contract from all other branches of legal obligation' indicates, closely related to these questions.[34] It will be recalled from the discussion, above, of the question of uncommunicated retraction of offers that Pothier suggested that, though contractual liability was (from his point of view) conceptually impossible, an equivalent liability might be imposed on a non-contractual basis. Suggestions of this sort have quite often been made in respect of various aspects of English contract law, with liability proposed to be based on concepts of property, equity, estoppel, tort, or unjust enrichment. This method appears to preserve principles of contract law, but the price is very high: the principles are only preserved by removing all inconvenient instances into other categories and foreclosing discussion of them. The method is weak as

---

32 Ibid., (9th ed. London, 1921) footnote (a), on page 1 of the text.
33 N. Duxbury, *Frederick Pollock and the English juristic tradition* (Oxford, 2004), p. 194.
34 See S. Waddams, *Dimensions of private law: categories and concepts in Anglo-American legal reasoning* (Cambridge, 2003).

a historical account of the actual reasons for decisions, and tends to produce a simplification more apparent than real, for the non-conforming legal issues, though apparently removed from the writer's and from the reader's agenda, do not disappear, and continue to require adjudication and resolution. Moreover, there is the same difficulty in identifying unifying principles in the other categories to which the issue may be displaced.

Anson, in contrast to Pollock, thought that the demarcation of contracts from other sources of legal obligation was an essential first step to understanding the principles of contract. Anson opened his first edition with this: 'In commencing an inquiry into the principles of the law of contract it is well to consider what are the main objects of the inquiry and in what order they arise for discussion. It would seem that the first thing to be considered is the relation of contract to other legal conceptions: if this can be ascertained, we get some definite notion of the subject of our inquiries.'[35] Anson recognized distinct categories of contractual, delictual, and quasi-contractual liability. But he also distinguished the liability to pay compensation for breach of contract from contractual liability itself, allocating the two kinds of obligation to entirely separate categories. He also recognized that the obligation to pay a judgment could not readily be accommodated under other headings, and that neither could matrimonial obligations nor obligations arising from trusts. He thus postulated six categories of obligation: contract, delict, quasi-contract, breach of contract, judgment, and miscellaneous. Whatever the merits of this scheme from the points of view of logic and elegance, it did not appear to correspond with the previous history of English contract law, nor, despite being carried through seventeen editions over a period of fifty years, did this aspect of Anson's work attract any following from his contemporaries or successors.

Many of the English nineteenth-century writers, including Pollock and Anson, made reference to civilian writings, especially to Pothier (1699–1772) and to the German jurist, Savigny (1779–1861). But the invocation of the names of Pothier and Savigny does not establish that Pollock and Anson were actually influenced by what they had written. The attraction of civilian writings was connected with a search for order, elegance, and a 'scientific' approach in the study of English law. The word 'principle' had a certain rhetorical component, indicating, usually, propositions favoured by the writer. But the relation of principles, as understood by the nineteenth-century writers, to the actual prior history of English law is by no means obvious. The assessment of the law as it is at the time of assessment is itself a complex process, involving elements of historical enquiry, of judgment, of synthesis, of aspiration, and of prediction. The issue is further complicated by what may be called the forensic convention, that is, the convention that

---

35 Anson, *Principles of the English law of contract*, 1879, p. 1.

the writers were indirectly addressing an English judge, as a barrister might do, and seeking to persuade him of the actual state of contemporary English law. The writer's view of what the law ought to be tended, therefore, to be expressed in terms of what the law already was – 'in accordance with the authorities of the common law when rightly understood,' as Pollock put it.[36]

Another aspect of these questions is the relation between 'principle' and changes in the law. Sir John Baker has said that the study of legal history is the study of legal change,[37] and no one doubts that the law has changed, sometimes radically, often in response to perceived social changes. Yet such changes are not easily reconcilable with the idea of eternal and immutable principles, unless expressed in the most general terms. The development of legal principles, it has sometimes been suggested, is for the courts, while their abrogation or radical alteration is for the legislature. But no infallible, or even workable, criterion has emerged for distinguishing in this context between development and abrogation, or between incremental and radical change.

The tentative conclusion would be, not that there have been no principles, nor that 'principle' has had no meaning, nor that observers are free to select the principle of their choice. The historical evidence tends to show that apparently conflicting principles have often represented different aspects of a single legal question. It is not a matter of choosing one aspect or the other: *both* are necessary for a complete understanding. In contract law certain 'bridge' concepts have enabled apparently conflicting principles to be accommodated. Thus the concept of 'promise' accommodates the ideas both of the promisor's intention, and of an assurance given to the promisee: a promise is something intended by the promisor, but it is also something received by the promisee. It would, therefore, be a mistake to attempt to simplify or purify the idea of promise by stripping it of either of these aspects, that is, by seeking to explain contract law solely in terms of intention, or, on the other hand, solely in terms of protection of the promisee's interests. The success of the concept of promise lies in its very impurity, that is, in its ability simultaneously to embrace both ideas.

Neil Duxbury, in a recent article (2005), recalls a question asked of him at a workshop he presented at an American law school: 'So, if you guys didn't have Langdell and legal realism, what *did* you have?' Duxbury recounts that his reply was that 'we just showed a profound dedication to underachievement and muddling along.'[38] The general tenor of Duxbury's article is, similarly, to compare English and American jurisprudence to the advantage

---

36 Note 14, above.
37 J. Baker, 'Why the history of English law has not been finished', *Cambridge Law Journal*, 59 (2000) 62 at 63.
38 Neil Duxbury, 'English jurisprudence between Austin and Hart,' *Virginia Law Review*, 91:1 (2005) 90.

of the latter. It is not to doubt this general assessment, however, to suggest that the lines of thought that animated Langdell[39] on the one hand and the American legal realists on the other were, in neither case, entirely original: they were both present in nineteenth-century English writing. Langdell himself did not go so far as Addison (1847) who spoke of contract law as 'a universal law adapted to all times and races, and all places and circumstances' and as 'immutable and eternal. And few of the realists would have found it necessary to differ greatly from Pollock's testing and reformulation of principle (1876), by considerations of 'common sense and convenience' for the avoidance of 'manifest injustice.'

In looking at the past I think we must accept that, in many instances, opposite ideas have been entertained simultaneously, and held in a kind of tension. The concept of principle has not supplied any simple resolution to such tensions, nor has it excluded general considerations of convenience, justice, and common sense. Moreover, the word 'principle' has been used in several different senses. But this does not show that the concept of principle has been unnecessary or unimportant. On the contrary, the constant appeal to principle by nineteenth-century writers and judges suggests that it played a very important role in enabling contract law to accommodate such general considerations and to avoid undue rigidity, while yet preserving (not only in appearance but also in reality) a substantial measure of predictability and stability and the efficacy of reasoned argument. General considerations of common sense, convenience, and justice played an important role. But it does not follow that the idea of principle could be or could have been dispensed with. The evidence suggests, rather, that it was an essential part of what made legal reasoning in the nineteenth century distinctively legal.

---

[39] Langdell's views were more complex than suggested by some of the realists. See Bruce A. Kimball, 'The Langdell problem: historicizing the century of historiography, 1906–2000', *Law and History Review*, 22 (2004) 277, especially at 302–11.

Urban commons: from customary use to community right on Scotland's bleaching greens

ANDREA LOUX JARMAN

COMMON LAND, AND THE customary rights exercised over the community's 'common good', were essential to the economic life of the inhabitants of Scotland's urban communities or 'burghs' in the eighteenth and nineteenth centuries. While commons historiography tends to focus on the history of agriculture and agricultural capitalism, the legal history of Scotland's urban commons highlights the importance of common land both to cottage industry and larger industrial concerns that replaced that industry during the industrial revolution.[1] This chapter, examines the legal history of one such common use – 'bleaching' – from the Union until the mid-nineteenth century.[2]

SCOTLAND'S TEXTILE INDUSTRY

In the eighteenth and nineteenth centuries, Scotland's linen industry grew from a small unimportant Scottish craft to become a major British industry. Prior to the Act of Union in 1707 Scotland's textile industry was largely a cottage industry carried out by agricultural workers. Whilst there was some

---

This chapter was produced with the assistance of a grant from the Pasold Research Foundation and the AHRC Research Centre for Law, Gender and Sexuality. Materials from the National Archives of Scotland, the Fife Council Archives, the Dick Institute and the Signet Library, Edinburgh, are cited with permission. The author would like to thank Professor John Cairns and Mr P.E. Jarman for their invaluable assistance with this chapter.

1 C. Hill, 'Customary liberties and legal rights' in *Liberty against the Law: some seventeenth century controversies* (London, 1997), J.M. Neeson, *Commoners: common right, enclosure and social change in England, 1700–1820* (Cambridge, 1993), E.P. Thompson, *Customs in common* (London, 1991), A.C. Loux, 'The persistence of the ancient regime: custom, utility and the common law in the nineteenth century', *Cornell Law Review*, 79:1 (1993), 183–218 and Peter King, 'Gleaners, farmers and the failure of legal sanction in England 1750–1850', *Past & Present*, 125:1 (1989), pp 116–50.
2 A.L. Jarman, *Custom, Community and common land: rights of access to land in Scotland from the Union to Devolution* (Dundee, forthcoming).

specialized production in Scotland's urban enclaves or 'burghs', the development of the industry was hampered by both lack of capital and lack of markets. Indeed, the promise of free access to the English, American and West Indian markets for Scotland's linen was one of the economic incentives for Union that was stressed in the debates leading up to 1707.

By the 1720's there is evidence of some capital investment in the industry by both 'improving landowners' and merchants. In 1727, after much groundwork by both the Convention of Royal Burghs and the Society of Improvers, parliament passed two acts establishing and funding the Board of Trustees for Fisheries and Manufacturers. The aim of the trustees was to improve the production of textiles through both regulation of production and capital investment.[3] It was Scotland's burghs, which were already centres of trade and manufacture, that used these funds to develop a modern, capitalist textile industry.

It was common practice for burgh trades such as textile producers to carry out the various processes required to produce and finish their products on burgh common land. Textile manufacturers needed large amounts of water to wash or treat their wool and linen and land on which to peg out their 'webs' to dry. Bleaching cases involve disputes over common land where the community is claiming the right to use land and water for the needs of their cottage industry, their households and, later in the eighteenth century, their manufactories.

The terms 'bleaching' and 'servitude of bleaching' are used in this chapter as they appear in the cases heard at the court of session in the eighteenth and nineteenth centuries. 'Bleaching' can refer to a wide range of processes carried out on a variety of textiles, all of which require the availability of water and land on which to dry the treated materials. Rights over 'bleaching greens' are most often claimed for both household and cottage industry, and later manufactories, and were often shared with other tradesmen of the burgh such as skinners and tanners.

The history of the right of bleaching from a mere custom in 1708 that the courts would not recognise to a community right in 1843 demonstrates how the court of session responded to commons litigation by protecting the rights in common land of local inhabitants, trades people and manufacturers against the predations of overlords, neighbouring landowners and town councils. Urban common land had always been important to local inhabitants and cottage industry, but with the arrival of capitalist investment post-Union, rights of common had new, wealthy advocates amongst the textile merchants and manufacturers of Scotland's burghs.[4] These individuals had both the

---

3 A.J. Durie, *The Scottish linen industry in the eighteenth century* (Edinburgh, 1979), pp 1–18; T.C. Smout, *Scottish trade on the eve of the Union* (Edinburgh, 1963).

4 On early capitalist investment and, more specifically the activities of the Board of Trustees, see Durie, 'The Scottish linen industry in the eighteenth century'.

money and interest to pursue litigation to protect urban bleaching greens for the use of manufactories and the cottage industry that supplied them. In Scotland in the eighteenth century, capitalist investment and industrial development encouraged the protection of communal greens to service the manufacturing needs of the inhabitants and community as a whole.

SCOTLAND'S URBAN CENTRES

The urban communities that are the subject of this chapter are the incorporated burghs of Scotland. There are three types of burghs: royal burghs, burghs of barony and burghs of regality. Royal burghs held their land direct of the king, whilst burghs of barony and burghs of regality were held of a subject superior, a baron or important churchman. Burghs were urban centres but could in population and geographical extent be more like a village.[5] A burgh was defined by its purpose, which was to engage in trade, and its special privileges, which varied to some extent from burgh to burgh, but usually included the right to appoint municipal government, hold their own courts, and regulate the markets, which they were exclusively permitted to hold.[6] A burgh was generally erected by charter, which would state the terms of its establishment and the extent of its privileges. These documents were drafted in the most general of terms, the meaning of which was often the subject of litigation when disputes arose.

The land and other assets of the burgh were managed by the magistrates. Royal burghs held their land directly of the monarch and the magistrates were infeft in the land. The magistrates both held the territory of the burgh and managed its affairs. Burghs of barony and regality on the other hand were incorporeal estates. The magistrates governed the affairs of the burgh in consultation with the superior lord, who held the land of the monarch. The magistrates were not infeft and as a corporate entity held no territory. The power of magistrates to control the disposition of burgh land was defined both by statute and by common law.

The disputes examined in this chapter concern land, or use rights held over land (servitudes), which were held in common by burgh inhabitants. Rights of common could be exercised over burgh land or on land outwith the burgh, and both were the subject of the actions discussed below.[7] The

---

5 E.P. Dennison, 'Medieval burghs' in D. Omand (ed.), *The Fife Book* (Edinburgh, 2000), pp 136–144, at 140.
6 Ibid., p. 137.
7 For a modern assessment of these rights, see A. Ferguson, *Common good law* (Edinburgh, 2006); D.J. Cusine & Roderick R.M. Paisley, *Servitudes and rights of way* (Edinburgh, 1998), pp 19–21.

geography of Scotland's burghs meant that the lives and livelihoods of the inhabitants often depended upon the use of the land of their neighbours, which was 'pertinent' to the burgh. The burghs typically had a single high street and often were defined in their extent by natural boundaries such as a river, high cliffs or the sea. Burgh activities that required a large piece of land were thus, inevitably, carried out on land outwith the burgh.

Whilst under the Division of Commonties Act, 1695, common land could be divided amongst those whose title contained written evidence of property in, or servitude over, the commonty, royal burghs were specifically exempt from the act.[8] In an 'action for division' of a commonty over which a burgh of barony held rights of common, where its charter included the terms 'with pertinents', 'common pasturage', 'privileges of commonty' or other indicators of rights of property, oral evidence would be taken regarding the community's customary use rights.[9] The court of session could then order that those rights be protected after division. Such customary use rights were recognized, defined and protected in law as 'positive servitudes'.

SERVITUDES

Servitudes are qualities of land and are constituted between tenements. In the case of a positive servitude, the servient tenement is the burdened land over which the dominant tenement has use rights. Positive servitudes could be constituted by prescription upon proof of forty years' uninterrupted use, or use from 'time immemorial', so long as charter and sasine in the dominant tenement was proved.[10]

Servitudes are real burdens and 'run with the land' — that is they are 'binding irrespective of changes in ownership of the dominant and servient tenements'.[11] Unlike most real burdens, servitudes need not appear on the title to the servient tenement.[12] Given the magnitude of the burden imposed, the courts imposed strict limits on the types of uses that the court would recognise as having given rise to a servitude.[13] The category of uses recognized, however, was not closed. With changes in land use, the courts would recognize new servitudes.[14]

8 Division of Commonties Act 1695 (c.69); Act Anent Lands Lying Run-rig 1695 (c. 36).
9 I.H. Adams, 'The legal geography of Scotland's common lands', *Revue de l'Institut de Sociologie*, 1973:2 (1973), pp 259–323, 267.
10 1617, c.12; J. Erskine, *The principles of the law of Scotland*, 3d ed. (Edinburgh, 1764), b. II. Tit. IX.3; Bell, § 993.
11 W.M. Gordon, *Scottish land law* (Edinburgh, 1989), p. 751.
12 Ibid., p. 751.
13 G.J. Bell, *Principles of the law of Scotland*, 4th ed. (Edinburgh, 1839), § 979.
14 James, Viscount of Stair, *The institutions of the law of Scotland* (Edinburgh, 1693), b.ii., tit.7. section 5; Erskine, b. II. Tit. IX.1.

In the eighteenth century, two issues were central to litigation by burghs and burgh inhabitants to establish servitudes. Firstly, did the burgh constitute a 'dominant tenement' such that it was capable of holding a servitude on behalf of its inhabitants? Secondly, if the burgh could hold a servitude on behalf of its inhabitants, was the use claimed a type of use that the court would recognise at law as creating a servitude?

DOMINANT TENEMENT

A proprietor only has title to sue and claim a right to servitude where he or she can produce charter and seisin to the dominant tenement. Until the mid-nineteenth century, courts held that royal burghs were capable of constituting a dominant tenement, whereas burghs of barony and regality were not. Baron Hume in his *Lectures*, delivered at the University of Edinburgh 1821–2, explained that this was because in the case of a burgh of barony,

> the incorporation (the united community), as such, do not hold any possession nor territory of any kind, to serve as dominant lands ... All they hold as a corporation is their immunities and privileges in point of trade and government, and internal administration, – a sort of incorporeal estate, which cannot be taken for a tenement, or connect with any such accessory or appendage.'[15]

Because royal burghs were infeft in the land of the burgh, a royal burgh could hold and claim servitudes on behalf of burgh's inhabitants. Such servitudes could be exercised over land outwith the burgh, or over burgh land that had been feued subject to the community's servitudes.[16]

Burghs of barony and regality, where the burgh was held not of the crown but of a subject superior, could not hold rights of servitude on behalf of their inhabitants because they were not infeft in the land.[17] In *Dunse v. Hay*[18] (1732) the burgesses and inhabitants of the village of Duns, acting as a corporation, sought a declarator of servitude of pasturage against the proprietor of a piece of land known as the 'commonty of Dunse'. The defender admitted that the burgesses and inhabitants had 'been in possession of the servitude past memory of man, by keeping a common town-herd, and

---

15 G. Campbell H. Paton (ed.), *Baron David Hume's lectures, 1786–1822*, iii, 15 Stair Society (Edinburgh, 1952) p. 265.
16 *Town of Falkland v. Carmichael* (1708) M. 10916; *Sinclair v. Mags of Dysart* (1779) Mor. 14519, 2 Pat. 554 (1789); *Dempster v. Cleghorn* (1805) M. 16141.
17 For an introduction to burgage tenure in Scotland, see G.L. Gretton, 'The feudal system', in K. Reid et al., *The law and property of Scotland* (Edinburgh, 1996), p. 72.
18 (1732) M. 1824.

pasturing their horse, nolt and sheep, promiscuously' over the land, but denied that a burgh of barony had title to acquire a servitude on behalf of its inhabitants.[19] The Court agreed and held that only those who were infeft in a house had title to claim a servitude of pasturage.[20]

'RECOGNIZED IN LAW'

Courts will only recognise a servitude where there is a dominant and servient tenement and where the use claimed is 'recognized in law'. Although courts could recognise new servitudes, they did not often do so because of the lasting burden that the recognition of a servitude created. The most prominent example of a 'new' servitude recognized in the eighteenth century was the servitude of bleaching.

FALKLAND v. CARMICHAEL

In 1708 Dr Carmichael sued the Town of Falkland. He claimed that the loaning at the foot of the Lomonds was his property and that the town enjoyed no servitudes over it.[21] For their part, the representatives of the town, which included members of the linen trade, raised a declarator claiming that the property belonged to it and that the inhabitants of the town had, for time immemorial or forty years, exercised rights of pasturing their animals, casting feal and divot, holding yearly fairs, and bleaching, scouring and washing their linen and wool on the ground by the mill dam.[22] The familiar pattern of claim, counter claim and 'self-help' appears to have preceded the litigation. Alongside their claim of property and servitude, the town accused the doctor of 'violently showering ... the pursuers webs in the milne damn, ... clandestinely under the cloud of night delving up the ... loan, [and] ... violently taking away ... the pursuers Linnen webs' and disposing of them 'without any order of law'.[23]

Like many towns in flax-growing Fife, Falkland had a significant cottage industry manufacturing linen. It is said that the industry helped provide for the needs of the royal palace located there and those of the important

---

19 Ibid., 1825.
20 Ibid., 1829.
21 *Town of Falkland v. Carmichael* (1708) M. 10916. A 'loan' was a type of common green found in southern Scotland that was created over land that had once been used as route way on which cattle were herded to hill pastures or commonties. Adams, 'Legal geography of common lands', 272.
22 *Town of Falkland v. Carmichael*, NAS CS239 F4/9 (13 February 1708).
23 Ibid.

families that followed the royal household to its holiday home, although royal visits had ceased altogether by the mid-seventeenth century.[24] Falkland had been erected into a royal burgh by James II in 1458 and had been granted all the rights associated with royal burghs, including the right to buy and sell merchandise and hold markets and the privilege of electing officers to manage the town, dispense justice and encourage trade and manufacture.

The lords of session found that the property in question belonged to Dr Carmichael but remitted the cause to the lord ordinary to determine whether the town could show that it had enjoyed forty years uninterrupted possession of pasturing, casting feal and divot, keeping fairs on the land and drawing their mill lead through it. Upon hearing further argument, the lords ordered that the lord ordinary also hear proof on the question of whether the town had immemorially possessed the privilege of bleaching linen on the ground.[25]

Dr Carmichael had claimed that the burgh had no dominant tenement in which to claim a servitude over a neighbouring proprietor's land. The charter erecting the burgh, however, had included the terms '*cum cummuni pastura*', and it was successfully argued by the town that such a charter gave sufficient title to claim rights arising by prescription. 'All the debate arose', however, with regard to the burgh's 'servitude of bleaching linen-cloth'.[26] A plurality of the court agreed with Carmichael that the bleaching of linen was not a servitude 'recognised at law' and that therefore proof of immemorial possession of such a use was 'not relevant to infer a servitude'. The use of the loaning was 'by mere tolerance favour and connivance, and not by way of right'.[27]

In *Falkland* it was reported that the lord president and others on the court thought that the practice of bleaching linen could be the subject of prescription or a right of servitude and therefore vest and be claimed as a legal right upon proof of immemorial (or forty years) use. Already in the early eighteenth century some judges were willing to recognise this use of common land (admitted by Carmichael to exist in other towns such as Edinburgh) as one which could give rise to a legal right.[28] By the middle of the eighteenth century, the members of court of session were in agreement that 'constant uninterrupted possession of whitening and drying ... linen upon' a piece of ground gave the inhabitants of a community the legal right to continue to do so.[29]

---

24 The Falkland Society, *A Falkland guide* (Falkland, 1988), p. 14.
25 *Town of Falkland v. Carmichael*, NAS CS239 F4/9 (13 February 1708).
26 *Town of Falkland v. Carmichael* (1708) M. 10916, 10917.
27 Ibid., at 10918.
28 *Town of Falkland v. Carmichael* (1708) M. 10916.
29 (1755) M. 2340, *rev. sub nom* (1757) *Duke of Roxburghe v. Jeffrey (Kelso Case)* 1 Pat. 632.

'KELSO'

The case of *Falkland* was a dispute between neighbours. The town, its inhabitants and, most importantly, its trades people were seeking to protect their traditional rights of access to land that was part of the estate of Balmblae and was owned by Dr Carmichael. Dr Carmichael believed the green to be his, rather than the town's resource, and sought to do with it what he liked. Whilst the right to bleach on the land was held not to be one that had vested in law upon forty years use, the other servitudes claimed by the town – that of pasturage, feal and divot and use of the land for a mill race, were recognised as legal rights that had been acquired by virtue of prescription. Dr Carmichael, therefore, held the land subject to these rights of servitude and could do nothing with the land that would interfere with the community's use.

Some of most important disputes over common land in Scotland, however, were not between mere neighbours but between the rulers and the ruled. Disputes would arise between barons and the inhabitants of the burghs of which they were the superior and between town councils and the inhabitants of the burgh. The case of *Jeffray* (on appeal *Jeffrey*) *v. Roxburgh* (*Kelso*)[30] and the dispute over bleaching on the island of Ana was a small battle in a much larger war that was being carried out by Robert, duke of Roxburghe with the townspeople and incorporated trades of the burgh of barony of Kelso.

Ninian Jeffrey was a successful linen merchant, and, at the time of the lawsuit by the Trades, Feuars, Heritors and Proprietors of Tenements in the burgh of Kelso was brought, treasurer to the merchant company of the burgh.[31] The pursuers were suing the duke because he had abolished the trades, revoked the regulations that governed manufacture and trade in the burgh, diverted the customs from the weekly markets for himself rather than for the 'common good' of the burgh, and was excluding bleachers, skinners and tanners, and local inhabitants from the mill island of Ana.

The duke claimed that the trades were excluding able craftsmen from the market of Kelso and squandering the money raised from the market on 'drinking, riot' and worst of all, 'projecting and carrying on groundless Lawsuits' (against himself).[32] In essence the duke was claiming that having allowed the trades to govern the burgh, he was now asserting his power of lordship to abolish them. As for the island of Ana, which had been created when the river Tweed had broken through the sand bed that had formerly

---

30 Ibid.
31 Durie, 'The Scottish linen industry in the eighteenth century', p. 90.
32 Information for the Duke of Roxburgh, Defender, Dec. 4, 1751, Session Papers Volume 39 (1749–56), No. 66, at 5. (Available at the Signet Library, Edinburgh.)

connected the island its banks, the duke claimed exclusive ownership. He owned the land on both banks of the river, and the townspeople of Kelso had no dominant tenement to which any servitude rights to the island could attach.

The court of session rejected all the defences of the duke. The trades were held to be incorporations with perpetual succession, albeit subject to the regulations of the duke, and the whole revenue of the weekly markets was to go to the good of the town. Finally, the court found that the burgesses and inhabitants of Kelso could continue whitening and drying their linen on the island of Ana, the duke having admitted that they had done so for 'time immemorial'.[33]

The court of session, whilst recognizing the rights of the duke of Roxburghe to regulate the trades of Kelso, nevertheless rejected the notion that his position as baron gave him absolute power over the burgh. Duke Robert died before his appeal was heard by the house of lords, but his heir continued the suit.[34] The house of lords upheld the court of session's finding that the trades were incorporations with perpetual succession and, indeed, strengthened the language of the interlocutor (or judgment) to state explicitly that the duke's power to make regulations for the corporations was 'without prejudice' to any claim by the trades regarding the reasonableness of any entrant, the conditions of their admission, or their 'exclusive privileges of trafficking or trading' in the burgh.

Their lordships, however, found in favour of the duke on the matter of the customs and duties and on the question of the right of the inhabitants of Kelso to bleach and tan skins on the island. No reasons were given for their decision and the meaning of the case of Kelso with regard to the servitude of bleaching would be debated by advocates and judges for nearly a century afterwards.

Lord Kames in his report of the case explains that the right to bleach on the island had been lost to the townspeople by 'negative prescription'.[35] In other words, the use itself had not been proved to their lordship's satisfaction. Other reporters claimed that the Lords had upheld the duke's defence that Scots law did not recognise a servitude of bleaching.[36] Hume stated that *Kelso* was not a 'bleaching' case at all but rather stood for the proposition that a burgh of barony does not constitute a dominant tenement and thus cannot claim a servitude at all.[37]

---

33 *Duke of Roxburghe v. Jeffrey (Kelso Case)* 1 Pat. 632.
34 *Duke of Roxburgh v. Jeffrey*, Petition of John, Duke of Roxburgh, NAS CS 228 R 2/63.
35 *Duke of Roxburghe v. Jeffrey (Kelso Case)* 1 Pat. 632, 639.
36 M. Napier, *Commentaries on the law of prescription in Scotland* (Edinburgh, 1854), pp 384–385 and authorities at n.1.
37 Hume, 'Lectures', p. 265.

The meaning of the decision in *Kelso* would form the centre-piece of the test case of *Home v. Young (Eyemouth)*[38] in the mid-nineteenth century, discussed below. There are, however, some strong indications that the lords did indeed accept the defence of the duke that a burgh of barony had no dominant tenement and thus no title to sue to claim a right of servitude. Firstly, it was this defence that the duke claimed before the court of session. The duke's counsel did not argue that bleaching was not a servitude recognized in Scots law.[39] The lack of argument might indicate that the view of the minority of the lords of session in *Falkland*, that bleaching could be claimed as a servitude, had by mid-century become the majority view and that the duke's counsel, therefore, chose not to argue the point. Secondly, the house of lords upheld a servitude of bleaching when claimed by a royal burgh only thirty years after the decision in *Kelso* in the case of *Dysart*.[40]

Before the question of whether bleaching was a recognized servitude could be resolved, however, the court of session heard a new form of bleaching case. In *Kilmarnock v. Wilson*, the townspeople asked the court to intervene and prevent the sale of the green on which they washed, bleached and dyed their cloth. They were not claiming a private law right of servitude but rather a public law right to good governance and management of burgh resources by the burgh's magistrates.

COMMUNITY RIGHTS

The burgh of Kilmarnock, like Kelso, was a centre of textile manufacturing and finishing. The town had profited from a scheme by the Commissioners for Trade and Industry to subsidize the establishment of wool manufacturers.[41] A wool factory was established in 1743 and a cloth finishing factory was built three years later.

Whilst some work was carried out on the premises of the factories, cottage industry contributed to the process of producing cloth and carpet with raw materials provided by the manufacturers. The washing, bleaching and dying of cloth was carried out on the town green, which the wool factory let from the magistrates with the proviso that the townspeople could continue to use the land for their washing and bleaching. Other trades, such as the skinners, came to arrangements with the wool manufacturers to also use the green. As it was in the interest of the town for the manufactories to be a success, deals

---

38 (1846) 9 D. 286
39 Information for the Duke of Roxburgh, Defender, Dec. 4, 1751, Session Papers Volume 39 (1749–56), No. 66.
40 *Sinclair v. Mags of Dysart* (1779) Mor. 14519, 2 Pat. 554 (1789).
41 John Hood, 'Two hundred fifty years of carpets' in P. Adams, D. Smith & S. Wilson (eds), *Kilmarnock: aspects of local history 2* (Kilmarnock, 1999), p. 61.

would be struck on the price of rent between manufacturers and the burgh council to encourage industry to develop.

The interests of manufacturers and town councils did not, however, always coincide. Town councils often fell into debt, and indeed many commons disputes began with the roup (or sale) of common land to pay off such debt.[42] The management of the business affairs of the burgh could create divisions within the town's elite. Corruption was rife, and self-dealing amongst the magistrates often resulted in schemes that would benefit individual magistrates, who were appointed not elected, rather than the town as a whole. Such divisions within the tiny body politic of a burgh often resulted in litigation.

In Kilmarnock in 1773 the superior, magistrates and town council decided to proceed with a housing scheme to be built on the green of Kilmarnock. Those who took the newly created feus would become burgesses and would be required to build houses, maintain their road, and use the town's mill and courts.[43] The new burgesses would pay handsomely for the privilege and help to relieve the town of its debt problems.[44] The woollen factory, however, was having its own problems. The business was due to be wound up and the owners, James Wilson, his son and other partners, were keen to attract new investors. To do so, they needed to be able to rent the green – and at a reasonable price.[45]

The Wilsons and others joined together and sought a suspension and interdict to prevent the sale of the green. The burgh of Kilmarnock at one time had been a royal burgh, but at the time of the commons litigation in the 1770's was a burgh of barony. The Wilsons and inhabitants of the burgh, however, were not claiming rights of servitude such as those at issue in *Kelso*; they were suing the magistrates to prevent them feuing assets of the burgh to the detriment of the community.

In 1776 the court of session held that the 'manufacturing inhabitants' had always had the use of the green for the purposes of 'bleaching, drying, etc.' and that whilst alienating the green might improve the public revenues; nonetheless, it would be improper of the magistrates to do so. In the words of Lord Hailes:

> Magistrates are administrators and guardians, not uncontrolled proprietors. They may feu waste ground, but not ground already

---

42 See, e.g., the forced sale of the links in *Dempster v. Cleghorn* (1805) M. 16141, *rem.* (1813) 2 Dow 40.
43 Kilmarnock Town Council Minutes, 14 January 1773, BK/1/1/2/1 (available at the Dick Institute, Kilmarnock) (hereinafter 'Kilmarnock Minutes').
44 For references to the town's borrowing see, e.g., Kilmarnock Minutes 14 January 1773 and 8 March 1774.
45 Kilmarnock Minutes 17 March 1773 and 3 November 1773.

occupied to its best advantage. Here, for the temptation of a ground rent of 15 shillings *per annum* from each house, they would deprive the whole inhabitants of a green which is at present useful, and which the inhabitants offer, at their own expense, to make render more useful. The Magistrates of Glasgow might build the noblest street in Scotland by feuing out the green of Glasgow, and yet the Court would never authorise such a plan.[46]

The action continued for another year, but ultimately the town settled with the manufacturers and inhabitants and 'renounce[d] the right they have or may have to sell or feu out the ... Common Town Green or any part thereof'.[47] As part of the settlement, the inhabitants agreed that the parties would each pay their own expenses. This was a great saving for the town against which expenses had been charged by the court. As early as 1774, the town council had had to borrow funds to cover their own costs of the litigation.[48] The settlement of the issue also allowed Wilson to proceed with his new venture, Wilson, Gregory and Co., which opened in 1778 and produced 'blankets, plush, damask and all kinds of Scotch carpets, narrow twilled cloths of different colours and horse and collar cloths fit for saddles.'[49]

A SERVITUDE OF BLEACHING

A month after the magistrates of Kilmarnock settled their action with the town's manufacturers and inhabitants, the court of session upheld the right of the inhabitants of the royal burgh of Dysart to wash, bleach and dry their linen on the property of the neighbouring barony of Colonel James Sinclair. Unlike in the case brought by the inhabitants of Kelso thirty years before, the house of lords upheld the servitude of bleaching found by the Scots court to belong to the inhabitants of the royal burgh, which was claimed by the magistrates and town council of the burgh on their behalf. Once again, no reasons for the decision of their Lordships were reported, and so the meaning of the case of *Kelso*, cited by counsel for the proposition that a servitude of bleaching is 'unknown in law', remained in doubt. The Lords did not state whether the fact that Dysart was a royal burgh (and therefore constituted a dominant tenement) distinguished the case from that of *Kelso*, or whether, like the court of session before it, the court had merely decided that societal developments required that the practice of bleaching be 'recognised' as a legal servitude.

46 *Mags of Kilmarnock v. Wilson* (1776) Hailes 738.
47 Kilmarnock Minutes 21 October 1777.
48 Kilmarnock Minutes 8 March 1774.
49 Hood, 'Two hundred fifty years of carpets', p. 61.

Like the litigation between Roxburghe and the inhabitants of Kelso, the action to exclude the inhabitants from bleaching their linen on the eight-acre site of Lethem Wells was one of a number of cases between Colonel Sinclair and the magistrates of Dysart. The town claimed that Sinclair had begun his campaign of litigation against it due to a dispute over who was to be the Member of Parliament for the district. Whether this was the sole cause of the animosity between the parties is unclear, but the town minutes do evidence a general 'ceasefire' and settlement of all outstanding cases in 1780, after the decision in *Dysart* had been announced.

For the townspeople, access to the wells for bleaching was vital. Like Falkland, Kelso and Kilmarnock, the manufacture and finishing of cloth was a growing industry in Dysart. Moreover, clean water with which to wash and bleach cloth was a scarce commodity because coal mining – the town's greatest industry – had polluted the wells and brooks of the town.[50] Sinclair, himself, may have recognised this. Rather than appeal the whole of the case, he conceded the right of the townspeople to take water for family use and only appealed the practice of bleaching on the site. The importance of the wells to the townspeople and their industry is highlighted by the long negotiation for their relinquishment with the heir and successor of Colonel Sinclair, Sir James St Clair–Erskine. After the decision of the house of lords, the townspeople of Dysart continued to use Lethem wells for another forty years until an alternative water supply and green was provided by the earl, with some investment by the magistrates.[51]

The confirmation by the house of lords that a servitude of bleaching was recognised at law and could be claimed by a royal burgh was an important development that bolstered the position of communities, the textile industries of which were dependent upon access to clean water and land on which to dry their cloth. Particularly in Fife, where royal burghs were often confined by the sea on one boundary and cliffs on the other, its was essential that access to greens on the land of neighbouring proprietors was secure. At the end of the eighteenth century, however, only the rights of inhabitants of royal burghs were protected. If *Kelso* remained good law – and there was nothing to indicate that it was not – then the use rights exercised by the inhabitants of burghs of barony, at least in so far as they were exercised over land outwith the burgh, could not be recognised at law as servitudes. A burgh of barony had no dominant tenement in which to claim such a legal right. The case of *Kilmarnock* offered such inhabitants protection from the predations of their magistrates as a matter of public law, but not from those of their neighbours or feudal superiors, where their rights had to be claimed

50 Respondent's Case House of Lords 1780, 1, NAS GD 164/445.
51 Minutes of Dysart Town Council, 20 January 1820.

as servitudes. In such cases, only feuars who could show that a servitude was pertinent to their property had title to sue to protect their customary use of another's land.[52]

EYEMOUTH

In 1845 a case came before the court of session that highlighted the injustice that could result when proof of proprietorship was required in order to vindicate a customary right held by the inhabitants of a burgh of barony. The Home family were the proprietors of the lands and barony of Eyemouth, which was erected by charter into a burgh of barony in 1597. David Milne, judicial factor over Eyemouth, and William Home, the first heir in entail of the lands, brought an action of declarator against five inhabitants of the burgh claiming an exclusive right of property in the land of the Fort of Eyemouth, including the Shore Well and adjacent land known as the Parade or Wellbraes, free from any 'burden or servitude of bleaching of linen, washing of clothes, drawing of water, or other burden or servitude whatsoever'. The action was raised against the wives of working men in the village: Alice Young, wife of a carpenter (along with her husband for his interest), Mary Gillie, wife of a fisher, and Elisabeth Pae and Agnes M'Kay, both wives of masons. The pursuers were able, in the words of their counsel, 'to single out five of the poorest inhabitants' of the village as defenders.[53]

The strategy of the pursuers was clear. In order to claim a servitude of taking water, washing clothes and bleaching linen on the basis of forty years use, the defenders would have to show charter and seisin in the dominant tenement. The houses of the defenders were owned by absentee landlords who, when sued directly by Home and Milne (having been contacted first by letter), disclaimed any servitude right.[54] The landlords of Young, Pae and M'Kay had ceased to live in the village and were 'not disposed to be at the expense of defending a privilege in which they were not personally interested'.[55] The pursuers were also able to settle the action with Mary Gillie or Leach, the only defender who was also a feuar. Her house was owned by her mother in liferent and herself in fee.[56]

---

52 *Dunse v. Hay*, (1732) M. 1824.
53 The defenders were enrolled on the Poor's Roll and received free legal representation. NAS 1P H/14/59. See C.N. Stoddart, 'A short history of legal aid in Scotland', *Juridical Review* (1972), pp 170–192.
54 Minute containing Condescendence of emerging fact for William F. Home Esq. of Billie & Paxton and David Milne (20 December 1844), NAS 1P H/14/59.
55 *Home v. Young* (1846) 9 D. 286; (27 Nov–12 Jan. 1846–47) General Coll. Session Papers, Vol. 417, Nos. 30–57, No. 46, Revised Minute of Debate for Alice Young or Grey and Others, No. VI, 30.
56 Deposition of Havers in *Cause Home & Milne v. Gray* (7 June 1844), NAS 1P H/14/59;

Once Home and Milne had settled with Gillie and the landlords of Gray, M'Kay and Pae, the defenders could not claim a servitude belonging to their houses. They could only claim the right of access to the well and adjoining land as either a right vested in the public at large or in the community of Eyemouth.[57] Access such as that claimed had, however, never been found as a public right. As for the community claim, whilst the house of lords had recently stated, *obiter dictum*, that a use right could be claimed by any 'inhabitant of a town' in the case of *Aikman v. Duke of Hamilton*,[58] the weight of authority held that the decisions in *Dunse* and *Kelso* stood for the proposition that a burgh of barony did not constitute a dominant tenement and could not hold a servitude on behalf of the community. Under the law as it was understood at the time, if a right of taking water, washing clothes and bleaching linen could be shown to have arisen by forty years use, these village women could only claim it by virtue of their landlords' interest in the land. By settling with the absentee landlords of the poor defenders, the claim of customary right of a whole community to a well and green had been undermined. Counsel for the defenders was keen to point out the cynical nature of this ploy.[59] The lord ordinary responded to this tactic by referring the case to the inner house and issuing a long note finding in favour of the inhabitants' right to defend the action.

He referred the case because it presented 'a question of great interest to the towns and villages throughout the country, – a numerous class, generally ill able to defend their own rights' and deserved 'the deliberate consideration of the Court'.[60] In *Eyemouth* the 'right to a partial use of ... a little piece of waste ground' was transformed into a test case that would establish the legal rights of inhabitants throughout Scotland and challenge the legal limitations on community rights created by courts adjudicating such rights under the rubric of the law of servitudes. The case, in the words of Lord Jeffrey, was

---

Minute for Mary Gillie or Leach, wife of Andrew Leach, Fisher in Eyemouth, and for the said Andrew Leach her husband as taking burden on him for his said wife, and also for the said Andrew Leach himself for his own right and interest in the premises (28 June 1844), NAS 1P H/14/59. It was a near fatal error to the strategy of the Pursuers to include Mrs. Leach in the action, according to the Defender. Prior to this Minute being lodged by Pursuers' Counsel, the defenders had hoped to rely on her title as a feuar to defend the action. No. 6 Revised Minute of debate for Alice Young/Gray NAS 1P H/14/59, 30.

57 Minute containing Condescendence of emerging fact for William F Home Esq. of Billie & Paxton and David Milne (20 December 1844), NAS 1P H/14/59, 5; No. 6 Revised Minute of debate for Alice Young/Gray NAS 1P H/14/59, 31–32; Minute of Debate for William F Home Esq. of Billie & Paxton and David Milne.
58 (1830) 8 S. 942, (1832) 6 W.S. 64, (1833) 5 S.J. 7.
59 Ibid., *Home v. Young* (1846) 9 D. 286; (27 Nov.–12 Jan. 1846–47) General Coll. Session Papers, Vol. 417, Nos. 30–57, No. 46, Revised Minute of Debate for Alice Young or Grey and Others, No. VI, 38.
60 *Home v. Young* (1846) 9 D. 286, 290.

'as elaborately considered, both at the bar' and by their lordships, 'as if the right to the whole barony' was being determined rather than the rights of the inhabitants to a small piece of ground.[61] The lords of session all commented on the skill, learning and extensive research displayed by counsel in the action.

For all that was at stake and ingenuity displayed by counsel, the judges appeared to come to their decision in favour of the inhabitants with a great deal of ease. This is because they did not view the case as one turning on the question of servitude – an area of law that was at once highly technical and lacking in reasoned and reported legal judgments.[62] Rather, *Eyemouth* was fundamentally a case about the rights of inhabitants of burgh communities *vis à vis* their magistrates or, in the absence of magistrates, the community's feudal superior. The lords of session removed the case of *Eyemouth* from the rubric of the Roman/Scots law of servitude and instead decided the case on public law principles of good governance and public trust.

In the view of their lordships, what the superior was claiming in *Eyemouth* was an absolute and arbitrary power to deprive eleven hundred burgh inhabitants of rights necessary for their survival and intrinsic to the purposes for which the burgh of barony was erected.[63] In the absence of elected magistrates, the superior was to be regarded as having taken upon himself the 'duties of superintendence and guardianship' of the burgh and became the 'protector' of the rights and privileges of the burgh.[64] The judges could see no reason for distinguishing between royal burghs and burghs of barony either with regard to the right of inhabitants to claim use rights or the responsibility of the magistrates (or in this case the baron who stood in their place) to protect them.

In order to reach this conclusion, the judges in *Eyemouth* had to explain why the authorities that had been previously understood as standing for the proposition that only a royal burgh could claim a servitude on behalf of its inhabitants did not apply. These included the case of *Dunse*,[65] where in 1732

---

61 Ibid., p. 303, per Lord Jeffrey.
62 In November, 1842 when approached for an opinion by the pursuers on the proposed *Eyemouth* action, advocate A. Wood wrote that '[t]he authorities bearing upon the point embraced in this query, are far from explicit, and I cannot venture to give any decided opinion in regard to it.' He concluded his opinion by suggesting that Home and Milne acquiesce in the use whilst guarding against its extension. He 'entertained considerable doubt of the expediency of embarking in a litigation ... [t]he matters at Issue not being clear in point of Law' and the facts being uncertain and rather likely to 'turn out against' them. Register of Legal Documents Relating to Billie Judicial Factor (1841–51), NAS GD267/25/132, 40.
63 *Home v. Young* (1846) 9 D. 286, 290.
64 Ibid., 295, per Lord President.
65 (1732) M. 1824.

it had been held that the burgh of barony of Duns could not hold a servitude of pasturage on behalf of its inhabitants, and the case of *Kelso*.[66]

Nearly a century after the *Kelso* judgment, commentators and judges alike still disagreed over the meaning of the reversal of the court of session's decision regarding the inhabitants' bleaching rights on the island of Ana by the house of lords.[67] The judgment of Lord Fullerton in *Eyemouth* that he did not know why the house of lords reversed the decision in Kelso is perhaps the most honest assessment of all of the explanations for the decision.[68] The other judges in *Eyemouth* proffered different theories of the grounds of reversal, but all agreed that, firstly, it had not been due to the burgh's lack of title and, secondly, that the decision was, in any case, inapposite. The case did not apply because the claim of the inhabitants of Kelso to a servitude of bleaching was over the land of another – the duke of Roxburghe. The claim made by the Eyemouth inhabitants was, in the view of a majority of the lords of session, over land that was part of the territory of the burgh and its pertinents'.[69] In fact the case of *Kelso* was almost identical to that of *Eyemouth*. In both cases the baron was seeking to deprive the inhabitants of their customary right to bleach on his property – property which the inhabitants claimed was either part of the barony or its pertinents.

The various *Eyemouth* judges claimed that in *Kelso* the house of lords held that possession of the servitude had not been proved,[70] that a servitude of bleaching was not recognized in law,[71] or that the servitude was not claimed over burgh property.[72] None of these explanations, however, are satisfactory. Baron Hume was probably correct that the lords found for the duke of Roxburghe on the defence claimed – that the burgh of barony had no title to hold a servitude on behalf of its inhabitants. This conclusion is supported by the fact that when the house of lords heard the case of *Dysart*, where a royal burgh claimed a servitude of bleaching, the right to servitude

---

66 *Duke of Roxburghe v. Jeffray* (1755) M. 2340, rev. sub nom (1757) *Duke of Roxburghe v. Jeffrey (Kelso Case)* 1 Pat. 632.
67 See Napier, *Commentaries on the law of prescription in Scotland*, 384–385 and authorities at n.1.
68 *Home v. Young* (1846) 9 D. 286, 301.
69 Ibid., 297, 300, 304 per Lord President and Lords Mackenzie and Jeffrey; *cf.* Ibid. at 302 per Lord Fullerton ('I have assumed that these wells are within the district of the burgh. I do not, however, care whether that be the case or not, as my principle would equally apply').
70 *Home v. Young* (1846) 9 D. 286, 295, per Lord President, but cf. *Dyce v. Hay* (1849) 11 D. 1266, 1271, per Lord Justice-Clerk ('Certainly I admit that the explanation given in one of the opinions in the Eyemouth case cannot be received, viz., that it appeared that the house of lords went on the insufficiency of the proof, since an erroneous view had been given to the Court in the Eyemouth case as to the state of that case of Kelso').
71 Ibid., p. 290, per Lord Ordinary.
72 Ibid., p. 300, per Lord Mackenzie.

was upheld.[73] The genuine difference between the decision of the court of session in *Eyemouth* and the house of lords in *Kelso* was the passage of time. Nineteenth-century courts simply refused to uphold arbitrary exercises of the power of lordship that had been regularly approved by courts in the eighteenth century.[74]

The task of reinterpreting *Kelso* was made easier by the lack of reasons for the decision of the house of lords. The case of *Dunse*, however, was arguably still good law. In *Dunse*, a burgh of barony had been held to be incapable of holding a servitude of pasturage on behalf of its inhabitants. This case had been thought by commentators like Napier and Hume, as well as generations of practicing advocates, to stand for the general proposition that a burgh of barony *qua* a corporation could not hold a servitude.[75] The clarity of this position had, however, been muddied by the decision of the house of lords in the recent case of *Aikman v. Duke of Hamilton* (1832).[76]

'AIKMAN v. HAMILTON' AND THE ENGLISH LAW OF CUSTOM

The duke of Hamilton sued George Robertson Aikman in the sheriff's court for taking gravel from his estate. The action was advocated to the court of session, where Aikman sought a declarator that he and the other inhabitants of the burgh of regality of Hamilton had a right, arising from positive prescription, to take sand and gravel from the banks of the Clyde.[77] The court of session found that Aikman had good title to claim a servitude and that in support of his claim before the jury court he could rely on 'the possession of persons proprietors and occupiers of houses and gardens in the town of Hamilton similarly situated' to his.[78] In other words, he could vindicate the right as one belonging to the community as a whole.

On appeal, there was much that the house of lords found unsatisfactory about the case. The interlocutors of the court of session were reversed and the case remitted to the court of session. In part this was because whilst 'Scotch law was the same as the laws of all countries where founded upon common sense', the Jury Court was a new institution.[79] The Scottish courts

---

73 2 Pat. 554 (1789).
74 A.C. Loux, 'The persistence of the ancient regime' (see note 1 above), 197.
75 See also, Bell in his *Principles* of 1839, 'Royal Burghs may, as the Crown's vassal, possess for individuals, but not burghs of barony'. § 993.
76 *Aikman v. Duke of Hamilton* (1830) 8 S. 942; (1832) 6 W.S. 64, (1833) 5 S.J. 7.
77 *Aikman v. Duke of Hamilton* (1833) 5 S.J. 7, at 9.
78 Ibid., p. 8.
79 Ibid., 9, col. 1.

lacked 'the habit' of stating causes using precise language and could not be expected to 'administer [such proceedings] with the same degree of accuracy and precision' as they were in England.[80] The form of words approved by the court of session to allow Aikman to found possession on evidence of the use of his neighbours was rejected.[81]

On the question of whether an inhabitant of a burgh of barony *qua* inhabitant could claim such a servitude, Lord Wynford opined that the laws of England and Scotland differed. In English law, a legal right to take sand and gravel would arise under the doctrine of custom.[82] There were two categories of custom: *profits à prendre*, where the right entailed pasturing animals or otherwise taking a product from the common; and easement customs, where a renewable resource such as a well is accessed or the land is used by a community for an activity such as playing games.[83] *Profits* could only be claimed by copyholders of a manor whereas easement customs could be claimed on the grounds of inhabitancy of a particular district. In English law, a right such as that claimed by Aikman would be a *profit à prendre* and could only be claimed by the holder of an estate.[84]

In Scotland, according to Lord Wynford, the right could be claimed by Aikman either as a property owner or as an inhabitant of a town.[85] On its face, therefore, the decision in *Aikman* appeared to control the case of *Eyemouth*. The house of lords held that Aikman, an inhabitant of a burgh of regality, could claim a servitude of taking sand and gravel on the grounds of that title alone. Their lordships, however, went on to say that the right of taking sand and gravel could only be claimed 'for the use of his own property'[86] or in the words of another reporter, '*in the right of* and for the use of his own properties' (emphasis added).[87] This language was very close to that of the court of session in *Dunse*, where the servitude of pasturage had been limited to feuars who could claim a servitude attached to their property.

---

80 Ibid., at 9, col. 2.
81 The Scottish court later held that the defect in the question had been one of form rather than substance. After the decision in *Aikman*, the court of session allowed the Writer (solicitor) James Thorburn of the royal burgh of Dumfries in *Thorburn v. Charters* to pose a question to a jury asking whether for a period of forty years the proprietors of his house, his tenants, 'and the other inhabitants of the ... street or neighbourhood' have had access to and drawn water from a local mill dam. (1841) 4 D. 169.
82 On the historical development of custom in England and its Roman roots, see J. Getzler, 'Roman and English prescription for incorporeal property' in J. Getzler (ed.), *rationalizing property, equity and trusts: essays in honour of Edward Burn* (London, 2003).
83 See, e.g., *Race v. Ward*, (1855) 4 E. & B. 702; *Fitch v. Rawling*, 2 Hy. Bl. 393, 126 Eng. Rep. 614 (C.P. 1795).
84 See A.C. Loux 'The persistence of the ancient regime', 197, 187 and 195–200.
85 *Aikman v. Duke of Hamilton* (1833) 5 S.J. 7, 9.
86 Ibid., 10.
87 *Aikman v. Duke of Hamilton* (1832) 6 W.S. 64.

The mischief that the lords were trying to prevent was the taking of the sand and gravel by the inhabitants to be sold. The concern was that if an unlimited right were approved, the entire *solum* could be carried off.[88] The house of lords, whilst recognizing the difference between English and Scots law with regard to the rights of inhabitants to claim a right in the nature of a *profit à prendre*, nonetheless adopted the reasoning of English courts in profit cases that in order to prevent the destruction of the resource, such a right had to be limited with reference to an interest in property.

George Aikman was not a mere inhabitant of the town. He was the proprietor of houses and gardens in Hamilton, and the lords ultimately vindicated his right to take sand and gravel for the use of those properties. Taken together with the refusal to allow Aikman to rely on the testimony of his neighbours to establish a community right, the view of Lord Wynford that inhabitants of a town could claim servitudes, in light of the final decision, was *obiter dictum*. In *Eyemouth*, where the owners of the houses had disclaimed the right to the rood and wells claimed by George Home in his suit against the occupying tenants, Lord Wynford's assertions with regard to rights of in the inhabitants of Scottish towns was to be tested by the court of session.

EYEMOUTH AND THE CREATION OF COMMUNITY RIGHTS IN SCOTS LAW

Like the law lords in *Aikman*, the Scots court, at least in part, looked not to the Scots law of servitudes but rather to the English law of custom to determine the rights of the inhabitants of Eyemouth. The lords of session distinguished the case of *Eyemouth* from the earlier case of *Dunse* by adopting the profit/easement distinction from English law. As the English courts had recognized since the early seventeenth century, rights in the nature of *profit à prendre* involve limited resources and when those rights are determined by a court, the category of users must somehow be restricted.[89] According to the *Eyemouth* court, this had been recognized in Scots law in the case of *Dunse*, where the court had limited the right of pasturage to those who were infeft in a house. But, according to Lord Fullerton, this was the extent of the court's holding in *Dunse*. Whilst a great deal of argument had been advanced in that case that a burgh of barony could not hold a servitude, the 'views of the Court' were not expressed. In his view, in *Dunse* 'there is no distinction taken there between the case of a burgh of barony and a royal burgh'. The

---

88 G. Hardin, 'The tragedy of the commons', *Science* 162: 3859 (1968), 1243.
89 Thompson, 'Customs in common', p. 133 (discussing the decision in *Gateward's Case*, 6 Co. Rep. 59b (KB 1607) and its invocation in cases in the eighteenth century).

whole of the argument employed against the corporation acquiring the servitude claimed, would be just as good against a royal burgh as against a burgh of barony.[90] *Dunse* did not control the court in *Eyemouth* because the limitations required to be placed on a right of pasturage did not apply where the right to take water and wash and bleach was being claimed.

Moreover, according to the court, *Eyemouth* could be distinguished from the servitude cases of *Dunse*, *Kelso* and *Aikman* on the grounds that in those cases the claims were made over the land of neighbouring proprietors. The claim of the Eyemouth inhabitants was a right of use over land that the court found belonged to the territory and pertinents of the burgh.[91] What was being sought in *Eyemouth* was not a servitude over another's property but an 'easement' over the burgh's own land. The court of session invoked not merely the substance of the English distinction between *profits* and easement customs, but the English nomenclature as well.[92] The right at issue in Eyemouth was a mere 'right of use' in the nature of an 'easement,' which as a matter of public law inured to all inhabitants regardless of whether they held property.[93] It was not the law of servitudes that should be applied to determine the title of the inhabitants to defend their rights but rather the public law of maladministration.[94] In the absence of magistrates, the Baron had stepped into their shoes and was as duty bound as the magistrates of Kilmarnock to protect the customary rights of the inhabitants.

PUBLIC TRUST AND COMMUNITY RIGHTS

Eyemouth consolidated the applicable decisions on the rights of inhabitants and imposed new duties on superiors of burghs of barony where there were no magistrates. Whilst the progressive nature of *Eyemouth* was cloaked in the eighteenth-century precedent governing the obligations of magistrates, the decision marked a significant change in the law. The *Eyemouth* Court found that the right at issue was not a servitude; nevertheless, both Lord Fullerton

---

90 Ibid., 301. See also *Burntisland*, as recounted in Lord Ordinary's Note in *Home v. Young* (1846) 9 D. 286, at 294.

91 Ibid., 298, per Lord President; 300, per Lord Mackenzie ('I don't know if it be disputed whether they are within the territory of the burgh or not, but an offer is made to prove immemorial possession. Can we doubt that it was just part of the territory and its pertinents?').

92 On the comparison between English easements and Scots servitudes, see A.G.M. Duncan, 'Servitudes and public rights of way', in K. Reid et al., *The law and property of Scotland*, p. 355.

93 *Home v. Young* (1846) 9 D. 286, at 300 per Lord Mackenzie ('I don't consider it necessary to enter into the question of servitude at all; for this is no servitude, – it is no more so than the right to the burgh jail').

94 Ibid., 304, per Lord Jeffrey.

and Lord Jeffrey left open the possibility that burghs of barony and regality could claim servitudes over land outwith the burgh on behalf of local inhabitants.[95] This view represented a significant change of the law as understood by commentators such as Baron Hume and Mark Napier.

In acting to protect the customary rights of all burgh inhabitants, the judges were following the lead of parliament, which had been investigating failures in the governance of royal burghs since the late eighteenth century with particular regard to the failure of magistrates to protect common land. The investigation would ultimately lead to burgh reform in 1833, when legislation was passed that established a system of election for magistrates of all Scottish burghs and required the magistrates to make annual accounts available to the public.[96]

The decision in *Eyemouth*, however, reflects more than a mere change of policy of the court of session. As was pointed out in the vitriolic attack by historian and Sheriff of Dumfries Mark Napier in his *Commentaries on the Law of Prescription in Scotland*, the decision in *Eyemouth*, and in particular the note of the lord ordinary, signalled a fundamental change in judicial ideology. The lord ordinary's note in favour of the rights of Eyemouth's inhabitants proceeded on the basis that 'there has been a great change and enlargement, in modern times, as to the principles on which claims of servitude, or of qualified uses of property, ought to receive effect'. In earlier times, 'under the influence of feudal notions, the leaning of the law was all in favour of the party holding ... [the] radical title of property', and servitudes and other burdens on property were 'held to be odious' and 'discouraged on the most strict and technical views of the law'. In modern times, though, those early precedents had been overruled by courts 'proceeding on more just views of the rights of property'.[97] Lord Cuninghame cited a wealth of examples in his Note of community uses upheld by the court of session in the nineteenth century. Courts had recognised community rights to take sand and gravel, to use drove roads and to establish a footpath. Even the right of inhabitants to claim a legal right to a game of golf had been upheld.[98] In his view, '[i]f such effect be given to mere rights of amusement claimed for the inhabitants of a town or district, how much more is due to the claims for water and bleaching, which, in many localities, are indispensable for the subsistence and health of the humblest members of the community.'[99]

---

95 Ibid., 302, per Lord Fullerton, 304, per Lord Jeffrey.
96 Royal Burghs (Scotland) Act 1833, 3 & 4 Will. IV, c.76; Parliamentary Burghs (Scotland) Act 1833 3 & 4 Will. IV, c.77.
97 *Home v. Young (Eyemouth)* (1846) 9 D. 286, 290, per the Lord Ordinary in his Note.
98 Ibid., at 290–1. See *Dempster v. Cleghorn* (1805) M. 16141, *rem.* (1813) 2 Dow 40; and cf. earlier cases of *spatiandi*, e.g., *Cochrane v. Fairholm* (1759) M. 14518.
99 *Home v. Young* (1846) 9 D. 286, 291, per the Lord Ordinary.

As Napier would point out in no case – except perhaps those of the drove roads – had a community other than a royal burgh been able to claim a community right to a servitude. Even 'enlightened' commentators on the law of servitudes had not countenanced the idea that a servitude could be claimed absent a dominant tenement.[1] The requirement that 'uses of the property of another' be founded upon a dominant tenement was not based on 'barbarous feudal notions'. It was based 'upon the simple proposition, and still prevailing maxim, that *meum* is not *tuum*'.[2] To do away with the requirement of a dominant tenement and allow inhabitants *qua* inhabitants to establish rights over others' property undermined the very principles upon which the law of servitudes was based.

Napier wrote his commentary after Lord Cuninghame referred the case to the inner house with his accompanying Note but before the final decision; nevertheless, his commentary on the lord ordinary's note remains untouched in the text of 1854. Napier was firm in his view that the *Eyemouth* Court was wrong to sanction the title of a burgh of barony to hold a servitude in the name of 'expediency'.[3]

In *Eyemouth*, the court modernized the feudal law that had held that royal burghs were a unique form of urban community. Burghs of barony had not been excluded from the terms of the 1695 Acts that permitted division of common land and had not, before *Eyemouth*, been recognised as having title to claim a servitude.[4] *Eyemouth* did away with the old distinctions and recognized as a matter of public law the modern burgh corporation, the legal nature of which was no longer defined by the identity of the burgh's superior. In this they were following the programme of modernization of burgh government that had been begun by Parliament with the acts of 1833 and continued with the abolition of the feudal privileges of the burgh incorporations the year *Eyemouth* was decided.[5]

Whilst driven by the reforming zeal of the court of session, and in particular its Whig judges, the decision in *Eyemouth* did not signal a wholesale revolution in the property law of Scotland. In 1860 when the inhabitants of the village of Lochgelly sued the earl of Minto to protect a variety of rights over the common muir, the court held that a group of villagers could not claim the same rights of servitude as an incorporated burgh.[6] More importantly for twenty-first century property law and politics, when lawyer-activists brought a test case based on the First Division's decision in *Eyemouth* to claim rights of recreation for the inhabitants of Old

1   Ibid., 382.
2   Ibid., 382.
3   Ibid., 374.
4   In 1764, the Commonty of Eyemouth had been divided. Ibid., 287–8.
5   T. Johnston, *The history of the working classes in Scotland* (1st edn, Glasgow, 1922), p. 146.
6   *Henderson v. Earl of Minto* (1860) 22 D. 1126.

Aberdeen on the land of Lady James Hay, the second division cut short the judicial innovations of their judicial brethren and held that the decision in *Eyemouth* could not be used to justify access to land of an 'unrelated third party'.[7] The decision in *Dyce v. Hay* hampered the efforts of campaigners for access to land for a century and a half, until the Land Reform Act 2003 was passed by the newly created Scottish parliament.

The fate of the innovations of the Scottish bleaching cases in the eighteenth and nineteenth centuries demonstrates the capacity of the common law, operating through legal doctrines that give legal legitimacy to community custom, to incorporate both innovations in land use and changes in political ideology. Paradoxically, they also demonstrate the limits of that capacity. The innovations of the *Eyemouth* court were hindered as much by the limits of doctrine as by those judges who opposed the 'introduction of new law' by judicial fiat.[8] By reconstructing the rights of access of the inhabitants as community rights protected by public law, the court both excluded the possibility that unincorporated localities could claim similar rights and left open the possibility that a more conservative court would limit rights of access where no pre-existing relationship existed between the parties.

CONCLUSION

In 1708 a majority of judges of the court of session in the case of *Falkland* were not yet willing to recognize a servitude of bleaching. By the middle of the century, the court of session recognised the right in the inhabitants of the burgh of barony of Kelso without especial comment or discussion in *Kelso v. Roxburgh*. When the duke of Roxburghe took his case to the house of lords, their lordships acted both to protect, and indeed strengthen, the rights of the regressive, monopolistic trades as well as the exclusive rights of property of one Britain's largest and most important landowners. Whilst the Lords would recognize a servitude of bleaching held by the royal burgh of Dysart in 1789, rights of common of inhabitants of burghs of barony would not be fully protected from appropriation by neighbours and feudal superiors until the middle of the nineteenth century. The decision of the house of lords in *Kelso* restricted the legal recognition of the servitude rights of the inhabitants of burghs of barony for nearly a century.

Marxist scholarship on common land in Scotland has emphasized the loss of urban common land to capitalists, agricultural land to enclosure and the abolition of custom as a source of right.[9] The history of the bleaching cases

---

7 *Dyce v. Hay* (1849) 11 D. 1266.
8 Ibid., 1270, per Lord Justice-Clerk.
9 T. Johnston, 'The history of the working classes in Scotland' and E.J. Hobsbawm, 'Scottish reformers of the eighteenth century and capitalist agriculture' in E.J. Hobsbawm, W. Kula,

in Scotland belies, at least in part, such assumptions. In cases brought on behalf of the inhabitants of Scotland's burghs, capitalist litigation served to protect communally held land and the interests of local inhabitants against improving landlords and town councils alike. In *Dysart*, Colonel Sinclair wished to be rid of the communal bleaching that was taking place too close to his home and private washing ground and to protect the trees he had planted nearby as part of an agricultural improvement scheme.[10] In *Kilmarnock*, the baron and town council wanted to build houses to fill the council's coffers.[11] The reasons for the actions of the duke of Roxburgh are more opaque, although it has been suggested that bleaching interfered with fishing on the Tweed. To be sure, such litigation was pursued to protect not the rights of independent cottage industry but rather the suppliers of emerging markets and growing manufacturing concerns. As Eric Hobsbawm points out, 'Scotland was not merely a part of British capitalism, but – both in its industry and in its agriculture – a pioneer of capitalist development, in certain respects superior to England.'[12] Such litigation did, however, protect common land and communal use for the burgh's inhabitants even as it contributed to the decline of cottage industry.

E.P. Thompson, in his seminal essay 'Custom, Law and Common Right' recognizes that in England urban common land remained open long after the majority of rural enclosures had taken place and attributes this to the money and resources of 'bourgeois commoners' who sued to protect their common rights.[13] Outside of these urban exceptions, however, Thompson argues that English judges prioritised ownership over common use because they 'shared the mentalities of improving landowners'.[14] In Scotland members of an emerging manufacturing and trading class similarly used the law to good effect to preserve the common good for their own and their communities' use. The bleaching cases of Scotland, however, cast doubt on the thesis that the results of custom cases were determined by the 'shared mentalities' or class bias of members of the judiciary.

Firstly, in Scotland as early as 1755 the court of session was willing to recognize that the customary uses of the people of Kelso took precedence over the legal title of the duke of Roxburghe to his island in the Tweed. Whilst the house of lords rejected this decision and sided with the duke in his dispute with the community of Kelso, by 1789 their lordships were

---

A. Mitra, K.N. Raj, I. Sachs (eds), *Peasants in history: essays in honour of Daniel Thorner* (Calcutta, 1980).
10 NAS GD 164/820 'Instructions for Mr. Jameson'; NAS GD164/445 Appellant's Case, house of lords, *Sinclair v. Dysart*.
11 Kilmarnock Town Council Minutes, 14 January 1773.
12 Hobsbawm, 'Scottish reformers of the eighteenth century and capitalist agriculture', p. 5.
13 Thompson, 'Customs in common', 121, 114.
14 Ibid., 137.

willing to uphold the claims of the inhabitants of Dysart to a bleaching ground as against the claims of the neighbouring landowner. By the mid-nineteenth century, the Scots court was expanding the range of communities that could claim customary rights as against their superior to include burghs of barony.

Secondly, it would be wrong to characterize the urban custom litigation in Scotland as cases of inter-class rivalry between a landed aristocracy and an emerging bourgeoisie. Much of the urban common land that was lost in Scotland was due to the mismanagement and greed of magistrates who came from the same class as the entrepreneurs that were trying to stop them. In *Kilmarnock*, the judges had to choose between two schemes for urban development – the housing scheme of the magistrates or Wilson's wool manufactory. In the early nineteenth century in the burgh of Burntisland, the court of session intervened to protect both the town's golf course and the inhabitants' right to bleach linen on the links adjoining the burgh by stopping the sale of the town's green to an industrialist with connections to the town's magistracy who wanted to build a vitriol factory.[15] Like the case of *Kilmarnock*, *Burntisland* was brought by local elites against the magistrates. The action was fought on the behalf of the society of golfers following on from the success of the St Andrews golfers in protecting their golfing ground in 1805.[16]

While it may be the case that, as Thompson and Hobsbawm have argued, Scotland's eighteenth-century judges shared the mentalité of Scotland's 'improvers', those improvers were not necessarily from the landed class, and many disputes over the disposition of common land were amongst members of the same class. Moreover, the thesis is cast into further doubt by the court of session's decisions in the cases of *Burntisland* and *St Andrews* in the opening decades of the nineteenth century. There, the court of session privileged community rights to recreation over the profit to be made on burgh common land from uses as various as keeping a rabbit warren and as a site for a factory to produce vitriol for the bleaching industry.

Without denying the deeply ideological nature of some custom decisions, it is nonetheless difficult to discern in Scotland's custom cases the work of a self-interested judiciary pursing a single class interest. The pattern that emerges is not the privileging of one class over another but rather the privileging of community use of common good land as against the 'capture' of common resources by an individual or small group of magistrates. Whether the community use was industrial or recreational, the court of

---

15 *Burntisland*, Session Papers 1811–1812, No. 26 (Available at the Signet Library, Edinburgh), reported in the Lord Ordinary's Note in *Home v. Young* (1846) 9 D. 286, 293–294.
16 *Dempster v. Cleghorn* (case of *St Andrews*) (1805) M. 16141, rem. (1813) 2 Dow 40; A.C. Loux, 'The Great Rabbit Massacre – A "Comedy of the Commons"? Custom, community and rights of public access to the links of St Andrews', *Liverpool Law Review*, 22 (2001), pp 123–55.

session acted to protect the rights of burgh inhabitants as against landlords, neighbouring landowners and magistrates alike. Far from reifying use rights into legal property rights, the judges of the court of session upheld a variety of community uses as good and lawful custom. In doing so, they did not preserve the pre-industrial past but rather laid the foundations for the creation of a modern, capitalist society by protecting the common land upon which Scotland's urban population both built their industries and took their leisure.